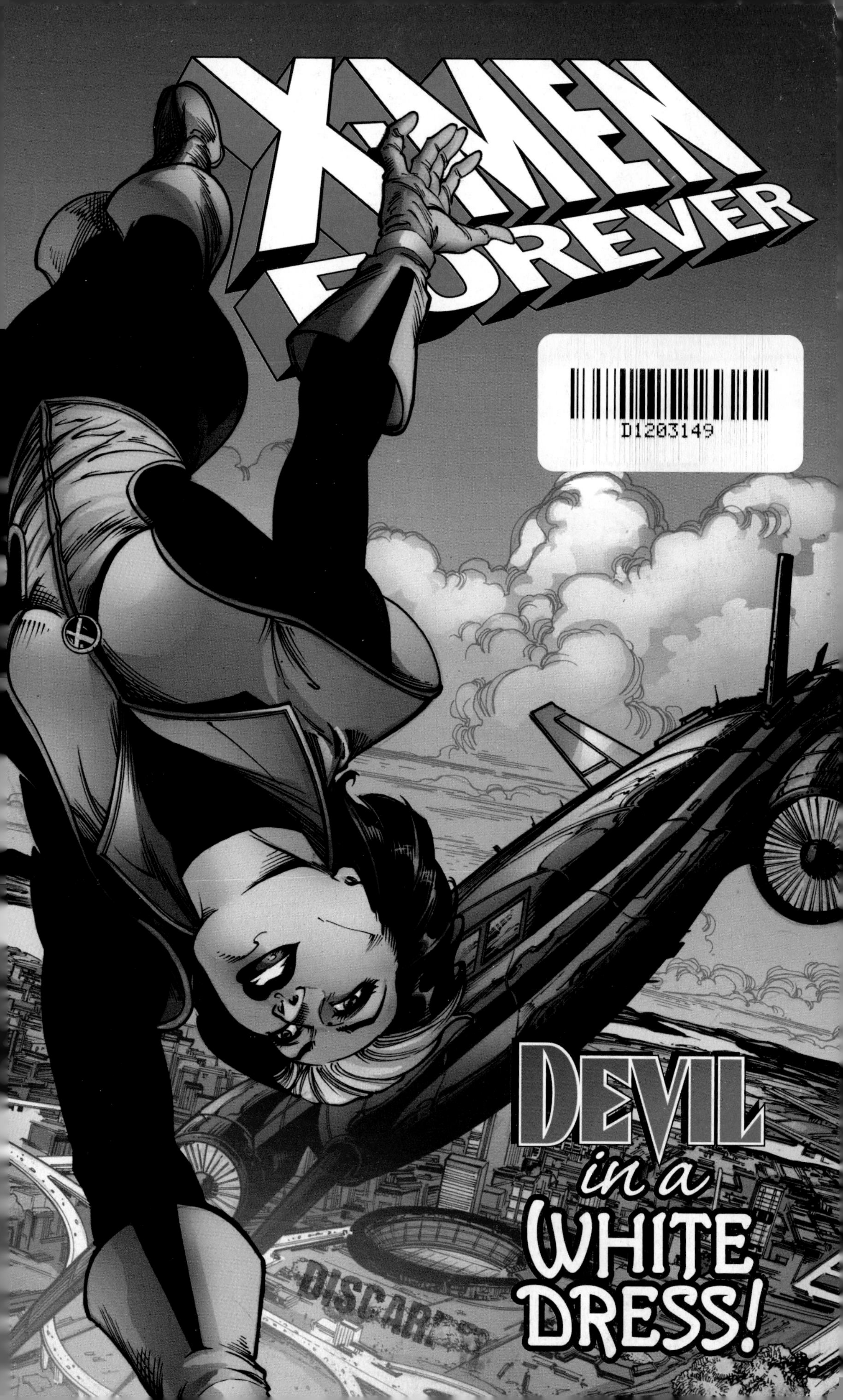
X-MEN
FOREVER
DEVIL
in a
WHITE
DRESS!

X-MEN FOREVER

DEVIL in a WHITE DRESS!

Writer:
CHRIS CLAREMONT

Pencilers:
GRAHAM NOLAN & TOM GRUMMETT

Inkers:
**VICENTE CIFUENTES, CORY HAMSCHER
& SCOTT KOBLISH**

Colorists:
SOTOCOLOR, WILFREDO QUINTANA & GUILLEM MARI

Artist, *Annual #1*:
SANA TAKEDA

Letterers:
TOM ORZECHOWSKI WITH DAVE SHARPE

Cover Art:
**TOM GRUMMETT WITH CORY HAMSCHER, TERRY AUSTIN,
MOOSE BAUMANN & MORRY HOLLOWELL**

Assistant Editors:
CHARLIE BECKERMAN & MICHAEL HORWITZ

Editor:
MARK PANICCIA

Collection Editor: **JENNIFER GRÜNWALD**
Editorial Assistants: **JAMES EMMETT & JOE HOCHSTEIN** • Assistant Editor: **ALEX STARBUCK**
Editor, Special Projects: **MARK D. BEAZLEY** • Senior Editor, Special Projects: **JEFF YOUNGQUIST**
Senior Vice President of Sales: **DAVID GABRIEL**

Editor in Chief: **JOE QUESADA** • Publisher: **DAN BUCKLEY**
Executive Producer: **ALAN FINE**

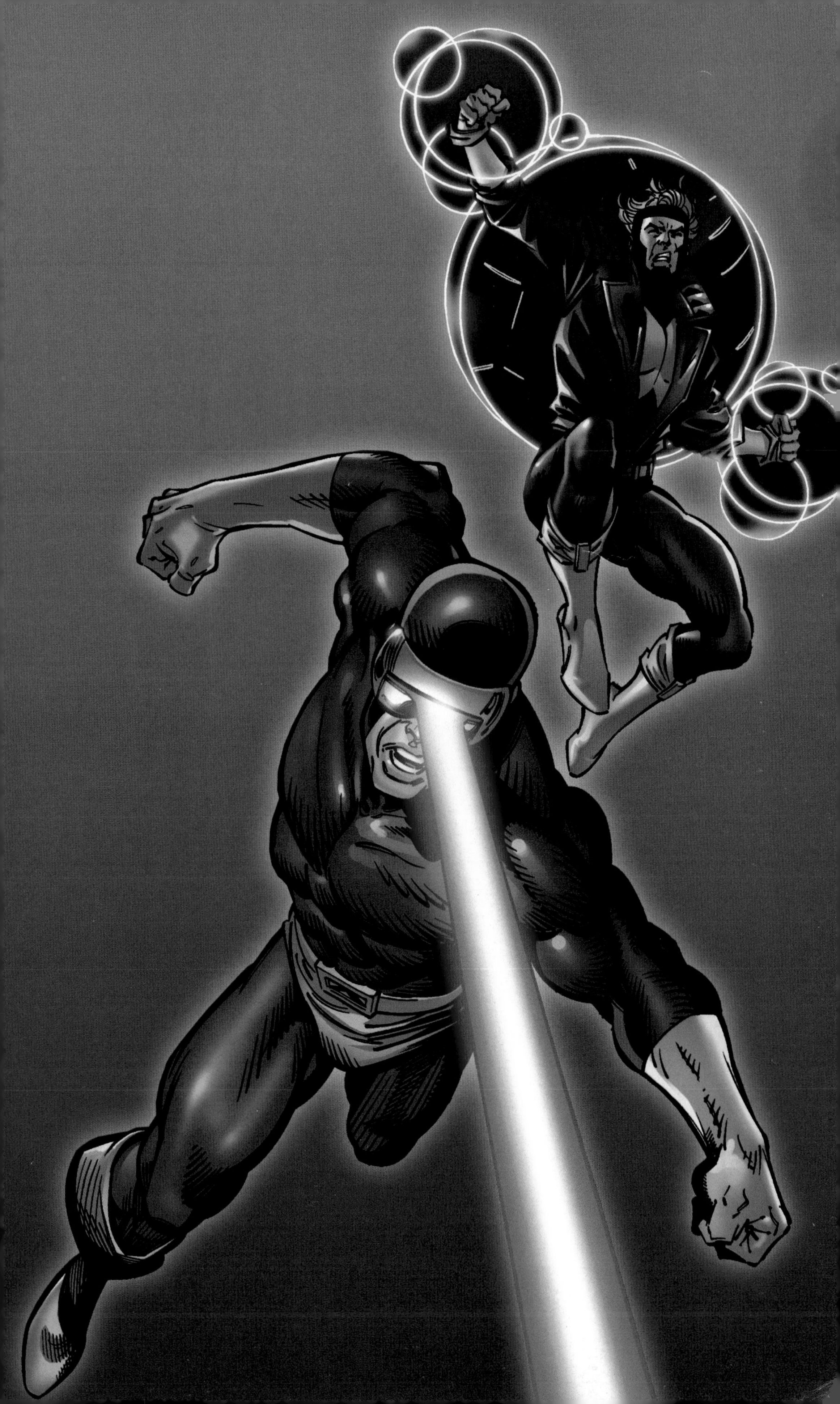

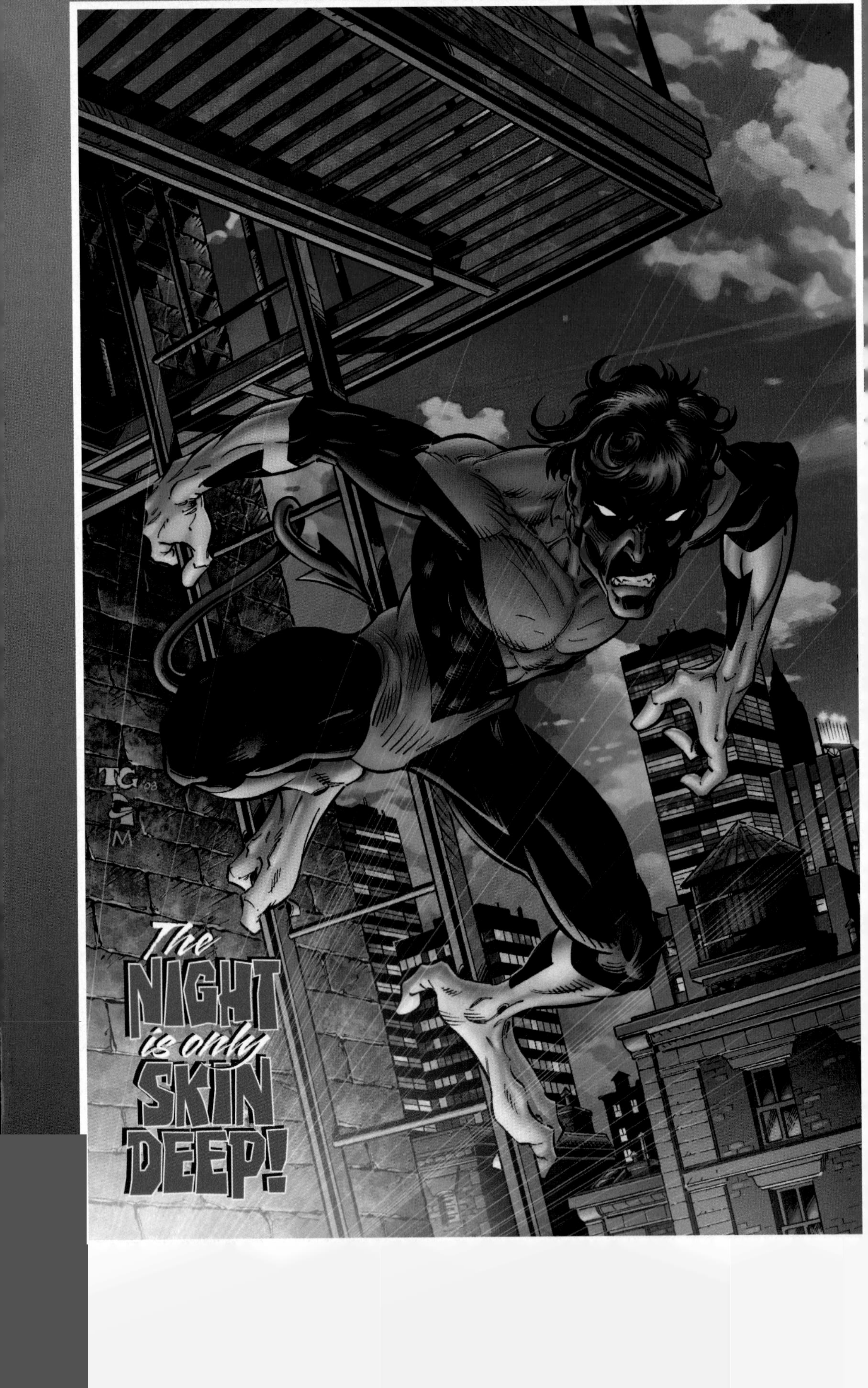
TG '98
M
The NIGHT is only SKIN DEEP!

mics legend *Chris Claremont* had an epic 16-year run on *X-MEN*, which concluded *h X-MEN: MUTANT GENESIS #1-3* in 1991. Now, in an unprecedented comics event, Claremont returns to his iconic run on the *X-MEN*.

ROFESSOR
X
Charles Xavier

PERFECT
STORM
Ororo Munroe?

CYCLOPS
Scott Summers

ROGUE
na Marie Raven

NIGHT-
CRAWLER
Kurt Wagner

Previously, in

BEAST
Hank McCoy

LIL' 'RO
Ororo Munroe?

JEAN GREY

GAMBIT
Remy Picard

SHADOWCAT
Kitty Pryde

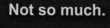

No rest for the weary.

Following the events on Asteroid M, the death of Magneto, the troubled Cortez mission, the death of Wolverine and the discovery and escape of an evil impostor Storm, and the revelations from deep within the South American jungle about a possible revival of the Sentinel Program, it seemed that, while Kitty, Gambit and Lil' 'Ro set off to Russia to check on former X-Men Piotr Rasputin, the rest of the team would finally get some rest.

Not so much.

A frantic call from Nightcrawler's former lover Amanda Sefton has him heading to Mississippi to see what's gone wrong. Fortunately for him, he has a bona fide Mississippi expert in the mansion — Rogue. The two of them take leave for the deep South, not knowing what awaits them…

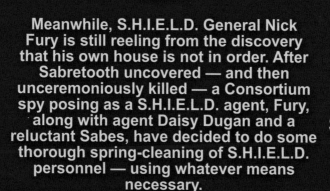

Meanwhile, S.H.I.E.L.D. General Nick Fury is still reeling from the discovery that his own house is not in order. After Sabretooth uncovered — and then unceremoniously killed — a Consortium spy posing as a S.H.I.E.L.D. agent, Fury, along with agent Daisy Dugan and a reluctant Sabes, have decided to do some thorough spring-cleaning of S.H.I.E.L.D. personnel — using whatever means necessary.

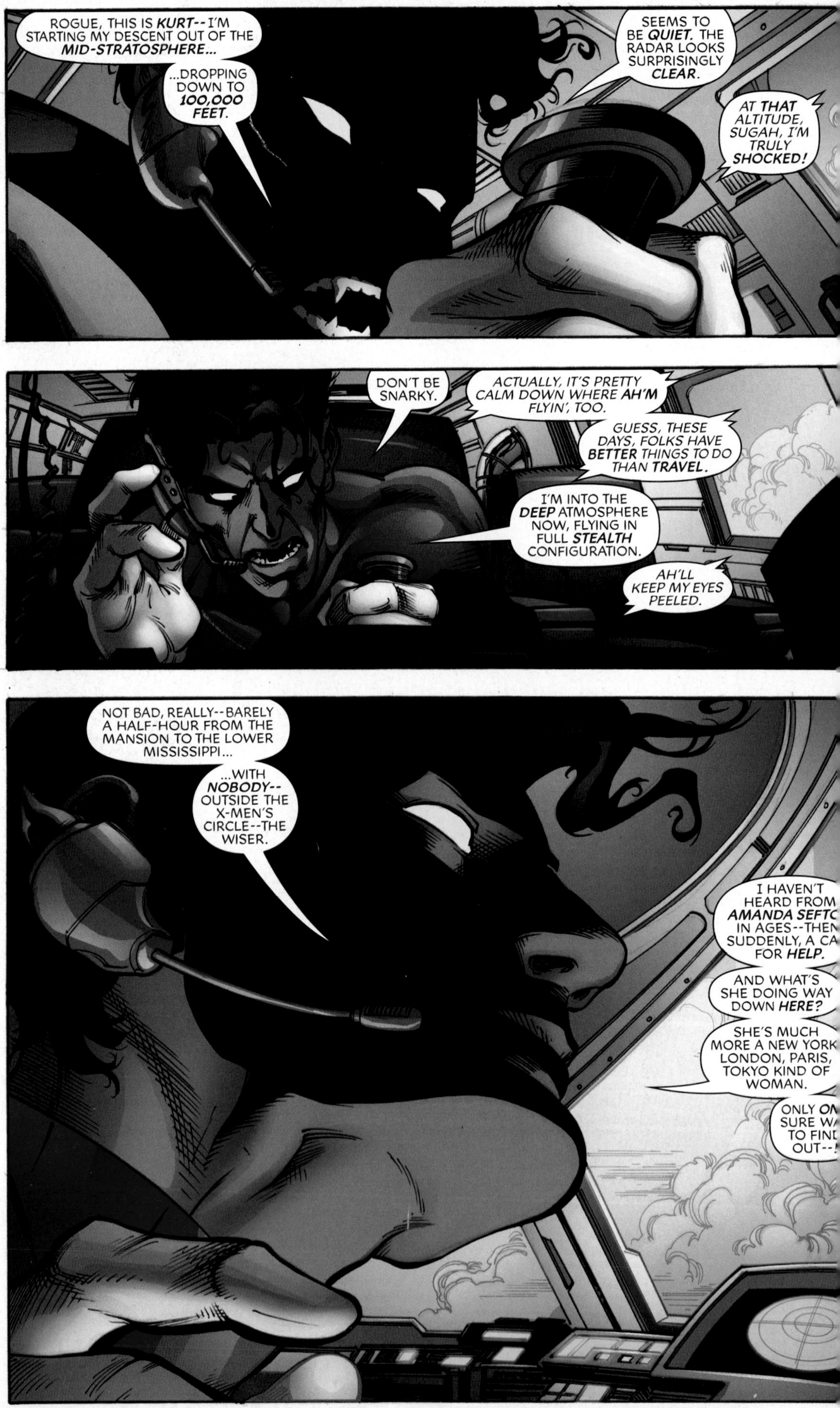
ROGUE, THIS IS KURT--I'M STARTING MY DESCENT OUT OF THE MID-STRATOSPHERE...
...DROPPING DOWN TO 100,000 FEET.
SEEMS TO BE QUIET. THE RADAR LOOKS SURPRISINGLY CLEAR.
AT THAT ALTITUDE, SUGAH, I'M TRULY SHOCKED!
DON'T BE SNARKY.
ACTUALLY, IT'S PRETTY CALM DOWN WHERE AH'M FLYIN', TOO.
GUESS, THESE DAYS, FOLKS HAVE BETTER THINGS TO DO THAN TRAVEL.
I'M INTO THE DEEP ATMOSPHERE NOW, FLYING IN FULL STEALTH CONFIGURATION.
AH'LL KEEP MY EYES PEELED.
NOT BAD, REALLY--BARELY A HALF-HOUR FROM THE MANSION TO THE LOWER MISSISSIPPI...
...WITH NOBODY--OUTSIDE THE X-MEN'S CIRCLE--THE WISER.
I HAVEN'T HEARD FROM AMANDA SEFTO IN AGES--THEN SUDDENLY, A CA FOR HELP.
AND WHAT'S SHE DOING WAY DOWN HERE?
SHE'S MUCH MORE A NEW YORK LONDON, PARIS, TOKYO KIND OF WOMAN.
ONLY ON SURE W TO FIND OUT--!

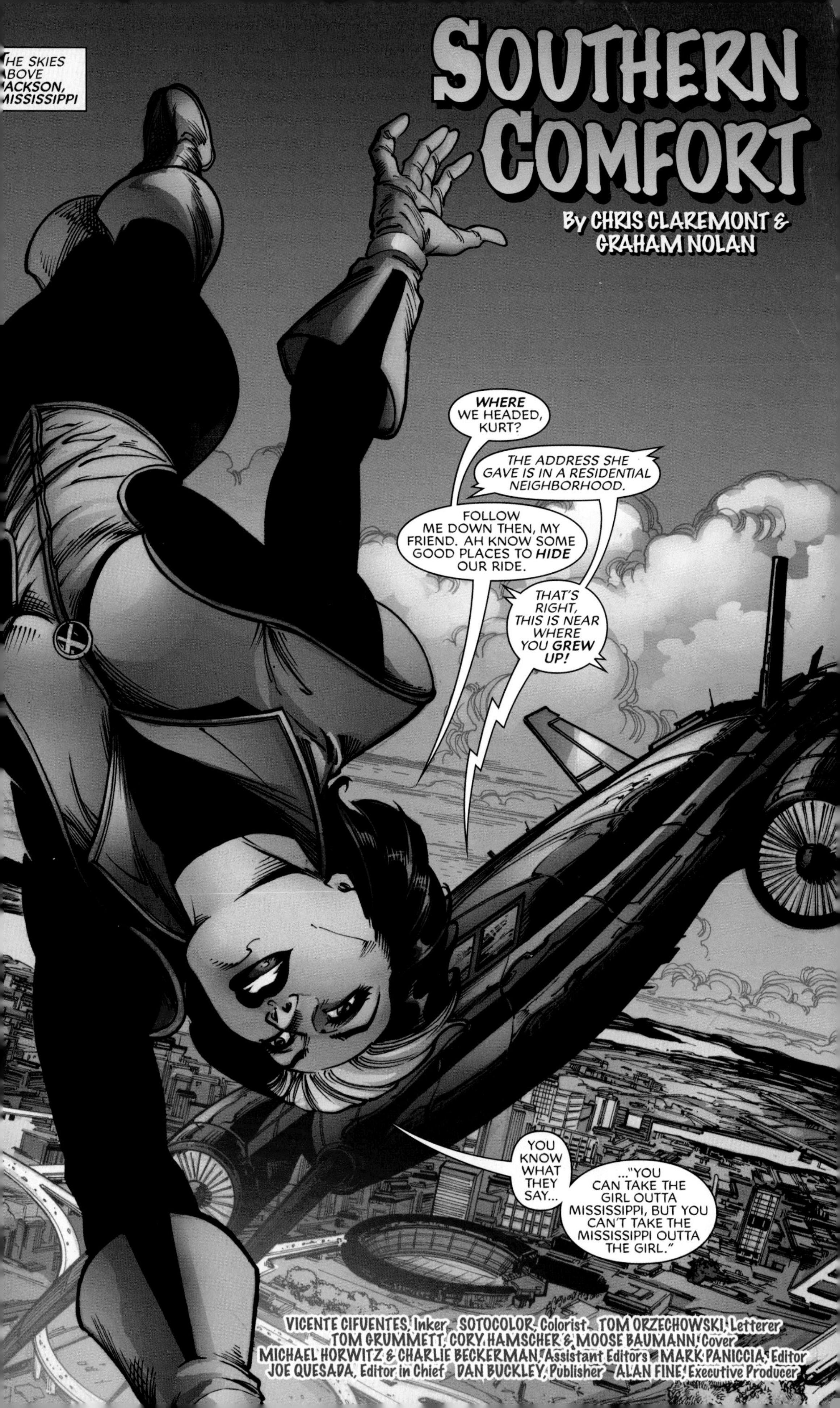
HE SKIES
BOVE
ACKSON,
MISSISSIPPI
SOUTHERN COMFORT
By CHRIS CLAREMONT & GRAHAM NOLAN
WHERE WE HEADED, KURT?
THE ADDRESS SHE GAVE IS IN A RESIDENTIAL NEIGHBORHOOD.
FOLLOW ME DOWN THEN, MY FRIEND. AH KNOW SOME GOOD PLACES TO HIDE OUR RIDE.
THAT'S RIGHT, THIS IS NEAR WHERE YOU GREW UP!
YOU KNOW WHAT THEY SAY...
..."YOU CAN TAKE THE GIRL OUTTA MISSISSIPPI, BUT YOU CAN'T TAKE THE MISSISSIPPI OUTTA THE GIRL."
VICENTE CIFUENTES, Inker SOTOCOLOR, Colorist TOM ORZECHOWSKI, Letterer
TOM GRUMMETT, CORY HAMSCHER & MOOSE BAUMANN, Cover
MICHAEL HORWITZ & CHARLIE BECKERMAN, Assistant Editors MARK PANICCIA, Editor
JOE QUESADA, Editor in Chief DAN BUCKLEY, Publisher ALAN FINE, Executive Producer

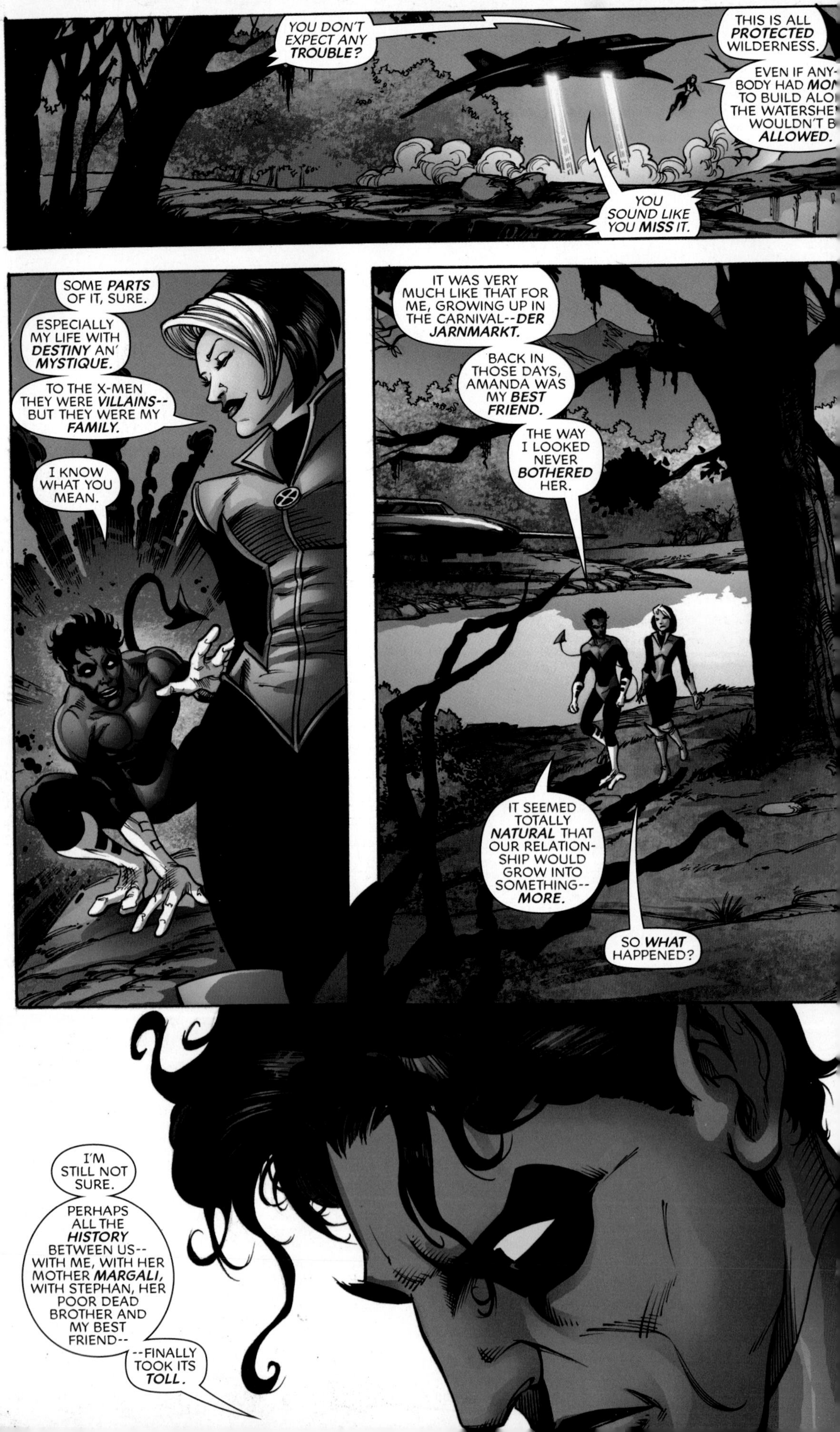

YOU DON'T EXPECT ANY TROUBLE?
THIS IS ALL PROTECTED WILDERNESS.
YOU SOUND LIKE YOU MISS IT.
SOME PARTS OF IT, SURE.
ESPECIALLY MY LIFE WITH DESTINY AN' MYSTIQUE.
TO THE X-MEN THEY WERE VILLAINS-- BUT THEY WERE MY FAMILY.
I KNOW WHAT YOU MEAN.
IT WAS VERY MUCH LIKE THAT FOR ME, GROWING UP IN THE CARNIVAL--DER JARNMARKT.
BACK IN THOSE DAYS, AMANDA WAS MY BEST FRIEND.
THE WAY I LOOKED NEVER BOTHERED HER.
IT SEEMED TOTALLY NATURAL THAT OUR RELATION-SHIP WOULD GROW INTO SOMETHING--MORE.
SO WHAT HAPPENED?
I'M STILL NOT SURE.
PERHAPS ALL THE HISTORY BETWEEN US-- WITH ME, WITH HER MOTHER MARGALI, WITH STEPHAN, HER POOR DEAD BROTHER AND MY BEST FRIEND--
--FINALLY TOOK ITS TOLL.

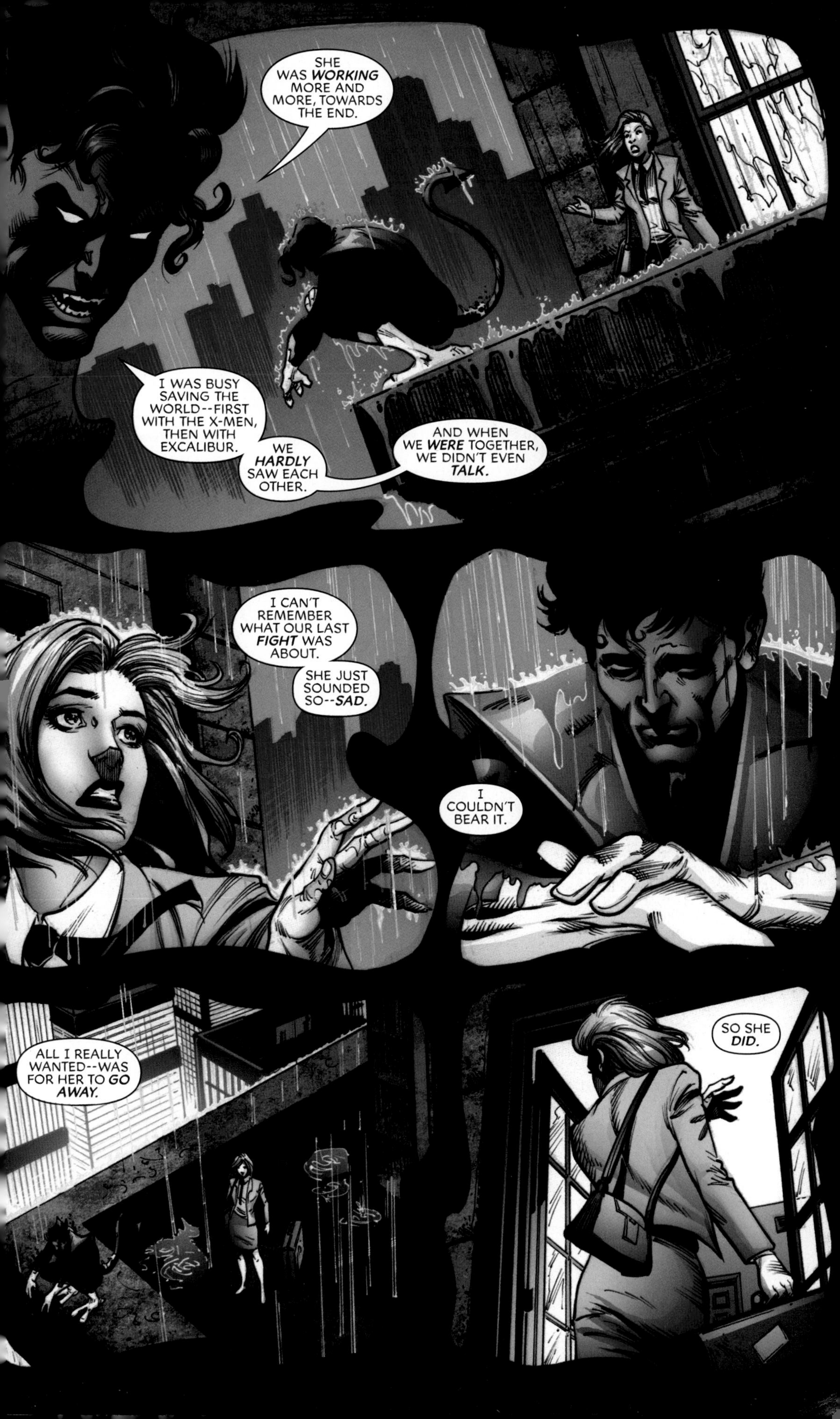
SHE WAS WORKING MORE AND MORE, TOWARDS THE END.
I WAS BUSY SAVING THE WORLD--FIRST WITH THE X-MEN, THEN WITH EXCALIBUR.
WE HARDLY SAW EACH OTHER.
AND WHEN WE WERE TOGETHER, WE DIDN'T EVEN TALK.
I CAN'T REMEMBER WHAT OUR LAST FIGHT WAS ABOUT.
SHE JUST SOUNDED SO--SAD.
I COULDN'T BEAR IT.
ALL I REALLY WANTED--WAS FOR HER TO GO AWAY.
SO SHE DID.

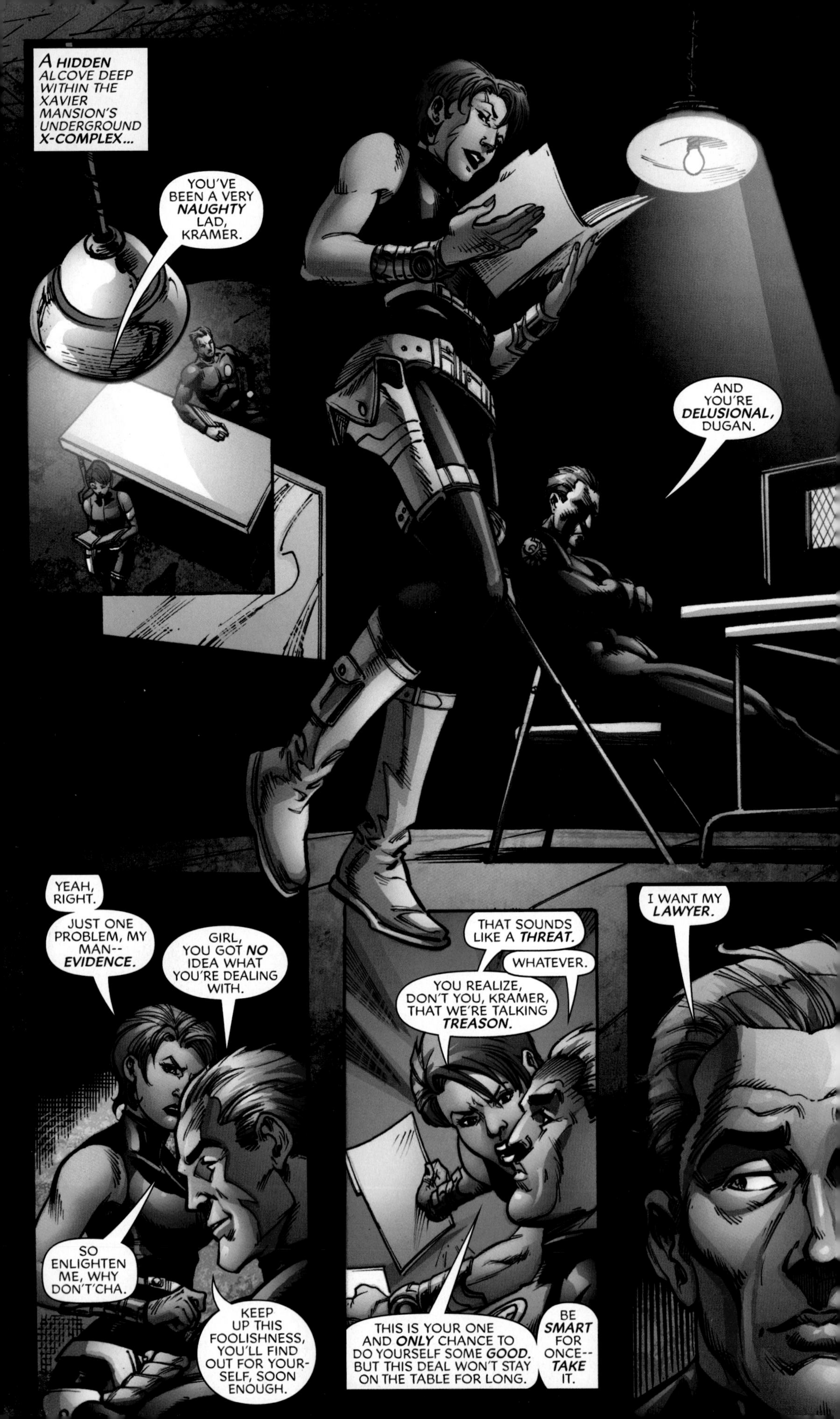
A HIDDEN ALCOVE DEEP WITHIN THE XAVIER MANSION'S UNDERGROUND X-COMPLEX...
YOU'VE BEEN A VERY NAUGHTY LAD, KRAMER.
AND YOU'RE DELUSIONAL, DUGAN.
YEAH, RIGHT.
JUST ONE PROBLEM, MY MAN-- EVIDENCE.
GIRL, YOU GOT NO IDEA WHAT YOU'RE DEALING WITH.
SO ENLIGHTEN ME, WHY DON'T'CHA.
KEEP UP THIS FOOLISHNESS, YOU'LL FIND OUT FOR YOURSELF, SOON ENOUGH.
THAT SOUNDS LIKE A THREAT.
WHATEVER.
YOU REALIZE, DON'T YOU, KRAMER, THAT WE'RE TALKING TREASON.
THIS IS YOUR ONE AND ONLY CHANCE TO DO YOURSELF SOME GOOD. BUT THIS DEAL WON'T STAY ON THE TABLE FOR LONG.
BE SMART FOR ONCE-- TAKE IT.
I WANT MY LAWYER.

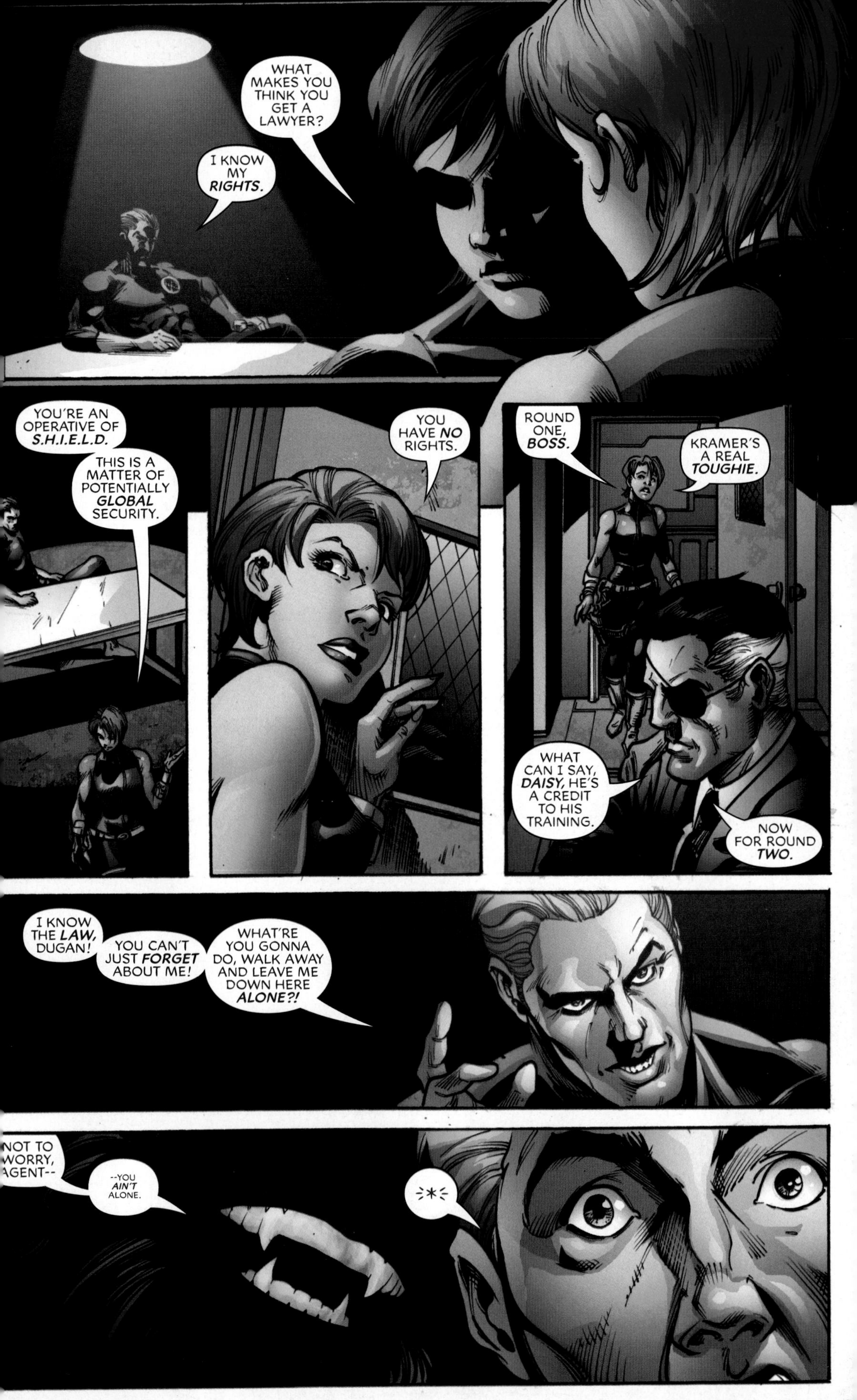

I KNOW MY RIGHTS.
WHAT MAKES YOU THINK YOU GET A LAWYER?
YOU'RE AN OPERATIVE OF S.H.I.E.L.D.
THIS IS A MATTER OF POTENTIALLY GLOBAL SECURITY.
YOU HAVE NO RIGHTS.
ROUND ONE, BOSS.
KRAMER'S A REAL TOUGHIE.
WHAT CAN I SAY, DAISY, HE'S A CREDIT TO HIS TRAINING.
NOW FOR ROUND TWO.
I KNOW THE LAW, DUGAN!
YOU CAN'T JUST FORGET ABOUT ME!
WHAT'RE YOU GONNA DO, WALK AWAY AND LEAVE ME DOWN HERE ALONE?!
NOT TO WORRY, AGENT--
--YOU AIN'T ALONE.
*

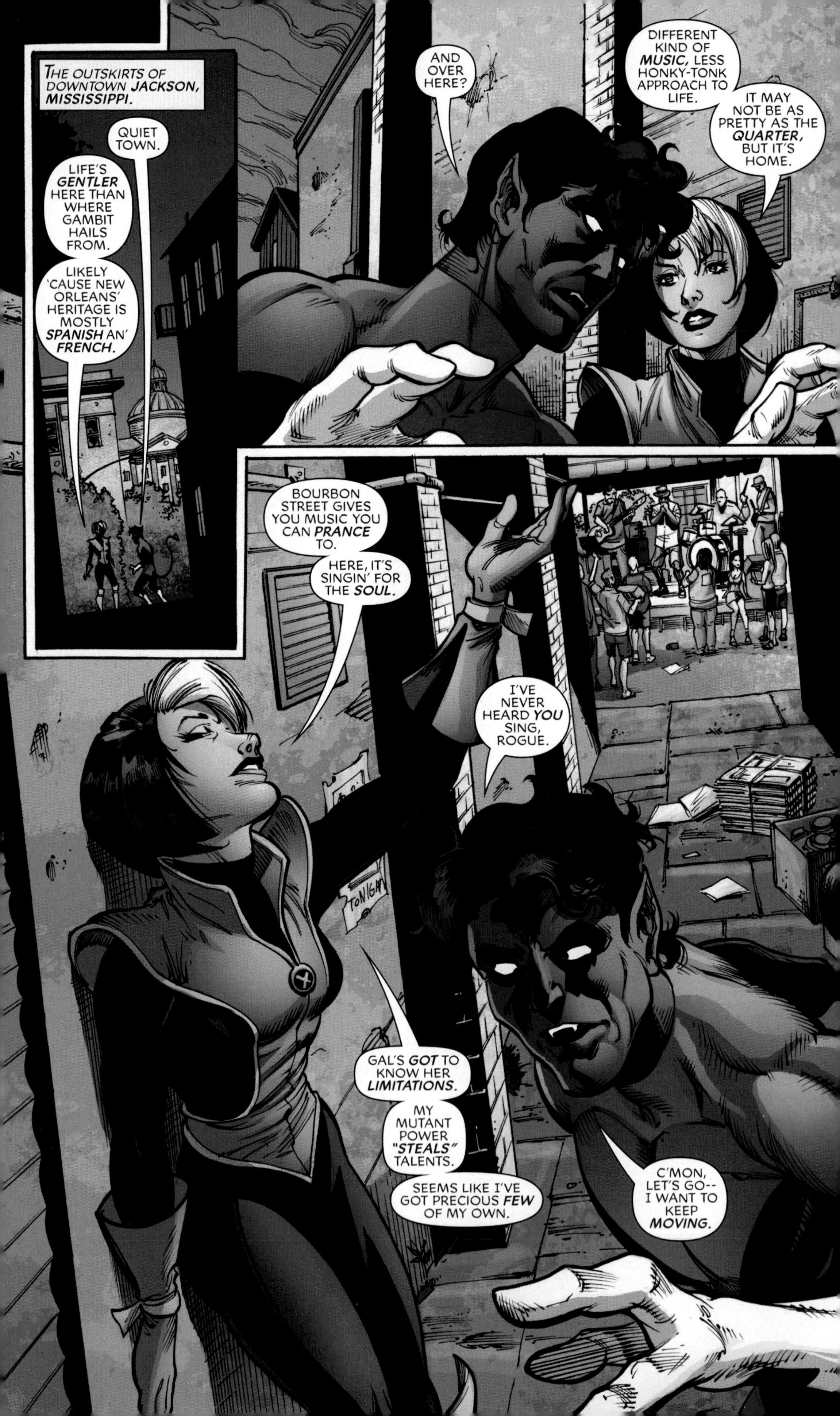
THE OUTSKIRTS OF DOWNTOWN JACKSON, MISSISSIPPI.
QUIET TOWN.
LIFE'S GENTLER HERE THAN WHERE GAMBIT HAILS FROM.
LIKELY 'CAUSE NEW ORLEANS' HERITAGE IS MOSTLY SPANISH AN' FRENCH.
AND OVER HERE?
DIFFERENT KIND OF MUSIC, LESS HONKY-TONK APPROACH TO LIFE.
IT MAY NOT BE AS PRETTY AS THE QUARTER, BUT IT'S HOME.
BOURBON STREET GIVES YOU MUSIC YOU CAN PRANCE TO.
HERE, IT'S SINGIN' FOR THE SOUL.
I'VE NEVER HEARD YOU SING, ROGUE.
GAL'S GOT TO KNOW HER LIMITATIONS.
MY MUTANT POWER "STEALS" TALENTS.
SEEMS LIKE I'VE GOT PRECIOUS FEW OF MY OWN.
C'MON, LET'S GO-- I WANT TO KEEP MOVING.

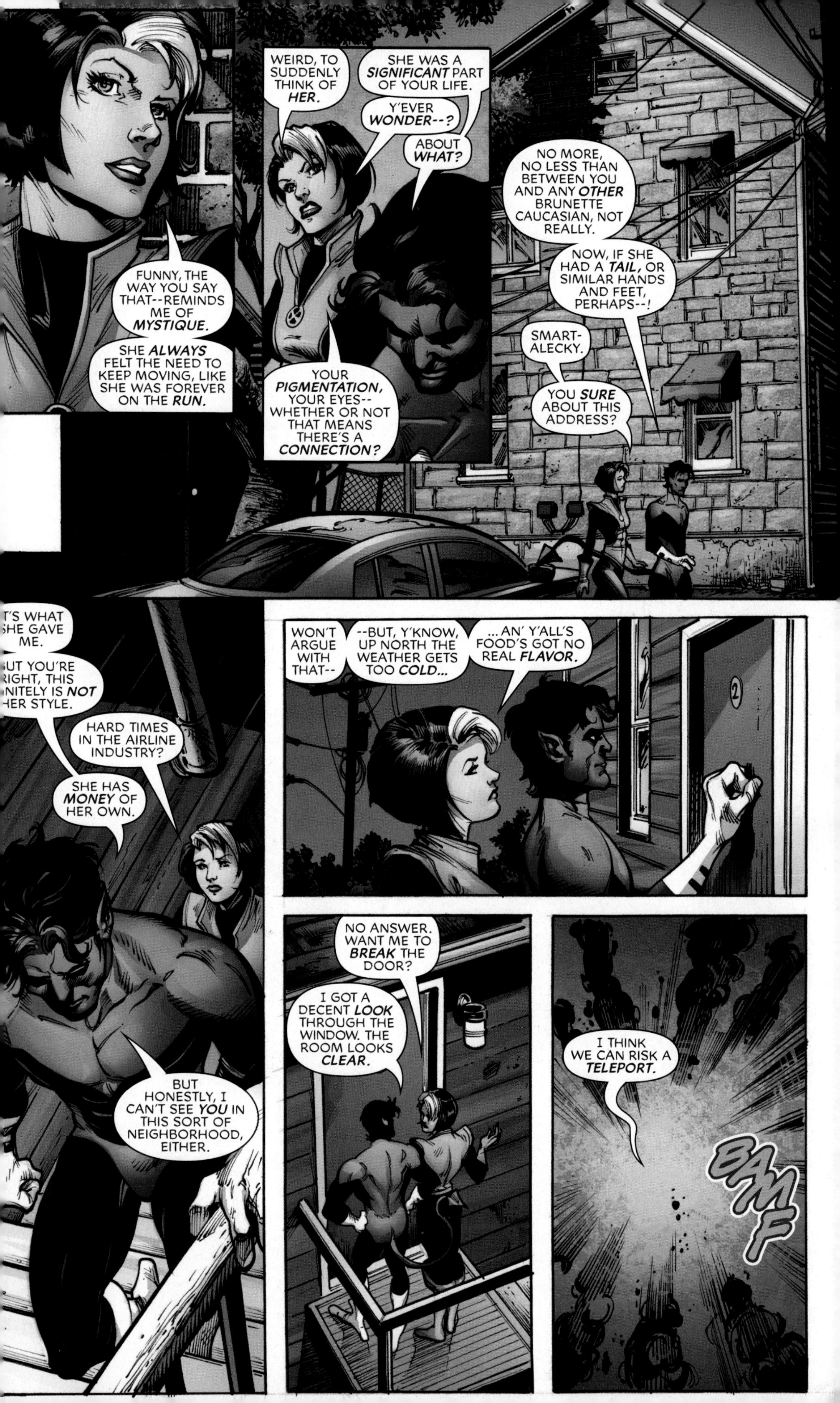
FUNNY, THE WAY YOU SAY THAT--REMINDS ME OF MYSTIQUE.
SHE ALWAYS FELT THE NEED TO KEEP MOVING, LIKE SHE WAS FOREVER ON THE RUN.
WEIRD, TO SUDDENLY THINK OF HER.
SHE WAS A SIGNIFICANT PART OF YOUR LIFE.
Y'EVER WONDER--?
ABOUT WHAT?
YOUR PIGMENTATION, YOUR EYES--WHETHER OR NOT THAT MEANS THERE'S A CONNECTION?
NO MORE, NO LESS THAN BETWEEN YOU AND ANY OTHER BRUNETTE CAUCASIAN, NOT REALLY.
NOW, IF SHE HAD A TAIL, OR SIMILAR HANDS AND FEET, PERHAPS--!
SMART-ALECKY.
YOU SURE ABOUT THIS ADDRESS?
T'S WHAT HE GAVE ME.
UT YOU'RE RIGHT, THIS NITELY IS NOT HER STYLE.
HARD TIMES IN THE AIRLINE INDUSTRY?
SHE HAS MONEY OF HER OWN.
BUT HONESTLY, I CAN'T SEE YOU IN THIS SORT OF NEIGHBORHOOD, EITHER.
WON'T ARGUE WITH THAT--
--BUT, Y'KNOW, UP NORTH THE WEATHER GETS TOO COLD...
...AN' Y'ALL'S FOOD'S GOT NO REAL FLAVOR.
NO ANSWER. WANT ME TO BREAK THE DOOR?
I GOT A DECENT LOOK THROUGH THE WINDOW. THE ROOM LOOKS CLEAR.
I THINK WE CAN RISK A TELEPORT.
BAMF

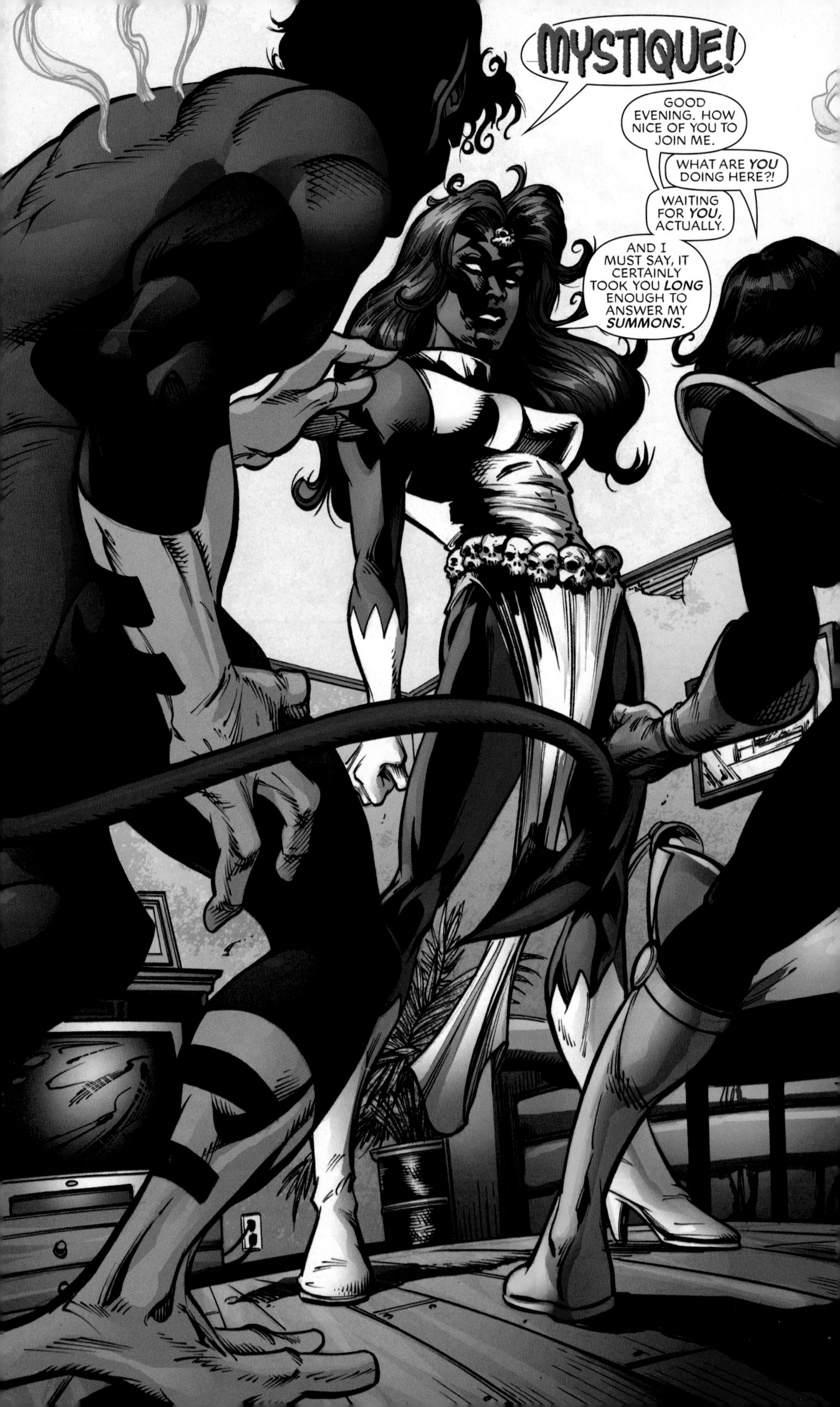
MYSTIQUE!
GOOD EVENING. HOW NICE OF YOU TO JOIN ME.
WHAT ARE *YOU* DOING HERE?!
WAITING FOR *YOU,* ACTUALLY.
AND I MUST SAY, IT CERTAINLY TOOK YOU *LONG* ENOUGH TO ANSWER MY *SUMMONS.*

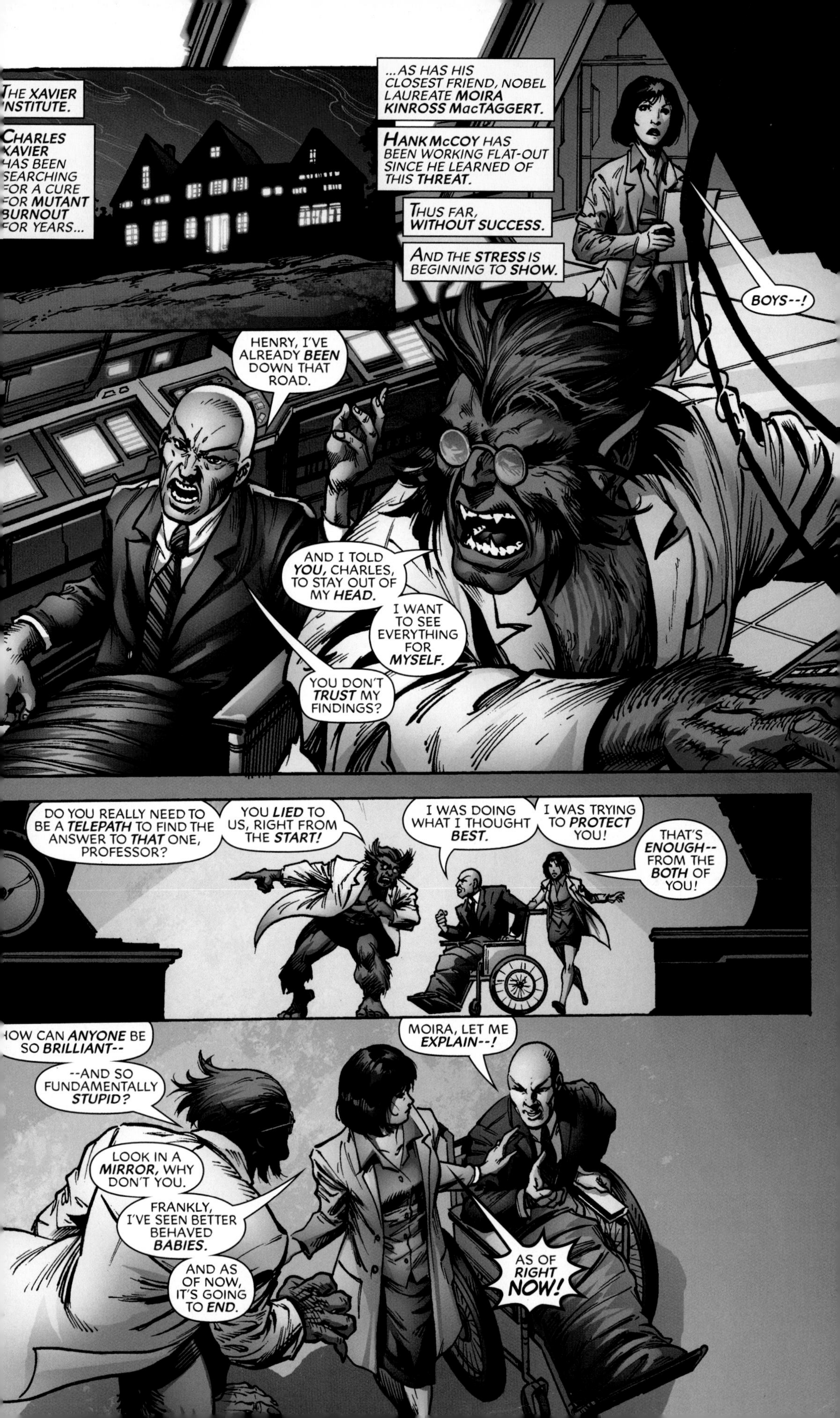
THE XAVIER INSTITUTE.
CHARLES XAVIER HAS BEEN SEARCHING FOR A CURE FOR MUTANT BURNOUT FOR YEARS...
...AS HAS HIS CLOSEST FRIEND, NOBEL LAUREATE MOIRA KINROSS MacTAGGERT.
HANK McCOY HAS BEEN WORKING FLAT-OUT SINCE HE LEARNED OF THIS THREAT.
THUS FAR, WITHOUT SUCCESS.
AND THE STRESS IS BEGINNING TO SHOW.
BOYS--!
HENRY, I'VE ALREADY BEEN DOWN THAT ROAD.
AND I TOLD YOU, CHARLES, TO STAY OUT OF MY HEAD.
I WANT TO SEE EVERYTHING FOR MYSELF.
YOU DON'T TRUST MY FINDINGS?
DO YOU REALLY NEED TO BE A TELEPATH TO FIND THE ANSWER TO THAT ONE, PROFESSOR?
YOU LIED TO US, RIGHT FROM THE START!
I WAS DOING WHAT I THOUGHT BEST.
I WAS TRYING TO PROTECT YOU!
THAT'S ENOUGH-- FROM THE BOTH OF YOU!
HOW CAN ANYONE BE SO BRILLIANT--
--AND SO FUNDAMENTALLY STUPID?
MOIRA, LET ME EXPLAIN--!
LOOK IN A MIRROR, WHY DON'T YOU.
FRANKLY, I'VE SEEN BETTER BEHAVED BABIES.
AND AS OF NOW, IT'S GOING TO END.
AS OF RIGHT NOW!

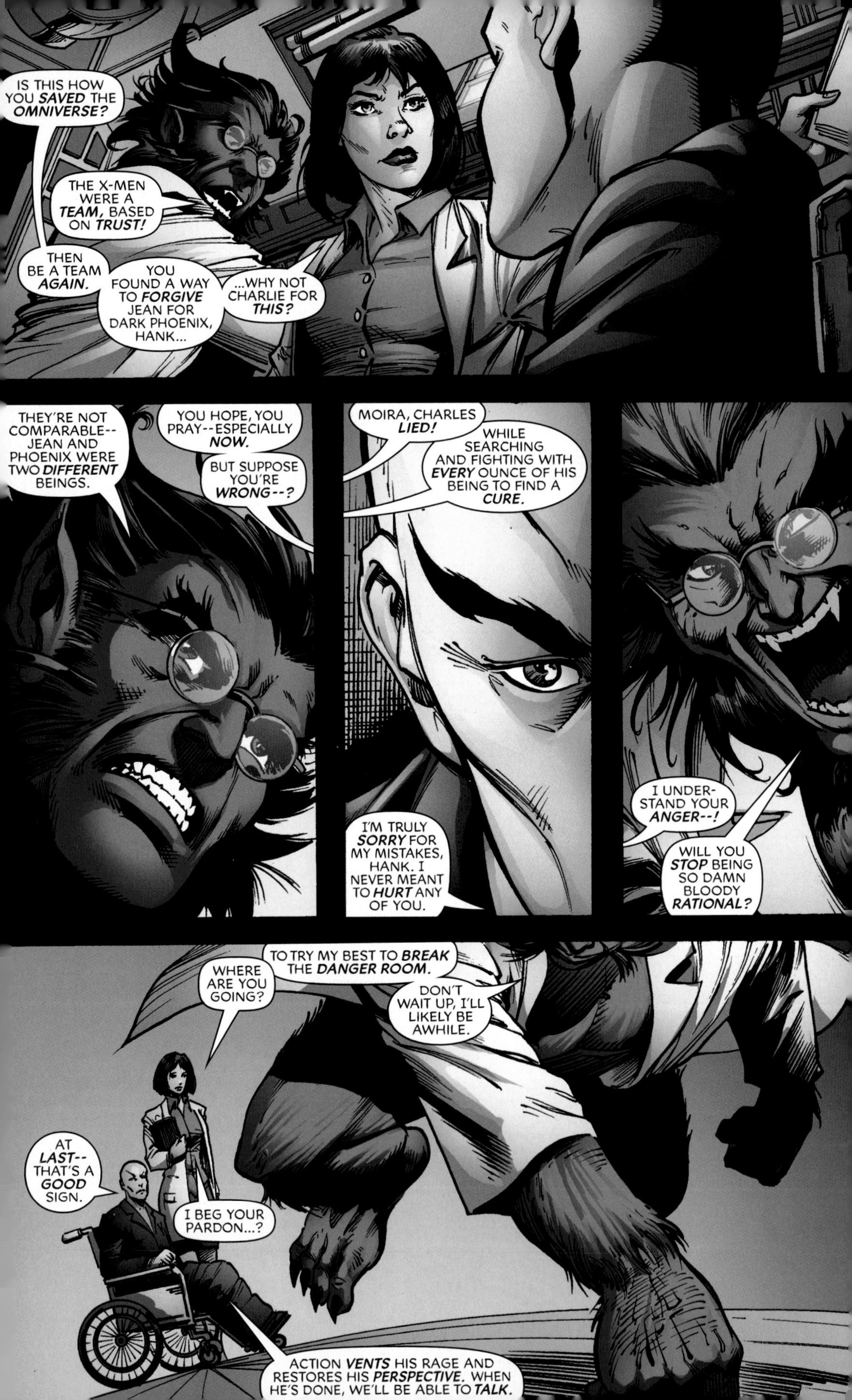
IS THIS HOW YOU *SAVED* THE *OMNIVERSE?*
THE X-MEN WERE A *TEAM,* BASED ON *TRUST!*
THEN BE A TEAM *AGAIN.*
YOU FOUND A WAY TO *FORGIVE* JEAN FOR DARK PHOENIX, HANK...
...WHY NOT CHARLIE FOR *THIS?*
THEY'RE NOT COMPARABLE-- JEAN AND PHOENIX WERE TWO *DIFFERENT* BEINGS.
YOU HOPE, YOU PRAY--ESPECIALLY *NOW.*
BUT SUPPOSE YOU'RE *WRONG--?*
MOIRA, CHARLES *LIED!*
WHILE SEARCHING AND FIGHTING WITH *EVERY* OUNCE OF HIS BEING TO FIND A *CURE.*
I'M TRULY *SORRY* FOR MY MISTAKES, HANK. I NEVER MEANT TO *HURT* ANY OF YOU.
I UNDERSTAND YOUR *ANGER--!*
WILL YOU *STOP* BEING SO DAMN BLOODY *RATIONAL?*
WHERE ARE YOU GOING?
TO TRY MY BEST TO *BREAK* THE *DANGER ROOM.*
DON'T WAIT UP, I'LL LIKELY BE AWHILE.
AT *LAST--* THAT'S A *GOOD* SIGN.
I BEG YOUR PARDON...?
ACTION *VENTS* HIS RAGE AND RESTORES HIS *PERSPECTIVE.* WHEN HE'S DONE, WE'LL BE ABLE TO *TALK.*

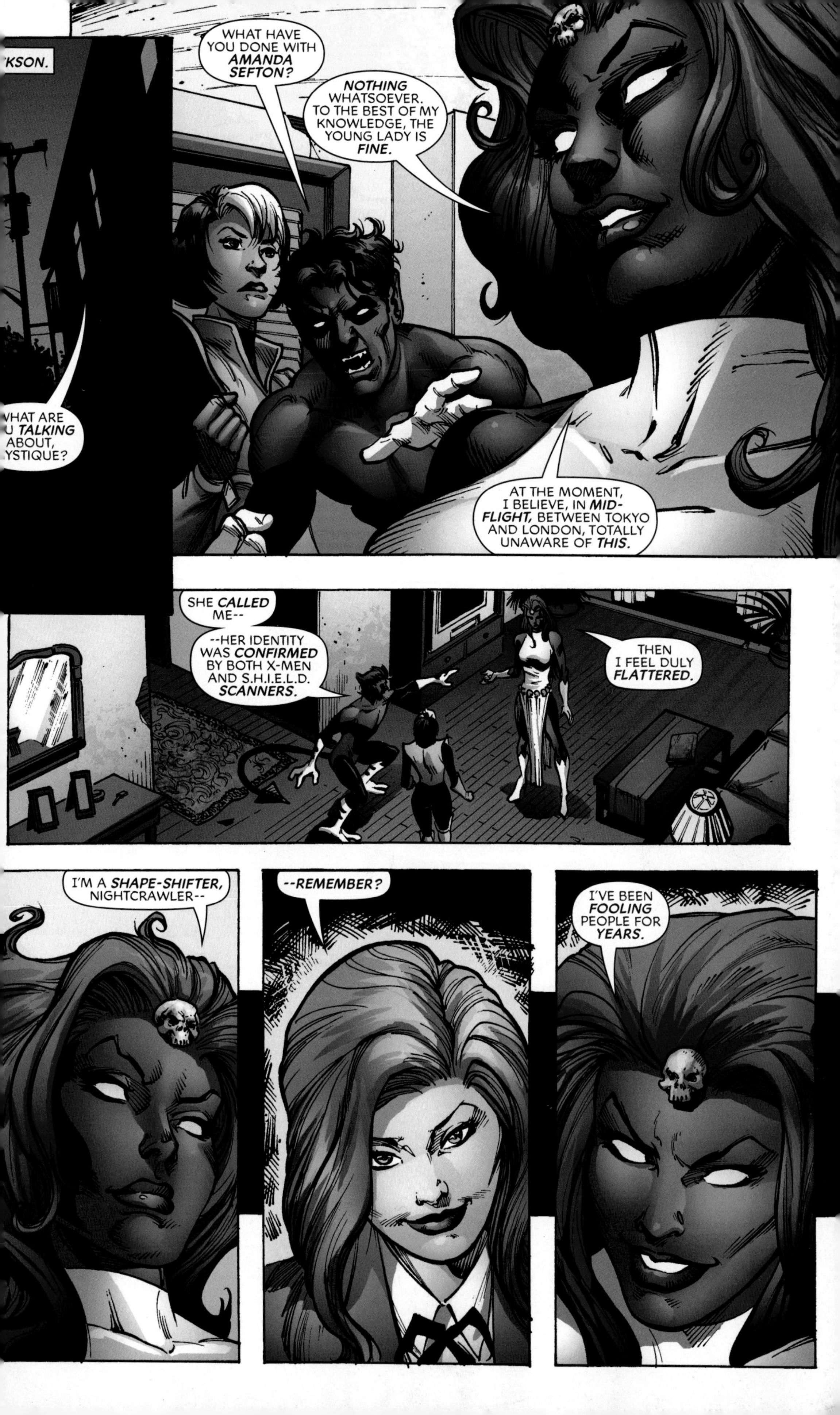

KSON.
WHAT HAVE YOU DONE WITH AMANDA SEFTON?
NOTHING WHATSOEVER. TO THE BEST OF MY KNOWLEDGE, THE YOUNG LADY IS FINE.
WHAT ARE U TALKING ABOUT, YSTIQUE?
AT THE MOMENT, I BELIEVE, IN MID-FLIGHT, BETWEEN TOKYO AND LONDON, TOTALLY UNAWARE OF THIS.
SHE CALLED ME--
--HER IDENTITY WAS CONFIRMED BY BOTH X-MEN AND S.H.I.E.L.D. SCANNERS.
THEN I FEEL DULY FLATTERED.
I'M A SHAPE-SHIFTER, NIGHTCRAWLER--
--REMEMBER?
I'VE BEEN FOOLING PEOPLE FOR YEARS.

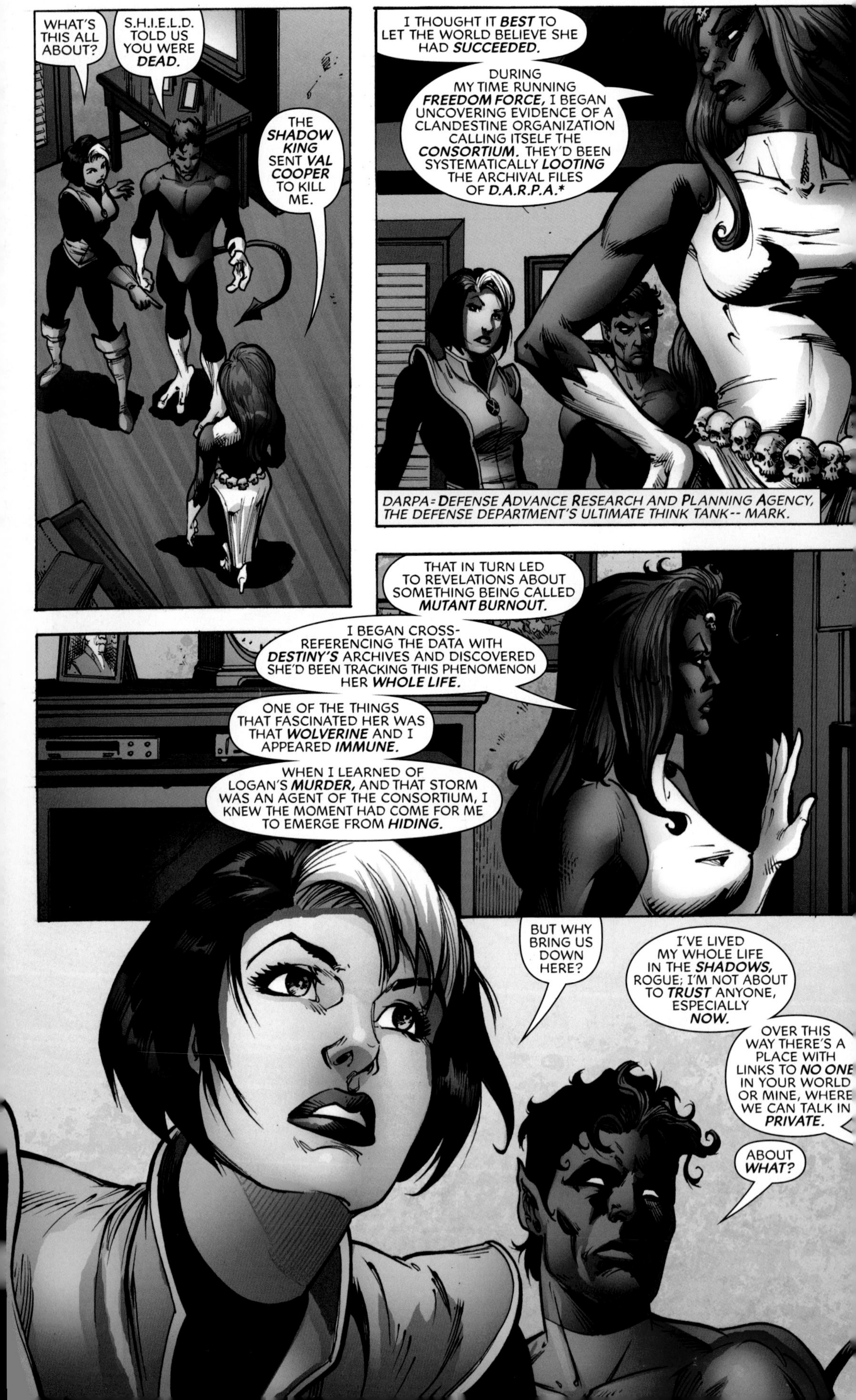

WHAT'S THIS ALL ABOUT?
S.H.I.E.L.D. TOLD US YOU WERE DEAD.
THE SHADOW KING SENT VAL COOPER TO KILL ME.
I THOUGHT IT BEST TO LET THE WORLD BELIEVE SHE HAD SUCCEEDED.
DURING MY TIME RUNNING FREEDOM FORCE, I BEGAN UNCOVERING EVIDENCE OF A CLANDESTINE ORGANIZATION CALLING ITSELF THE CONSORTIUM. THEY'D BEEN SYSTEMATICALLY LOOTING THE ARCHIVAL FILES OF D.A.R.P.A.*
DARPA= DEFENSE ADVANCE RESEARCH AND PLANNING AGENCY, THE DEFENSE DEPARTMENT'S ULTIMATE THINK TANK-- MARK.
THAT IN TURN LED TO REVELATIONS ABOUT SOMETHING BEING CALLED MUTANT BURNOUT.
I BEGAN CROSS-REFERENCING THE DATA WITH DESTINY'S ARCHIVES AND DISCOVERED SHE'D BEEN TRACKING THIS PHENOMENON HER WHOLE LIFE.
ONE OF THE THINGS THAT FASCINATED HER WAS THAT WOLVERINE AND I APPEARED IMMUNE.
WHEN I LEARNED OF LOGAN'S MURDER, AND THAT STORM WAS AN AGENT OF THE CONSORTIUM, I KNEW THE MOMENT HAD COME FOR ME TO EMERGE FROM HIDING.
BUT WHY BRING US DOWN HERE?
I'VE LIVED MY WHOLE LIFE IN THE SHADOWS, ROGUE; I'M NOT ABOUT TO TRUST ANYONE, ESPECIALLY NOW.
OVER THIS WAY THERE'S A PLACE WITH LINKS TO NO ONE IN YOUR WORLD OR MINE, WHERE WE CAN TALK IN PRIVATE.
ABOUT WHAT?

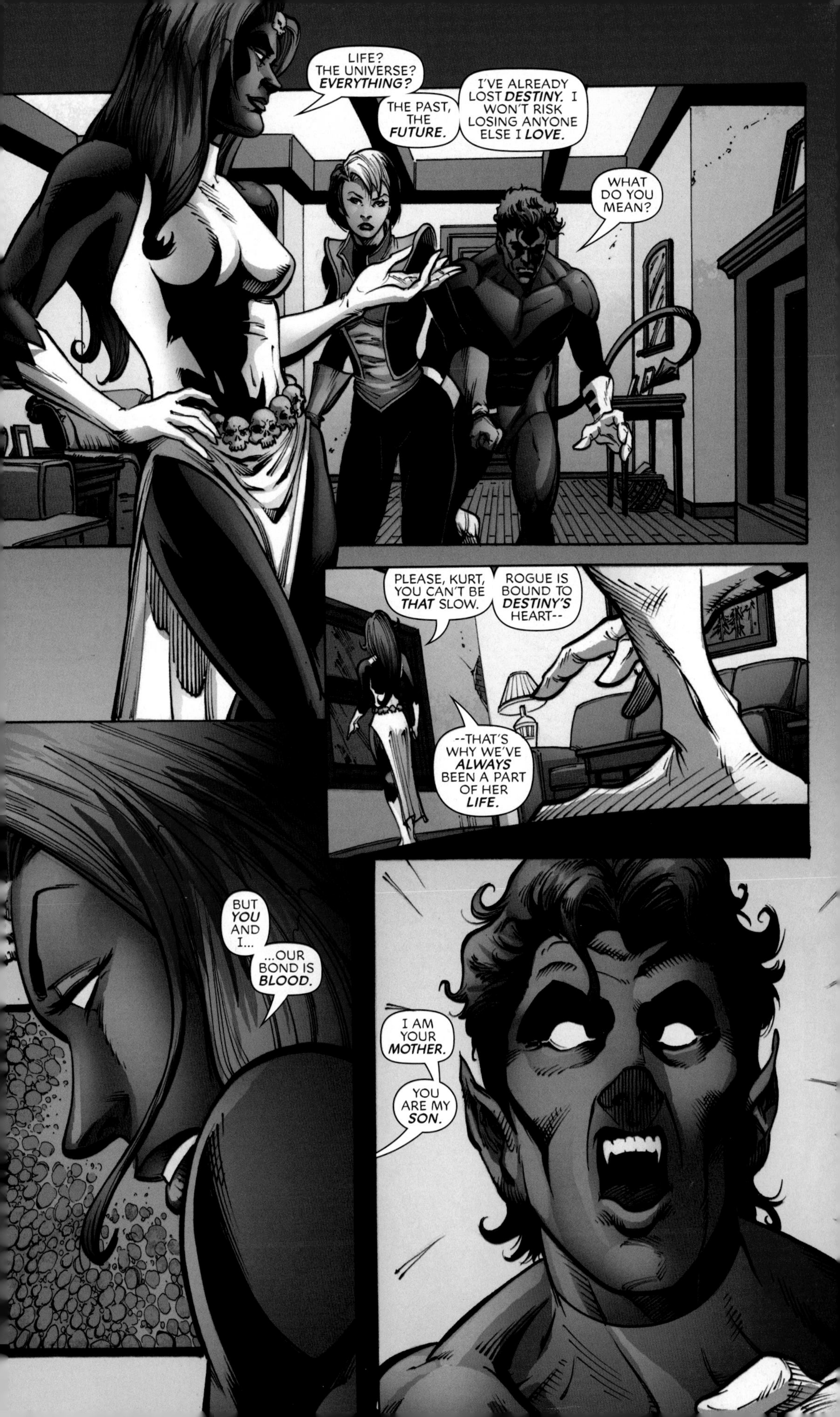
LIFE? THE UNIVERSE? EVERYTHING?
THE PAST, THE FUTURE.
I'VE ALREADY LOST DESTINY. I WON'T RISK LOSING ANYONE ELSE I LOVE.
WHAT DO YOU MEAN?
PLEASE, KURT, YOU CAN'T BE THAT SLOW.
ROGUE IS BOUND TO DESTINY'S HEART--
--THAT'S WHY WE'VE ALWAYS BEEN A PART OF HER LIFE.
BUT YOU AND I...
...OUR BOND IS BLOOD.
I AM YOUR MOTHER.
YOU ARE MY SON.

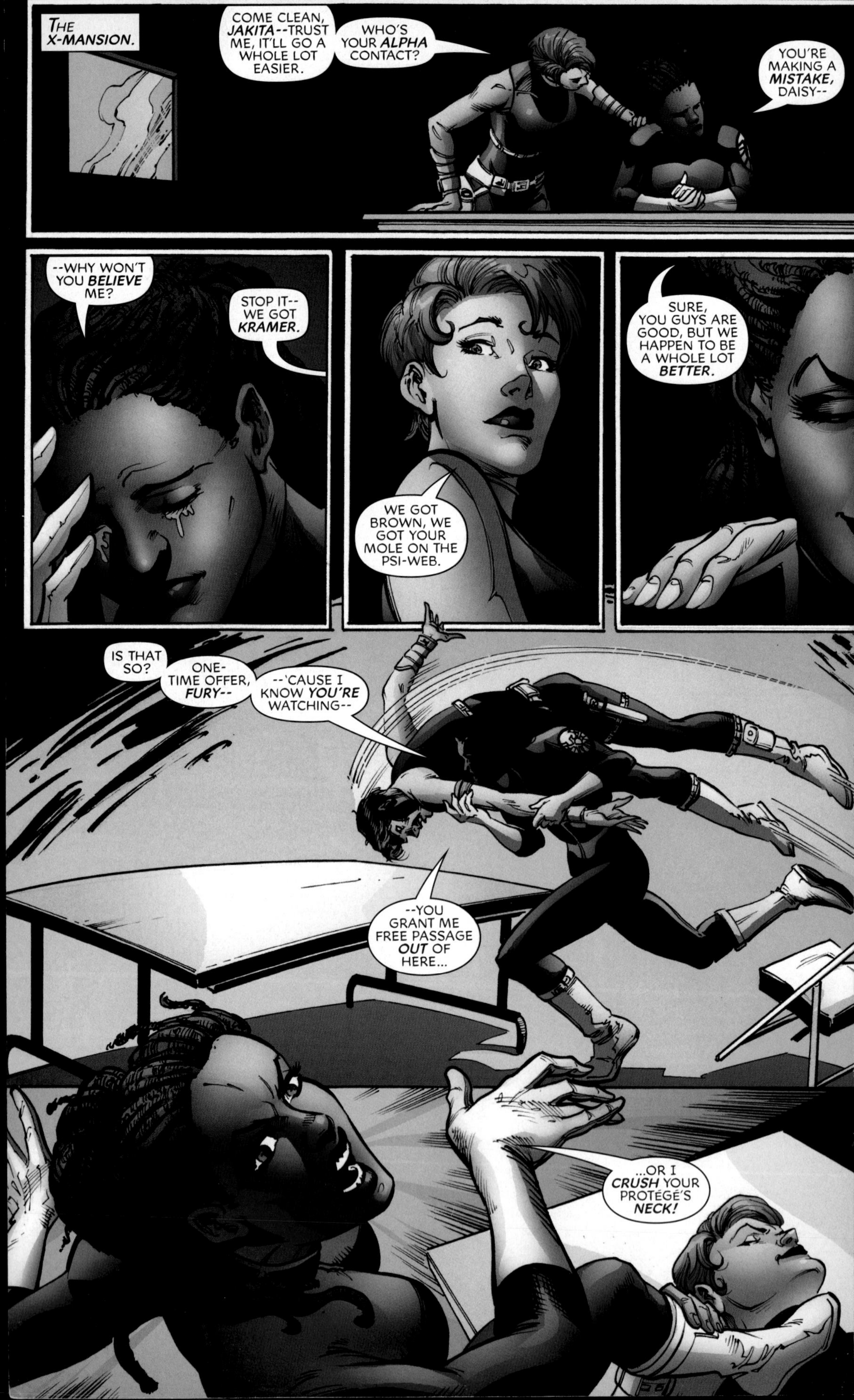
THE X-MANSION.
COME CLEAN, JAKITA--TRUST ME, IT'LL GO A WHOLE LOT EASIER.
WHO'S YOUR ALPHA CONTACT?
YOU'RE MAKING A MISTAKE, DAISY--
--WHY WON'T YOU BELIEVE ME?
STOP IT-- WE GOT KRAMER.
WE GOT BROWN, WE GOT YOUR MOLE ON THE PSI-WEB.
SURE, YOU GUYS ARE GOOD, BUT WE HAPPEN TO BE A WHOLE LOT BETTER.
IS THAT SO?
ONE-TIME OFFER, FURY--
--'CAUSE I KNOW YOU'RE WATCHING--
--YOU GRANT ME FREE PASSAGE OUT OF HERE...
...OR I CRUSH YOUR PROTÉGÉ'S NECK!

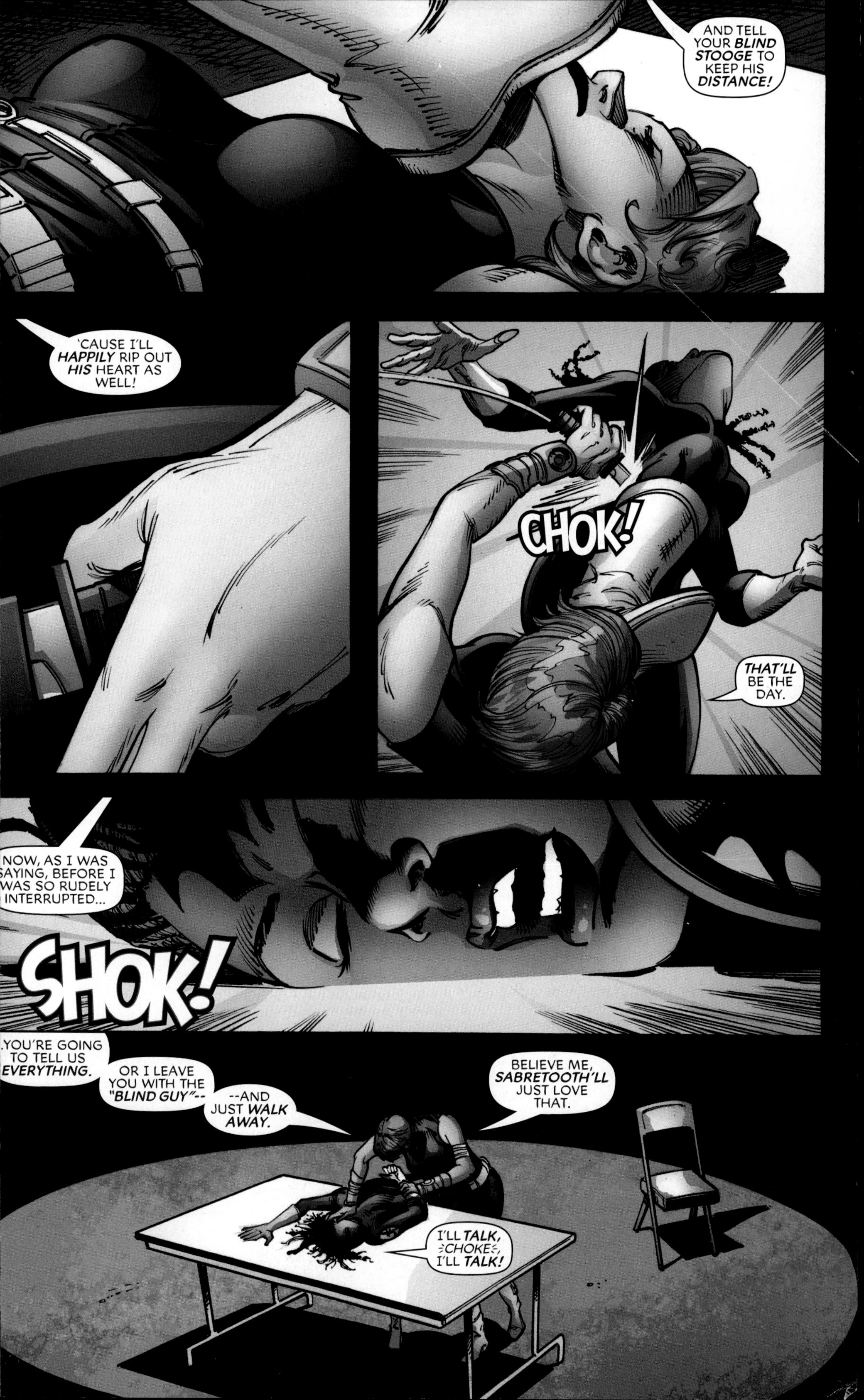
AND TELL YOUR BLIND STOOGE TO KEEP HIS DISTANCE!
'CAUSE I'LL HAPPILY RIP OUT HIS HEART AS WELL!
CHOK!
THAT'LL BE THE DAY.
NOW, AS I WAS SAYING, BEFORE I WAS SO RUDELY INTERRUPTED...
SHOK!
...YOU'RE GOING TO TELL US EVERYTHING.
OR I LEAVE YOU WITH THE "BLIND GUY"--
--AND JUST WALK AWAY.
BELIEVE ME, SABRETOOTH'LL JUST LOVE THAT.
I'LL TALK, CHOKE, I'LL TALK!

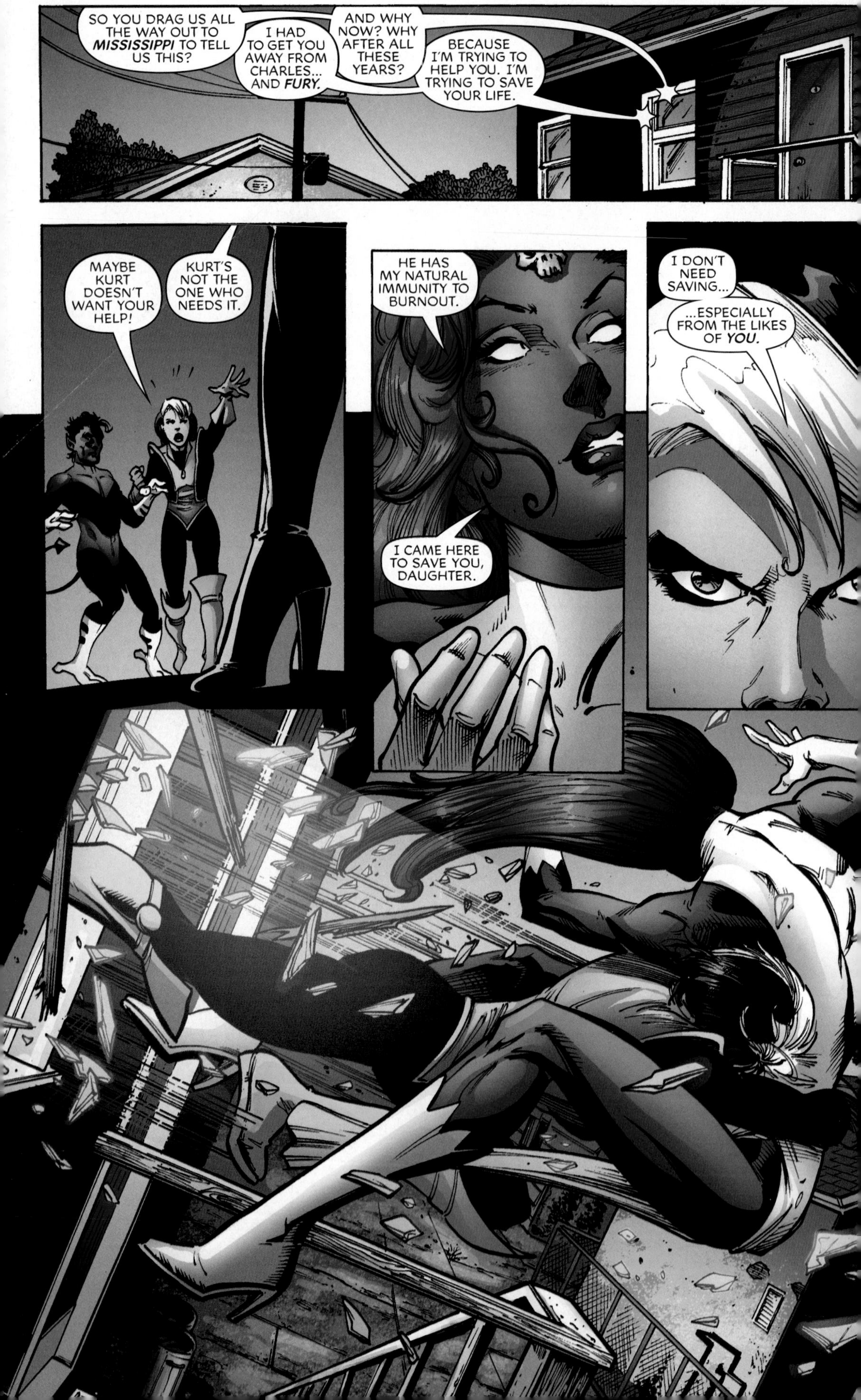

SO YOU DRAG US ALL THE WAY OUT TO *MISSISSIPPI* TO TELL US THIS?
I HAD TO GET YOU AWAY FROM CHARLES... AND *FURY.*
AND WHY NOW? WHY AFTER ALL THESE YEARS?
BECAUSE I'M TRYING TO HELP YOU. I'M TRYING TO SAVE YOUR LIFE.
MAYBE KURT DOESN'T WANT YOUR HELP!
KURT'S NOT THE ONE WHO NEEDS IT.
HE HAS MY NATURAL IMMUNITY TO BURNOUT.
I CAME HERE TO SAVE YOU, DAUGHTER.
I DON'T NEED SAVING...
...ESPECIALLY FROM THE LIKES OF *YOU.*

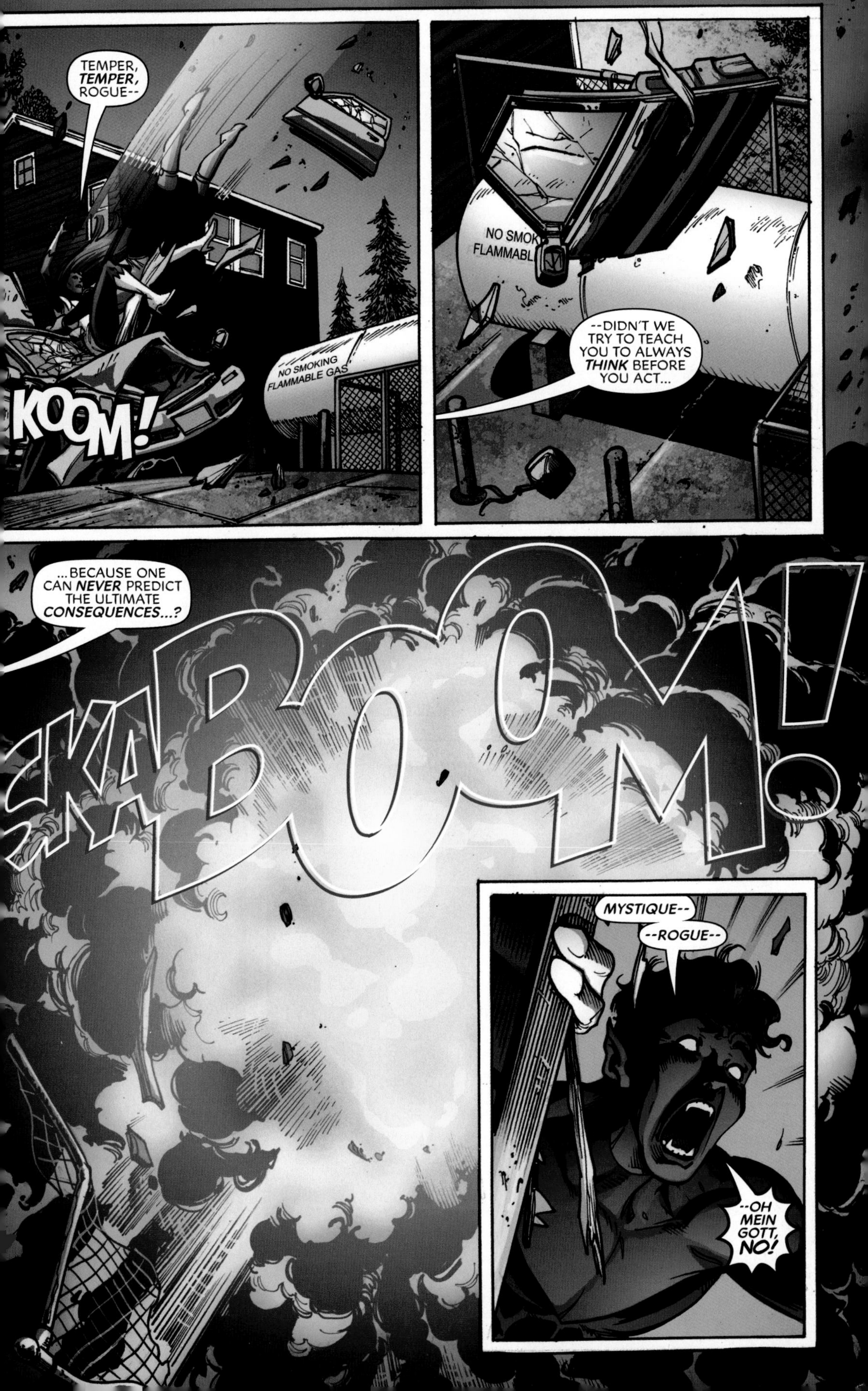
TEMPER, TEMPER, ROGUE--
NO SMOKING FLAMMABLE GAS
KOOM!
NO SMOK FLAMMABL
--DIDN'T WE TRY TO TEACH YOU TO ALWAYS THINK BEFORE YOU ACT...
...BECAUSE ONE CAN NEVER PREDICT THE ULTIMATE CONSEQUENCES...?
SKABOOM!
MYSTIQUE--
--ROGUE--
--OH MEIN GOTT, NO!

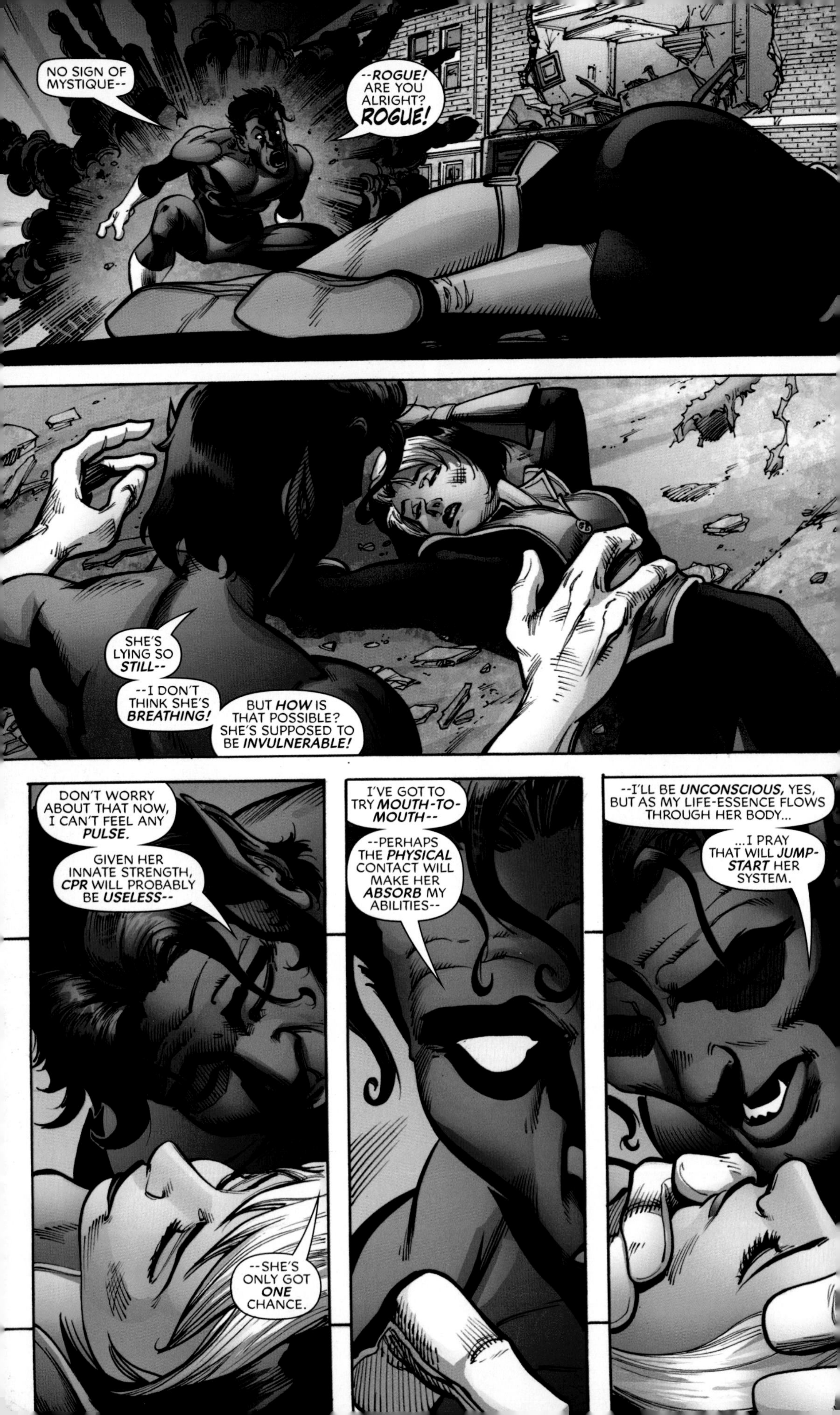
NO SIGN OF MYSTIQUE--
--ROGUE! ARE YOU ALRIGHT? ROGUE!
SHE'S LYING SO STILL--
--I DON'T THINK SHE'S BREATHING!
BUT HOW IS THAT POSSIBLE? SHE'S SUPPOSED TO BE INVULNERABLE!
DON'T WORRY ABOUT THAT NOW, I CAN'T FEEL ANY PULSE.
GIVEN HER INNATE STRENGTH, CPR WILL PROBABLY BE USELESS--
--SHE'S ONLY GOT ONE CHANCE.
I'VE GOT TO TRY MOUTH-TO-MOUTH--
--PERHAPS THE PHYSICAL CONTACT WILL MAKE HER ABSORB MY ABILITIES--
--I'LL BE UNCONSCIOUS, YES, BUT AS MY LIFE-ESSENCE FLOWS THROUGH HER BODY...
...I PRAY THAT WILL JUMP-START HER SYSTEM.

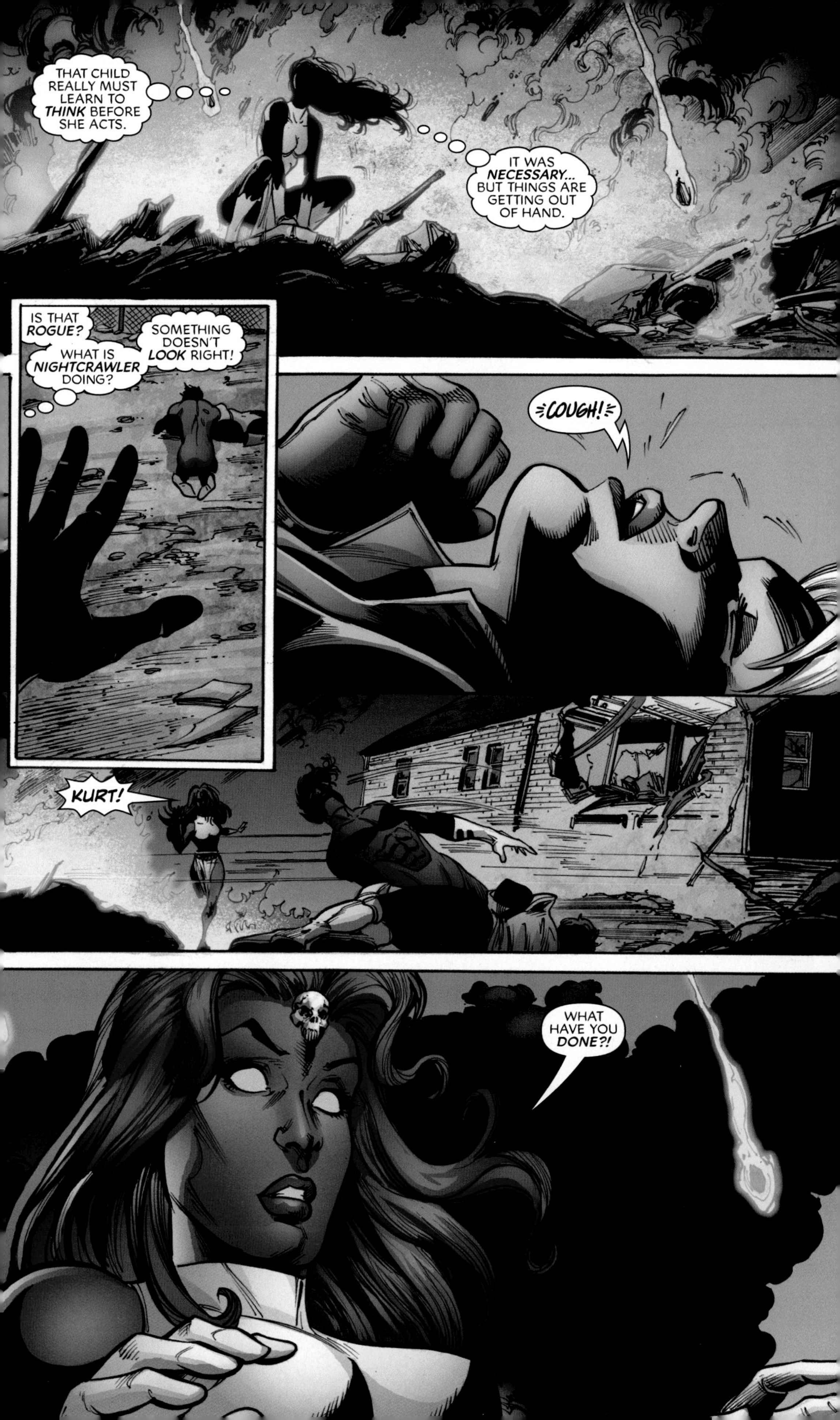
THAT CHILD REALLY MUST LEARN TO THINK BEFORE SHE ACTS.
IT WAS NECESSARY... BUT THINGS ARE GETTING OUT OF HAND.
IS THAT ROGUE?
WHAT IS NIGHTCRAWLER DOING?
SOMETHING DOESN'T LOOK RIGHT!
COUGH!
KURT!
WHAT HAVE YOU DONE?!

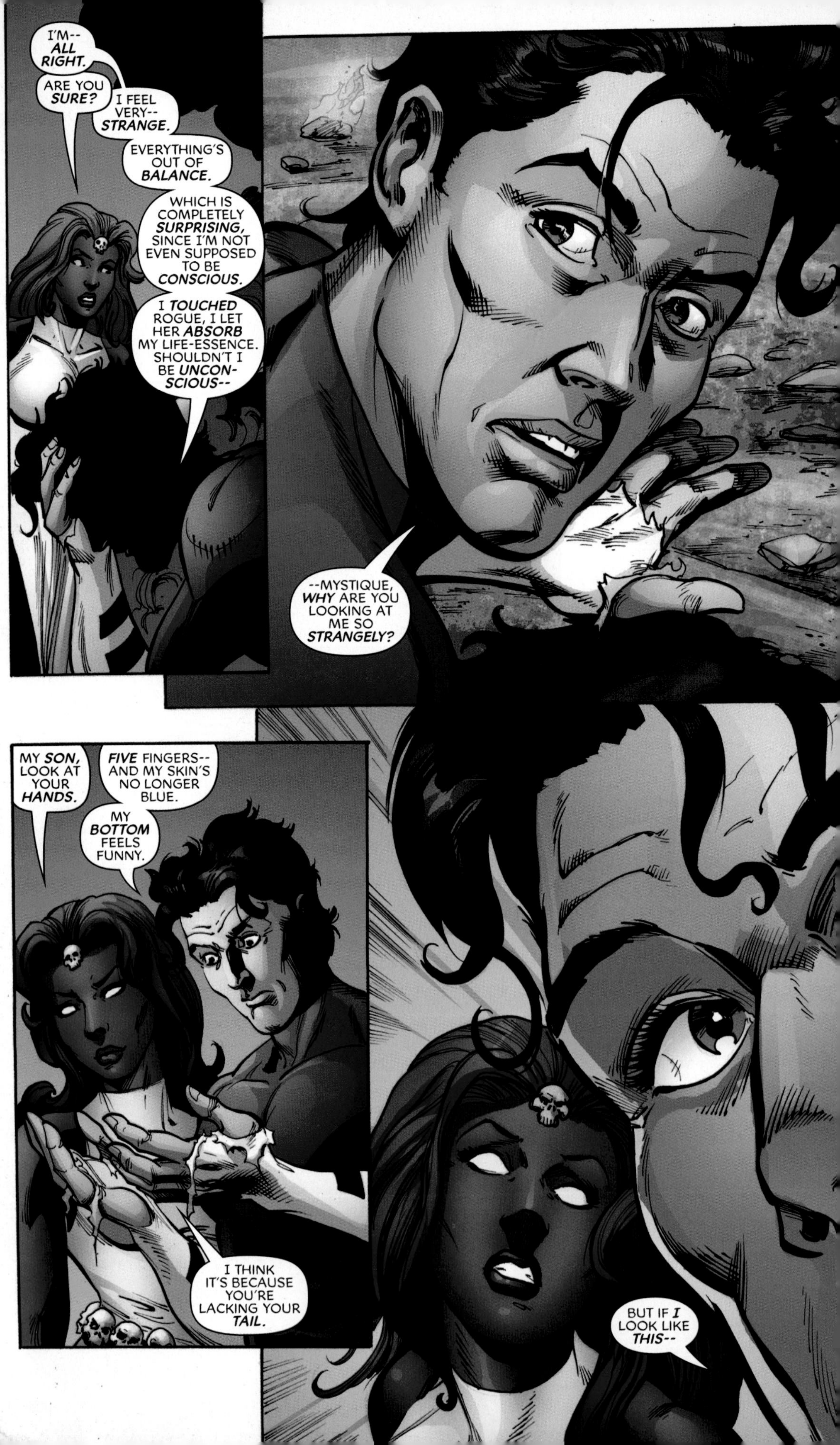

I'M-- ALL RIGHT.
ARE YOU SURE?
I FEEL VERY-- STRANGE.
EVERYTHING'S OUT OF BALANCE.
WHICH IS COMPLETELY SURPRISING, SINCE I'M NOT EVEN SUPPOSED TO BE CONSCIOUS.
I TOUCHED ROGUE, I LET HER ABSORB MY LIFE-ESSENCE. SHOULDN'T I BE UNCON-SCIOUS--
--MYSTIQUE, WHY ARE YOU LOOKING AT ME SO STRANGELY?
MY SON, LOOK AT YOUR HANDS.
FIVE FINGERS-- AND MY SKIN'S NO LONGER BLUE.
MY BOTTOM FEELS FUNNY.
I THINK IT'S BECAUSE YOU'RE LACKING YOUR TAIL.
BUT IF I LOOK LIKE THIS--

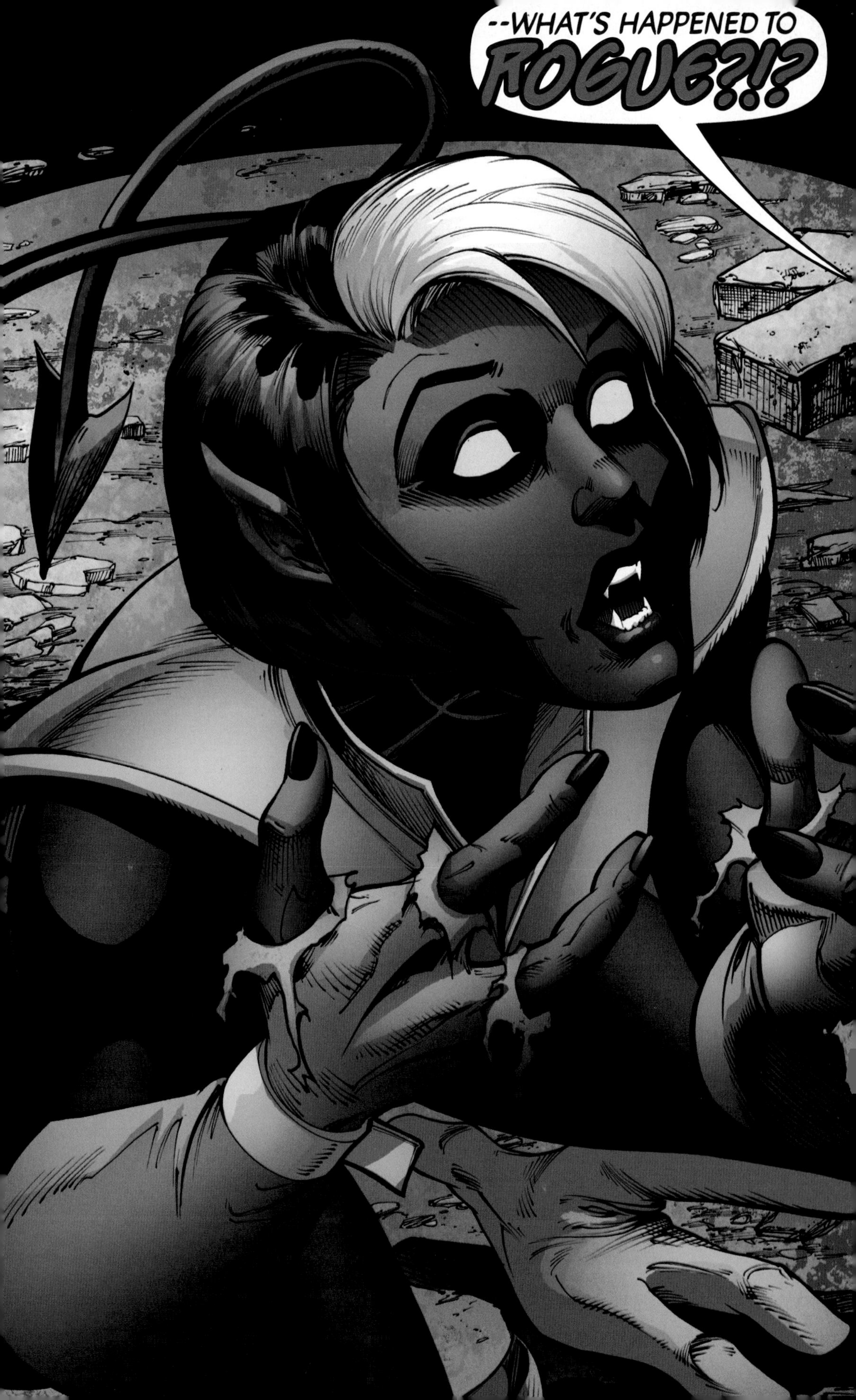
--WHAT'S HAPPENED TO
ROGUE?!?

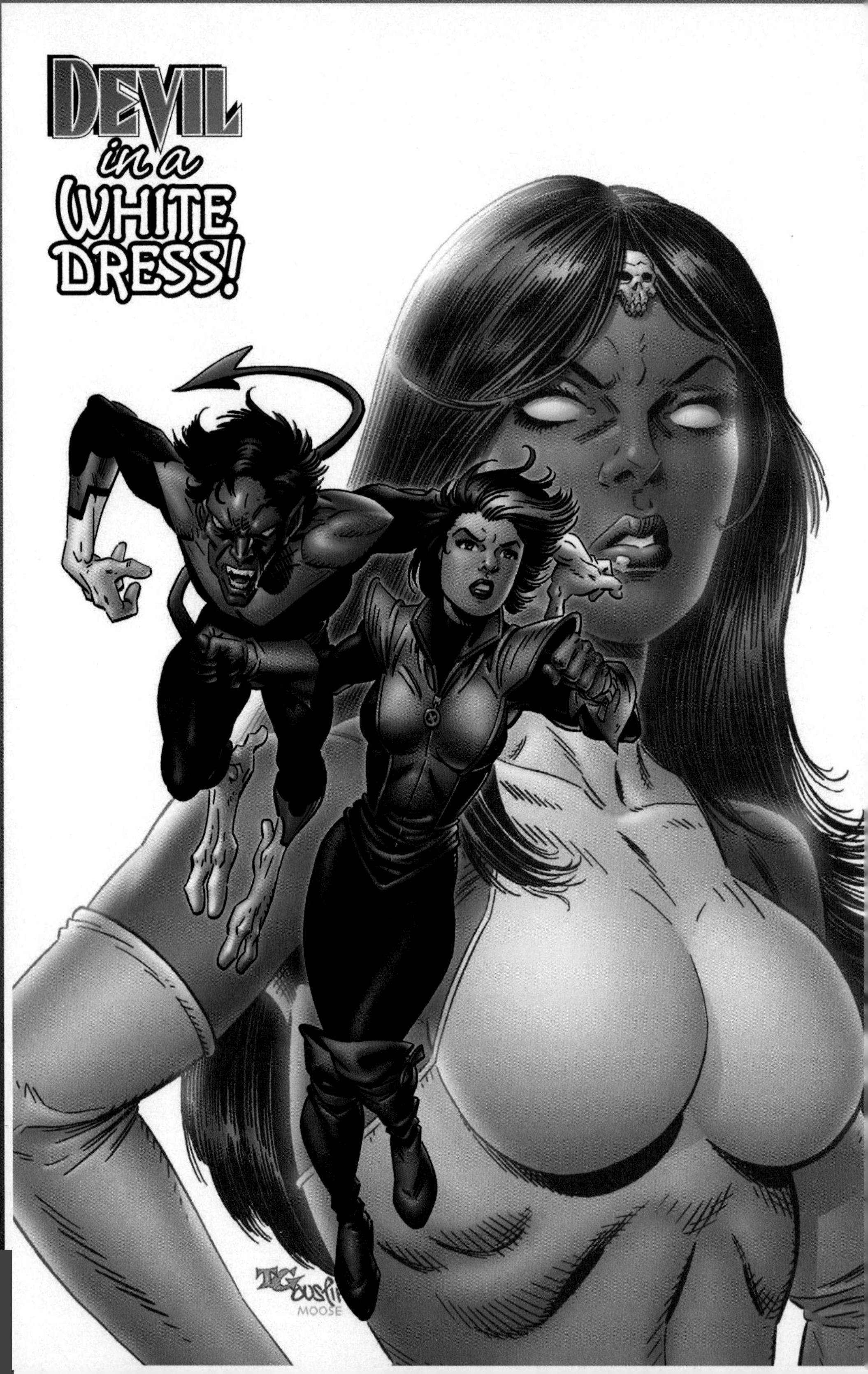
DEVIL
in a
WHITE
DRESS!

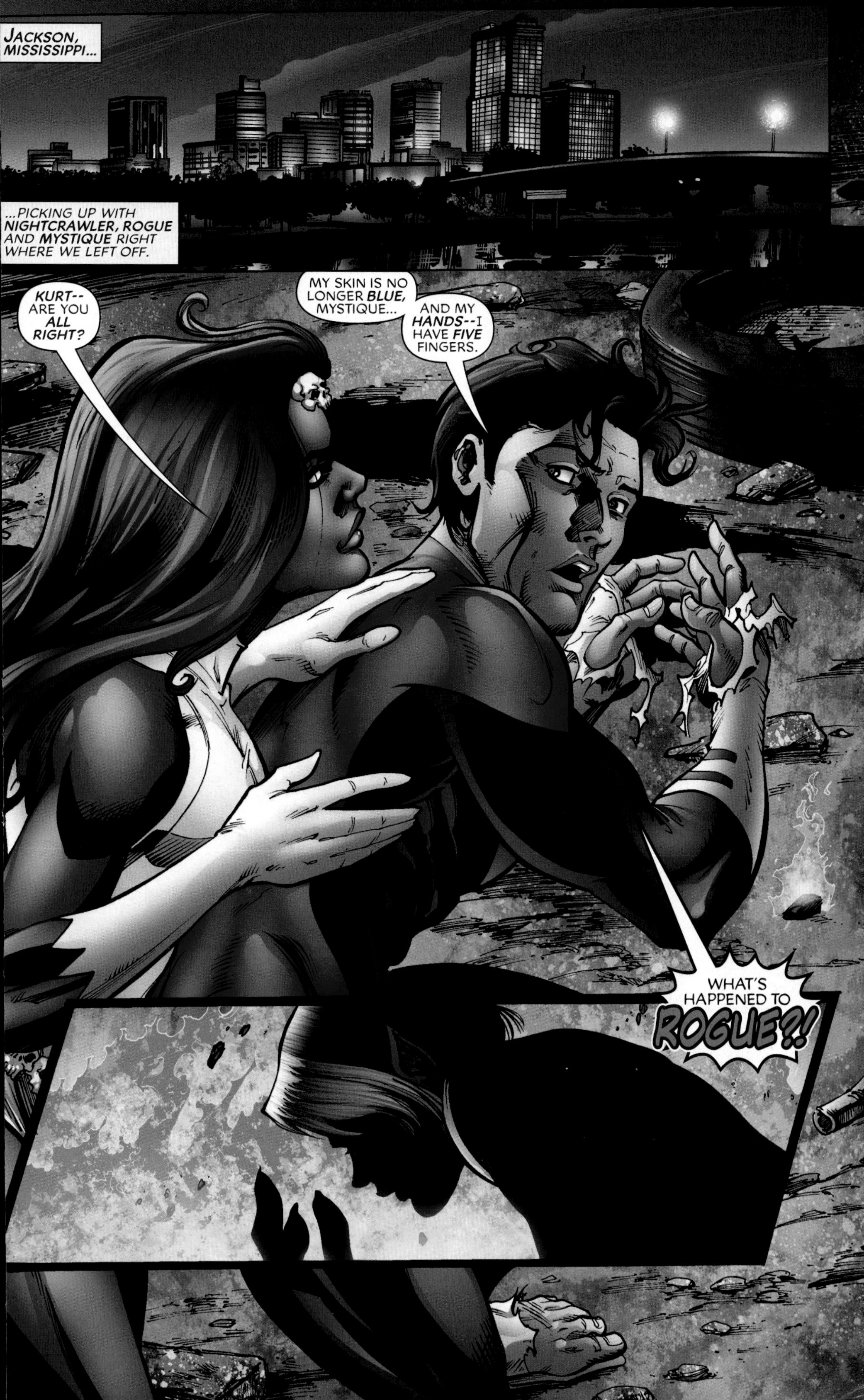

JACKSON, MISSISSIPPI...
...PICKING UP WITH NIGHTCRAWLER, ROGUE AND MYSTIQUE RIGHT WHERE WE LEFT OFF.
KURT-- ARE YOU ALL RIGHT?
MY SKIN IS NO LONGER BLUE, MYSTIQUE...
AND MY HANDS--I HAVE FIVE FINGERS.
WHAT'S HAPPENED TO ROGUE?!

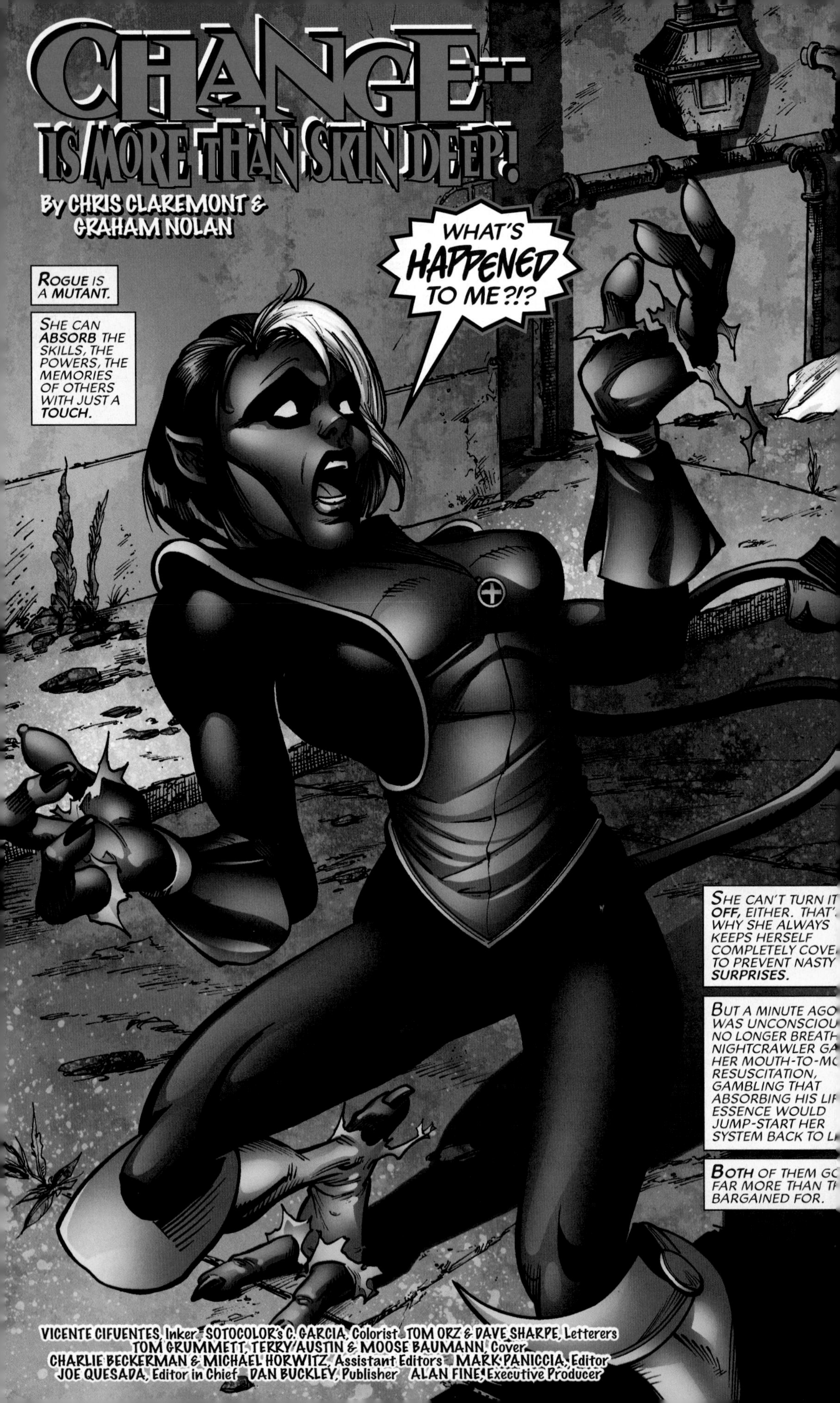

CHANGE--
IS MORE THAN SKIN DEEP!
By CHRIS CLAREMONT & GRAHAM NOLAN
ROGUE IS A MUTANT.
SHE CAN ABSORB THE SKILLS, THE POWERS, THE MEMORIES OF OTHERS WITH JUST A TOUCH.
WHAT'S HAPPENED TO ME?!?
SHE CAN'T TURN IT OFF, EITHER. THAT' WHY SHE ALWAYS KEEPS HERSELF COMPLETELY COVE TO PREVENT NASTY SURPRISES.
BUT A MINUTE AGO WAS UNCONSCIOU NO LONGER BREATH NIGHTCRAWLER GA HER MOUTH-TO-MO RESUSCITATION, GAMBLING THAT ABSORBING HIS LIF ESSENCE WOULD JUMP-START HER SYSTEM BACK TO L
BOTH OF THEM GO FAR MORE THAN T BARGAINED FOR.
VICENTE CIFUENTES, Inker SOTOCOLOR's C. GARCIA, Colorist TOM ORZ & DAVE SHARPE, Letterers
TOM GRUMMETT, TERRY AUSTIN & MOOSE BAUMANN, Cover
CHARLIE BECKERMAN & MICHAEL HORWITZ, Assistant Editors MARK PANICCIA, Editor
JOE QUESADA, Editor in Chief DAN BUCKLEY, Publisher ALAN FINE, Executive Producer

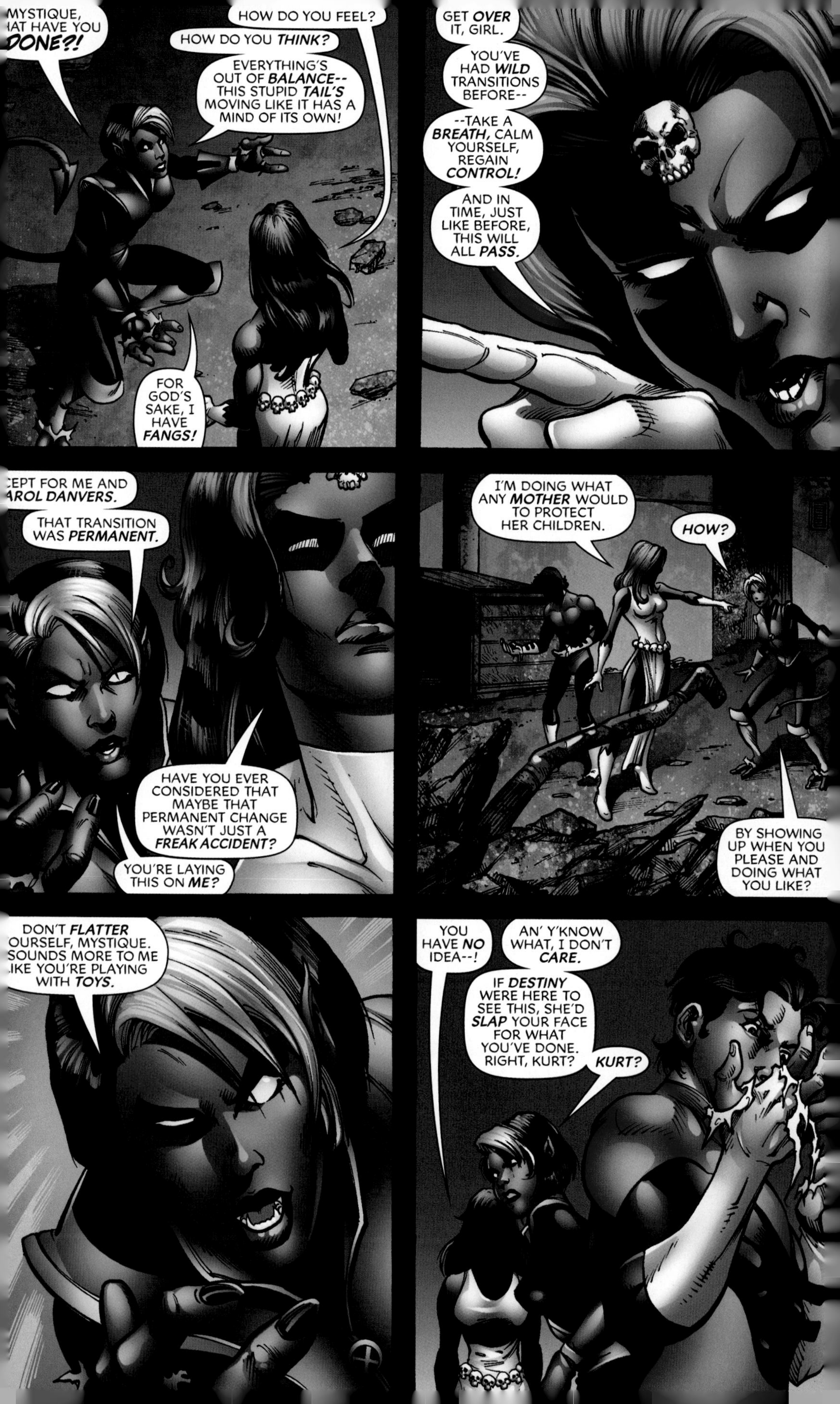
MYSTIQUE, (W)HAT HAVE YOU DONE?!
HOW DO YOU FEEL?
HOW DO YOU THINK?
EVERYTHING'S OUT OF BALANCE-- THIS STUPID TAIL'S MOVING LIKE IT HAS A MIND OF ITS OWN!
FOR GOD'S SAKE, I HAVE FANGS!
GET OVER IT, GIRL.
YOU'VE HAD WILD TRANSITIONS BEFORE--
--TAKE A BREATH, CALM YOURSELF, REGAIN CONTROL!
AND IN TIME, JUST LIKE BEFORE, THIS WILL ALL PASS.
CEPT FOR ME AND AROL DANVERS.
THAT TRANSITION WAS PERMANENT.
HAVE YOU EVER CONSIDERED THAT MAYBE THAT PERMANENT CHANGE WASN'T JUST A FREAK ACCIDENT?
YOU'RE LAYING THIS ON ME?
I'M DOING WHAT ANY MOTHER WOULD TO PROTECT HER CHILDREN.
HOW?
BY SHOWING UP WHEN YOU PLEASE AND DOING WHAT YOU LIKE?
DON'T FLATTER OURSELF, MYSTIQUE. SOUNDS MORE TO ME LIKE YOU'RE PLAYING WITH TOYS.
YOU HAVE NO IDEA--!
AN' Y'KNOW WHAT, I DON'T CARE.
IF DESTINY WERE HERE TO SEE THIS, SHE'D SLAP YOUR FACE FOR WHAT YOU'VE DONE. RIGHT, KURT?
KURT?

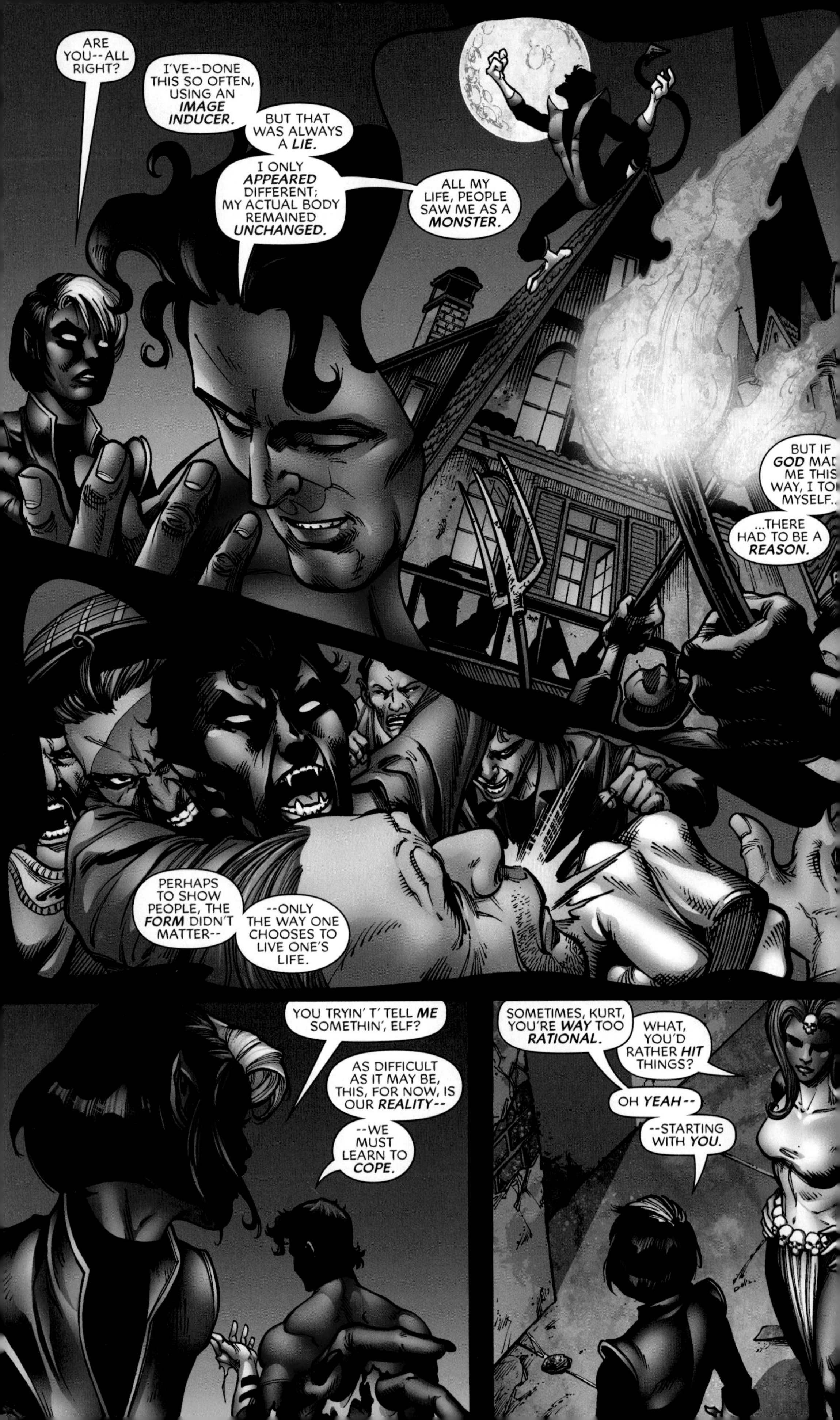
ARE YOU--ALL RIGHT?
I'VE--DONE THIS SO OFTEN, USING AN IMAGE INDUCER.
BUT THAT WAS ALWAYS A LIE.
I ONLY APPEARED DIFFERENT; MY ACTUAL BODY REMAINED UNCHANGED.
ALL MY LIFE, PEOPLE SAW ME AS A MONSTER.
BUT IF GOD MAD ME THIS WAY, I TO MYSELF...
...THERE HAD TO BE A REASON.
PERHAPS TO SHOW PEOPLE, THE FORM DIDN'T MATTER--
--ONLY THE WAY ONE CHOOSES TO LIVE ONE'S LIFE.
YOU TRYIN' T' TELL ME SOMETHIN', ELF?
AS DIFFICULT AS IT MAY BE, THIS, FOR NOW, IS OUR REALITY--
--WE MUST LEARN TO COPE.
SOMETIMES, KURT, YOU'RE WAY TOO RATIONAL.
WHAT, YOU'D RATHER HIT THINGS?
OH YEAH--
--STARTING WITH YOU.

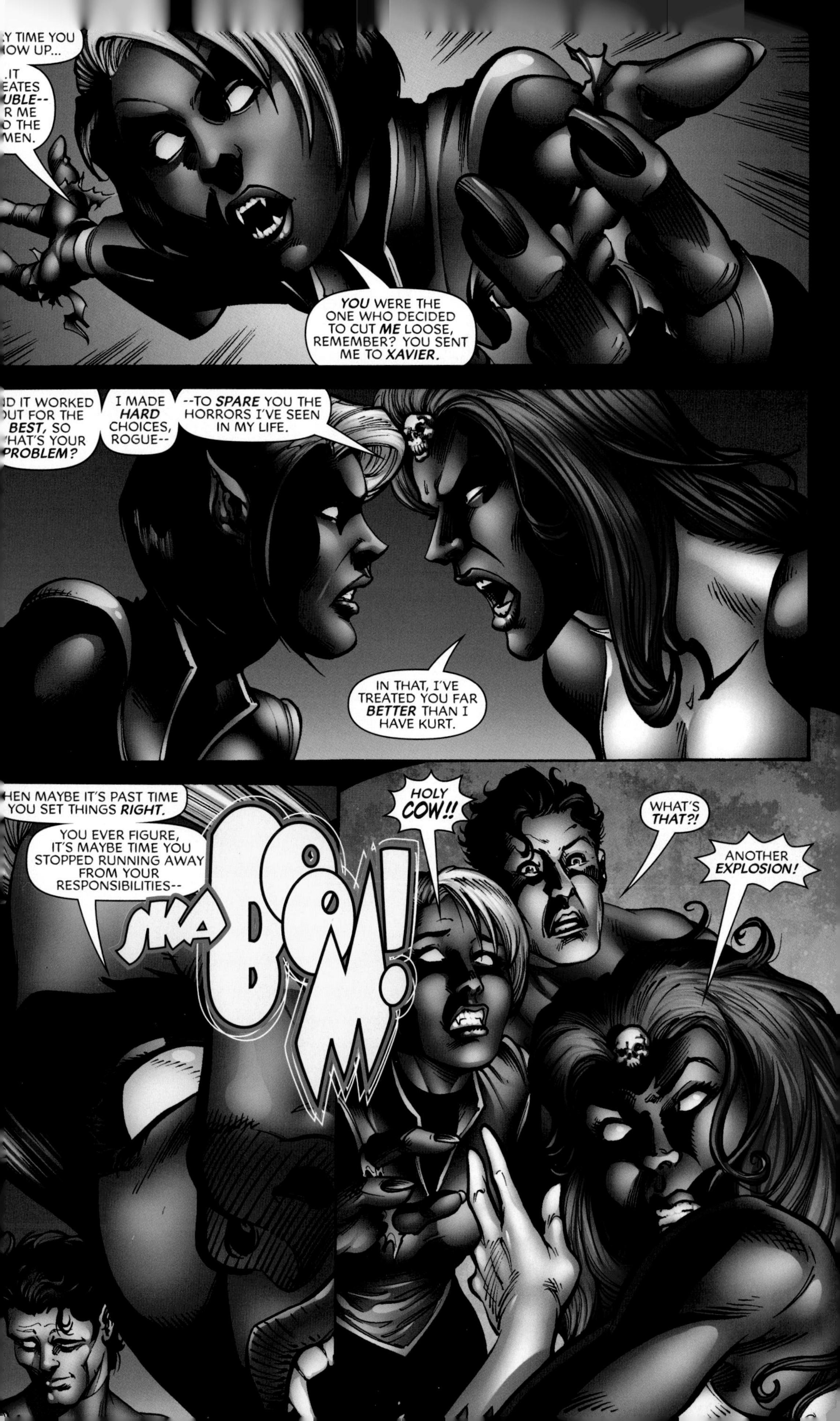

Y TIME YOU
IOW UP...
..IT
EATES
UBLE--
R ME
D THE
MEN.
YOU WERE THE ONE WHO DECIDED TO CUT ME LOOSE, REMEMBER? YOU SENT ME TO XAVIER.
D IT WORKED
UT FOR THE
BEST, SO
HAT'S YOUR
PROBLEM?
I MADE HARD CHOICES, ROGUE--
--TO SPARE YOU THE HORRORS I'VE SEEN IN MY LIFE.
IN THAT, I'VE TREATED YOU FAR BETTER THAN I HAVE KURT.
HEN MAYBE IT'S PAST TIME
YOU SET THINGS RIGHT.
YOU EVER FIGURE, IT'S MAYBE TIME YOU STOPPED RUNNING AWAY FROM YOUR RESPONSIBILITIES--
SKA BOOM!
HOLY COW!!
WHAT'S THAT?!
ANOTHER EXPLOSION!

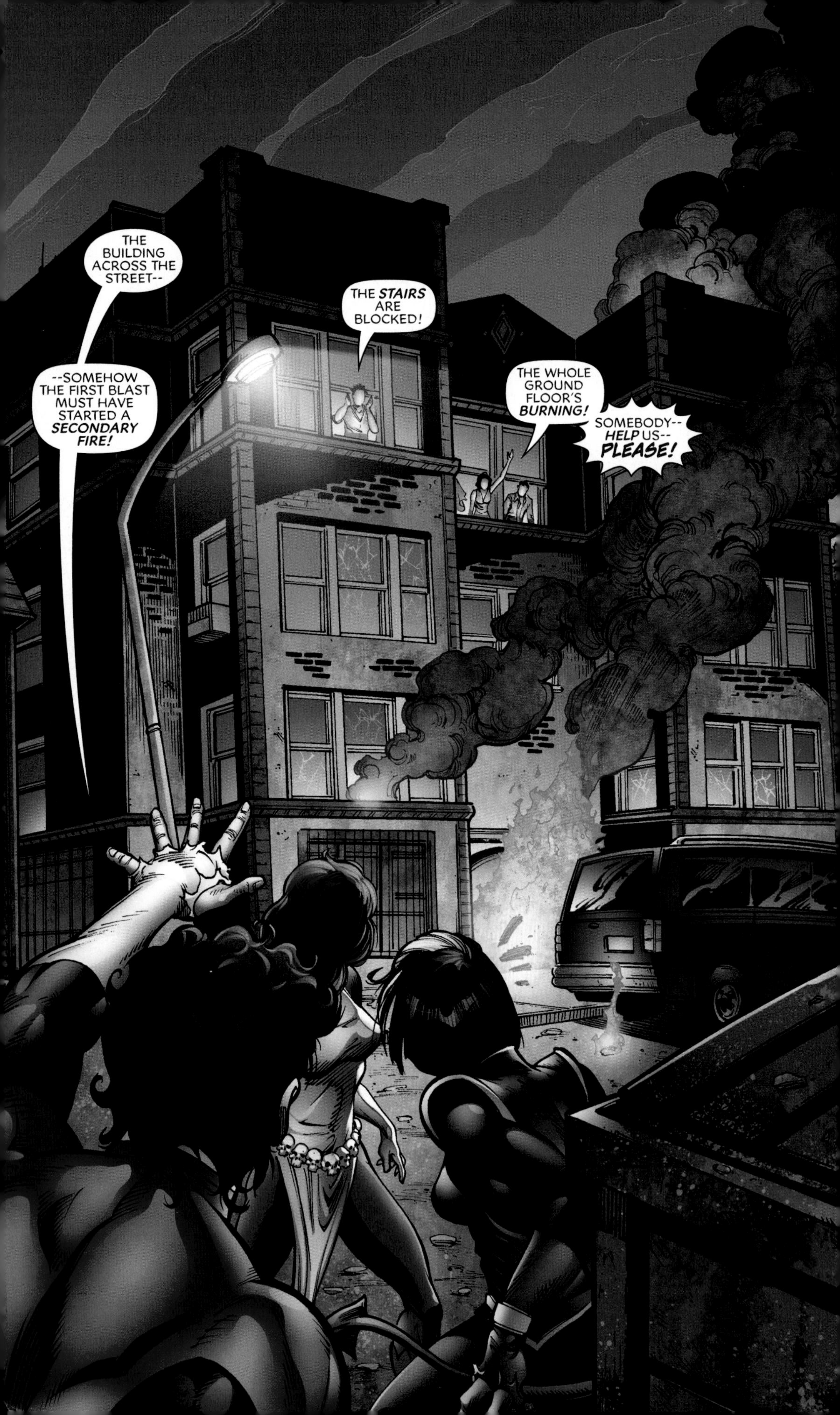
THE BUILDING ACROSS THE STREET--
--SOMEHOW THE FIRST BLAST MUST HAVE STARTED A SECONDARY FIRE!
THE STAIRS ARE BLOCKED!
THE WHOLE GROUND FLOOR'S BURNING!
SOMEBODY-- HELP US-- PLEASE!

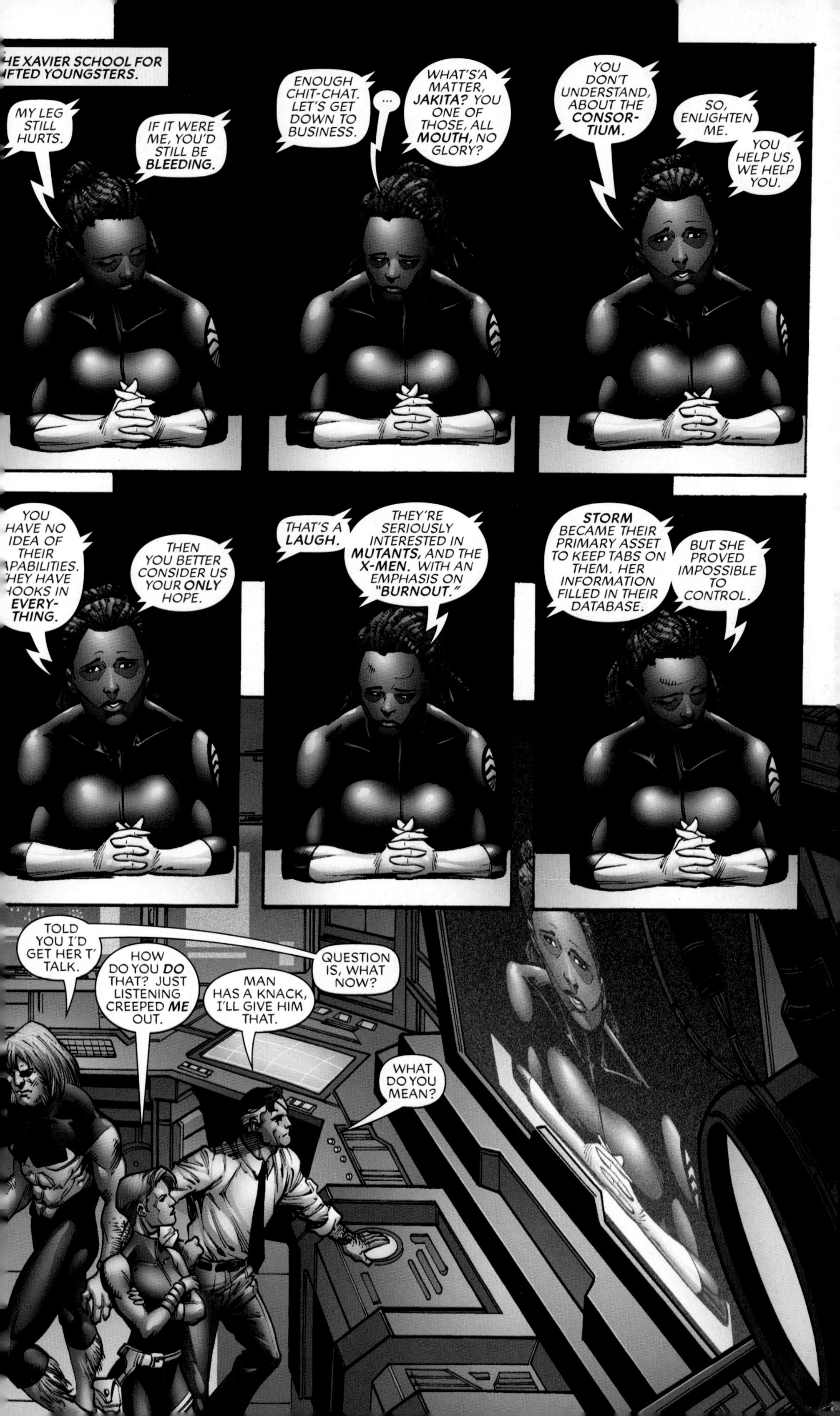
HE XAVIER SCHOOL FOR
IFTED YOUNGSTERS.
MY LEG STILL HURTS.
IF IT WERE ME, YOU'D STILL BE BLEEDING.
ENOUGH CHIT-CHAT. LET'S GET DOWN TO BUSINESS.
...
WHAT'S'A MATTER, JAKITA? YOU ONE OF THOSE, ALL MOUTH, NO GLORY?
YOU DON'T UNDERSTAND, ABOUT THE CONSORTIUM.
SO, ENLIGHTEN ME.
YOU HELP US, WE HELP YOU.
YOU HAVE NO IDEA OF THEIR APABILITIES. HEY HAVE HOOKS IN EVERYTHING.
THEN YOU BETTER CONSIDER US YOUR ONLY HOPE.
THAT'S A LAUGH.
THEY'RE SERIOUSLY INTERESTED IN MUTANTS, AND THE X-MEN. WITH AN EMPHASIS ON "BURNOUT."
STORM BECAME THEIR PRIMARY ASSET TO KEEP TABS ON THEM. HER INFORMATION FILLED IN THEIR DATABASE.
BUT SHE PROVED IMPOSSIBLE TO CONTROL.
TOLD YOU I'D GET HER T' TALK.
HOW DO YOU DO THAT? JUST LISTENING CREEPED ME OUT.
MAN HAS A KNACK, I'LL GIVE HIM THAT.
QUESTION IS, WHAT NOW?
WHAT DO YOU MEAN?

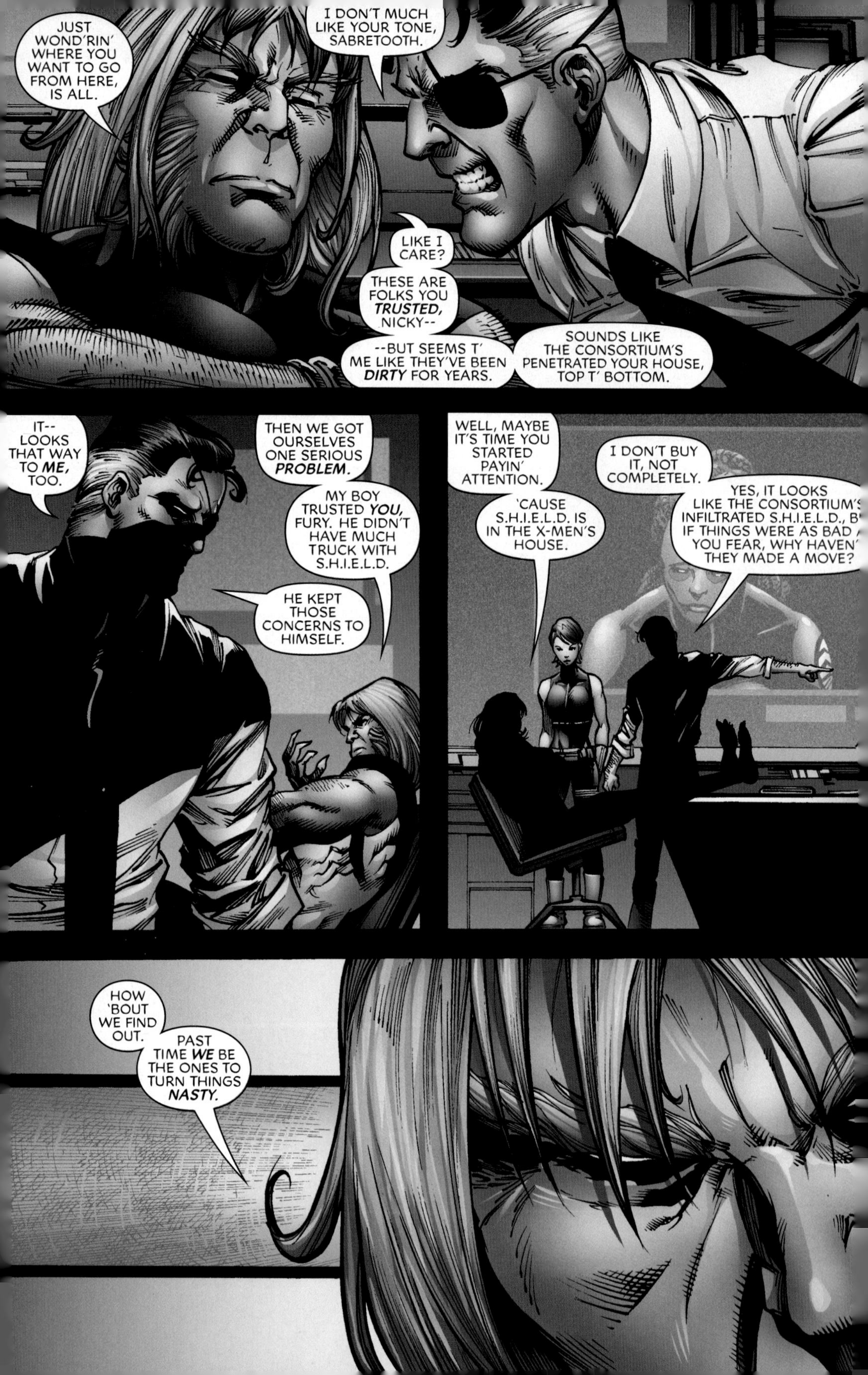
JUST WOND'RIN' WHERE YOU WANT TO GO FROM HERE, IS ALL.
I DON'T MUCH LIKE YOUR TONE, SABRETOOTH.
LIKE I CARE?
THESE ARE FOLKS YOU TRUSTED, NICKY--
--BUT SEEMS T' ME LIKE THEY'VE BEEN DIRTY FOR YEARS.
SOUNDS LIKE THE CONSORTIUM'S PENETRATED YOUR HOUSE, TOP T' BOTTOM.
IT-- LOOKS THAT WAY TO ME, TOO.
THEN WE GOT OURSELVES ONE SERIOUS PROBLEM.
MY BOY TRUSTED YOU, FURY. HE DIDN'T HAVE MUCH TRUCK WITH S.H.I.E.L.D.
HE KEPT THOSE CONCERNS TO HIMSELF.
WELL, MAYBE IT'S TIME YOU STARTED PAYIN' ATTENTION.
'CAUSE S.H.I.E.L.D. IS IN THE X-MEN'S HOUSE.
I DON'T BUY IT, NOT COMPLETELY.
YES, IT LOOKS LIKE THE CONSORTIUM'S INFILTRATED S.H.I.E.L.D., BUT IF THINGS WERE AS BAD AS YOU FEAR, WHY HAVEN'T THEY MADE A MOVE?
HOW 'BOUT WE FIND OUT.
PAST TIME WE BE THE ONES TO TURN THINGS NASTY.

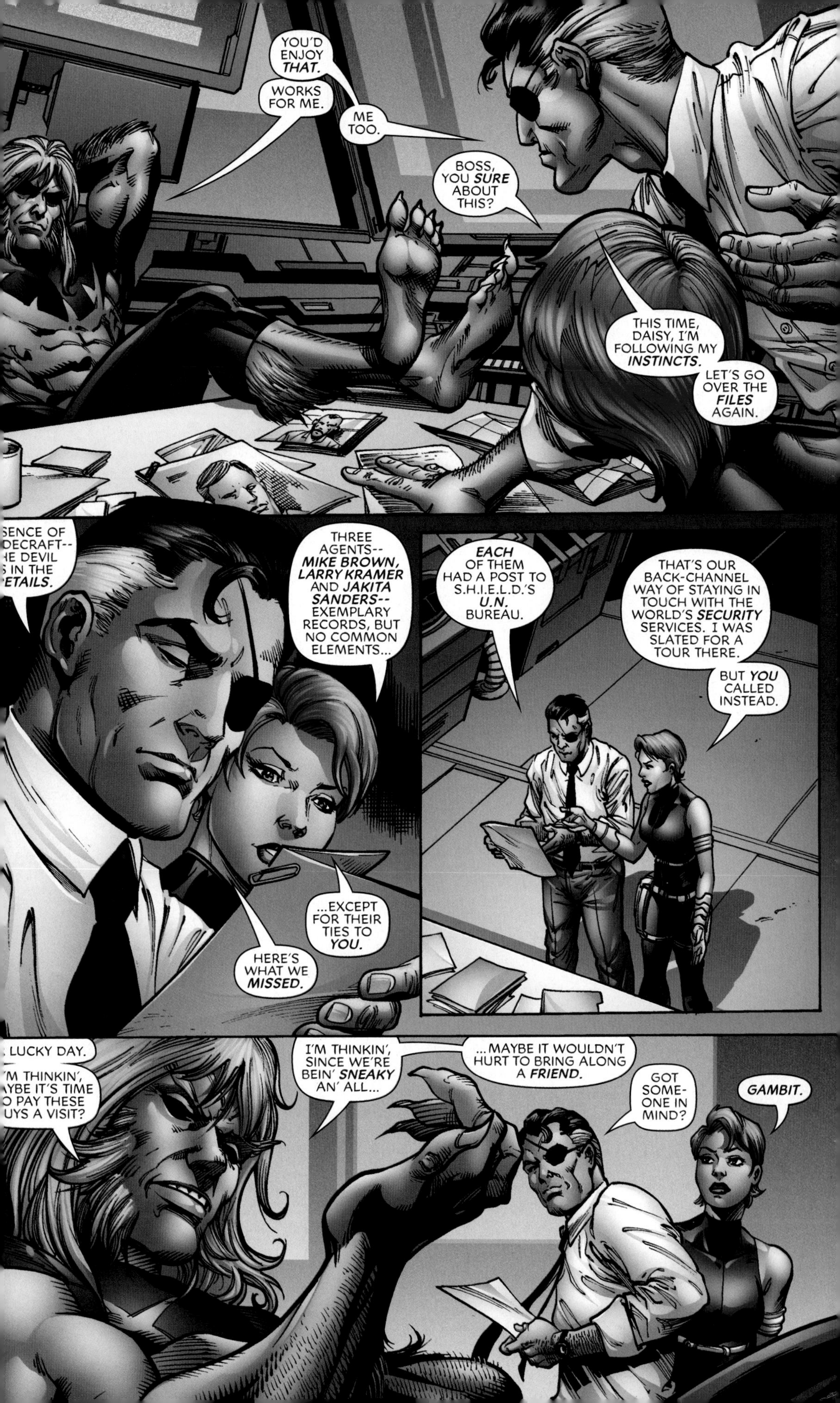

YOU'D ENJOY THAT.
WORKS FOR ME.
ME TOO.
BOSS, YOU SURE ABOUT THIS?
THIS TIME, DAISY, I'M FOLLOWING MY INSTINCTS.
LET'S GO OVER THE FILES AGAIN.
SENCE OF DECRAFT-- HE DEVIL S IN THE ETAILS.
THREE AGENTS-- MIKE BROWN, LARRY KRAMER AND JAKITA SANDERS-- EXEMPLARY RECORDS, BUT NO COMMON ELEMENTS...
...EXCEPT FOR THEIR TIES TO YOU.
HERE'S WHAT WE MISSED.
EACH OF THEM HAD A POST TO S.H.I.E.L.D.'S U.N. BUREAU.
THAT'S OUR BACK-CHANNEL WAY OF STAYING IN TOUCH WITH THE WORLD'S SECURITY SERVICES. I WAS SLATED FOR A TOUR THERE.
BUT YOU CALLED INSTEAD.
LUCKY DAY.
'M THINKIN', AYBE IT'S TIME O PAY THESE UYS A VISIT?
I'M THINKIN', SINCE WE'RE BEIN' SNEAKY AN' ALL...
...MAYBE IT WOULDN'T HURT TO BRING ALONG A FRIEND.
GOT SOME-ONE IN MIND?
GAMBIT.

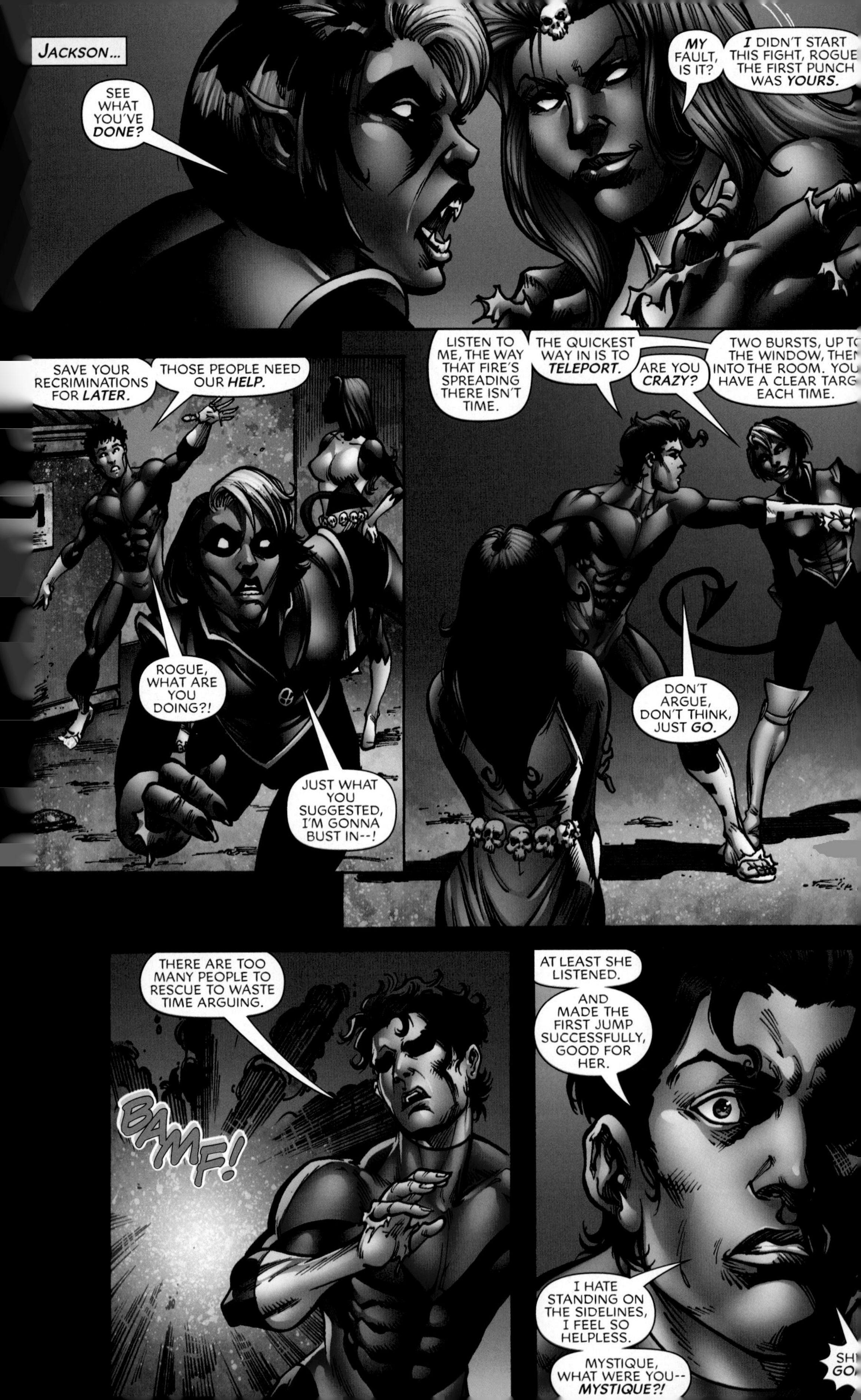
JACKSON...
SEE WHAT YOU'VE DONE?
MY FAULT, IS IT?
I DIDN'T START THIS FIGHT, ROGUE. THE FIRST PUNCH WAS YOURS.
SAVE YOUR RECRIMINATIONS FOR LATER.
THOSE PEOPLE NEED OUR HELP.
ROGUE, WHAT ARE YOU DOING?!
JUST WHAT YOU SUGGESTED, I'M GONNA BUST IN--!
LISTEN TO ME, THE WAY THAT FIRE'S SPREADING THERE ISN'T TIME.
THE QUICKEST WAY IN IS TO TELEPORT.
ARE YOU CRAZY?
TWO BURSTS, UP TO THE WINDOW, THEN INTO THE ROOM. YOU HAVE A CLEAR TARG EACH TIME.
DON'T ARGUE, DON'T THINK, JUST GO.
THERE ARE TOO MANY PEOPLE TO RESCUE TO WASTE TIME ARGUING.
BAMF!
AT LEAST SHE LISTENED.
AND MADE THE FIRST JUMP SUCCESSFULLY, GOOD FOR HER.
I HATE STANDING ON THE SIDELINES, I FEEL SO HELPLESS.
MYSTIQUE, WHAT WERE YOU-- MYSTIQUE?!

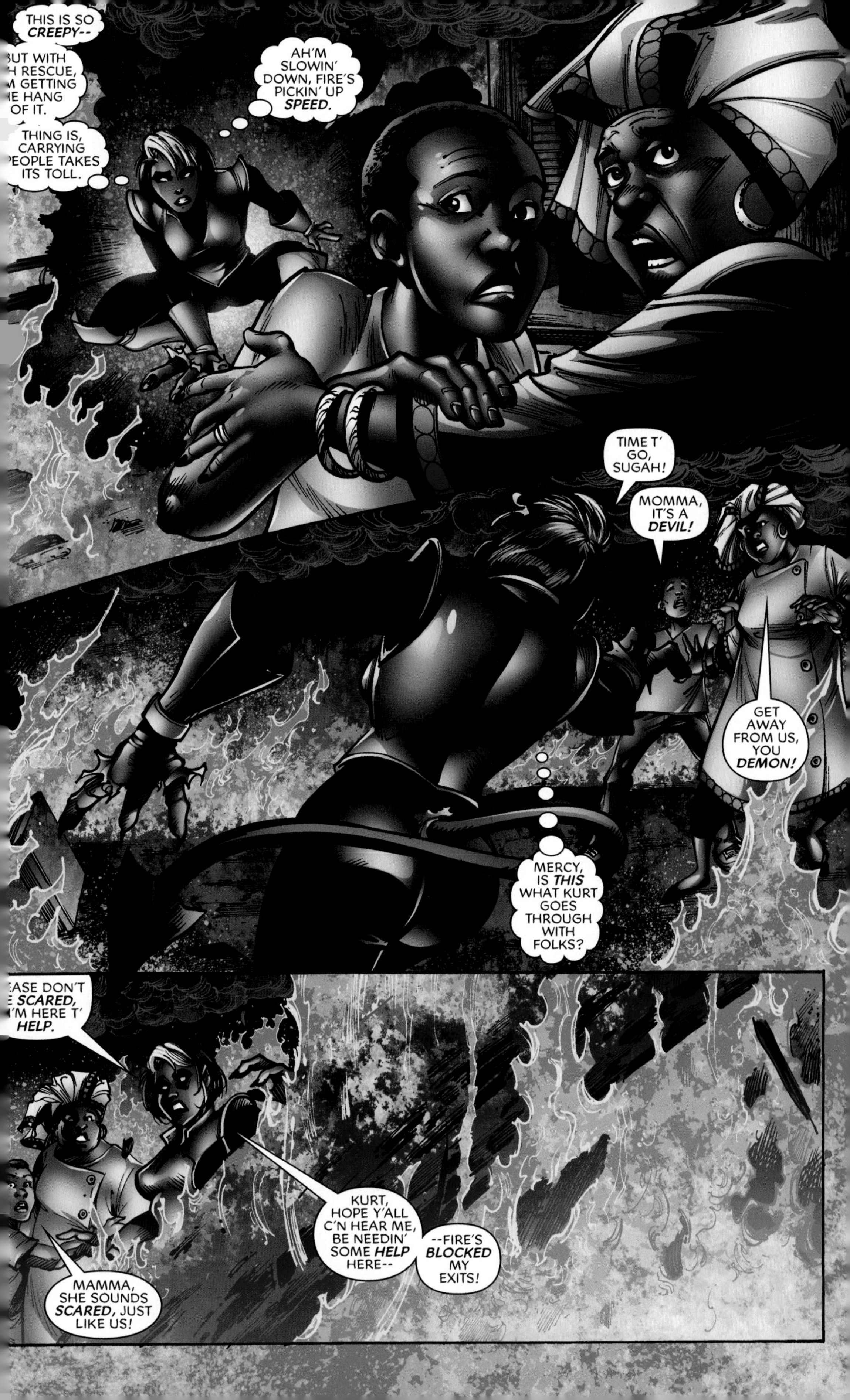
THIS IS SO *CREEPY--*
BUT WITH H RESCUE, M GETTING E HANG OF IT.
THING IS, CARRYING EOPLE TAKES ITS TOLL.
AH'M SLOWIN' DOWN, FIRE'S PICKIN' UP *SPEED.*
TIME T' GO, SUGAH!
MOMMA, IT'S A *DEVIL!*
GET AWAY FROM US, YOU *DEMON!*
MERCY, IS *THIS* WHAT KURT GOES THROUGH WITH FOLKS?
EASE DON'T E *SCARED,* 'M HERE T' *HELP.*
MAMMA, SHE SOUNDS *SCARED,* JUST LIKE US!
KURT, HOPE Y'ALL C'N HEAR ME, BE NEEDIN' SOME *HELP* HERE--
--FIRE'S *BLOCKED* MY EXITS!

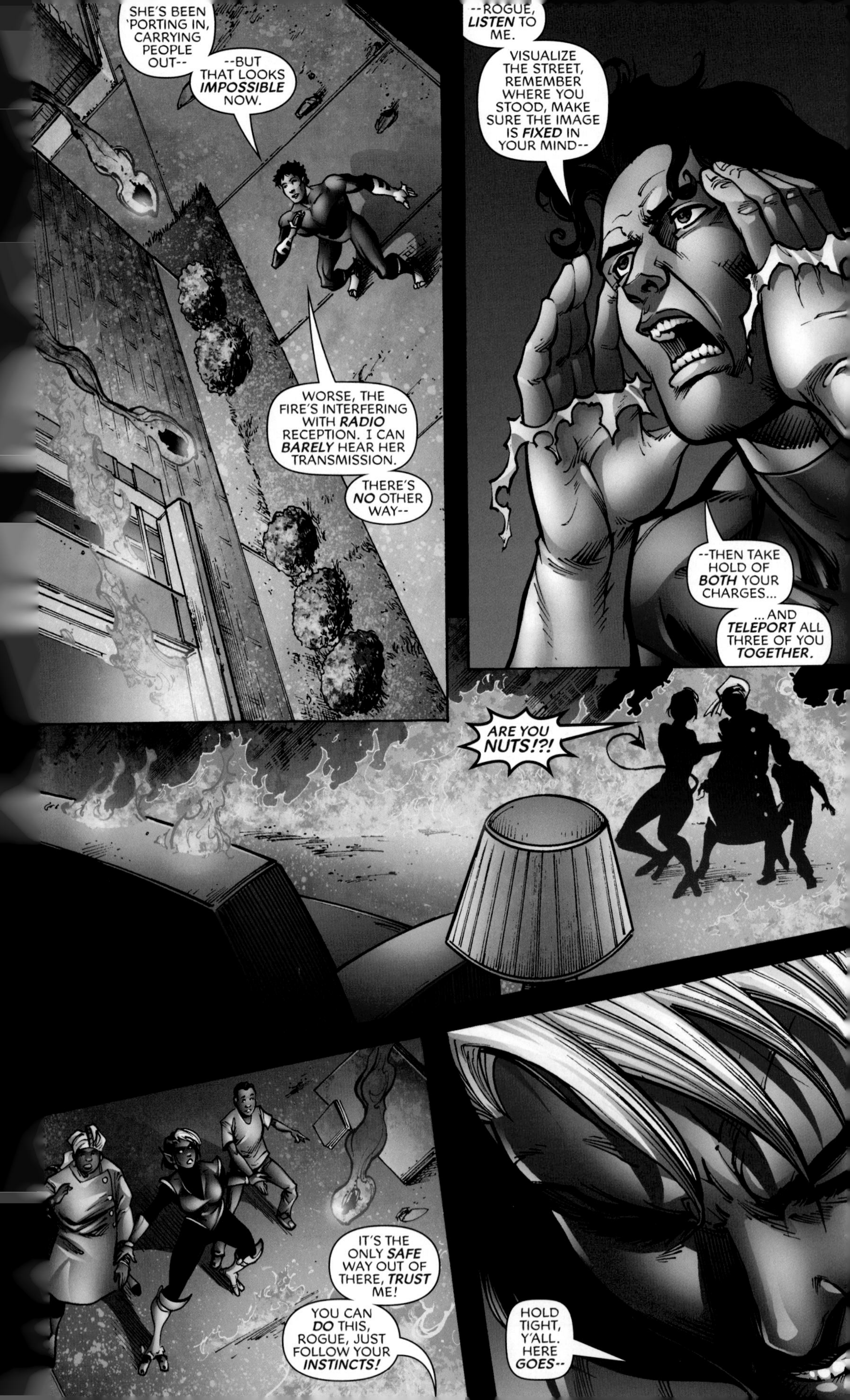
SHE'S BEEN 'PORTING IN, CARRYING PEOPLE OUT--
--BUT THAT LOOKS IMPOSSIBLE NOW.
WORSE, THE FIRE'S INTERFERING WITH RADIO RECEPTION. I CAN BARELY HEAR HER TRANSMISSION.
THERE'S NO OTHER WAY--
--ROGUE, LISTEN TO ME.
VISUALIZE THE STREET, REMEMBER WHERE YOU STOOD, MAKE SURE THE IMAGE IS FIXED IN YOUR MIND--
--THEN TAKE HOLD OF BOTH YOUR CHARGES...
...AND TELEPORT ALL THREE OF YOU TOGETHER.
ARE YOU NUTS!?!
IT'S THE ONLY SAFE WAY OUT OF THERE, TRUST ME!
YOU CAN DO THIS, ROGUE, JUST FOLLOW YOUR INSTINCTS!
HOLD TIGHT, Y'ALL. HERE GOES--

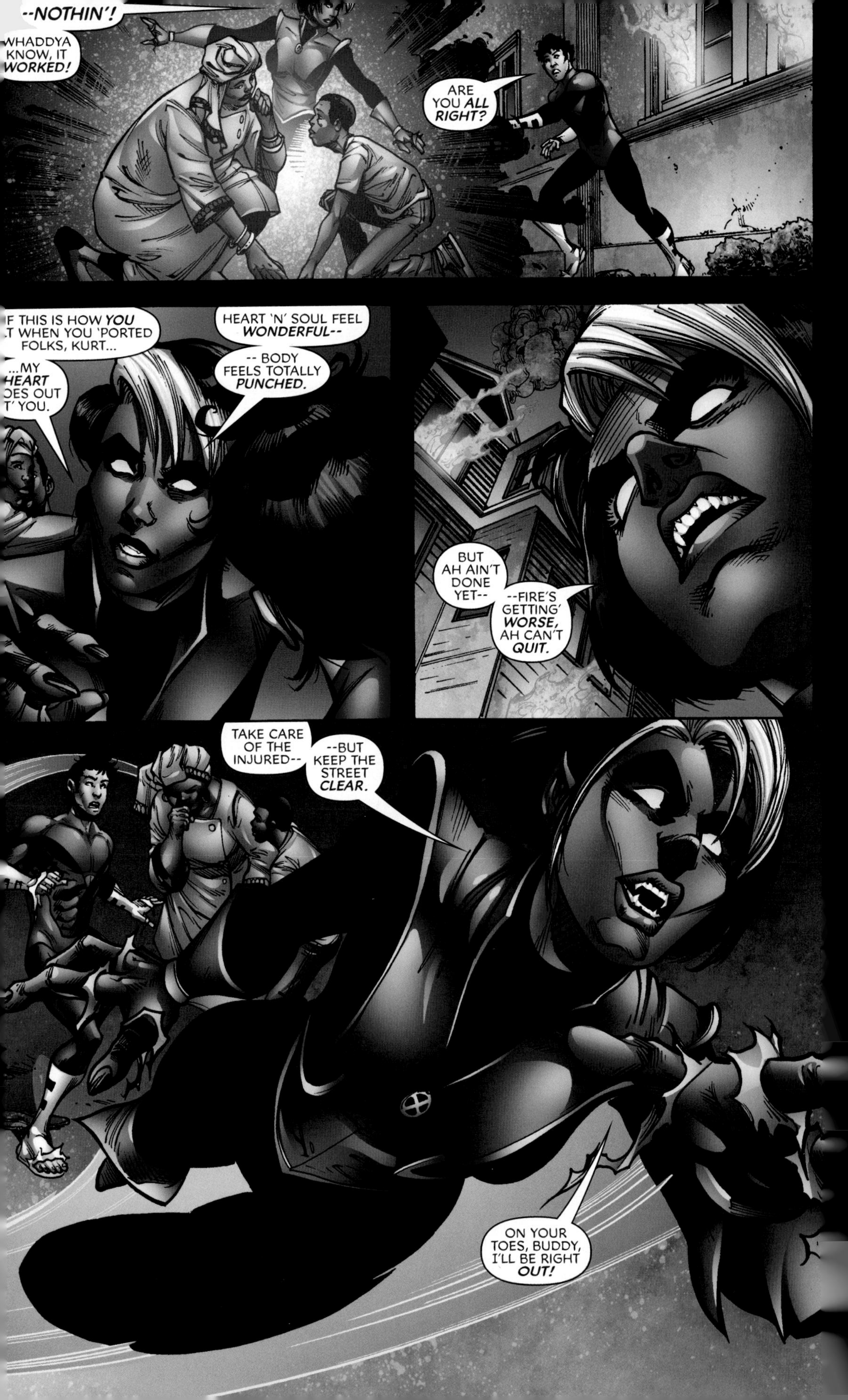
--NOTHIN'!
WHADDYA KNOW, IT WORKED!
ARE YOU ALL RIGHT?
F THIS IS HOW YOU
T WHEN YOU 'PORTED FOLKS, KURT...
...MY HEART
OES OUT
T' YOU.
HEART 'N' SOUL FEEL WONDERFUL--
-- BODY FEELS TOTALLY PUNCHED.
BUT AH AIN'T DONE YET--
--FIRE'S GETTING' WORSE, AH CAN'T QUIT.
TAKE CARE OF THE INJURED--
--BUT KEEP THE STREET CLEAR.
ON YOUR TOES, BUDDY, I'LL BE RIGHT OUT!

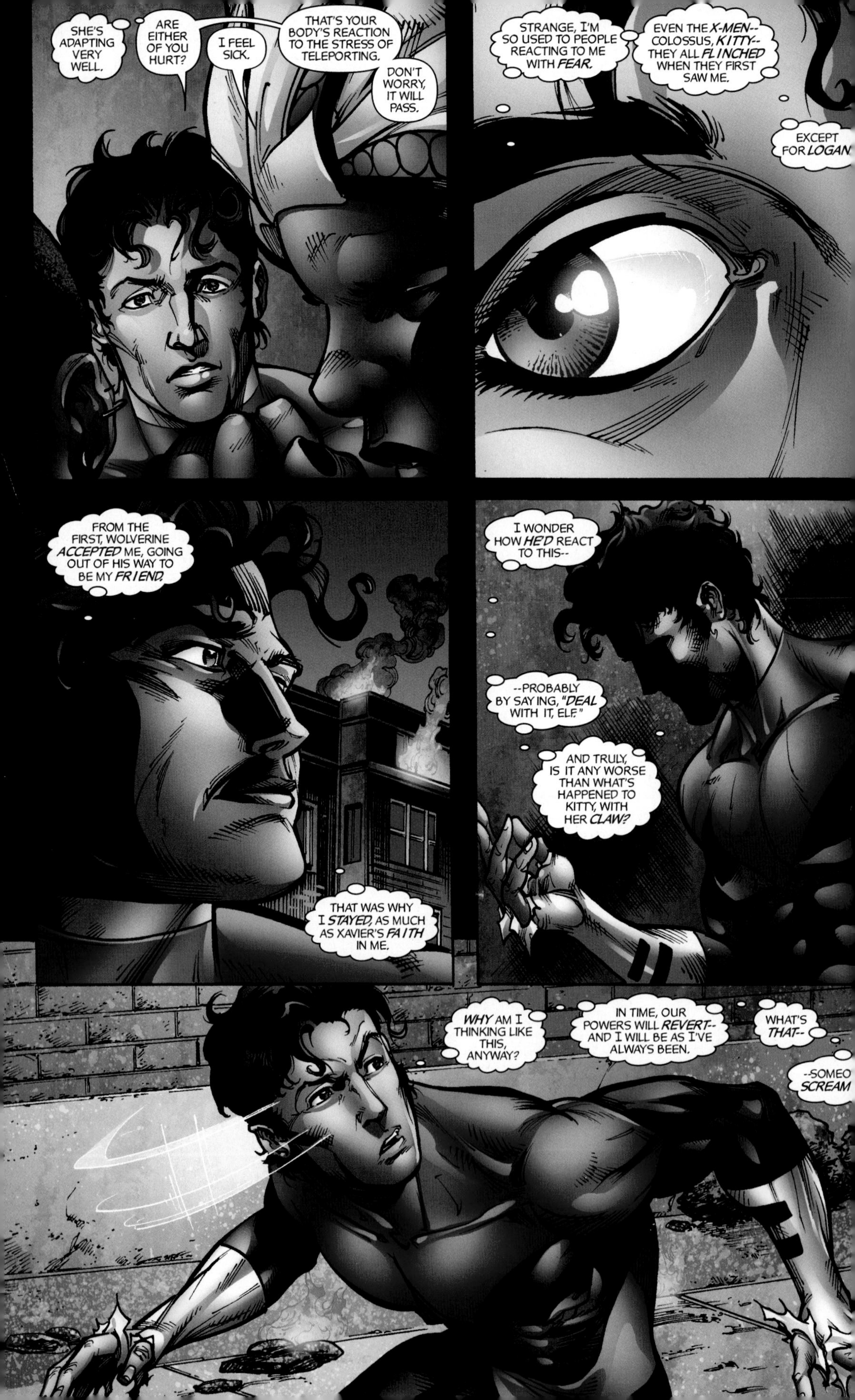
SHE'S ADAPTING VERY WELL.
ARE EITHER OF YOU HURT?
I FEEL SICK.
THAT'S YOUR BODY'S REACTION TO THE STRESS OF TELEPORTING.
DON'T WORRY, IT WILL PASS.
STRANGE, I'M SO USED TO PEOPLE REACTING TO ME WITH FEAR.
EVEN THE X-MEN-- COLOSSUS, KITTY-- THEY ALL FLINCHED WHEN THEY FIRST SAW ME.
EXCEPT FOR LOGAN.
FROM THE FIRST, WOLVERINE ACCEPTED ME, GOING OUT OF HIS WAY TO BE MY FRIEND.
THAT WAS WHY I STAYED, AS MUCH AS XAVIER'S FAITH IN ME.
I WONDER HOW HE'D REACT TO THIS--
--PROBABLY BY SAYING, "DEAL WITH IT, ELF."
AND TRULY, IS IT ANY WORSE THAN WHAT'S HAPPENED TO KITTY, WITH HER CLAW?
WHY AM I THINKING LIKE THIS, ANYWAY?
IN TIME, OUR POWERS WILL REVERT-- AND I WILL BE AS I'VE ALWAYS BEEN.
WHAT'S THAT--
--SOMEO SCREAM

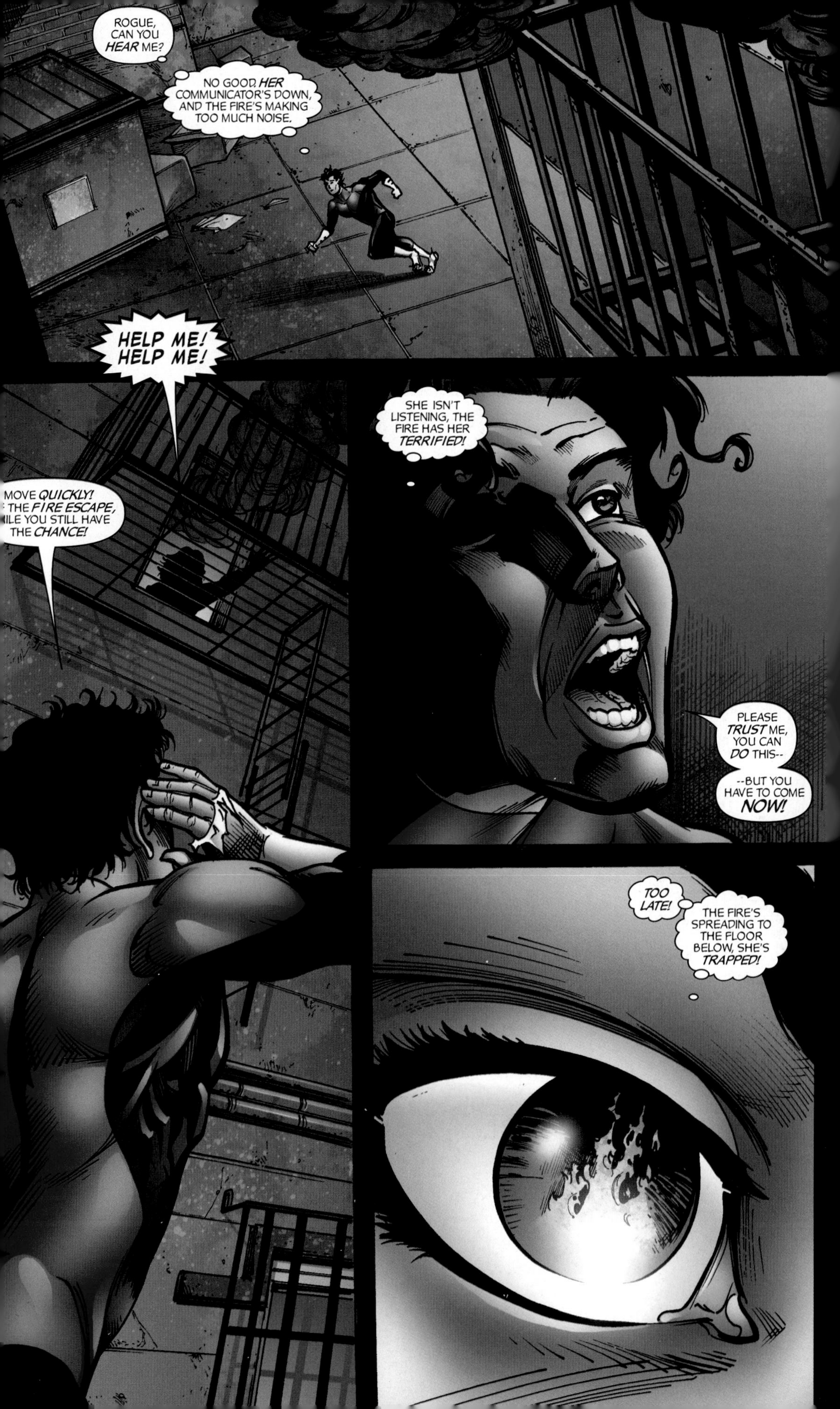

ROGUE, CAN YOU HEAR ME?
NO GOOD. HER COMMUNICATOR'S DOWN, AND THE FIRE'S MAKING TOO MUCH NOISE.
HELP ME! HELP ME!
MOVE QUICKLY! ...F THE FIRE ESCAPE, ...ILE YOU STILL HAVE THE CHANCE!
SHE ISN'T LISTENING, THE FIRE HAS HER TERRIFIED!
PLEASE TRUST ME, YOU CAN DO THIS--
--BUT YOU HAVE TO COME NOW!
TOO LATE!
THE FIRE'S SPREADING TO THE FLOOR BELOW, SHE'S TRAPPED!

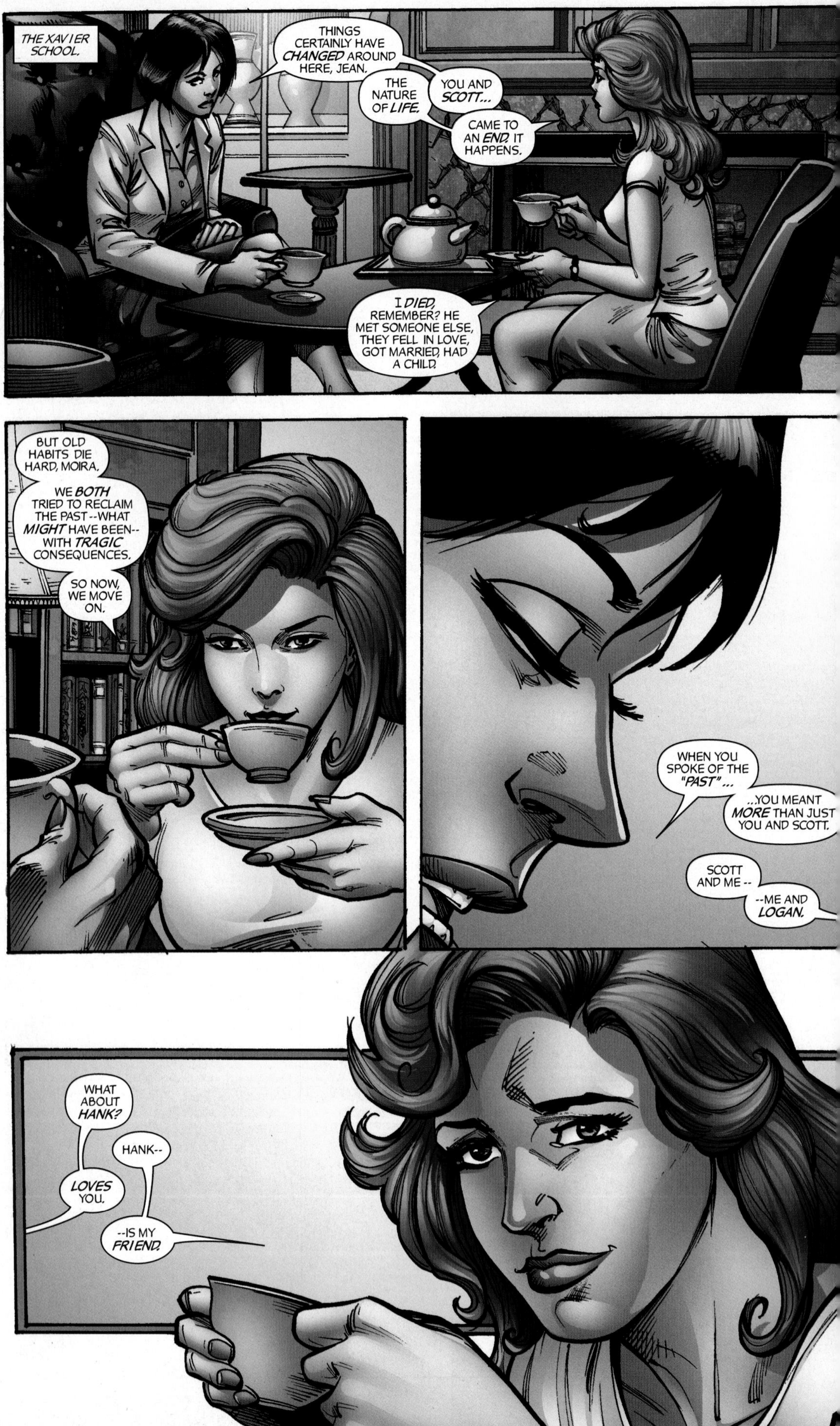
THE XAVIER SCHOOL.
THINGS CERTAINLY HAVE CHANGED AROUND HERE, JEAN.
YOU AND SCOTT...
THE NATURE OF LIFE.
CAME TO AN END. IT HAPPENS.
I DIED, REMEMBER? HE MET SOMEONE ELSE, THEY FELL IN LOVE, GOT MARRIED, HAD A CHILD.
BUT OLD HABITS DIE HARD, MOIRA.
WE BOTH TRIED TO RECLAIM THE PAST--WHAT MIGHT HAVE BEEN--WITH TRAGIC CONSEQUENCES.
SO NOW, WE MOVE ON.
WHEN YOU SPOKE OF THE "PAST"...
...YOU MEANT MORE THAN JUST YOU AND SCOTT.
SCOTT AND ME --
--ME AND LOGAN.
WHAT ABOUT HANK?
HANK--
LOVES YOU.
--IS MY FRIEND.

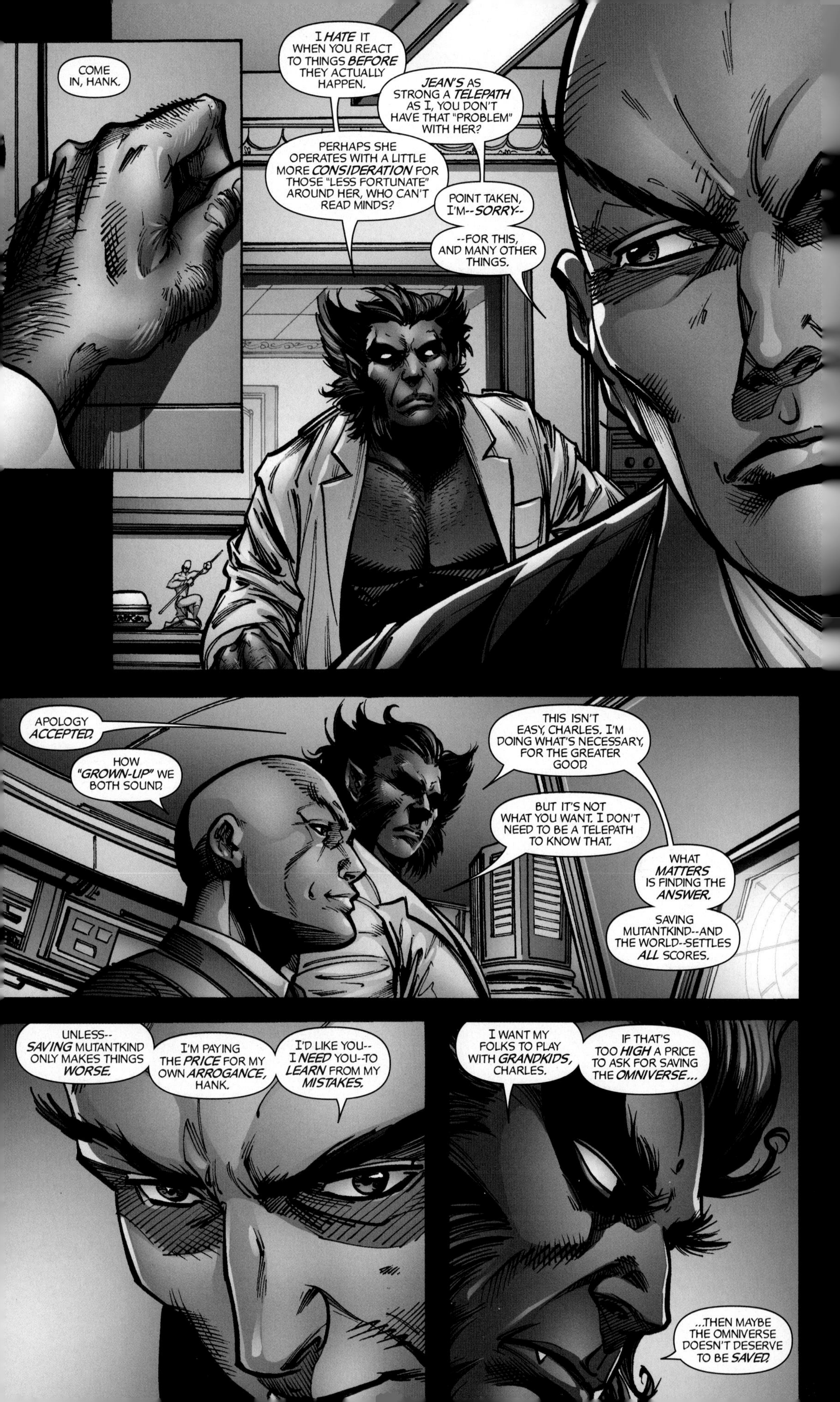
COME IN, HANK.
I *HATE* IT WHEN YOU REACT TO THINGS *BEFORE* THEY ACTUALLY HAPPEN.
JEAN'S AS STRONG A *TELEPATH* AS I, YOU DON'T HAVE THAT "PROBLEM" WITH HER?
PERHAPS SHE OPERATES WITH A LITTLE MORE *CONSIDERATION* FOR THOSE "LESS FORTUNATE" AROUND HER, WHO CAN'T READ MINDS?
POINT TAKEN, I'M--*SORRY*--
--FOR THIS, AND MANY OTHER THINGS.
APOLOGY *ACCEPTED.*
HOW *"GROWN-UP"* WE BOTH SOUND.
THIS ISN'T EASY, CHARLES. I'M DOING WHAT'S NECESSARY, FOR THE GREATER GOOD.
BUT IT'S NOT WHAT YOU WANT. I DON'T NEED TO BE A TELEPATH TO KNOW THAT.
WHAT *MATTERS* IS FINDING THE *ANSWER.*
SAVING MUTANTKIND--AND THE WORLD--SETTLES *ALL* SCORES.
UNLESS--*SAVING* MUTANTKIND ONLY MAKES THINGS *WORSE.*
I'M PAYING THE *PRICE* FOR MY OWN *ARROGANCE,* HANK.
I'D LIKE YOU--I *NEED* YOU--TO *LEARN* FROM MY *MISTAKES.*
I WANT MY FOLKS TO PLAY WITH *GRANDKIDS,* CHARLES.
IF THAT'S TOO *HIGH* A PRICE TO ASK FOR SAVING THE *OMNIVERSE...*
...THEN MAYBE THE OMNIVERSE DOESN'T DESERVE TO BE *SAVED.*

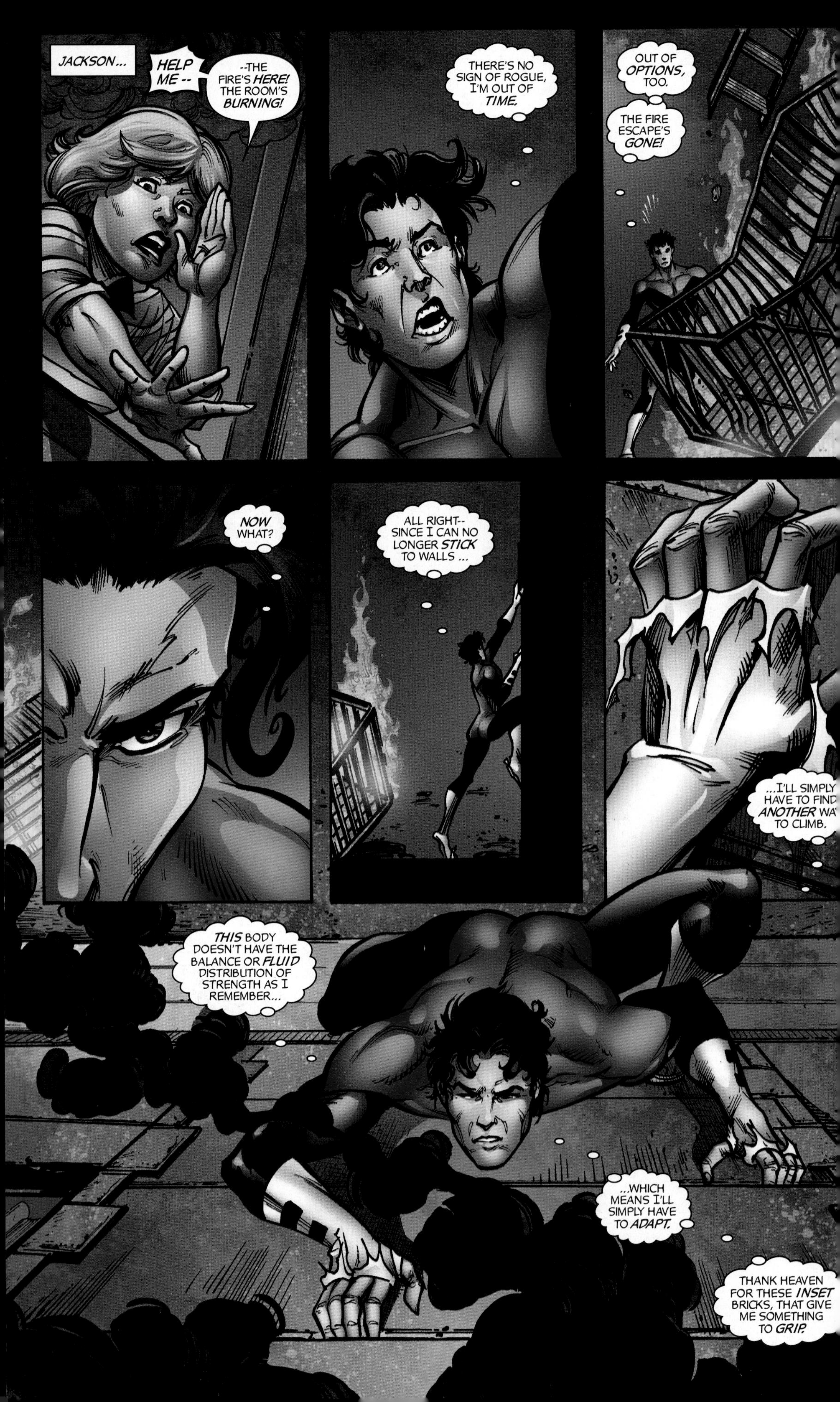

JACKSON...
HELP ME --
--THE FIRE'S HERE! THE ROOM'S BURNING!
THERE'S NO SIGN OF ROGUE, I'M OUT OF TIME.
OUT OF OPTIONS, TOO.
THE FIRE ESCAPE'S GONE!
NOW WHAT?
ALL RIGHT-- SINCE I CAN NO LONGER STICK TO WALLS ...
...I'LL SIMPLY HAVE TO FIND ANOTHER WA TO CLIMB.
THIS BODY DOESN'T HAVE THE BALANCE OR FLUID DISTRIBUTION OF STRENGTH AS I REMEMBER...
...WHICH MEANS I'LL SIMPLY HAVE TO ADAPT.
THANK HEAVEN FOR THESE INSET BRICKS, THAT GIVE ME SOMETHING TO GRIP.

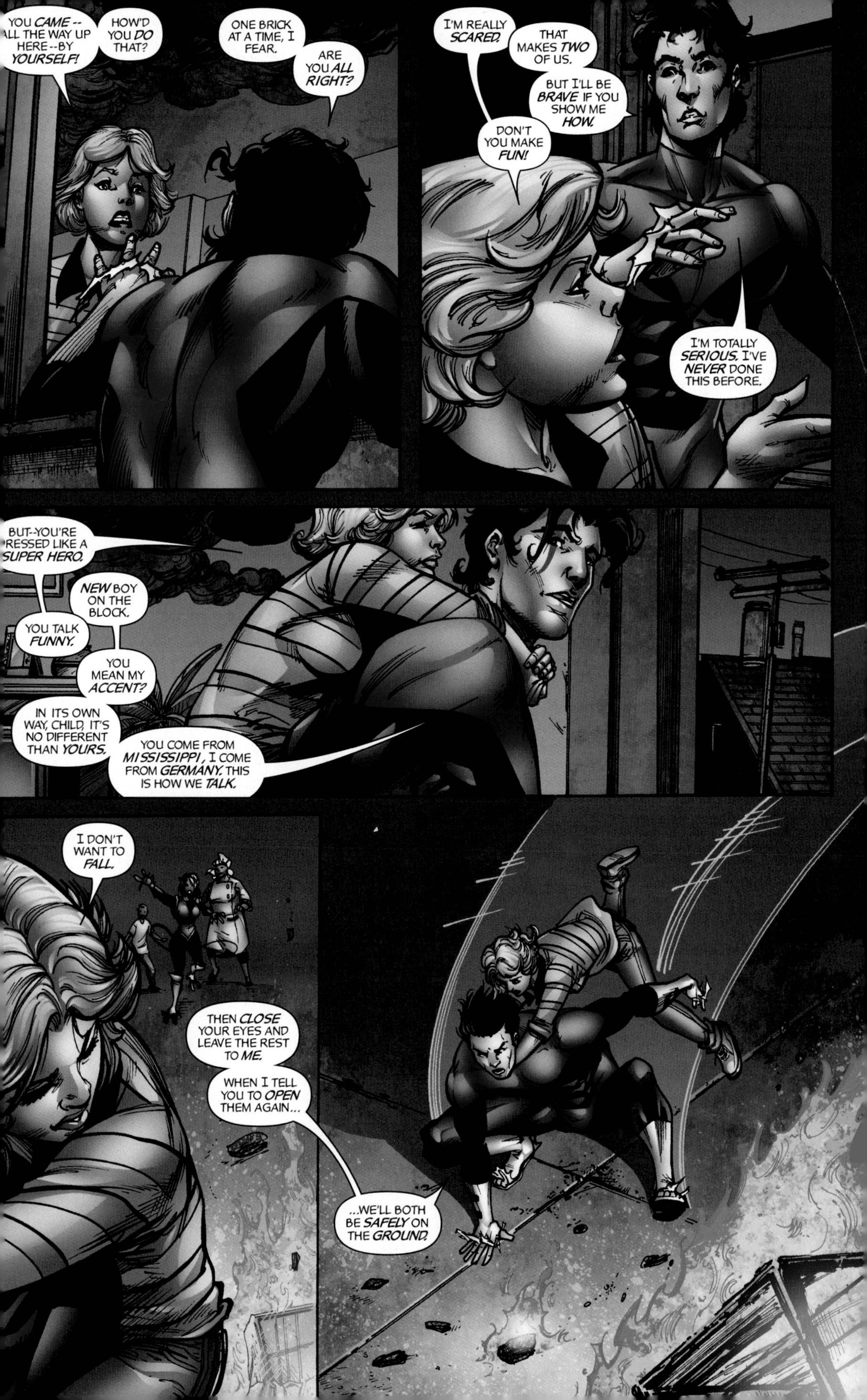

YOU CAME -- ALL THE WAY UP HERE--BY YOURSELF!
HOW'D YOU DO THAT?
ONE BRICK AT A TIME, I FEAR.
ARE YOU ALL RIGHT?
I'M REALLY SCARED.
THAT MAKES TWO OF US.
BUT I'LL BE BRAVE IF YOU SHOW ME HOW.
DON'T YOU MAKE FUN!
I'M TOTALLY SERIOUS. I'VE NEVER DONE THIS BEFORE.
BUT-YOU'RE DRESSED LIKE A SUPER HERO.
NEW BOY ON THE BLOCK.
YOU TALK FUNNY.
YOU MEAN MY ACCENT?
IN ITS OWN WAY, CHILD, IT'S NO DIFFERENT THAN YOURS.
YOU COME FROM MISSISSIPPI, I COME FROM GERMANY. THIS IS HOW WE TALK.
I DON'T WANT TO FALL.
THEN CLOSE YOUR EYES AND LEAVE THE REST TO ME.
WHEN I TELL YOU TO OPEN THEM AGAIN...
...WE'LL BOTH BE SAFELY ON THE GROUND.

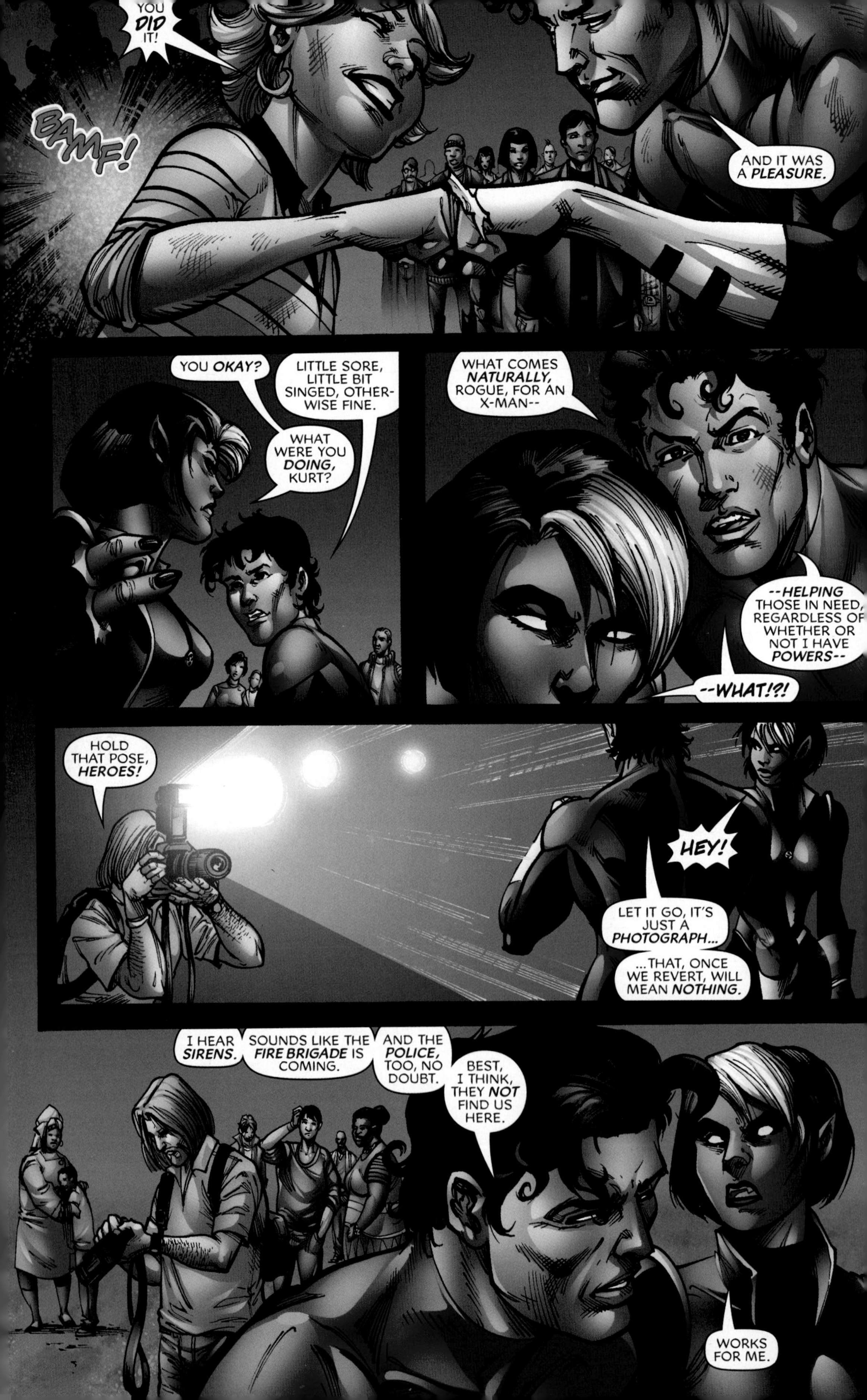

YOU DID IT!
BAMF!
AND IT WAS A PLEASURE.
YOU OKAY?
LITTLE SORE, LITTLE BIT SINGED, OTHER-WISE FINE.
WHAT WERE YOU DOING, KURT?
WHAT COMES NATURALLY, ROGUE, FOR AN X-MAN--
--HELPING THOSE IN NEED, REGARDLESS OF WHETHER OR NOT I HAVE POWERS--
--WHAT!?!
HOLD THAT POSE, HEROES!
HEY!
LET IT GO, IT'S JUST A PHOTOGRAPH...
...THAT, ONCE WE REVERT, WILL MEAN NOTHING.
I HEAR SIRENS.
SOUNDS LIKE THE FIRE BRIGADE IS COMING.
AND THE POLICE, TOO, NO DOUBT.
BEST, I THINK, THEY NOT FIND US HERE.
WORKS FOR ME.

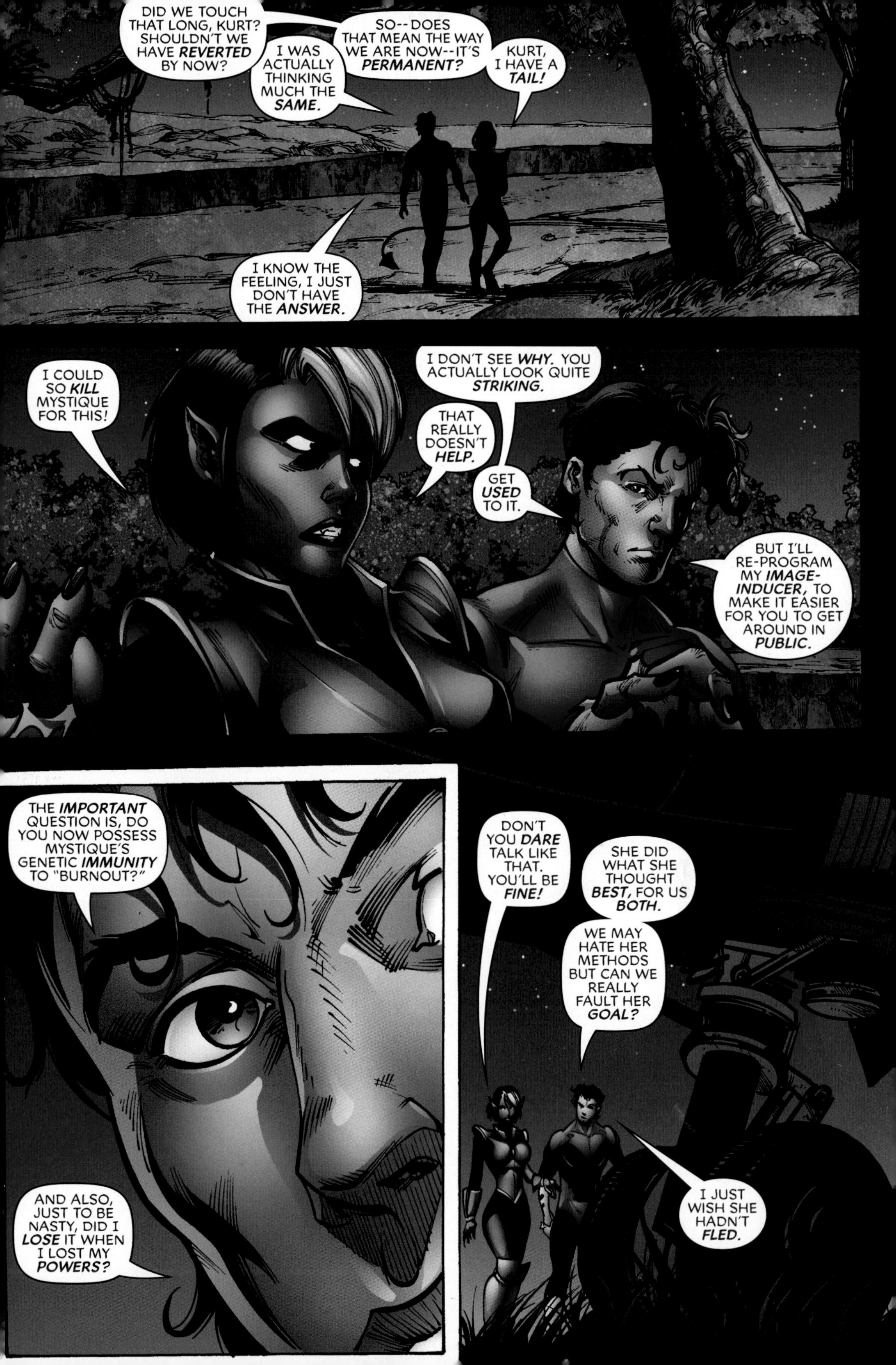
DID WE TOUCH THAT LONG, KURT? SHOULDN'T WE HAVE REVERTED BY NOW?
I WAS ACTUALLY THINKING MUCH THE SAME.
SO-- DOES THAT MEAN THE WAY WE ARE NOW--IT'S PERMANENT?
KURT, I HAVE A TAIL!
I KNOW THE FEELING, I JUST DON'T HAVE THE ANSWER.
I COULD SO KILL MYSTIQUE FOR THIS!
I DON'T SEE WHY. YOU ACTUALLY LOOK QUITE STRIKING.
THAT REALLY DOESN'T HELP.
GET USED TO IT.
BUT I'LL RE-PROGRAM MY IMAGE-INDUCER, TO MAKE IT EASIER FOR YOU TO GET AROUND IN PUBLIC.
THE IMPORTANT QUESTION IS, DO YOU NOW POSSESS MYSTIQUE'S GENETIC IMMUNITY TO "BURNOUT?"
AND ALSO, JUST TO BE NASTY, DID I LOSE IT WHEN I LOST MY POWERS?
DON'T YOU DARE TALK LIKE THAT. YOU'LL BE FINE!
SHE DID WHAT SHE THOUGHT BEST, FOR US BOTH.
WE MAY HATE HER METHODS BUT CAN WE REALLY FAULT HER GOAL?
I JUST WISH SHE HADN'T FLED.

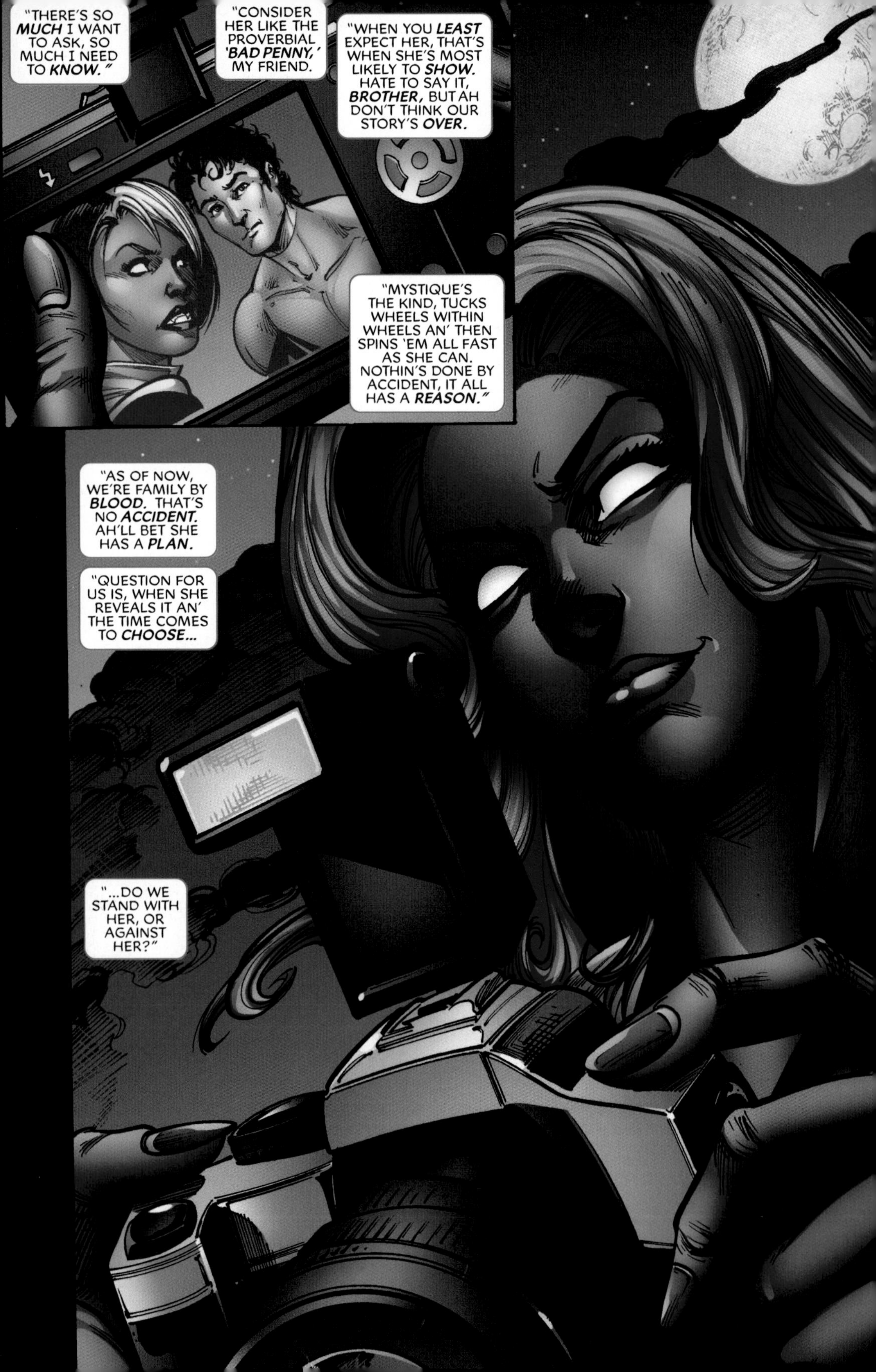
"THERE'S SO MUCH I WANT TO ASK, SO MUCH I NEED TO KNOW."
"CONSIDER HER LIKE THE PROVERBIAL 'BAD PENNY,' MY FRIEND.
"WHEN YOU LEAST EXPECT HER, THAT'S WHEN SHE'S MOST LIKELY TO SHOW. HATE TO SAY IT, BROTHER, BUT AH DON'T THINK OUR STORY'S OVER.
"MYSTIQUE'S THE KIND, TUCKS WHEELS WITHIN WHEELS AN' THEN SPINS 'EM ALL FAST AS SHE CAN. NOTHIN'S DONE BY ACCIDENT, IT ALL HAS A REASON."
"AS OF NOW, WE'RE FAMILY BY BLOOD. THAT'S NO ACCIDENT. AH'LL BET SHE HAS A PLAN.
"QUESTION FOR US IS, WHEN SHE REVEALS IT AN' THE TIME COMES TO CHOOSE...
"...DO WE STAND WITH HER, OR AGAINST HER?"

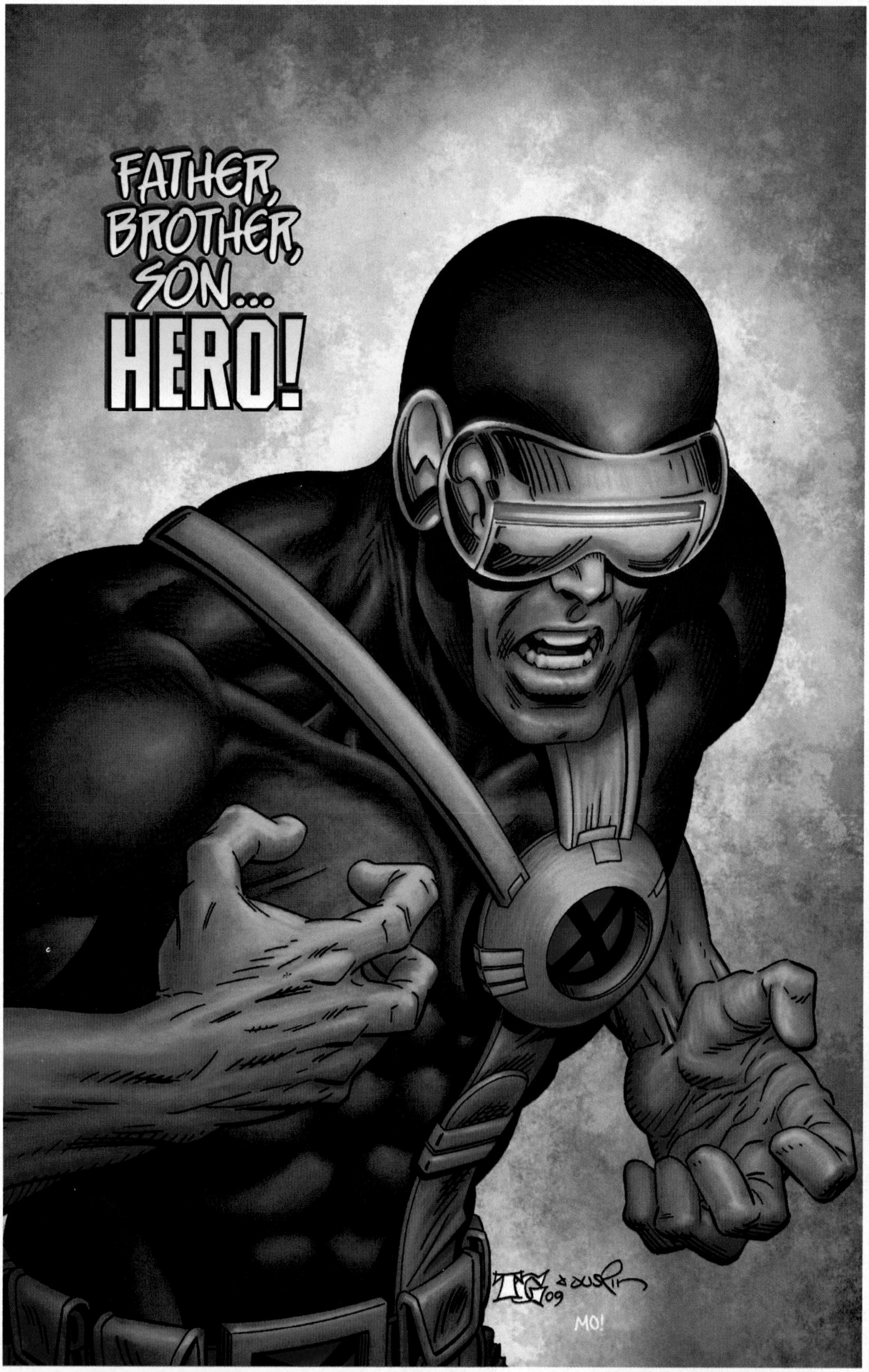
FATHER, BROTHER, SON... HERO!
MO!

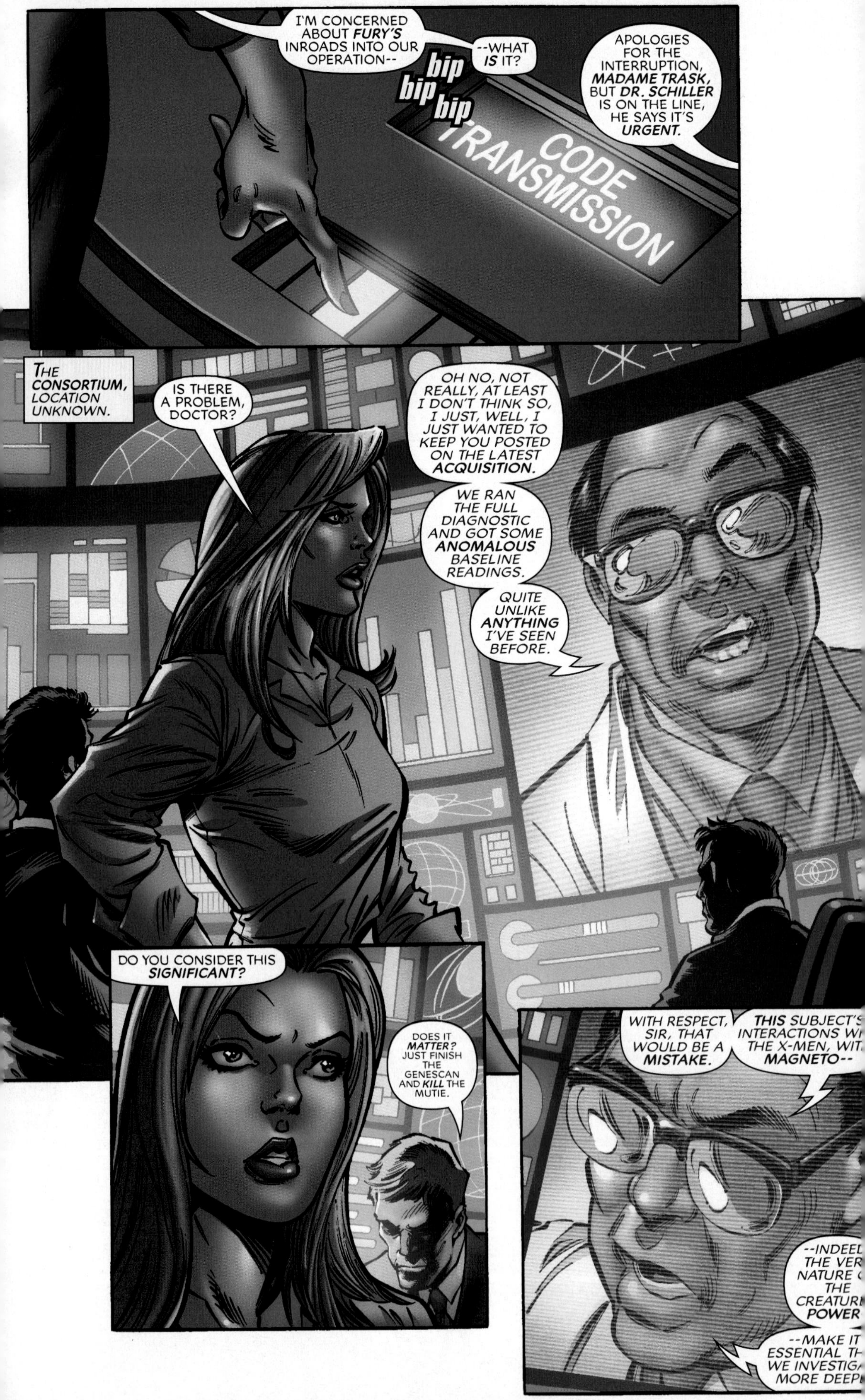

I'M CONCERNED ABOUT FURY'S INROADS INTO OUR OPERATION--
--WHAT IS IT?
bip bip bip
CODE TRANSMISSION
APOLOGIES FOR THE INTERRUPTION, MADAME TRASK, BUT DR. SCHILLER IS ON THE LINE, HE SAYS IT'S URGENT.
THE CONSORTIUM, LOCATION UNKNOWN.
IS THERE A PROBLEM, DOCTOR?
OH NO, NOT REALLY, AT LEAST I DON'T THINK SO, I JUST, WELL, I JUST WANTED TO KEEP YOU POSTED ON THE LATEST ACQUISITION.
WE RAN THE FULL DIAGNOSTIC AND GOT SOME ANOMALOUS BASELINE READINGS.
QUITE UNLIKE ANYTHING I'VE SEEN BEFORE.
DO YOU CONSIDER THIS SIGNIFICANT?
DOES IT MATTER? JUST FINISH THE GENESCAN AND KILL THE MUTIE.
WITH RESPECT, SIR, THAT WOULD BE A MISTAKE.
THIS SUBJECT'S INTERACTIONS WI THE X-MEN, WIT MAGNETO--
--INDEEL THE VER NATURE THE CREATUR POWER
--MAKE IT ESSENTIAL TH WE INVESTIG MORE DEEP

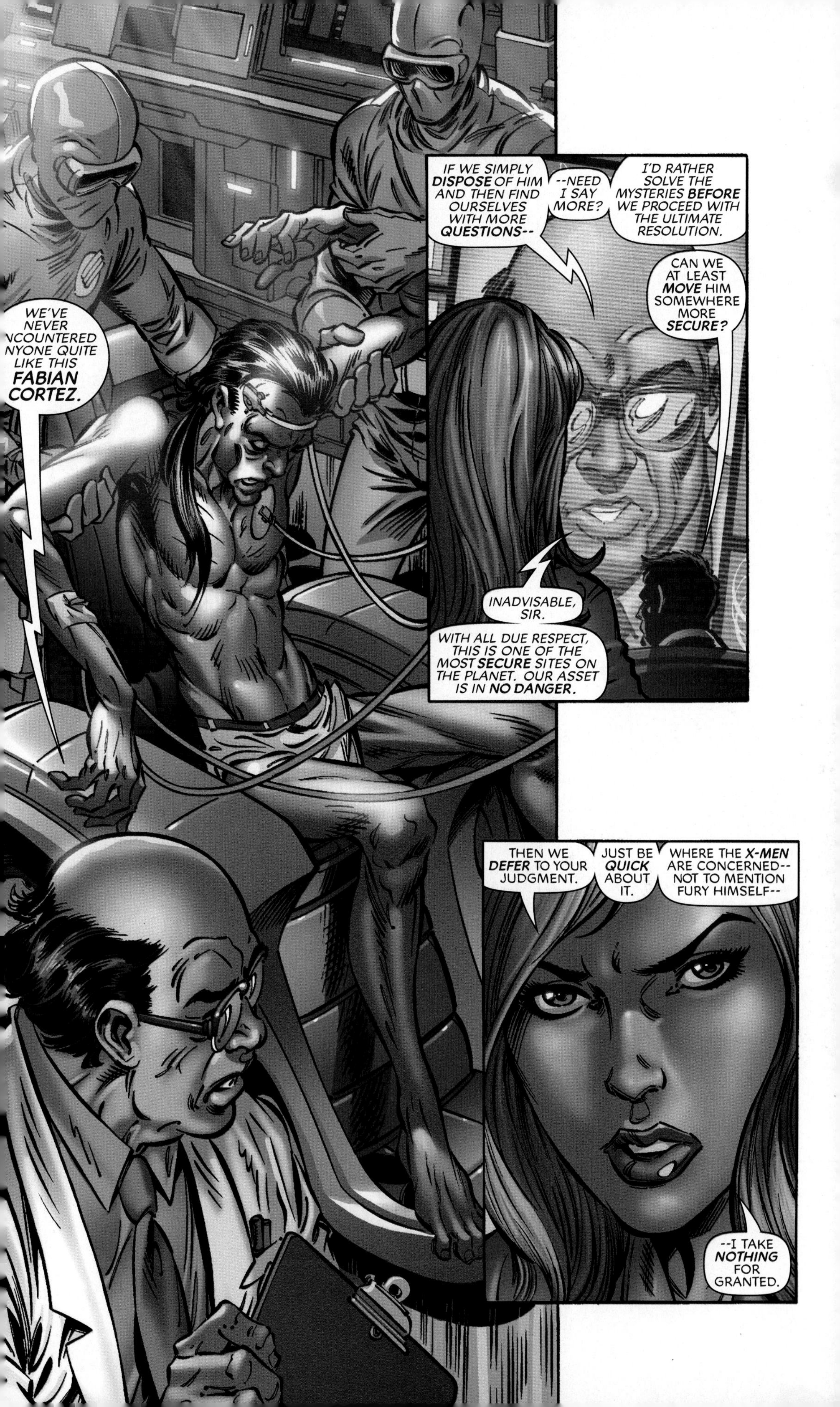
WE'VE NEVER NCOUNTERED NYONE QUITE LIKE THIS FABIAN CORTEZ.
IF WE SIMPLY DISPOSE OF HIM AND THEN FIND OURSELVES WITH MORE QUESTIONS--
--NEED I SAY MORE?
I'D RATHER SOLVE THE MYSTERIES BEFORE WE PROCEED WITH THE ULTIMATE RESOLUTION.
CAN WE AT LEAST MOVE HIM SOMEWHERE MORE SECURE?
INADVISABLE, SIR.
WITH ALL DUE RESPECT, THIS IS ONE OF THE MOST SECURE SITES ON THE PLANET. OUR ASSET IS IN NO DANGER.
THEN WE DEFER TO YOUR JUDGMENT.
JUST BE QUICK ABOUT IT.
WHERE THE X-MEN ARE CONCERNED-- NOT TO MENTION FURY HIMSELF--
--I TAKE NOTHING FOR GRANTED.

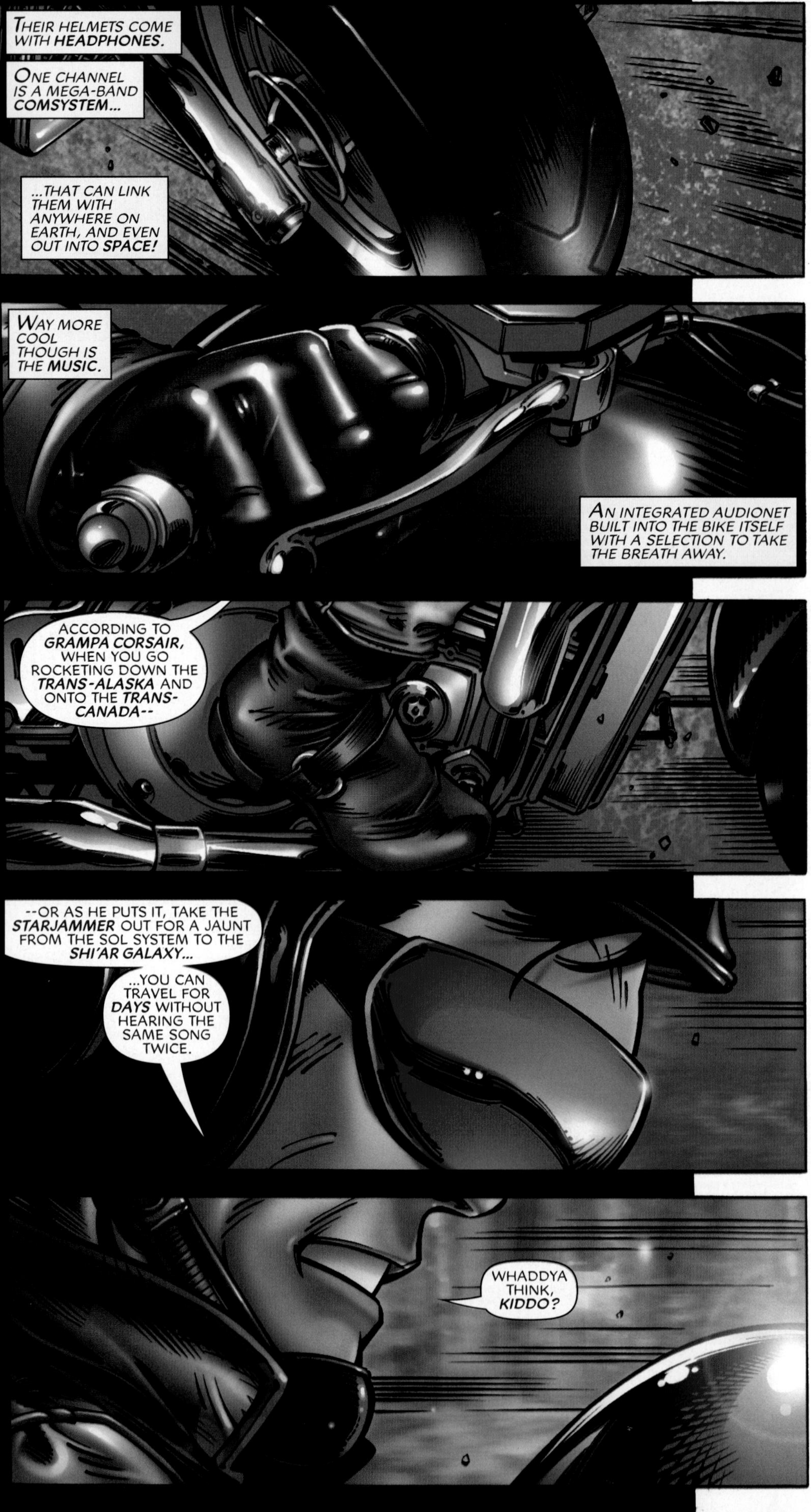
THEIR HELMETS COME WITH HEADPHONES.
ONE CHANNEL IS A MEGA-BAND COMSYSTEM...
...THAT CAN LINK THEM WITH ANYWHERE ON EARTH, AND EVEN OUT INTO SPACE!
WAY MORE COOL THOUGH IS THE MUSIC.
AN INTEGRATED AUDIONET BUILT INTO THE BIKE ITSELF WITH A SELECTION TO TAKE THE BREATH AWAY.
ACCORDING TO GRAMPA CORSAIR, WHEN YOU GO ROCKETING DOWN THE TRANS-ALASKA AND ONTO THE TRANS-CANADA--
--OR AS HE PUTS IT, TAKE THE STARJAMMER OUT FOR A JAUNT FROM THE SOL SYSTEM TO THE SHI'AR GALAXY...
...YOU CAN TRAVEL FOR DAYS WITHOUT HEARING THE SAME SONG TWICE.
WHADDYA THINK, KIDDO?

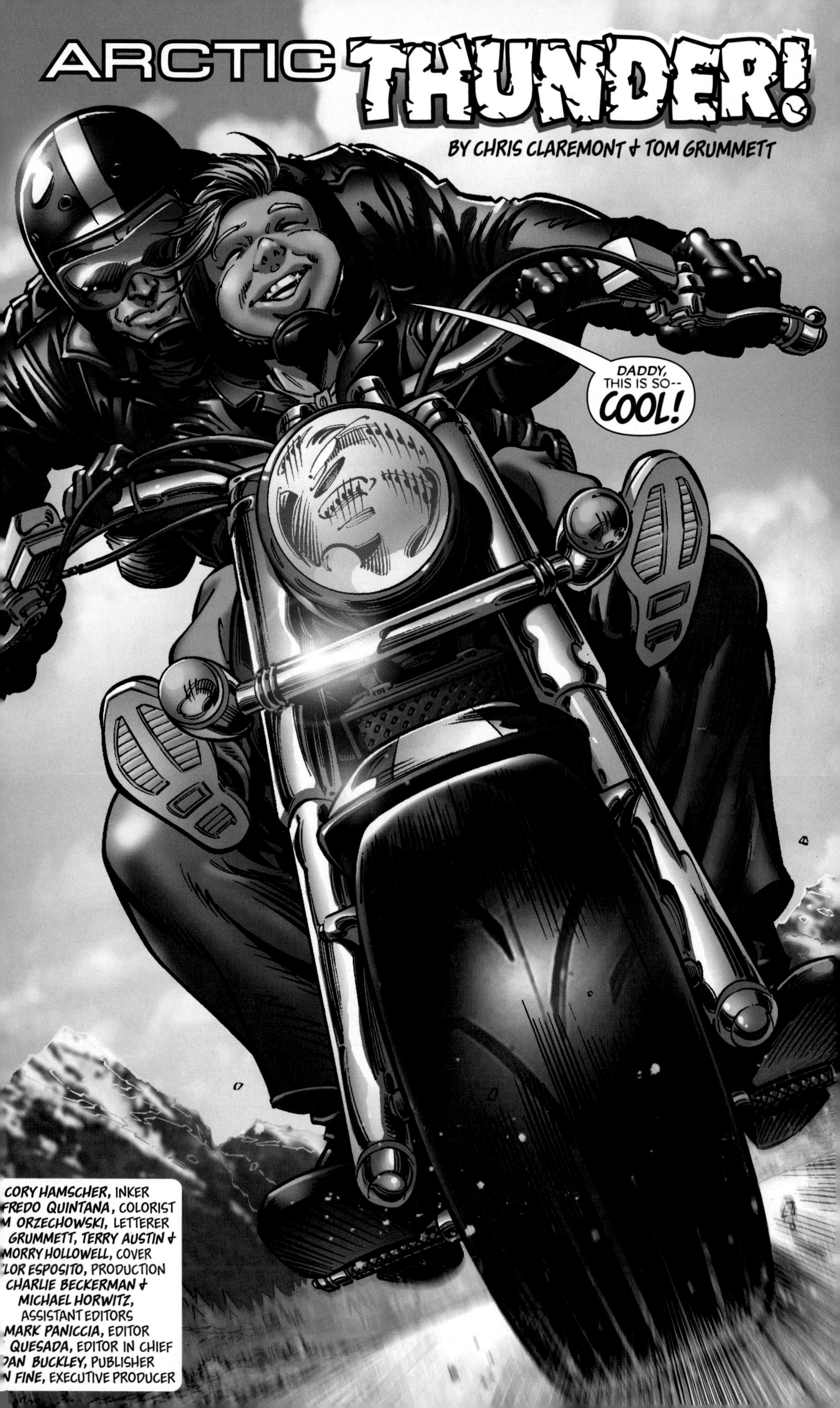

ARCTIC THUNDER!
BY CHRIS CLAREMONT & TOM GRUMMETT
DADDY, THIS IS SO-- COOL!
CORY HAMSCHER, INKER
FREDO QUINTANA, COLORIST
M ORZECHOWSKI, LETTERER
GRUMMETT, TERRY AUSTIN &
MORRY HOLLOWELL, COVER
LOR ESPOSITO, PRODUCTION
CHARLIE BECKERMAN &
MICHAEL HORWITZ,
ASSISTANT EDITORS
MARK PANICCIA, EDITOR
QUESADA, EDITOR IN CHIEF
AN BUCKLEY, PUBLISHER
N FINE, EXECUTIVE PRODUCER

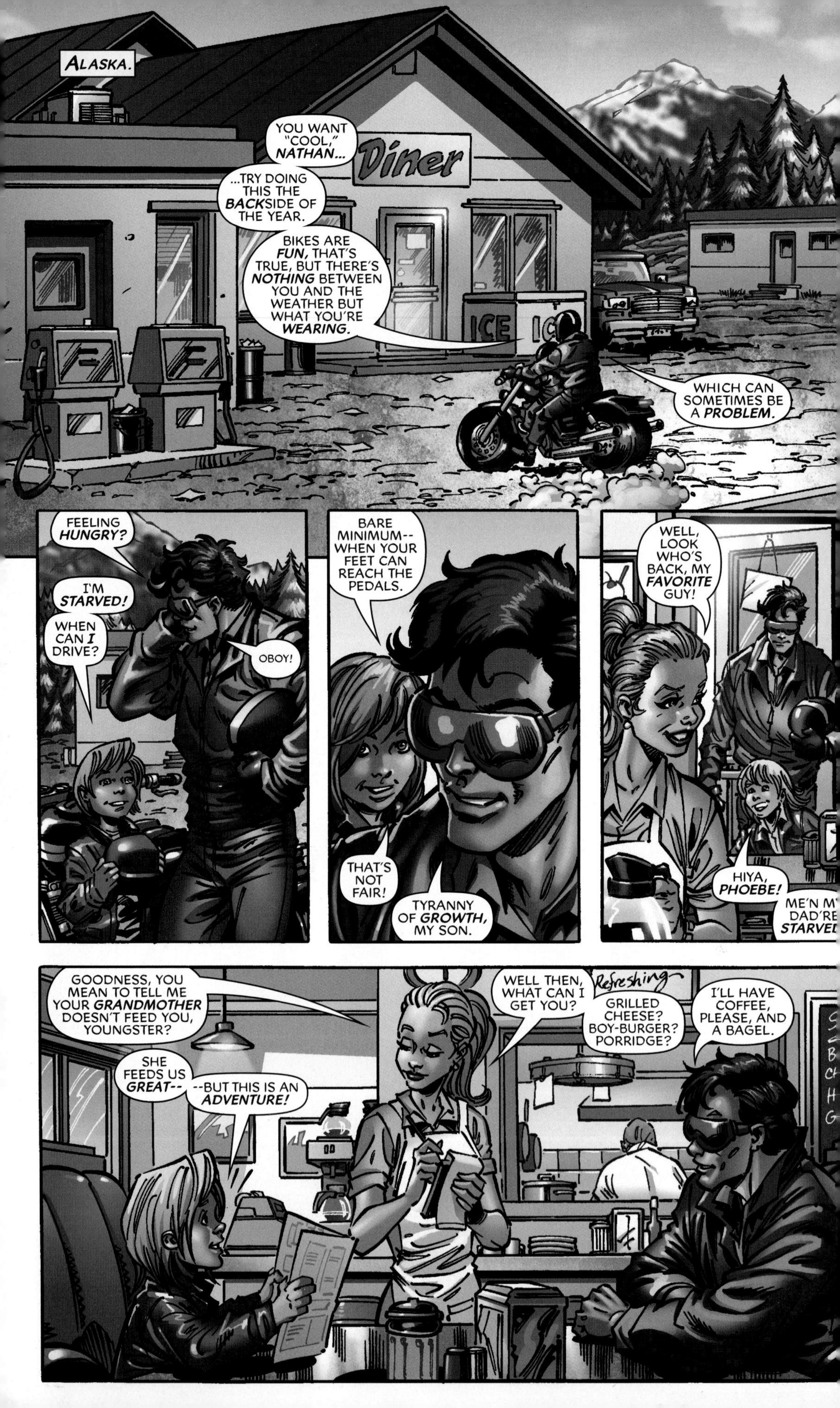

ALASKA.
YOU WANT "COOL," NATHAN...
...TRY DOING THIS THE BACKSIDE OF THE YEAR.
Diner
BIKES ARE FUN, THAT'S TRUE, BUT THERE'S NOTHING BETWEEN YOU AND THE WEATHER BUT WHAT YOU'RE WEARING.
ICE
WHICH CAN SOMETIMES BE A PROBLEM.
FEELING HUNGRY?
I'M STARVED!
WHEN CAN I DRIVE?
OBOY!
BARE MINIMUM--WHEN YOUR FEET CAN REACH THE PEDALS.
THAT'S NOT FAIR!
TYRANNY OF GROWTH, MY SON.
WELL, LOOK WHO'S BACK, MY FAVORITE GUY!
HIYA, PHOEBE!
GOODNESS, YOU MEAN TO TELL ME YOUR GRANDMOTHER DOESN'T FEED YOU, YOUNGSTER?
SHE FEEDS US GREAT--
--BUT THIS IS AN ADVENTURE!
WELL THEN, WHAT CAN I GET YOU?
Refreshing
GRILLED CHEESE? BOY-BURGER? PORRIDGE?
I'LL HAVE COFFEE, PLEASE, AND A BAGEL.

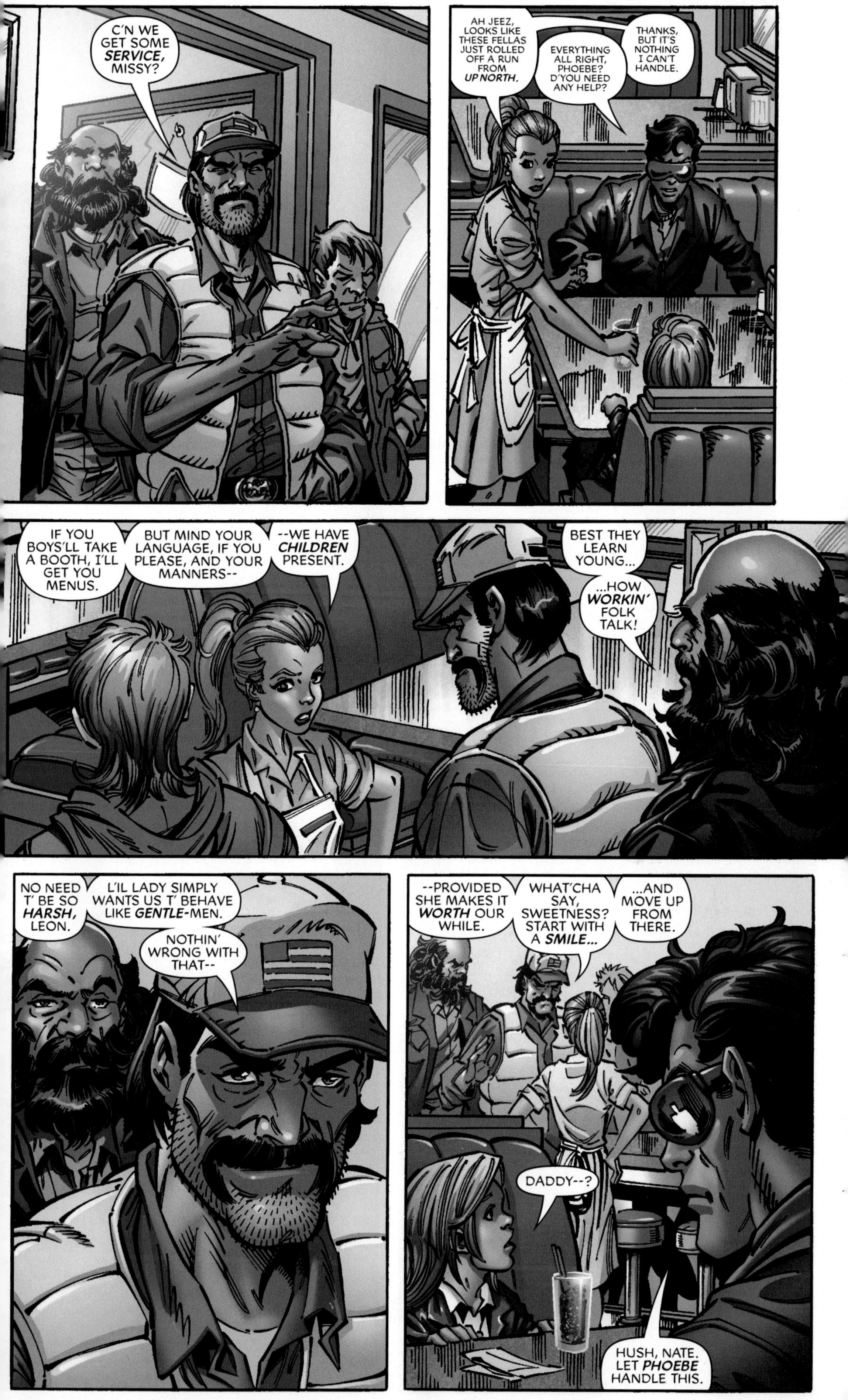
C'N WE GET SOME SERVICE, MISSY?
AH JEEZ, LOOKS LIKE THESE FELLAS JUST ROLLED OFF A RUN FROM UP NORTH.
EVERYTHING ALL RIGHT, PHOEBE? D'YOU NEED ANY HELP?
THANKS, BUT IT'S NOTHING I CAN'T HANDLE.
IF YOU BOYS'LL TAKE A BOOTH, I'LL GET YOU MENUS.
BUT MIND YOUR LANGUAGE, IF YOU PLEASE, AND YOUR MANNERS--
--WE HAVE CHILDREN PRESENT.
BEST THEY LEARN YOUNG...
...HOW WORKIN' FOLK TALK!
NO NEED T' BE SO HARSH, LEON.
L'IL LADY SIMPLY WANTS US T' BEHAVE LIKE GENTLE-MEN.
NOTHIN' WRONG WITH THAT--
--PROVIDED SHE MAKES IT WORTH OUR WHILE.
WHAT'CHA SAY, SWEETNESS? START WITH A SMILE...
...AND MOVE UP FROM THERE.
DADDY--?
HUSH, NATE. LET PHOEBE HANDLE THIS.

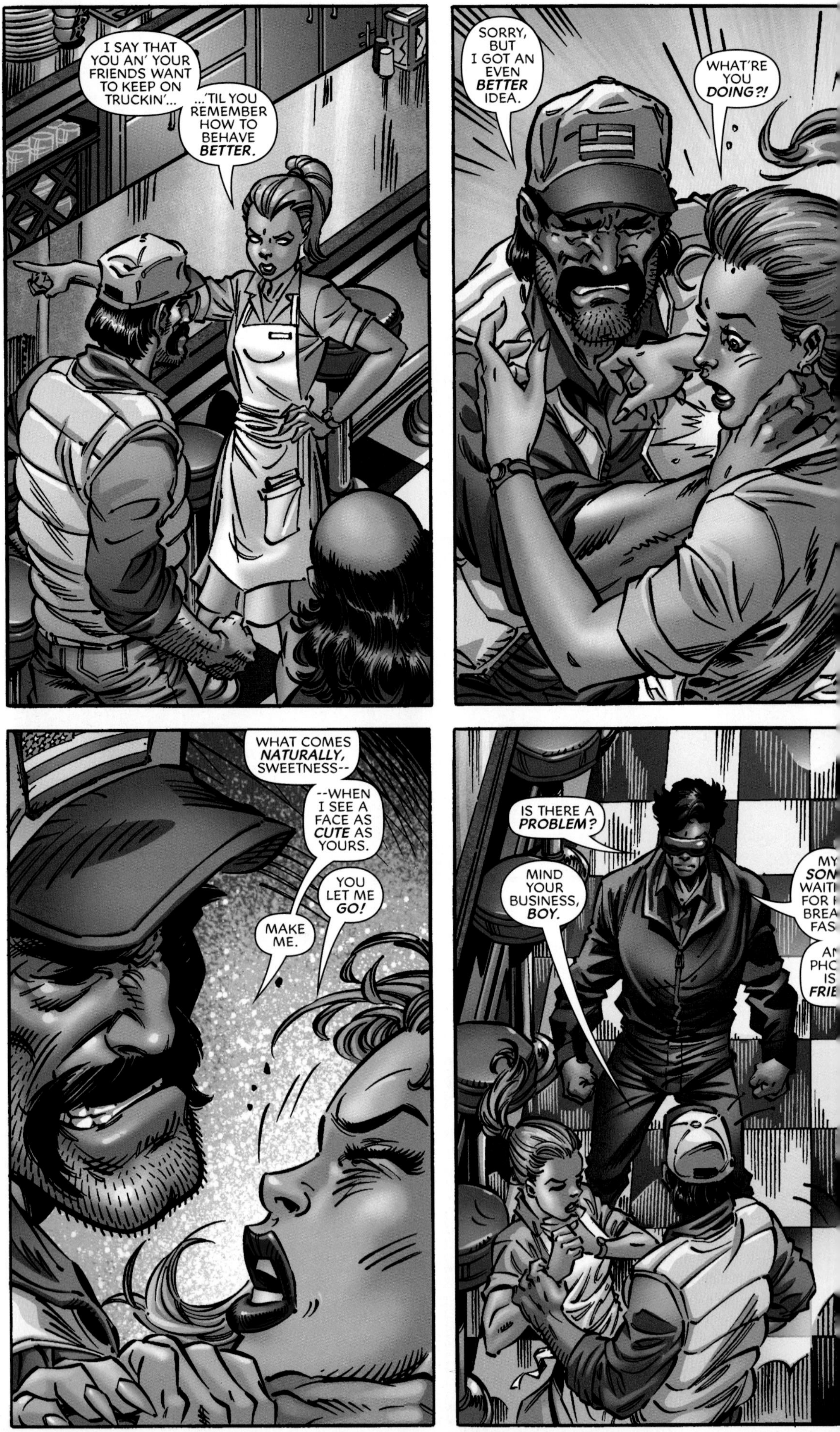
I SAY THAT YOU AN' YOUR FRIENDS WANT TO KEEP ON TRUCKIN'...
...'TIL YOU REMEMBER HOW TO BEHAVE BETTER.
SORRY, BUT I GOT AN EVEN BETTER IDEA.
WHAT'RE YOU DOING?!
WHAT COMES NATURALLY, SWEETNESS--
--WHEN I SEE A FACE AS CUTE AS YOURS.
YOU LET ME GO!
MAKE ME.
IS THERE A PROBLEM?
MIND YOUR BUSINESS, BOY.

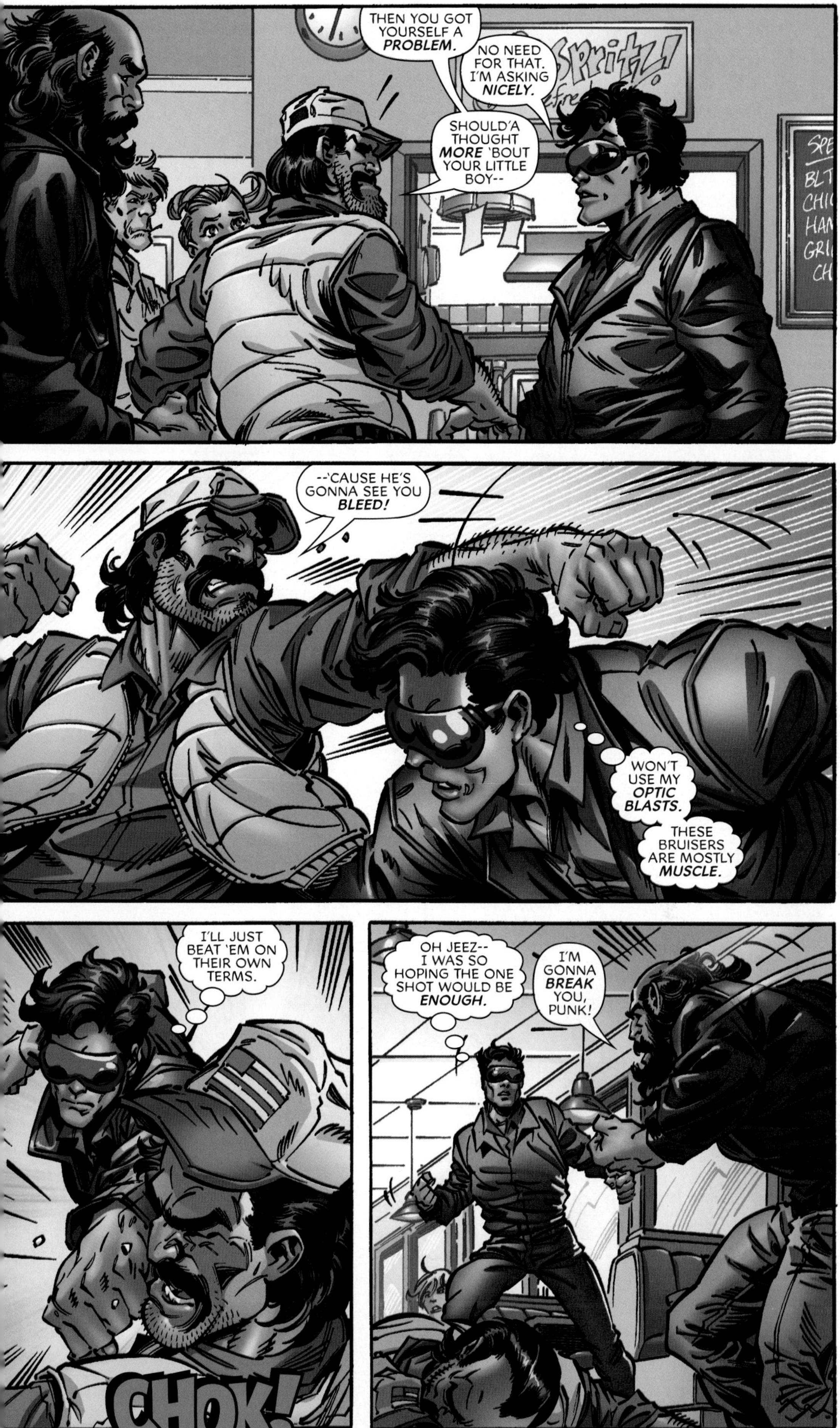
THEN YOU GOT YOURSELF A PROBLEM.
NO NEED FOR THAT. I'M ASKING NICELY.
SHOULD'A THOUGHT MORE 'BOUT YOUR LITTLE BOY--
--'CAUSE HE'S GONNA SEE YOU BLEED!
WON'T USE MY OPTIC BLASTS.
THESE BRUISERS ARE MOSTLY MUSCLE.
I'LL JUST BEAT 'EM ON THEIR OWN TERMS.
CHOK!
OH JEEZ-- I WAS SO HOPING THE ONE SHOT WOULD BE ENOUGH.
I'M GONNA BREAK YOU, PUNK!

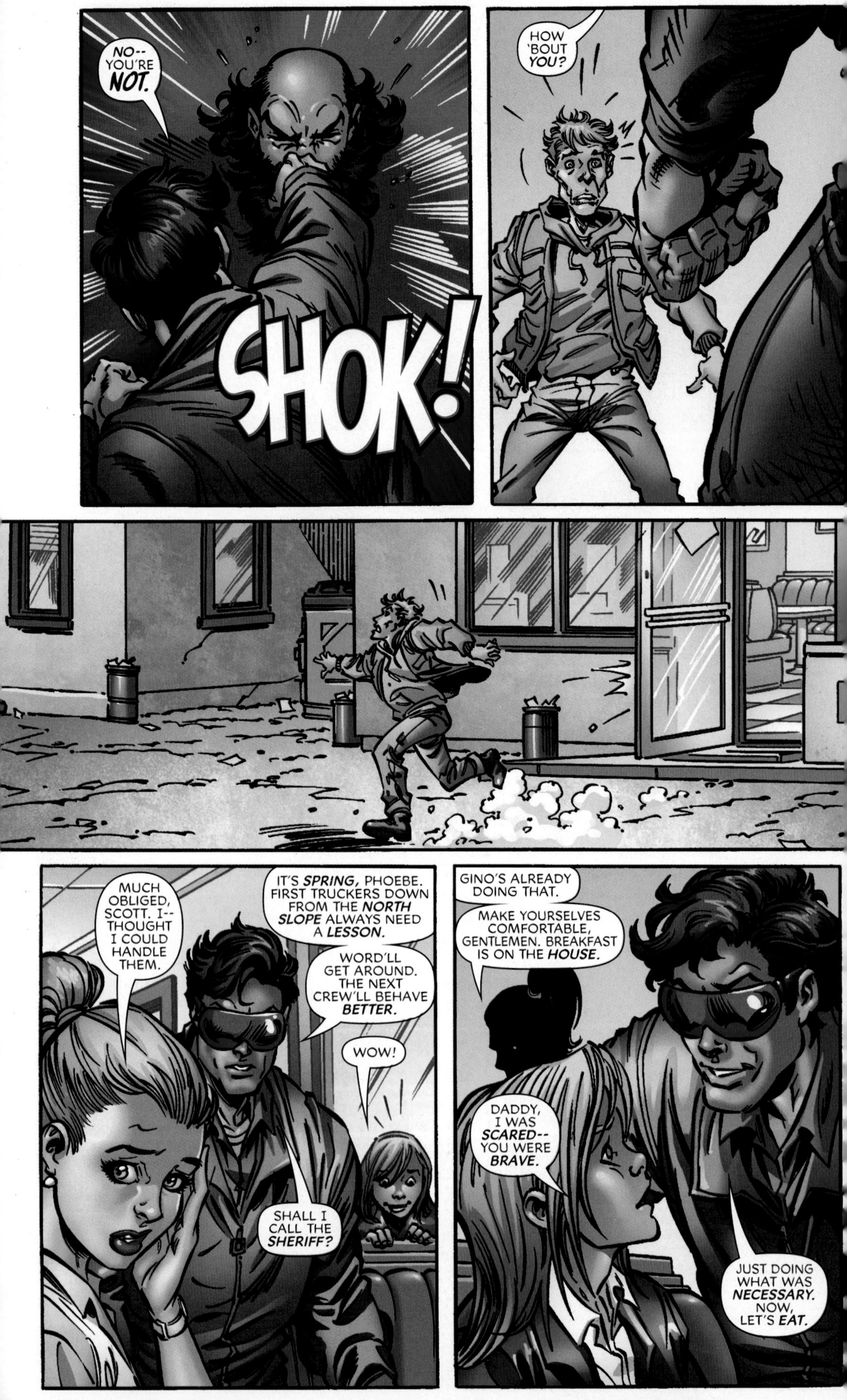
NO-- YOU'RE NOT.
SHOK!
HOW 'BOUT YOU?
MUCH OBLIGED, SCOTT. I-- THOUGHT I COULD HANDLE THEM.
IT'S SPRING, PHOEBE. FIRST TRUCKERS DOWN FROM THE NORTH SLOPE ALWAYS NEED A LESSON.
WORD'LL GET AROUND. THE NEXT CREW'LL BEHAVE BETTER.
WOW!
SHALL I CALL THE SHERIFF?
GINO'S ALREADY DOING THAT.
MAKE YOURSELVES COMFORTABLE, GENTLEMEN. BREAKFAST IS ON THE HOUSE.
DADDY, I WAS SCARED-- YOU WERE BRAVE.
JUST DOING WHAT WAS NECESSARY. NOW, LET'S EAT.

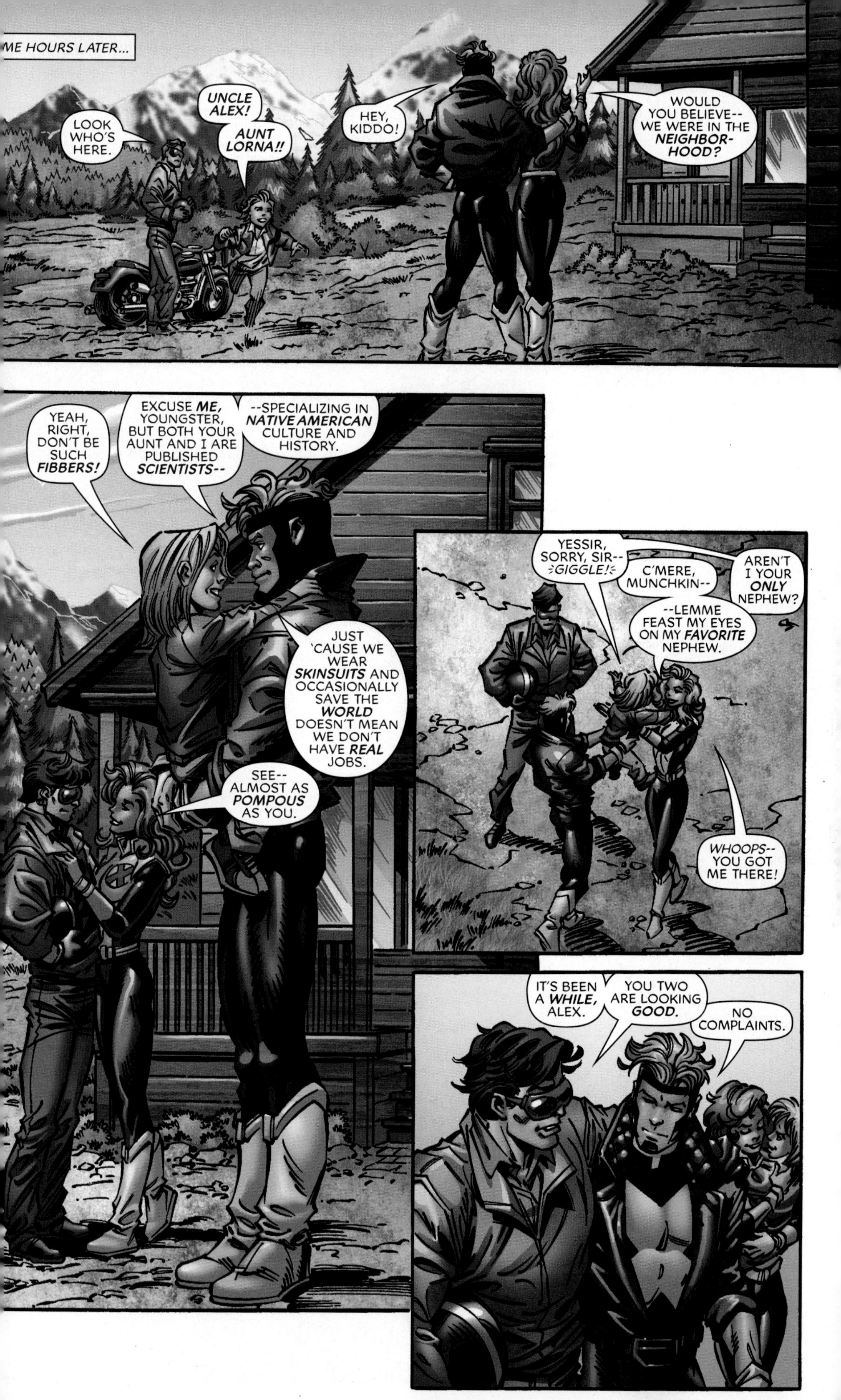
ME HOURS LATER...
LOOK WHO'S HERE.
UNCLE ALEX!
AUNT LORNA!!
HEY, KIDDO!
WOULD YOU BELIEVE-- WE WERE IN THE NEIGHBOR-HOOD?
YEAH, RIGHT, DON'T BE SUCH FIBBERS!
EXCUSE ME, YOUNGSTER, BUT BOTH YOUR AUNT AND I ARE PUBLISHED SCIENTISTS--
--SPECIALIZING IN NATIVE AMERICAN CULTURE AND HISTORY.
JUST 'CAUSE WE WEAR SKINSUITS AND OCCASIONALLY SAVE THE WORLD DOESN'T MEAN WE DON'T HAVE REAL JOBS.
SEE-- ALMOST AS POMPOUS AS YOU.
YESSIR, SORRY, SIR-- GIGGLE!
C'MERE, MUNCHKIN--
--LEMME FEAST MY EYES ON MY FAVORITE NEPHEW.
AREN'T I YOUR ONLY NEPHEW?
WHOOPS-- YOU GOT ME THERE!
IT'S BEEN A WHILE, ALEX.
YOU TWO ARE LOOKING GOOD.
NO COMPLAINTS.

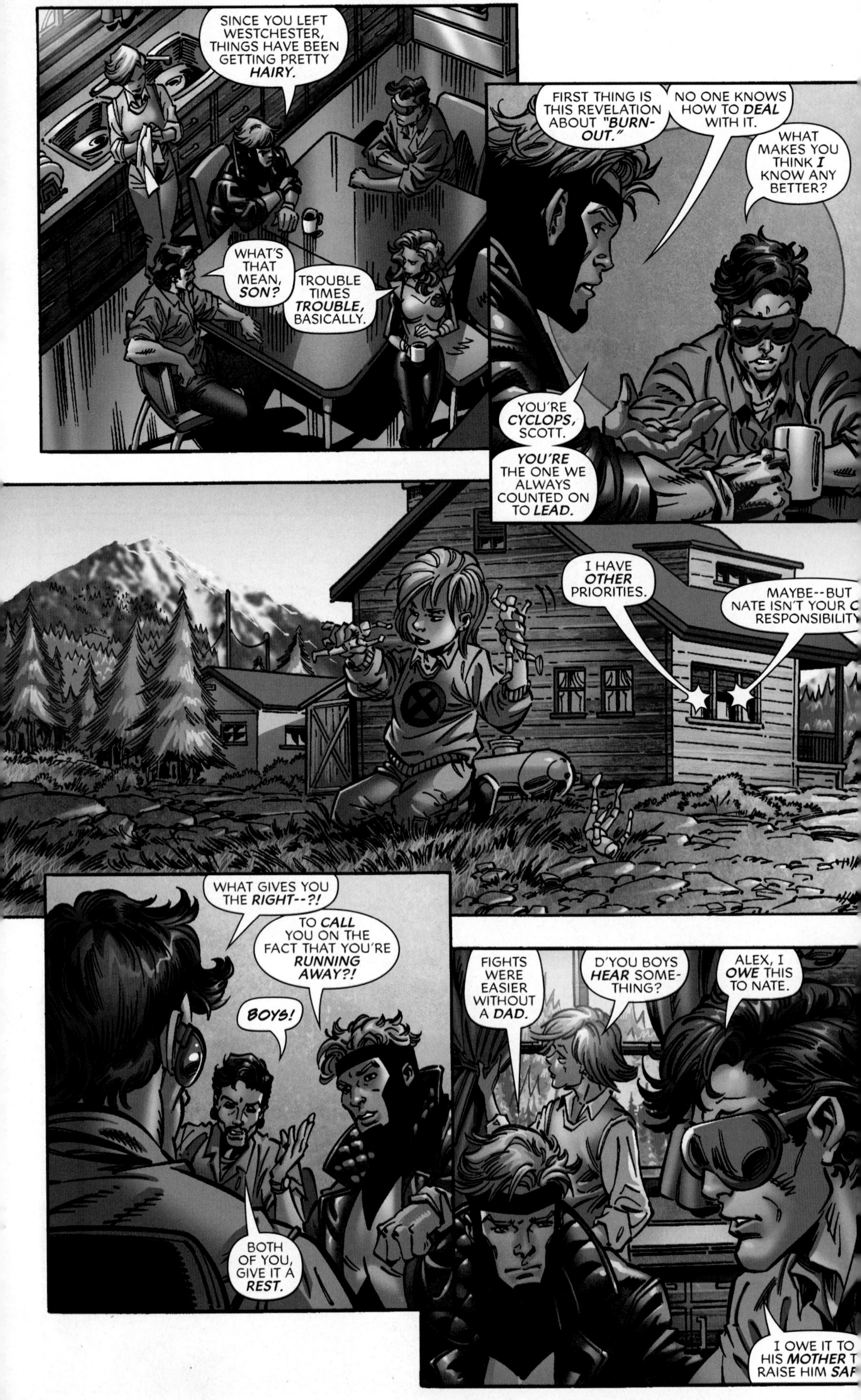
SINCE YOU LEFT WESTCHESTER, THINGS HAVE BEEN GETTING PRETTY HAIRY.
WHAT'S THAT MEAN, SON?
TROUBLE TIMES TROUBLE, BASICALLY.
FIRST THING IS THIS REVELATION ABOUT "BURN-OUT."
NO ONE KNOWS HOW TO DEAL WITH IT.
WHAT MAKES YOU THINK I KNOW ANY BETTER?
YOU'RE CYCLOPS, SCOTT.
YOU'RE THE ONE WE ALWAYS COUNTED ON TO LEAD.
I HAVE OTHER PRIORITIES.
MAYBE--BUT NATE ISN'T YOUR
RESPONSIBILITY
WHAT GIVES YOU THE RIGHT--?!
TO CALL YOU ON THE FACT THAT YOU'RE RUNNING AWAY?!
BOYS!
BOTH OF YOU, GIVE IT A REST.
FIGHTS WERE EASIER WITHOUT A DAD.
D'YOU BOYS HEAR SOME-THING?
ALEX, I OWE THIS TO NATE.
I OWE IT TO HIS MOTHER
RAISE HIM

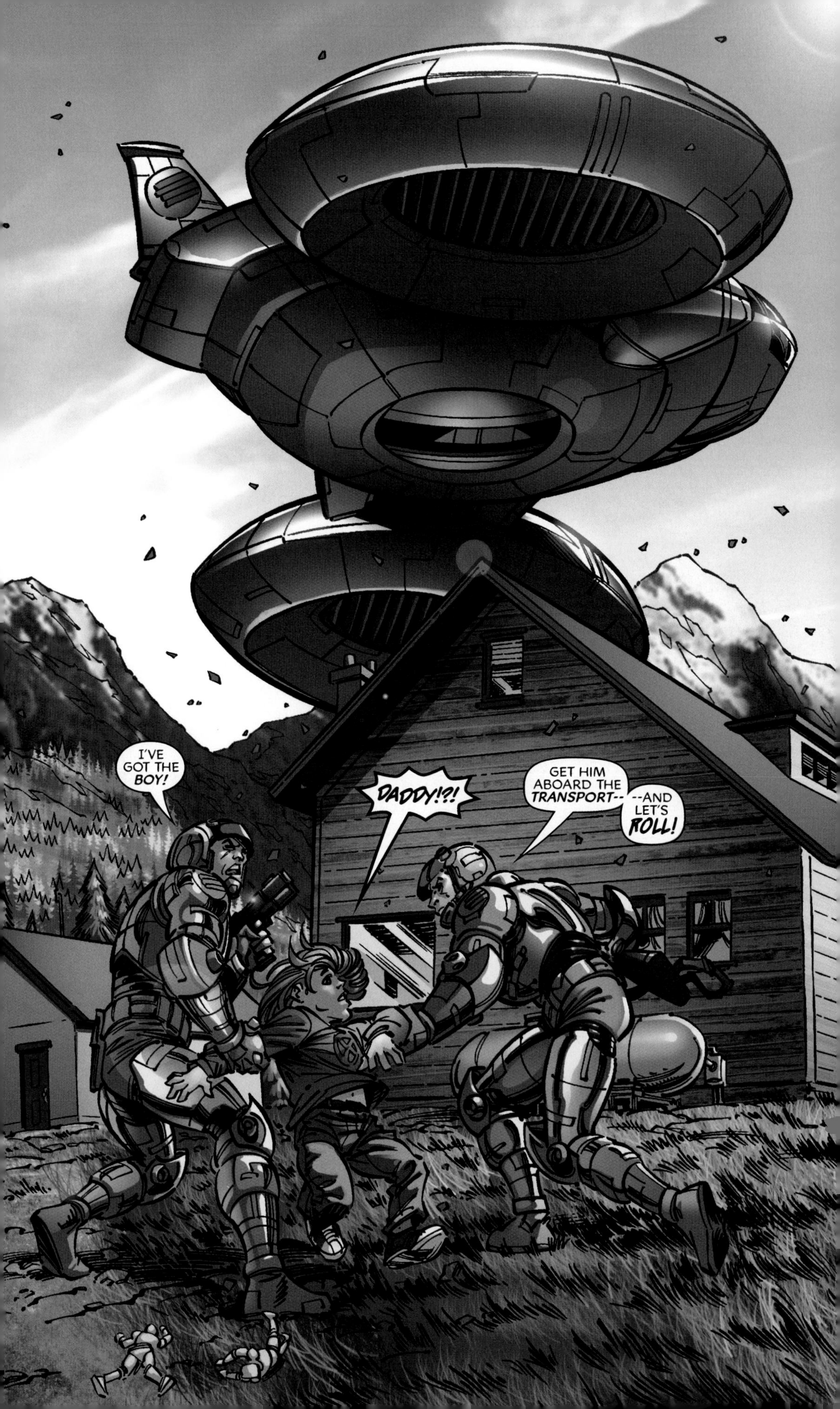

I'VE GOT THE BOY!
DADDY!?!
GET HIM ABOARD THE TRANSPORT--
--AND LET'S ROLL!

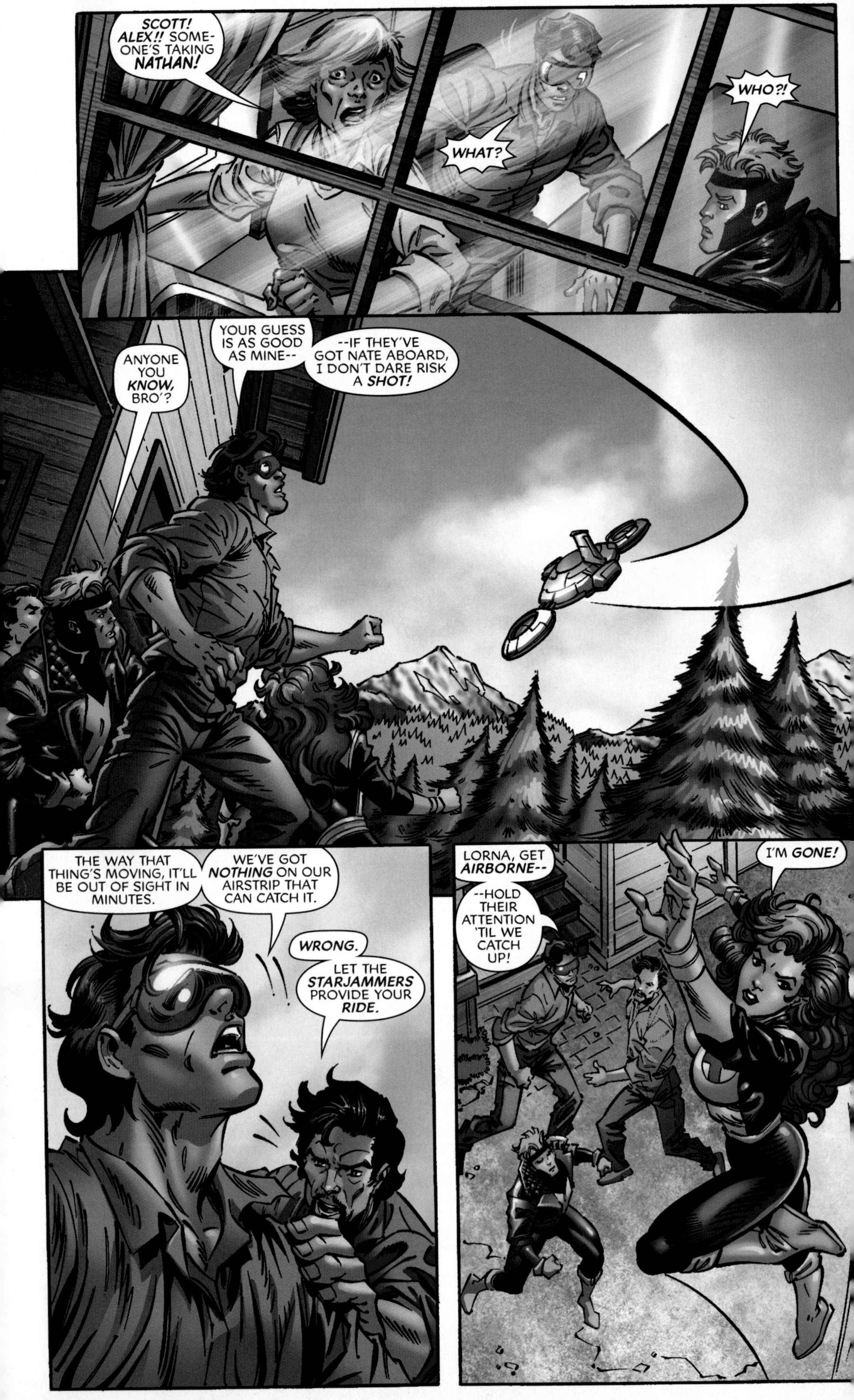
SCOTT! ALEX!! SOME-ONE'S TAKING NATHAN!
WHAT?
WHO?!
ANYONE YOU KNOW, BRO'?
YOUR GUESS IS AS GOOD AS MINE--
--IF THEY'VE GOT NATE ABOARD, I DON'T DARE RISK A SHOT!
THE WAY THAT THING'S MOVING, IT'LL BE OUT OF SIGHT IN MINUTES.
WE'VE GOT NOTHING ON OUR AIRSTRIP THAT CAN CATCH IT.
WRONG.
LET THE STARJAMMERS PROVIDE YOUR RIDE.
LORNA, GET AIRBORNE--
--HOLD THEIR ATTENTION 'TIL WE CATCH UP!
I'M GONE!

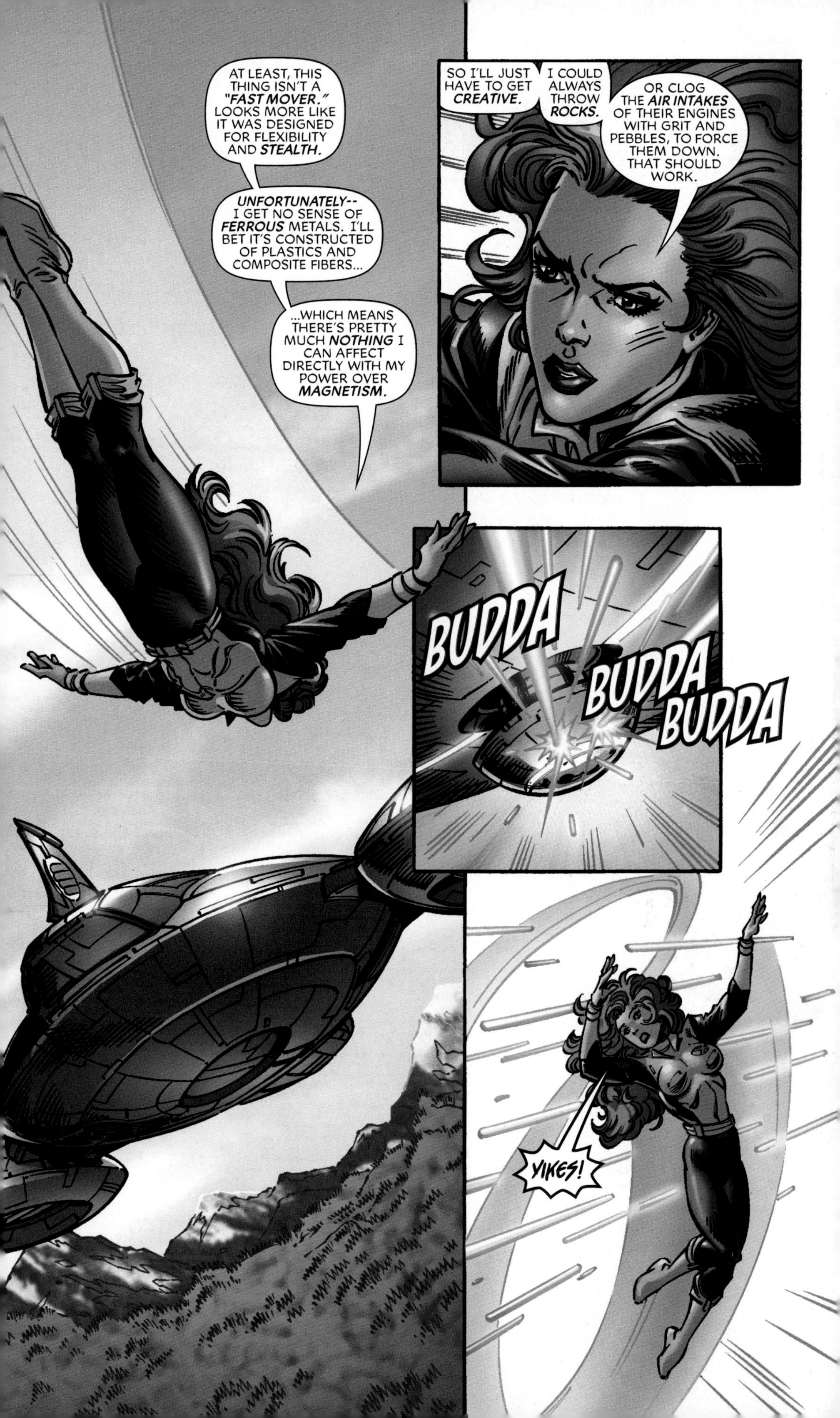

AT LEAST, THIS THING ISN'T A "FAST MOVER." LOOKS MORE LIKE IT WAS DESIGNED FOR FLEXIBILITY AND STEALTH.
UNFORTUNATELY-- I GET NO SENSE OF FERROUS METALS. I'LL BET IT'S CONSTRUCTED OF PLASTICS AND COMPOSITE FIBERS...
...WHICH MEANS THERE'S PRETTY MUCH NOTHING I CAN AFFECT DIRECTLY WITH MY POWER OVER MAGNETISM.
SO I'LL JUST HAVE TO GET CREATIVE.
I COULD ALWAYS THROW ROCKS.
OR CLOG THE AIR INTAKES OF THEIR ENGINES WITH GRIT AND PEBBLES, TO FORCE THEM DOWN. THAT SHOULD WORK.
BUDDA
BUDDA
BUDDA
YIKES!

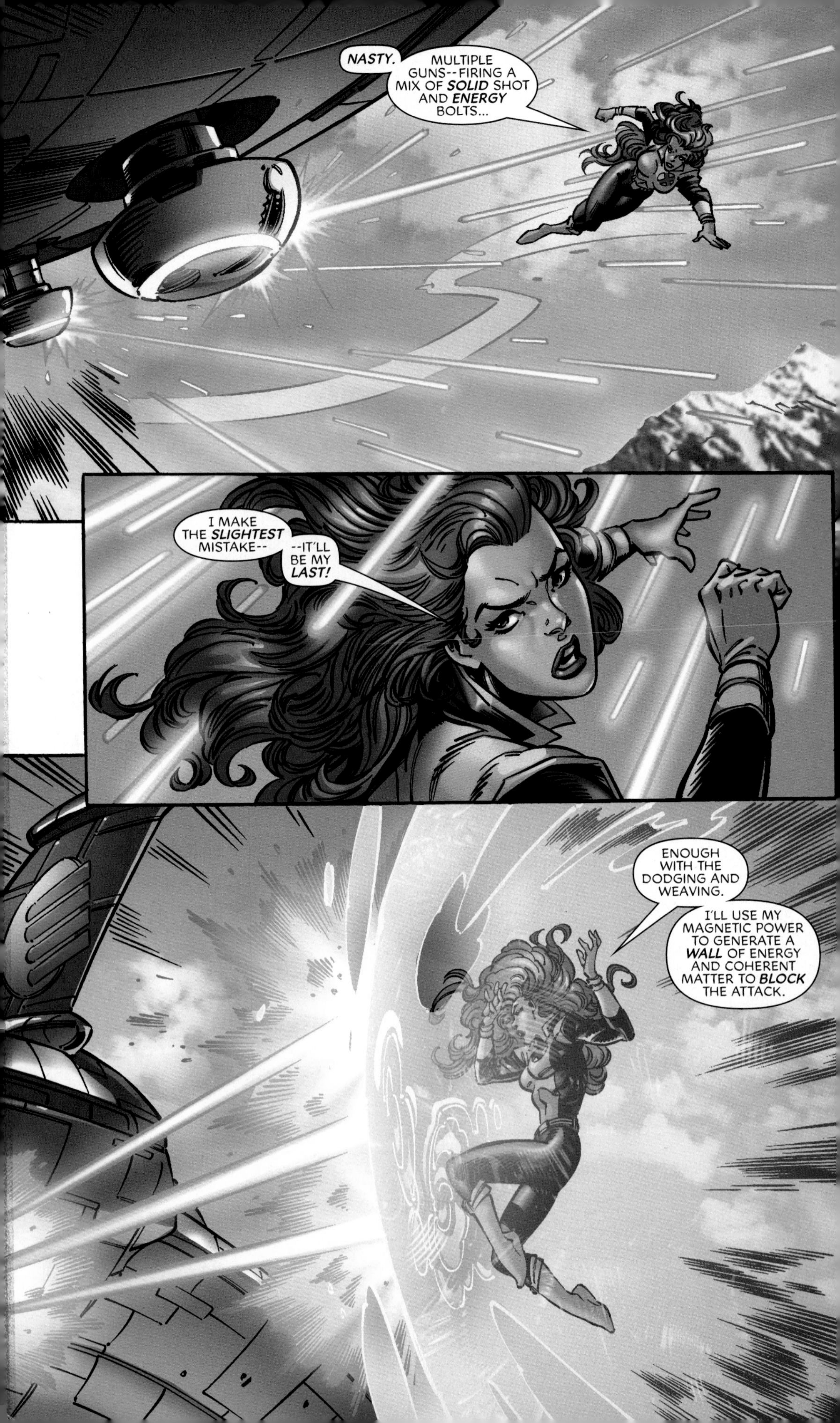
NASTY.
MULTIPLE GUNS--FIRING A MIX OF SOLID SHOT AND ENERGY BOLTS...
I MAKE THE SLIGHTEST MISTAKE--
--IT'LL BE MY LAST!
ENOUGH WITH THE DODGING AND WEAVING.
I'LL USE MY MAGNETIC POWER TO GENERATE A WALL OF ENERGY AND COHERENT MATTER TO BLOCK THE ATTACK.

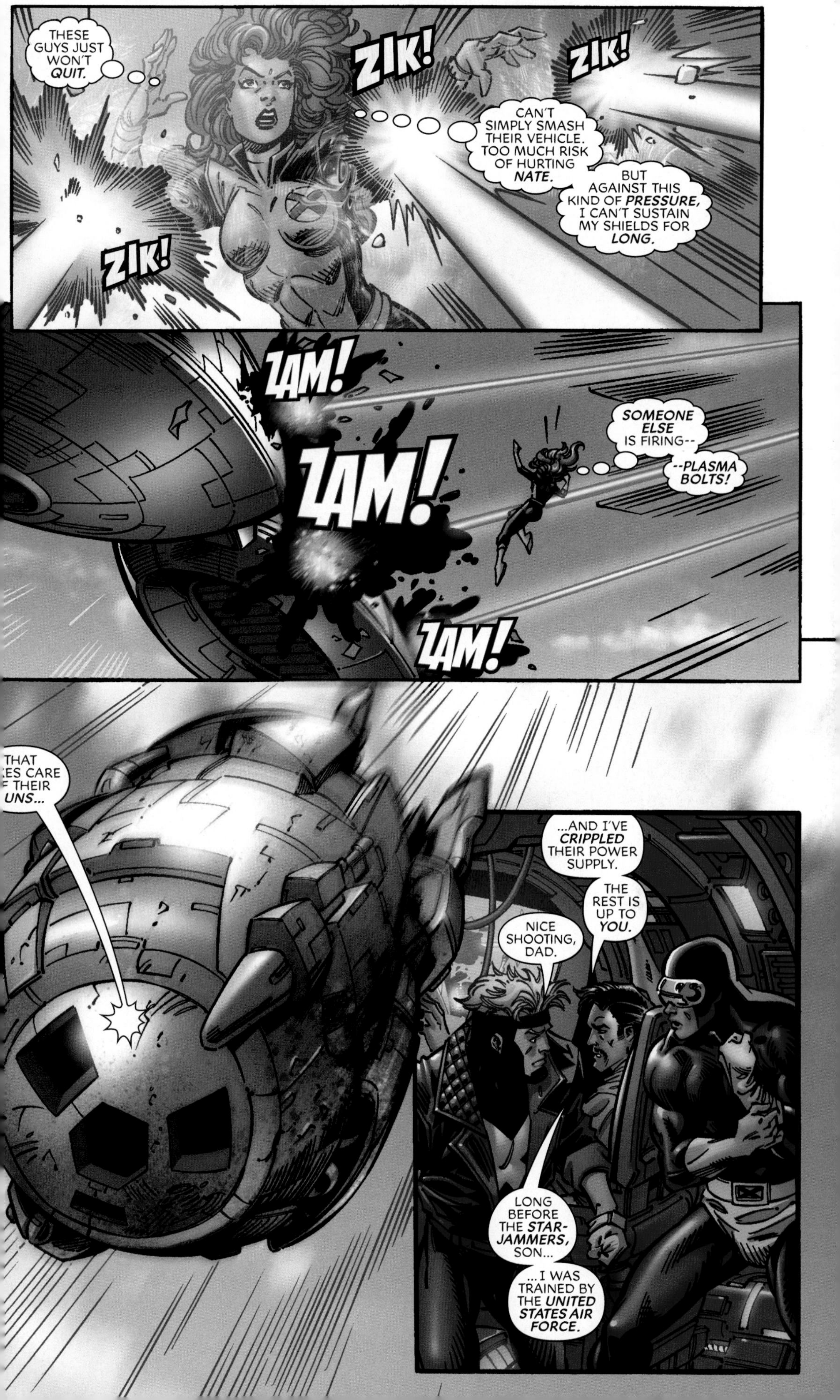
THESE GUYS JUST WON'T *QUIT.*
ZIK!
ZIK!
CAN'T SIMPLY SMASH THEIR VEHICLE. TOO MUCH RISK OF HURTING *NATE.*
BUT AGAINST THIS KIND OF *PRESSURE,* I CAN'T SUSTAIN MY SHIELDS FOR *LONG.*
ZIK!
ZAM!
SOMEONE ELSE IS FIRING--
--*PLASMA BOLTS!*
ZAM!
ZAM!
THAT
ES CARE
F THEIR
UNS...
...AND I'VE *CRIPPLED* THEIR POWER SUPPLY.
THE REST IS UP TO *YOU.*
NICE SHOOTING, DAD.
LONG BEFORE THE *STAR-JAMMERS,* SON...
...I WAS TRAINED BY THE *UNITED STATES AIR FORCE.*

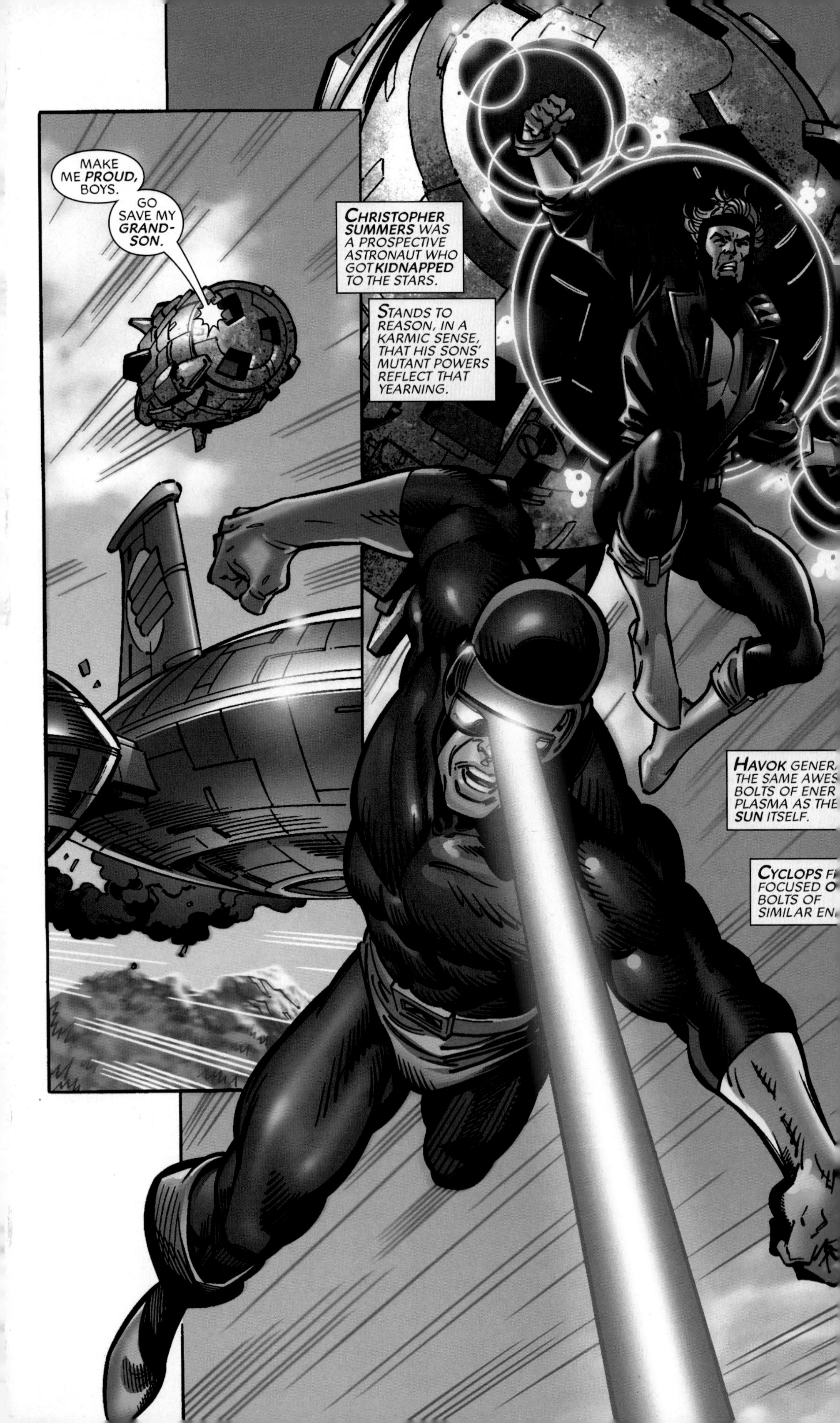
MAKE ME PROUD, BOYS.
GO SAVE MY GRAND-SON.
CHRISTOPHER SUMMERS WAS A PROSPECTIVE ASTRONAUT WHO GOT KIDNAPPED TO THE STARS.
STANDS TO REASON, IN A KARMIC SENSE, THAT HIS SONS' MUTANT POWERS REFLECT THAT YEARNING.
HAVOK GENER
THE SAME AWES
BOLTS OF ENER
PLASMA AS THE
SUN ITSELF.
CYCLOPS F
FOCUSED O
BOLTS OF
SIMILAR EN

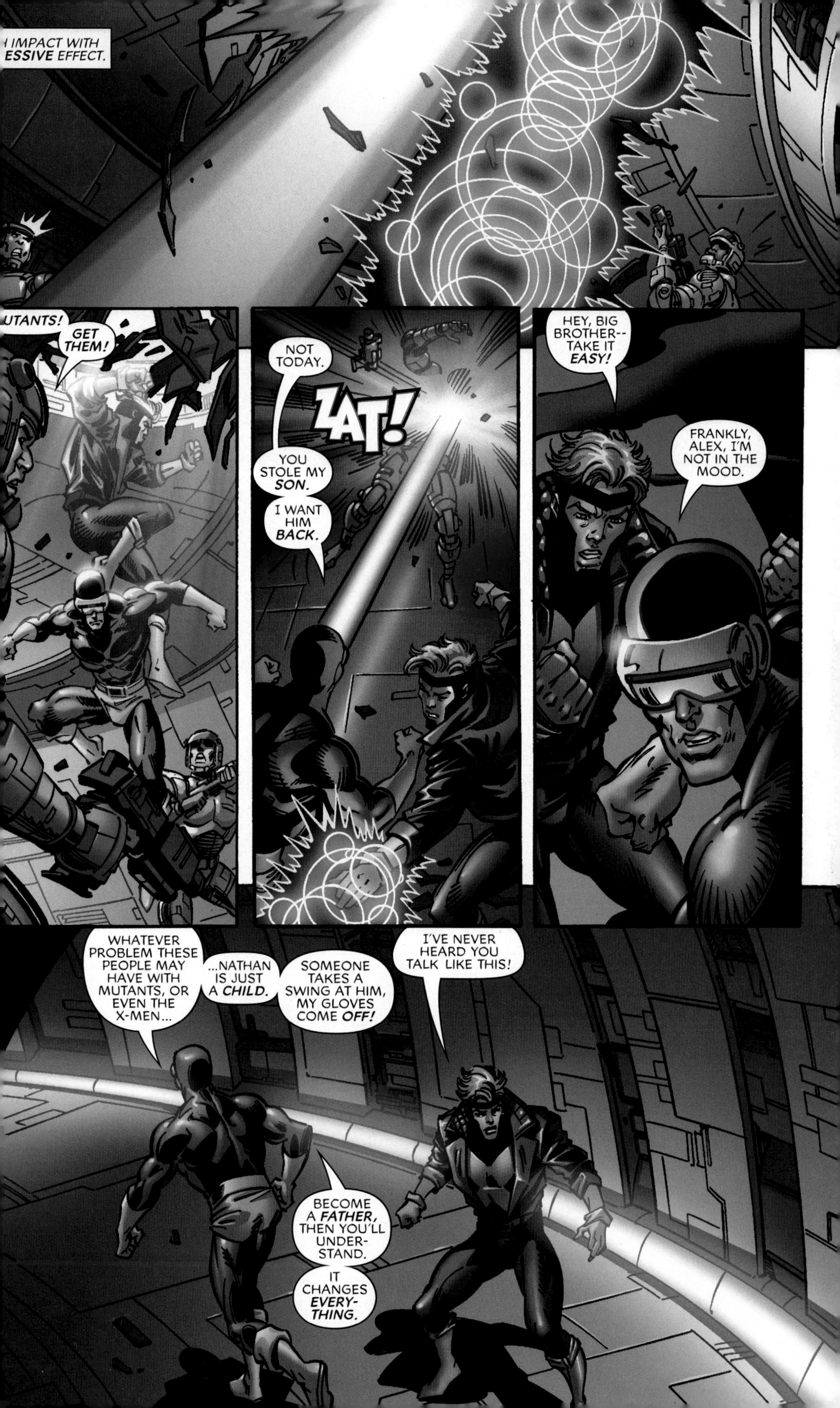

...H IMPACT WITH ...ESSIVE EFFECT.
...UTANTS!
GET THEM!
NOT TODAY.
ZAT!
YOU STOLE MY SON.
I WANT HIM BACK.
HEY, BIG BROTHER-- TAKE IT EASY!
FRANKLY, ALEX, I'M NOT IN THE MOOD.
WHATEVER PROBLEM THESE PEOPLE MAY HAVE WITH MUTANTS, OR EVEN THE X-MEN...
...NATHAN IS JUST A CHILD.
SOMEONE TAKES A SWING AT HIM, MY GLOVES COME OFF!
I'VE NEVER HEARD YOU TALK LIKE THIS!
BECOME A FATHER, THEN YOU'LL UNDERSTAND.
IT CHANGES EVERYTHING.

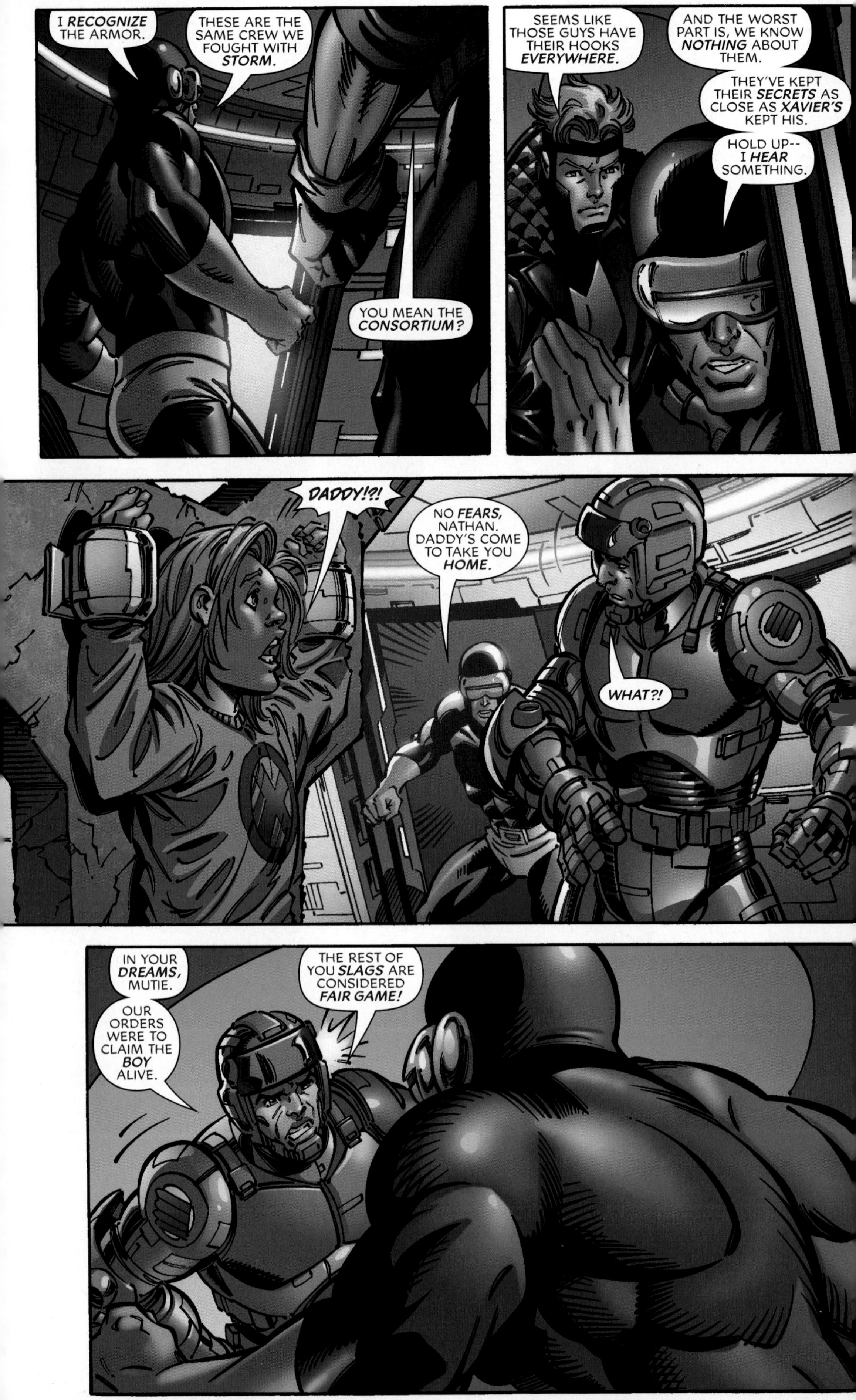

I RECOGNIZE THE ARMOR.
THESE ARE THE SAME CREW WE FOUGHT WITH STORM.
YOU MEAN THE CONSORTIUM?
SEEMS LIKE THOSE GUYS HAVE THEIR HOOKS EVERYWHERE.
AND THE WORST PART IS, WE KNOW NOTHING ABOUT THEM.
THEY'VE KEPT THEIR SECRETS AS CLOSE AS XAVIER'S KEPT HIS.
HOLD UP-- I HEAR SOMETHING.
DADDY!?!
NO FEARS, NATHAN. DADDY'S COME TO TAKE YOU HOME.
WHAT?!
IN YOUR DREAMS, MUTIE.
OUR ORDERS WERE TO CLAIM THE BOY ALIVE.
THE REST OF YOU SLAGS ARE CONSIDERED FAIR GAME!

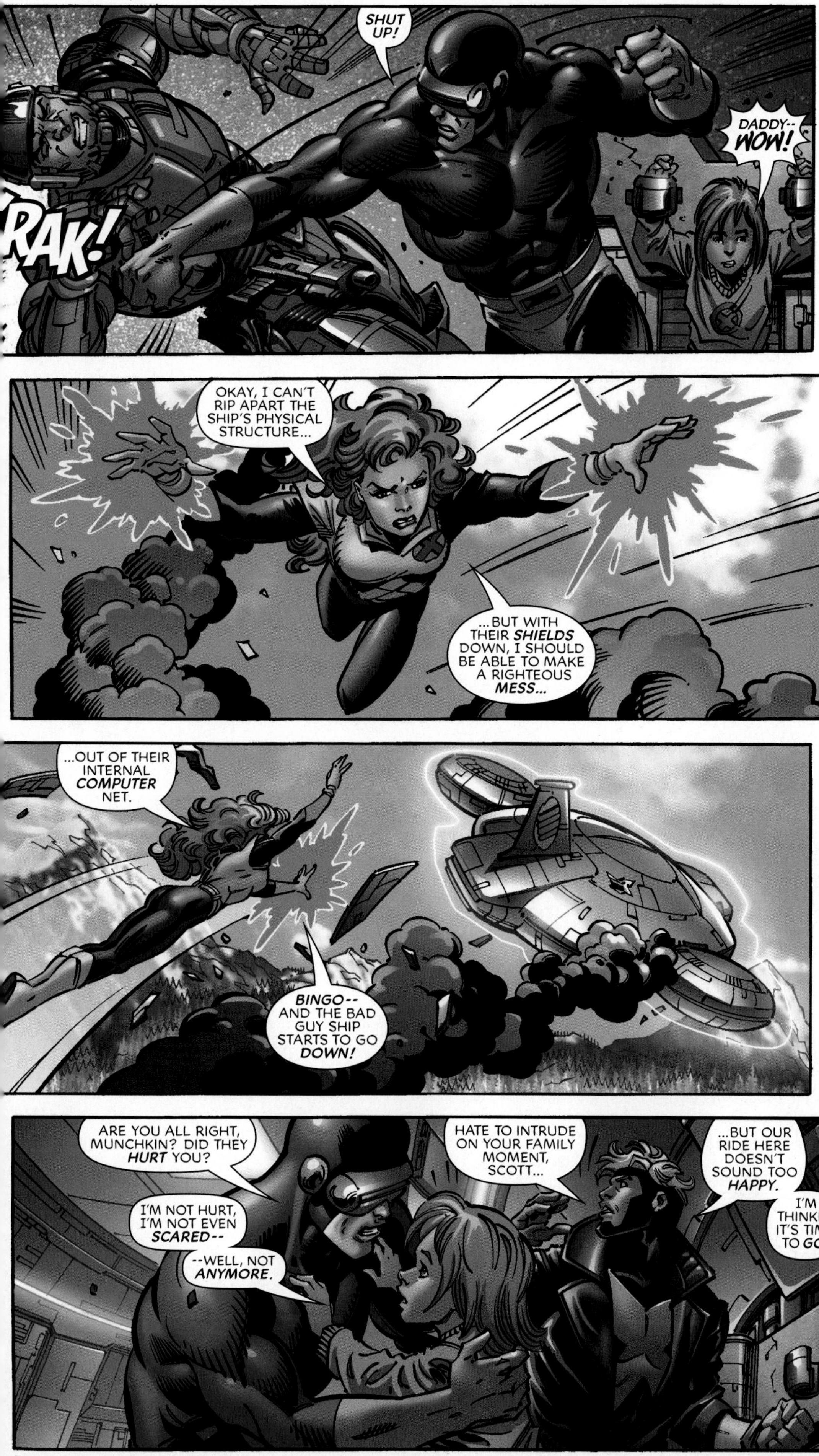

SHUT UP!
RAK!
DADDY-- WOW!
OKAY, I CAN'T RIP APART THE SHIP'S PHYSICAL STRUCTURE...
...BUT WITH THEIR SHIELDS DOWN, I SHOULD BE ABLE TO MAKE A RIGHTEOUS MESS...
...OUT OF THEIR INTERNAL COMPUTER NET.
BINGO-- AND THE BAD GUY SHIP STARTS TO GO DOWN!
ARE YOU ALL RIGHT, MUNCHKIN? DID THEY HURT YOU?
I'M NOT HURT, I'M NOT EVEN SCARED--
--WELL, NOT ANYMORE.
HATE TO INTRUDE ON YOUR FAMILY MOMENT, SCOTT...
...BUT OUR RIDE HERE DOESN'T SOUND TOO HAPPY.
I'M THINKIN' IT'S TIME TO GO!

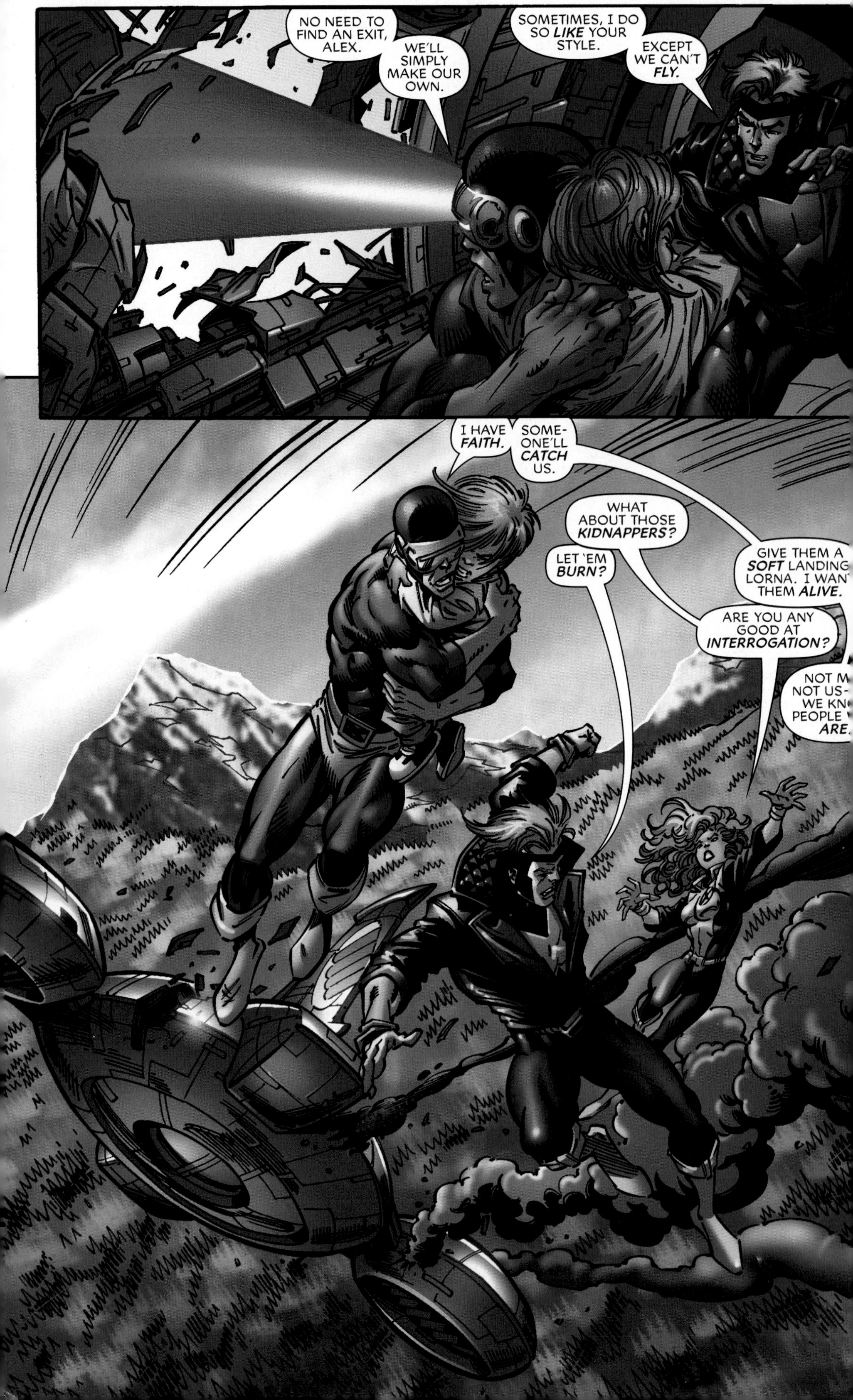
NO NEED TO FIND AN EXIT, ALEX.
WE'LL SIMPLY MAKE OUR OWN.
SOMETIMES, I DO SO LIKE YOUR STYLE.
EXCEPT WE CAN'T FLY.
I HAVE FAITH.
SOME-ONE'LL CATCH US.
WHAT ABOUT THOSE KIDNAPPERS?
LET 'EM BURN?
GIVE THEM A SOFT LANDING LORNA. I WAN THEM ALIVE.
ARE YOU ANY GOOD AT INTERROGATION?
NOT M NOT US- WE KN PEOPLE ARE.

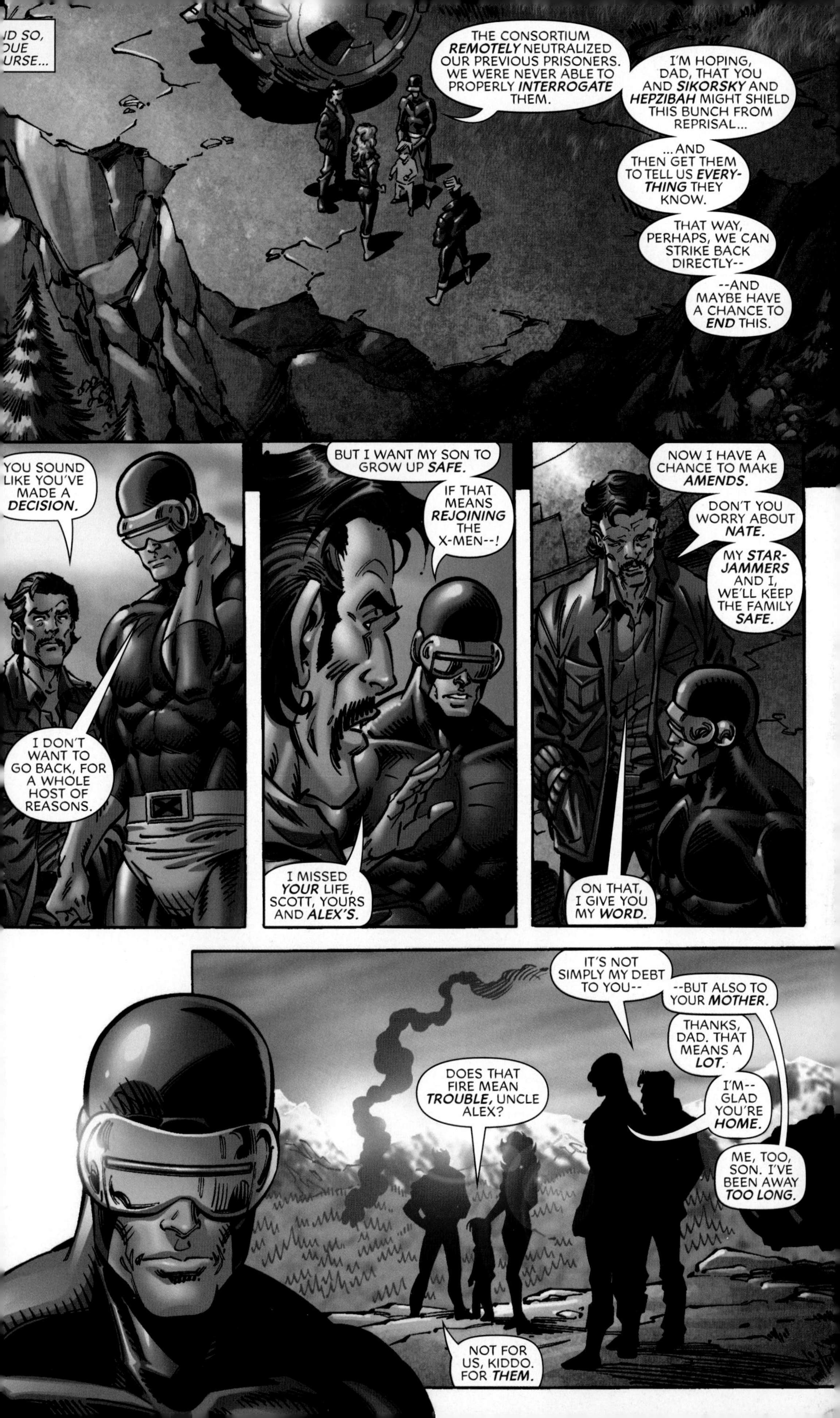

...ID SO, ...DUE ...URSE...
THE CONSORTIUM REMOTELY NEUTRALIZED OUR PREVIOUS PRISONERS. WE WERE NEVER ABLE TO PROPERLY INTERROGATE THEM.
I'M HOPING, DAD, THAT YOU AND SIKORSKY AND HEPZIBAH MIGHT SHIELD THIS BUNCH FROM REPRISAL...
...AND THEN GET THEM TO TELL US EVERYTHING THEY KNOW.
THAT WAY, PERHAPS, WE CAN STRIKE BACK DIRECTLY--
--AND MAYBE HAVE A CHANCE TO END THIS.
YOU SOUND LIKE YOU'VE MADE A DECISION.
I DON'T WANT TO GO BACK, FOR A WHOLE HOST OF REASONS.
BUT I WANT MY SON TO GROW UP SAFE.
IF THAT MEANS REJOINING THE X-MEN--!
I MISSED YOUR LIFE, SCOTT, YOURS AND ALEX'S.
NOW I HAVE A CHANCE TO MAKE AMENDS.
DON'T YOU WORRY ABOUT NATE.
MY STAR-JAMMERS AND I, WE'LL KEEP THE FAMILY SAFE.
ON THAT, I GIVE YOU MY WORD.
IT'S NOT SIMPLY MY DEBT TO YOU--
--BUT ALSO TO YOUR MOTHER.
THANKS, DAD. THAT MEANS A LOT.
I'M-- GLAD YOU'RE HOME.
ME, TOO, SON. I'VE BEEN AWAY TOO LONG.
DOES THAT FIRE MEAN TROUBLE, UNCLE ALEX?
NOT FOR US, KIDDO. FOR THEM.

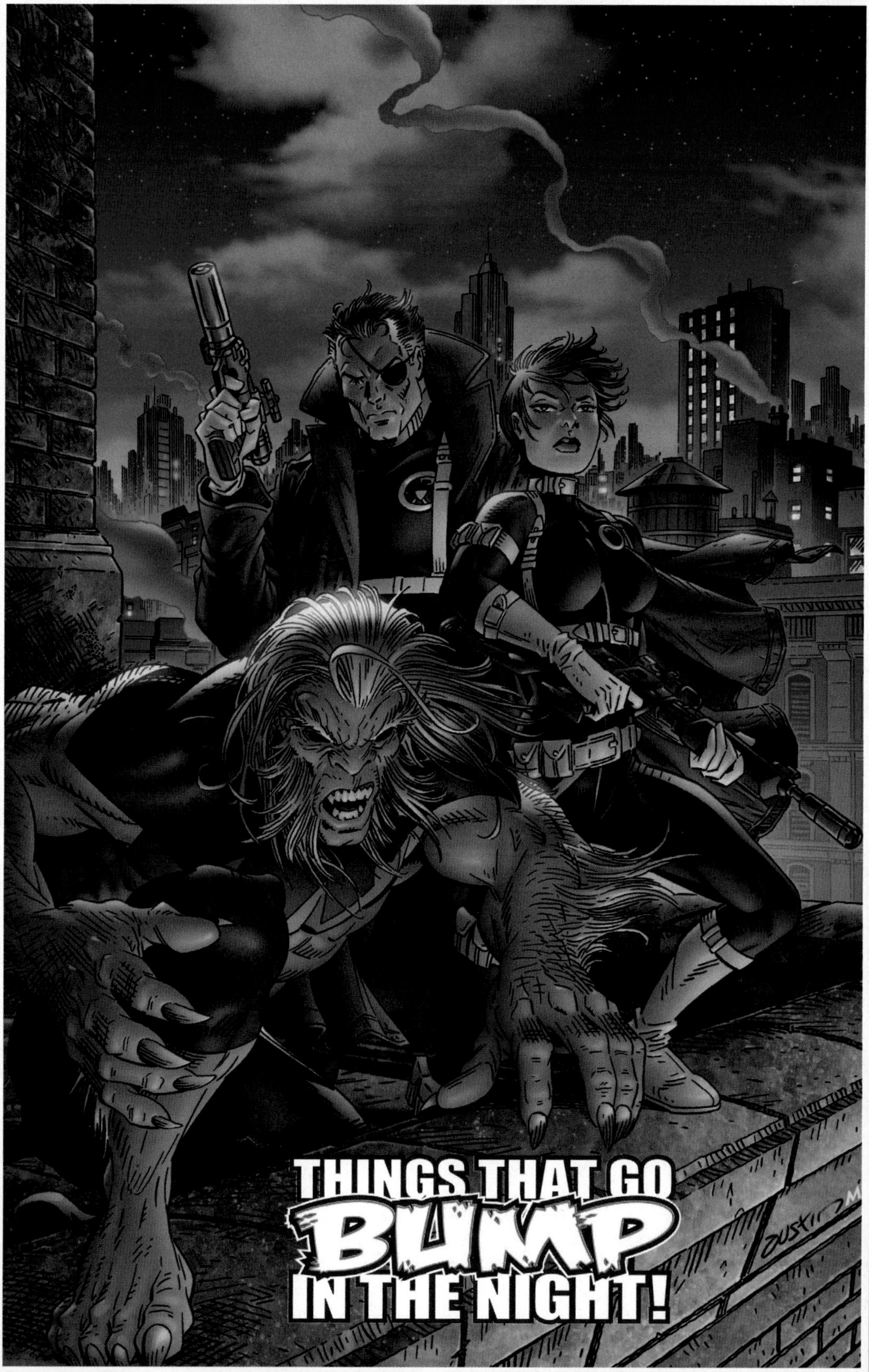
THINGS THAT GO
BUMP
IN THE NIGHT!

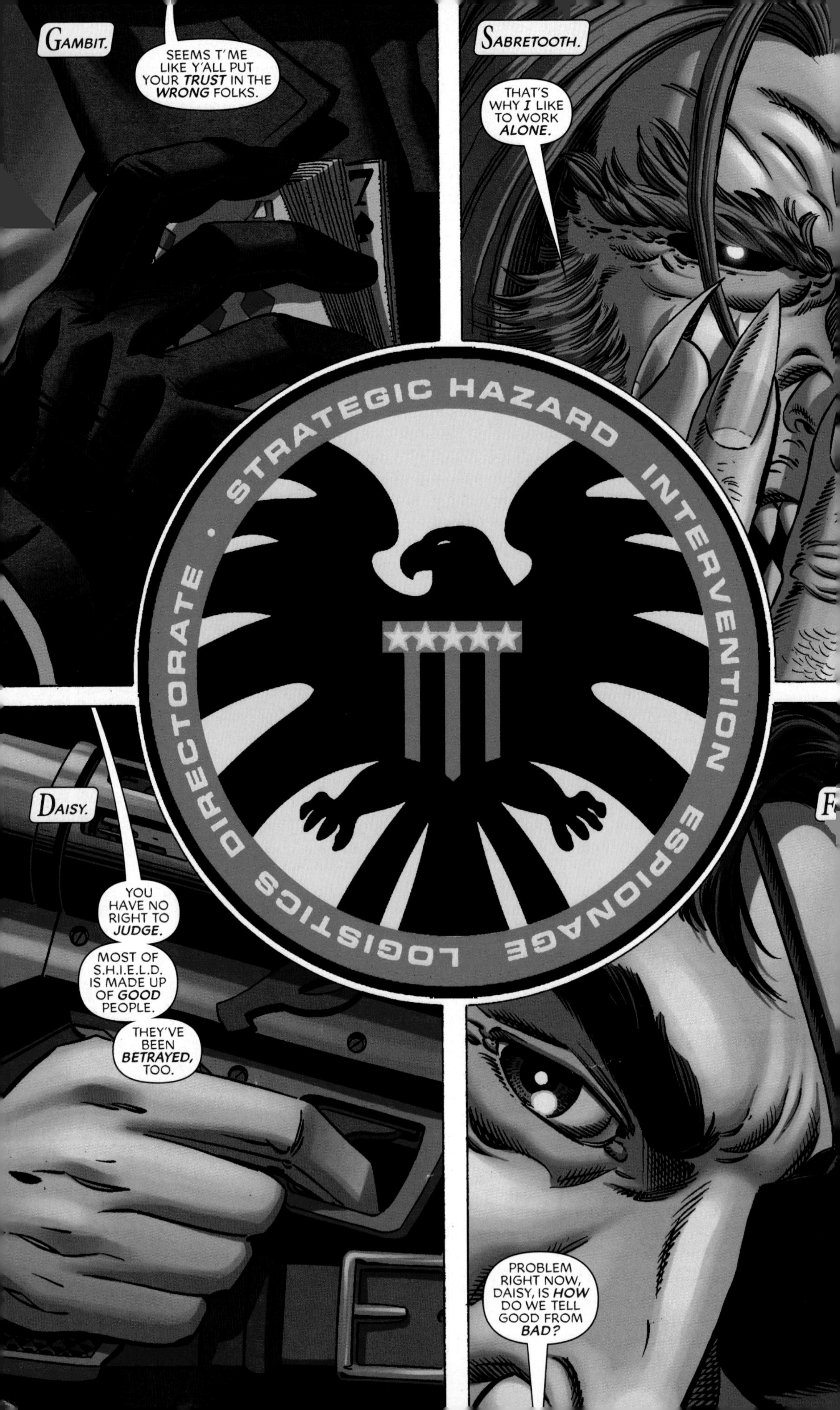

GAMBIT.
SEEMS T'ME LIKE Y'ALL PUT YOUR TRUST IN THE WRONG FOLKS.
SABRETOOTH.
THAT'S WHY I LIKE TO WORK ALONE.
STRATEGIC HAZARD INTERVENTION ESPIONAGE LOGISTICS DIRECTORATE
DAISY.
YOU HAVE NO RIGHT TO JUDGE.
MOST OF S.H.I.E.L.D. IS MADE UP OF GOOD PEOPLE.
THEY'VE BEEN BETRAYED, TOO.
PROBLEM RIGHT NOW, DAISY, IS HOW DO WE TELL GOOD FROM BAD?

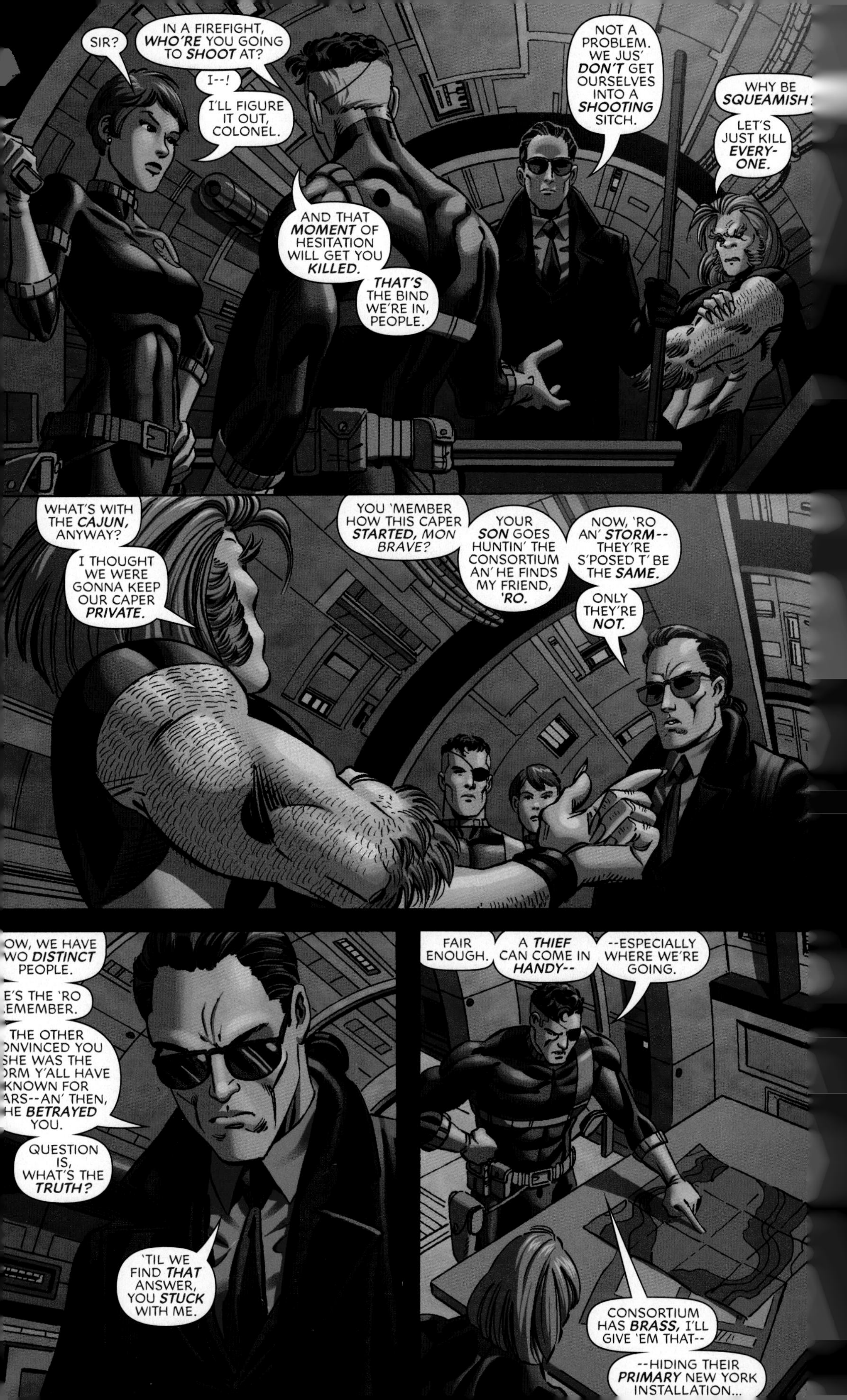

SIR?
IN A FIREFIGHT, WHO'RE YOU GOING TO SHOOT AT?
I--!
I'LL FIGURE IT OUT, COLONEL.
AND THAT MOMENT OF HESITATION WILL GET YOU KILLED.
THAT'S THE BIND WE'RE IN, PEOPLE.
NOT A PROBLEM. WE JUS' DON'T GET OURSELVES INTO A SHOOTING SITCH.
WHY BE SQUEAMISH?
LET'S JUST KILL EVERY-ONE.
WHAT'S WITH THE CAJUN, ANYWAY?
I THOUGHT WE WERE GONNA KEEP OUR CAPER PRIVATE.
YOU 'MEMBER HOW THIS CAPER STARTED, MON BRAVE?
YOUR SON GOES HUNTIN' THE CONSORTIUM AN' HE FINDS MY FRIEND, 'RO.
NOW, 'RO AN' STORM-- THEY'RE S'POSED T' BE THE SAME.
ONLY THEY'RE NOT.
OW, WE HAVE WO DISTINCT PEOPLE.
E'S THE 'RO EMEMBER.
THE OTHER ONVINCED YOU SHE WAS THE ORM Y'ALL HAVE KNOWN FOR ARS--AN' THEN, HE BETRAYED YOU.
QUESTION IS, WHAT'S THE TRUTH?
'TIL WE FIND THAT ANSWER, YOU STUCK WITH ME.
FAIR ENOUGH.
A THIEF CAN COME IN HANDY--
--ESPECIALLY WHERE WE'RE GOING.
CONSORTIUM HAS BRASS, I'LL GIVE 'EM THAT--
--HIDING THEIR PRIMARY NEW YORK INSTALLATION...

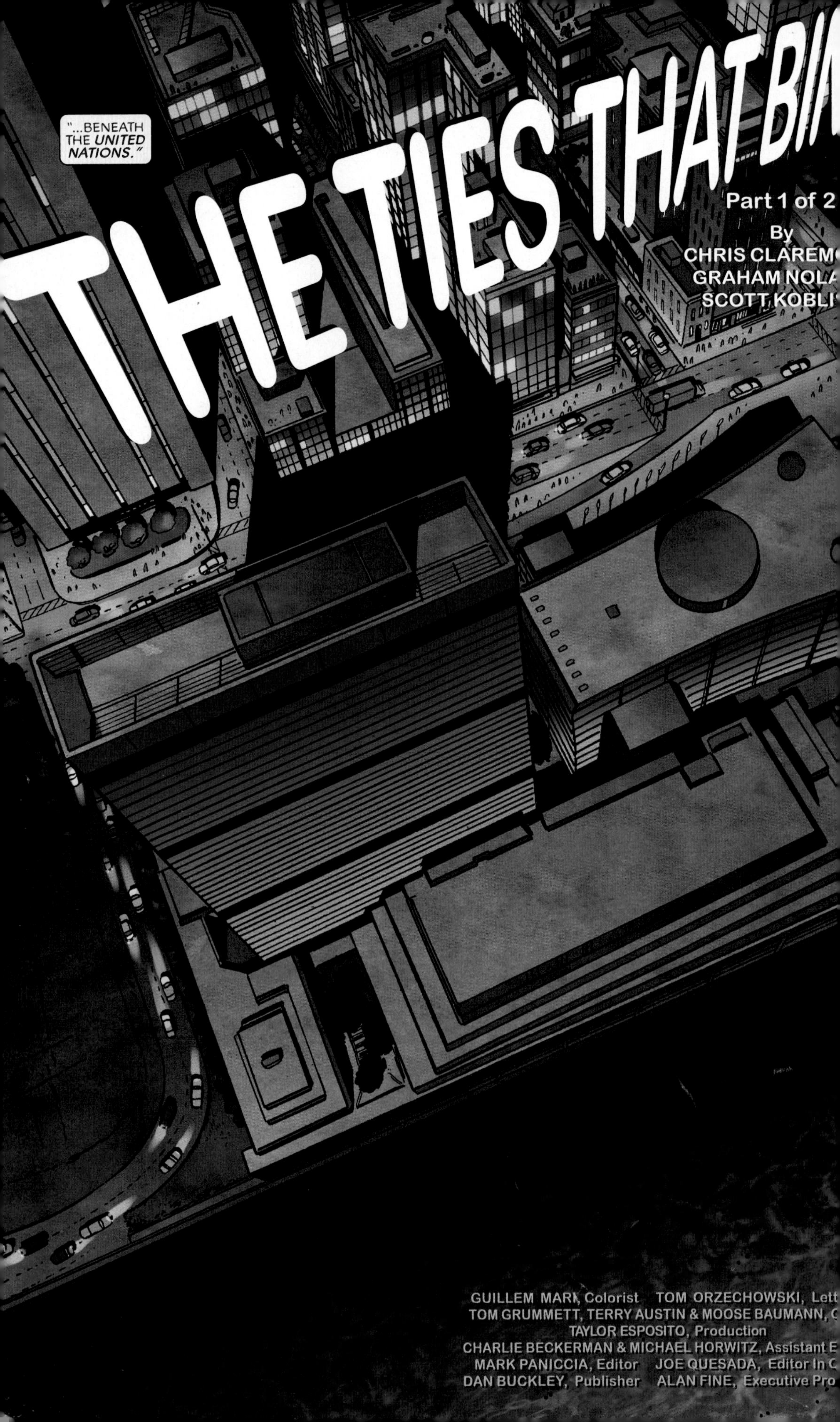

"...BENEATH THE *UNITED NATIONS.*"
THE TIES THAT BIN
Part 1 of 2
By
CHRIS CLAREM
GRAHAM NOLA
SCOTT KOBLI
GUILLEM MARI, Colorist TOM ORZECHOWSKI, Lett
TOM GRUMMETT, TERRY AUSTIN & MOOSE BAUMANN, C
TAYLOR ESPOSITO, Production
CHARLIE BECKERMAN & MICHAEL HORWITZ, Assistant E
MARK PANICCIA, Editor JOE QUESADA, Editor In C
DAN BUCKLEY, Publisher ALAN FINE, Executive Pro

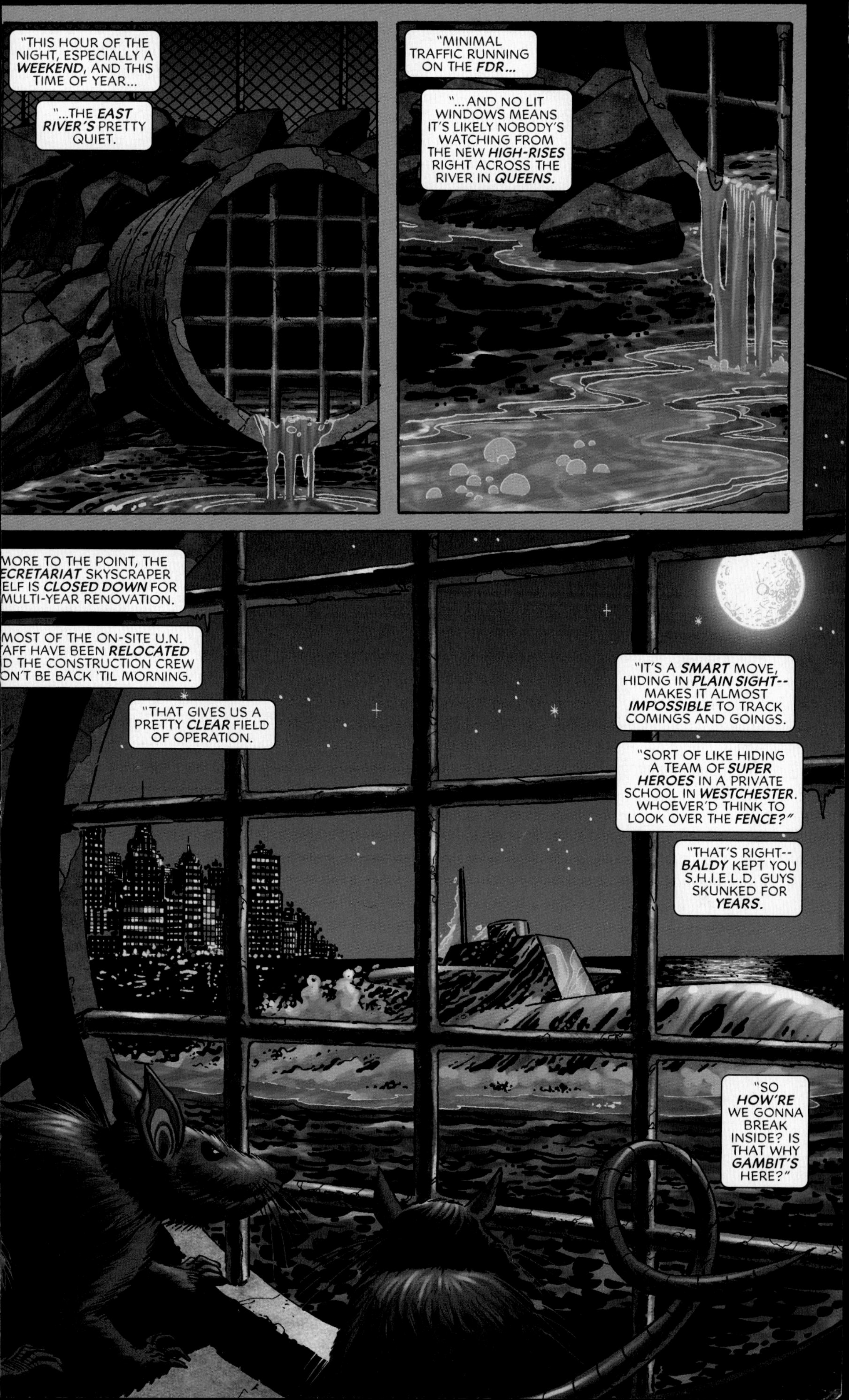
"THIS HOUR OF THE NIGHT, ESPECIALLY A WEEKEND, AND THIS TIME OF YEAR...
"...THE EAST RIVER'S PRETTY QUIET.
"MINIMAL TRAFFIC RUNNING ON THE FDR...
"...AND NO LIT WINDOWS MEANS IT'S LIKELY NOBODY'S WATCHING FROM THE NEW HIGH-RISES RIGHT ACROSS THE RIVER IN QUEENS.
MORE TO THE POINT, THE ECRETARIAT SKYSCRAPER ELF IS CLOSED DOWN FOR MULTI-YEAR RENOVATION.
MOST OF THE ON-SITE U.N. AFF HAVE BEEN RELOCATED D THE CONSTRUCTION CREW ON'T BE BACK 'TIL MORNING.
"THAT GIVES US A PRETTY CLEAR FIELD OF OPERATION.
"IT'S A SMART MOVE, HIDING IN PLAIN SIGHT-- MAKES IT ALMOST IMPOSSIBLE TO TRACK COMINGS AND GOINGS.
"SORT OF LIKE HIDING A TEAM OF SUPER HEROES IN A PRIVATE SCHOOL IN WESTCHESTER. WHOEVER'D THINK TO LOOK OVER THE FENCE?"
"THAT'S RIGHT-- BALDY KEPT YOU S.H.I.E.L.D. GUYS SKUNKED FOR YEARS.
"SO HOW'RE WE GONNA BREAK INSIDE? IS THAT WHY GAMBIT'S HERE?"

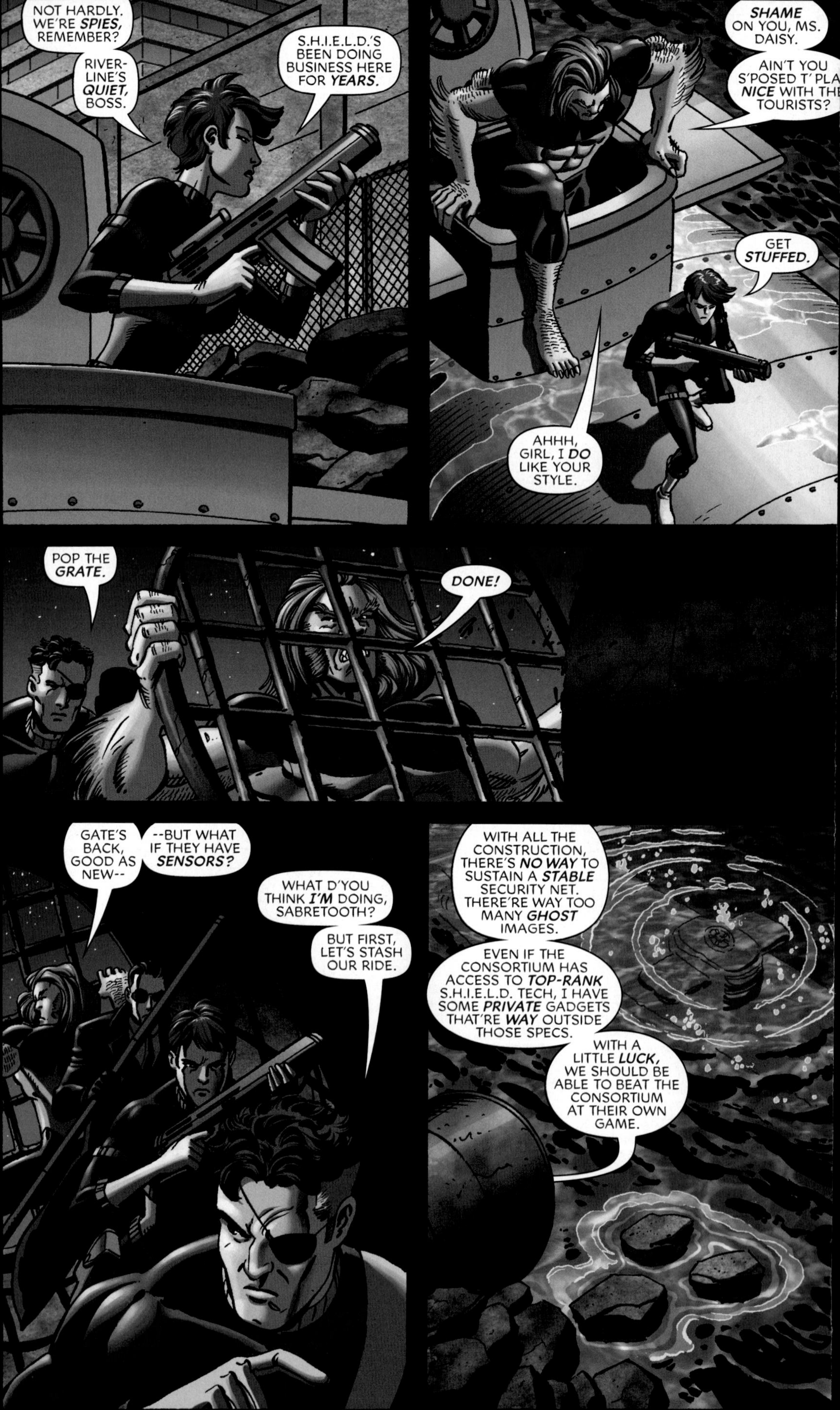
NOT HARDLY. WE'RE SPIES, REMEMBER?
RIVER-LINE'S QUIET, BOSS.
S.H.I.E.L.D.'S BEEN DOING BUSINESS HERE FOR YEARS.
SHAME ON YOU, MS. DAISY.
AIN'T YOU S'POSED T' PLA NICE WITH THE TOURISTS?
GET STUFFED.
AHHH, GIRL, I DO LIKE YOUR STYLE.
POP THE GRATE.
DONE!
GATE'S BACK, GOOD AS NEW--
--BUT WHAT IF THEY HAVE SENSORS?
WHAT D'YOU THINK I'M DOING, SABRETOOTH?
BUT FIRST, LET'S STASH OUR RIDE.
WITH ALL THE CONSTRUCTION, THERE'S NO WAY TO SUSTAIN A STABLE SECURITY NET. THERE'RE WAY TOO MANY GHOST IMAGES.
EVEN IF THE CONSORTIUM HAS ACCESS TO TOP-RANK S.H.I.E.L.D. TECH, I HAVE SOME PRIVATE GADGETS THAT'RE WAY OUTSIDE THOSE SPECS.
WITH A LITTLE LUCK, WE SHOULD BE ABLE TO BEAT THE CONSORTIUM AT THEIR OWN GAME.

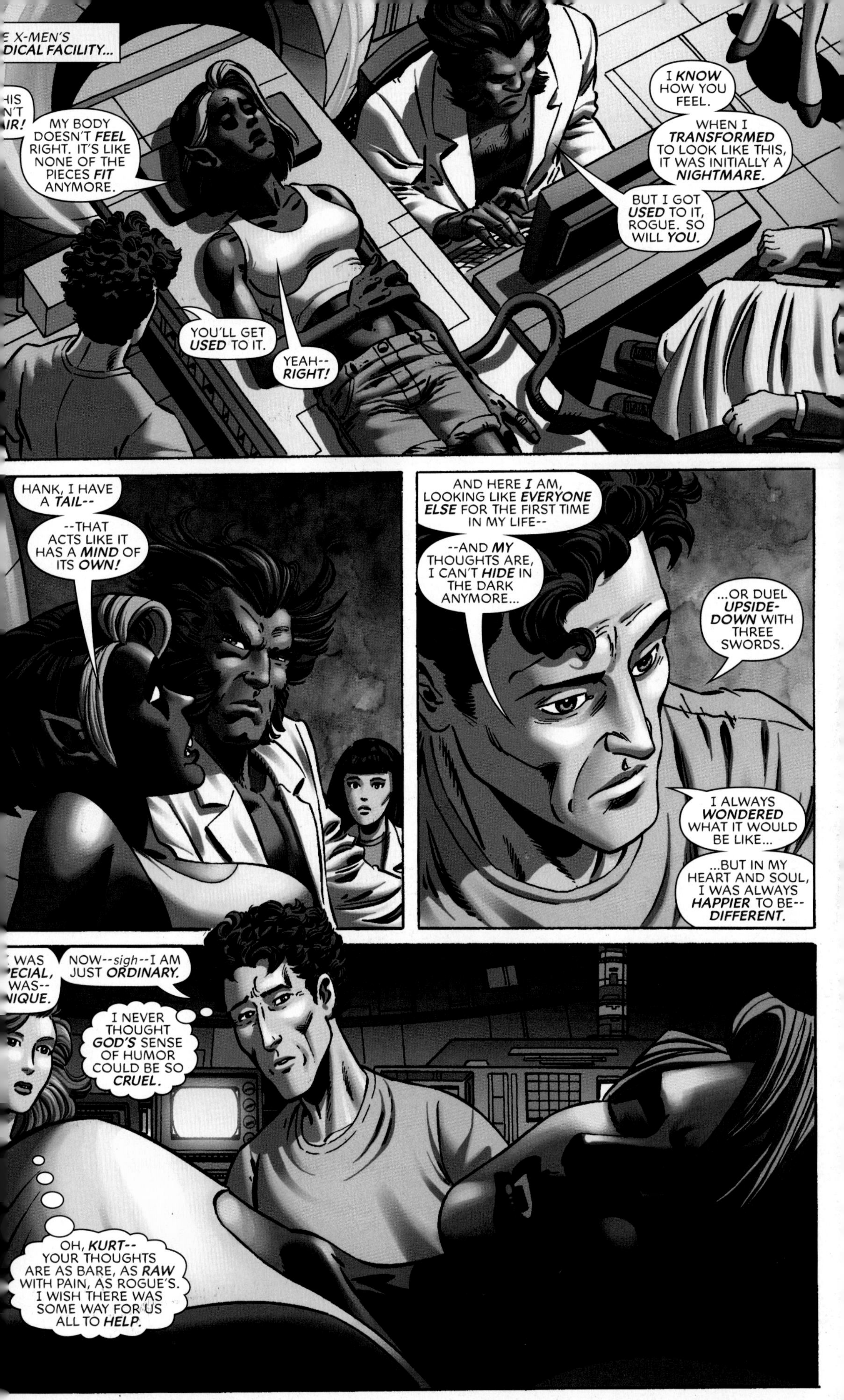
E X-MEN'S DICAL FACILITY...
HIS N'T IR!
MY BODY DOESN'T FEEL RIGHT. IT'S LIKE NONE OF THE PIECES FIT ANYMORE.
I KNOW HOW YOU FEEL.
WHEN I TRANSFORMED TO LOOK LIKE THIS, IT WAS INITIALLY A NIGHTMARE.
BUT I GOT USED TO IT, ROGUE. SO WILL YOU.
YOU'LL GET USED TO IT.
YEAH-- RIGHT!
HANK, I HAVE A TAIL--
--THAT ACTS LIKE IT HAS A MIND OF ITS OWN!
AND HERE I AM, LOOKING LIKE EVERYONE ELSE FOR THE FIRST TIME IN MY LIFE--
--AND MY THOUGHTS ARE, I CAN'T HIDE IN THE DARK ANYMORE...
...OR DUEL UPSIDE-DOWN WITH THREE SWORDS.
I ALWAYS WONDERED WHAT IT WOULD BE LIKE...
...BUT IN MY HEART AND SOUL, I WAS ALWAYS HAPPIER TO BE-- DIFFERENT.
WAS PECIAL, WAS-- NIQUE.
NOW--sigh--I AM JUST ORDINARY.
I NEVER THOUGHT GOD'S SENSE OF HUMOR COULD BE SO CRUEL.
OH, KURT-- YOUR THOUGHTS ARE AS BARE, AS RAW WITH PAIN, AS ROGUE'S. I WISH THERE WAS SOME WAY FOR US ALL TO HELP.

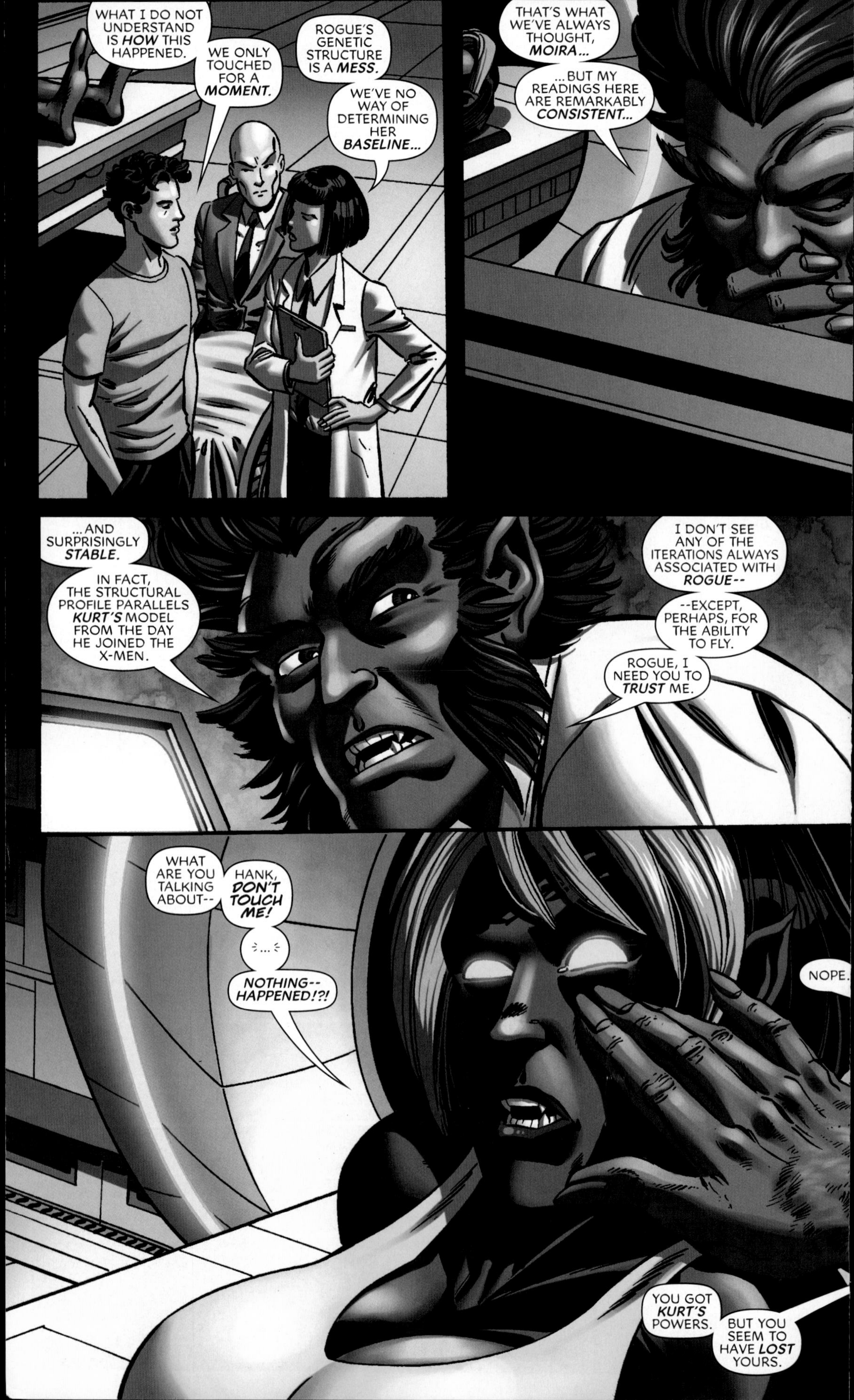
WHAT I DO NOT UNDERSTAND IS HOW THIS HAPPENED.
WE ONLY TOUCHED FOR A MOMENT.
ROGUE'S GENETIC STRUCTURE IS A MESS.
WE'VE NO WAY OF DETERMINING HER BASELINE...
THAT'S WHAT WE'VE ALWAYS THOUGHT, MOIRA...
...BUT MY READINGS HERE ARE REMARKABLY CONSISTENT...
...AND SURPRISINGLY STABLE.
IN FACT, THE STRUCTURAL PROFILE PARALLELS KURT'S MODEL FROM THE DAY HE JOINED THE X-MEN.
I DON'T SEE ANY OF THE ITERATIONS ALWAYS ASSOCIATED WITH ROGUE--
--EXCEPT, PERHAPS, FOR THE ABILITY TO FLY.
ROGUE, I NEED YOU TO TRUST ME.
WHAT ARE YOU TALKING ABOUT--
HANK, DON'T TOUCH ME!
...
NOTHING-- HAPPENED!?!
NOPE.
YOU GOT KURT'S POWERS.
BUT YOU SEEM TO HAVE LOST YOURS.

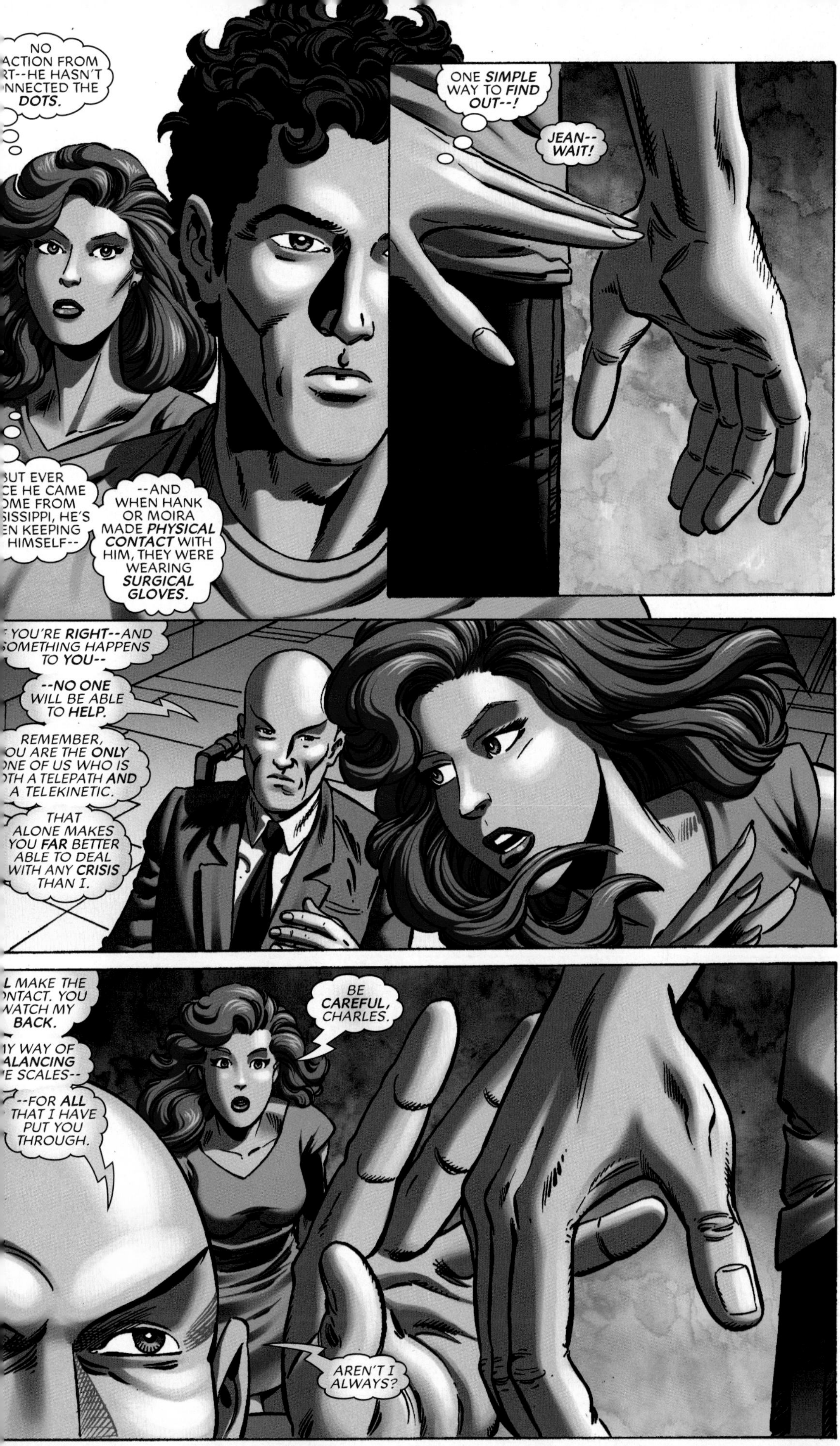

NO ACTION FROM RT--HE HASN'T NNECTED THE DOTS.
ONE SIMPLE WAY TO FIND OUT--!
JEAN-- WAIT!
BUT EVER CE HE CAME OME FROM SISSIPPI, HE'S EN KEEPING HIMSELF--
--AND WHEN HANK OR MOIRA MADE PHYSICAL CONTACT WITH HIM, THEY WERE WEARING SURGICAL GLOVES.
YOU'RE RIGHT--AND SOMETHING HAPPENS TO YOU--
--NO ONE WILL BE ABLE TO HELP.
REMEMBER, OU ARE THE ONLY ONE OF US WHO IS OTH A TELEPATH AND A TELEKINETIC.
THAT ALONE MAKES YOU FAR BETTER ABLE TO DEAL WITH ANY CRISIS THAN I.
L MAKE THE NTACT. YOU WATCH MY BACK.
Y WAY OF ALANCING E SCALES--
--FOR ALL THAT I HAVE PUT YOU THROUGH.
BE CAREFUL, CHARLES.
AREN'T I ALWAYS?

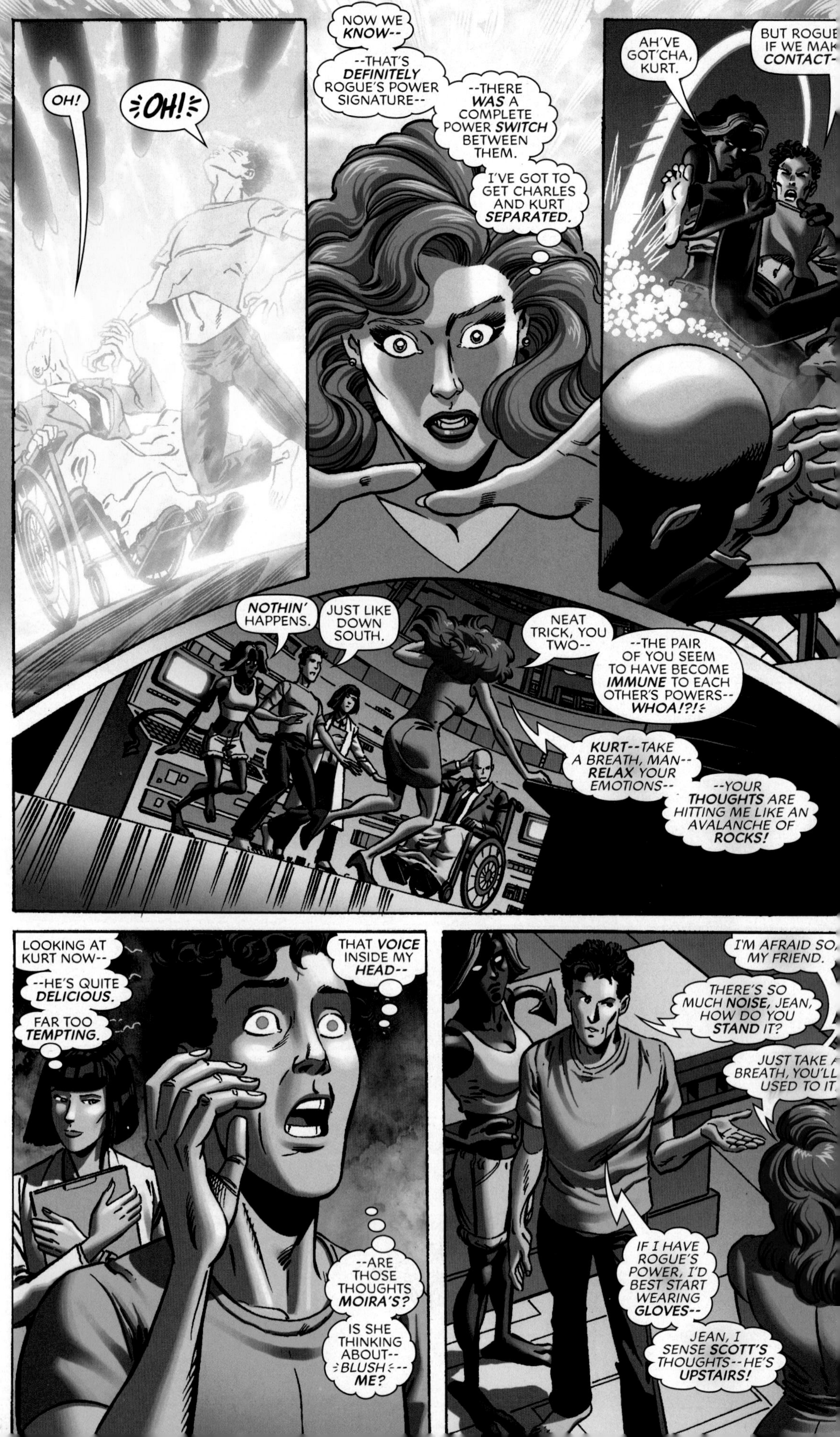

OH!
OH!
NOW WE KNOW--
--THAT'S DEFINITELY ROGUE'S POWER SIGNATURE--
--THERE WAS A COMPLETE POWER SWITCH BETWEEN THEM.
I'VE GOT TO GET CHARLES AND KURT SEPARATED.
AH'VE GOT'CHA, KURT.
BUT ROGUE IF WE MAK CONTACT-
NOTHIN' HAPPENS.
JUST LIKE DOWN SOUTH.
NEAT TRICK, YOU TWO--
--THE PAIR OF YOU SEEM TO HAVE BECOME IMMUNE TO EACH OTHER'S POWERS-- WHOA!?!
KURT--TAKE A BREATH, MAN-- RELAX YOUR EMOTIONS--
--YOUR THOUGHTS ARE HITTING ME LIKE AN AVALANCHE OF ROCKS!
LOOKING AT KURT NOW--
--HE'S QUITE DELICIOUS.
FAR TOO TEMPTING.
THAT VOICE INSIDE MY HEAD--
--ARE THOSE THOUGHTS MOIRA'S?
IS SHE THINKING ABOUT-- BLUSH-- ME?
I'M AFRAID SO, MY FRIEND.
THERE'S SO MUCH NOISE, JEAN, HOW DO YOU STAND IT?
JUST TAKE A BREATH, YOU'LL USED TO IT.
IF I HAVE ROGUE'S POWER, I'D BEST START WEARING GLOVES--
JEAN, I SENSE SCOTT'S THOUGHTS--HE'S UPSTAIRS!

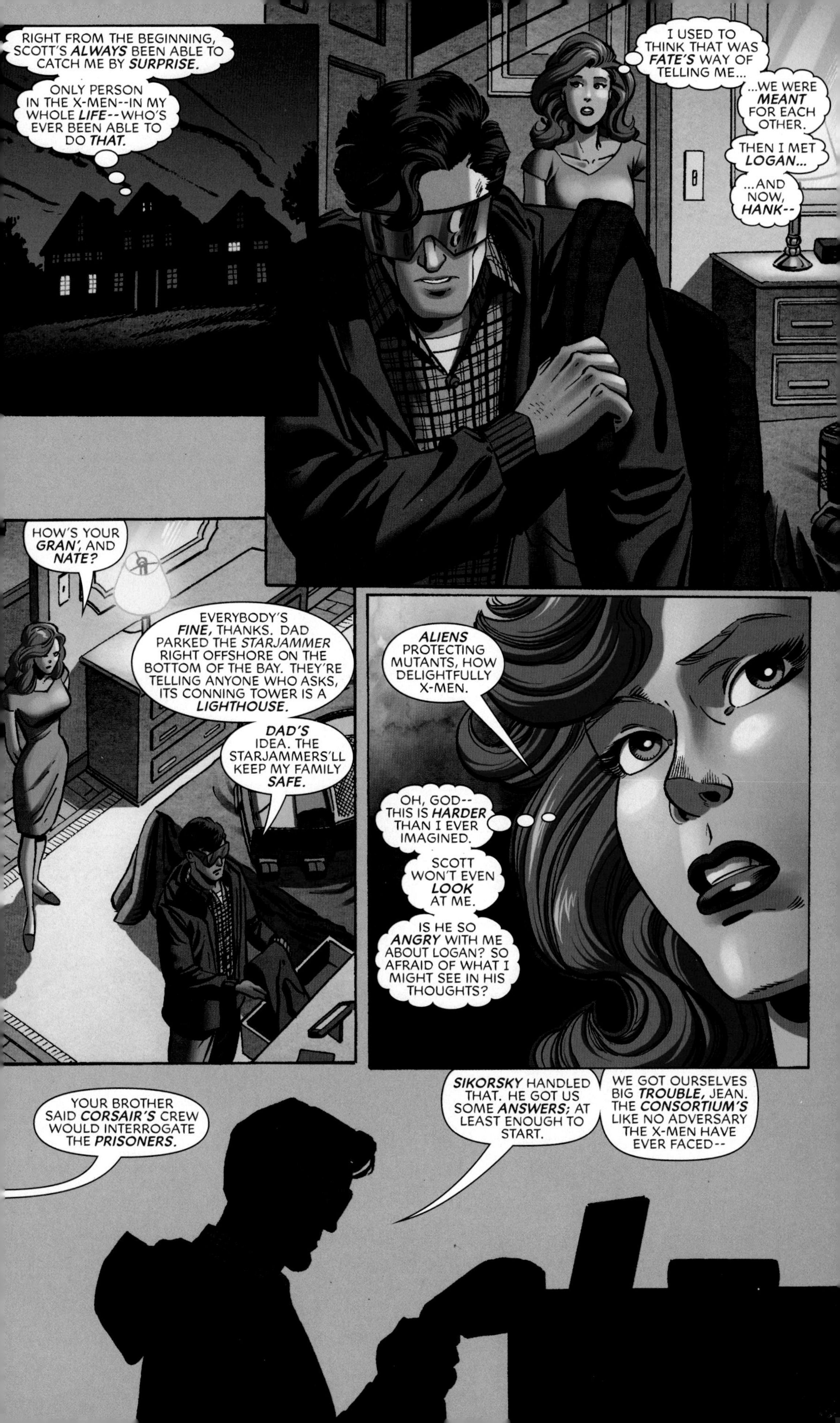

RIGHT FROM THE BEGINNING, SCOTT'S *ALWAYS* BEEN ABLE TO CATCH ME BY *SURPRISE*.
ONLY PERSON IN THE X-MEN--IN MY WHOLE *LIFE*--WHO'S EVER BEEN ABLE TO DO *THAT.*
I USED TO THINK THAT WAS *FATE'S* WAY OF TELLING ME...
...WE WERE *MEANT* FOR EACH OTHER.
THEN I MET *LOGAN...*
...AND NOW, *HANK*--
HOW'S YOUR *GRAN',* AND *NATE?*
EVERYBODY'S *FINE,* THANKS. DAD PARKED THE *STARJAMMER* RIGHT OFFSHORE ON THE BOTTOM OF THE BAY. THEY'RE TELLING ANYONE WHO ASKS, ITS CONNING TOWER IS A *LIGHTHOUSE.*
DAD'S IDEA. THE STARJAMMERS'LL KEEP MY FAMILY *SAFE.*
ALIENS PROTECTING MUTANTS, HOW DELIGHTFULLY X-MEN.
OH, GOD-- THIS IS *HARDER* THAN I EVER IMAGINED.
SCOTT WON'T EVEN *LOOK* AT ME.
IS HE SO *ANGRY* WITH ME ABOUT LOGAN? SO AFRAID OF WHAT I MIGHT SEE IN HIS THOUGHTS?
YOUR BROTHER SAID *CORSAIR'S* CREW WOULD INTERROGATE THE *PRISONERS.*
SIKORSKY HANDLED THAT. HE GOT US SOME *ANSWERS;* AT LEAST ENOUGH TO START.
WE GOT OURSELVES BIG *TROUBLE,* JEAN. THE *CONSORTIUM'S* LIKE NO ADVERSARY THE X-MEN HAVE EVER FACED--

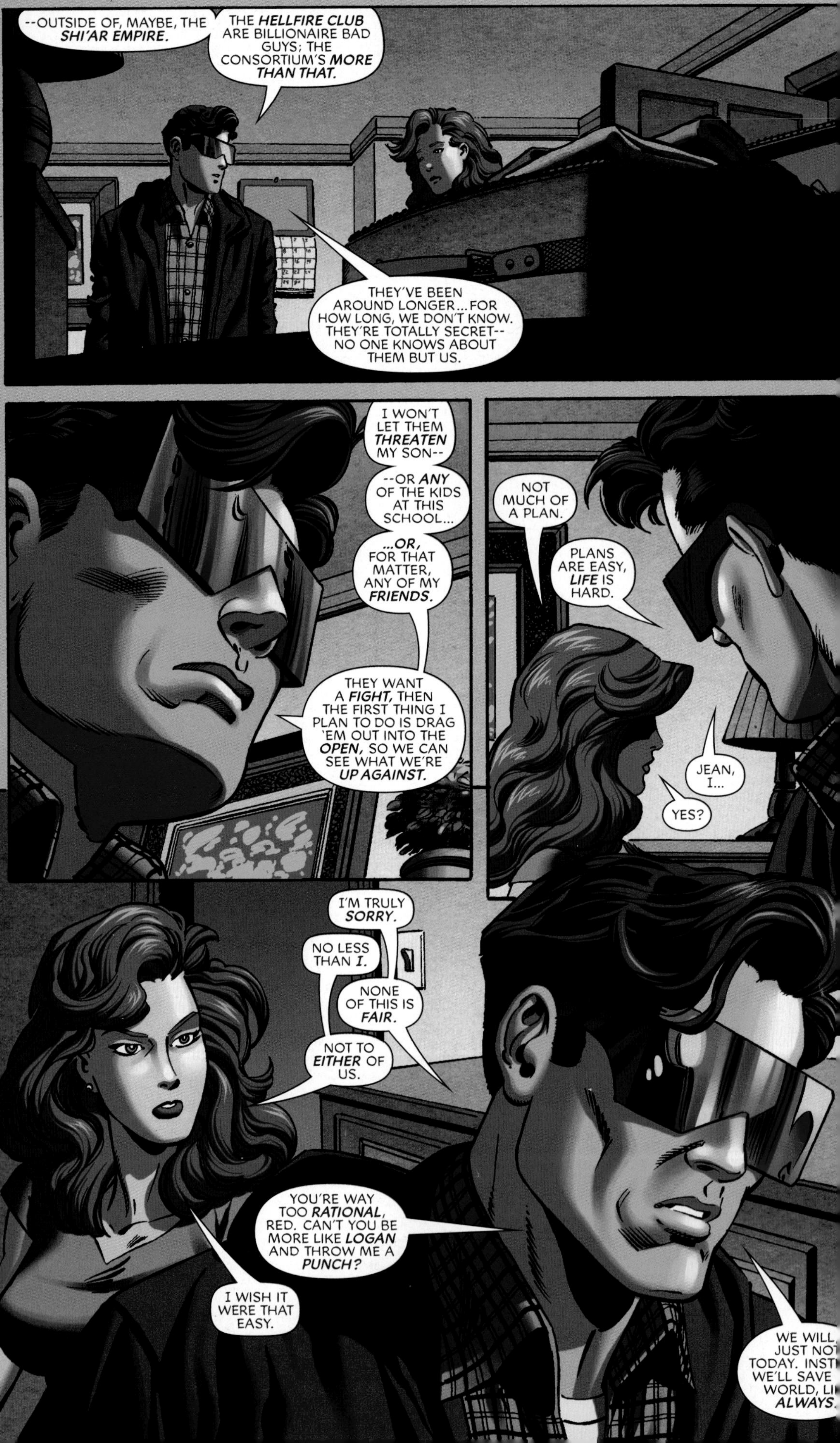

--OUTSIDE OF, MAYBE, THE SHI'AR EMPIRE.
THE HELLFIRE CLUB ARE BILLIONAIRE BAD GUYS; THE CONSORTIUM'S MORE THAN THAT.
THEY'VE BEEN AROUND LONGER... FOR HOW LONG, WE DON'T KNOW. THEY'RE TOTALLY SECRET-- NO ONE KNOWS ABOUT THEM BUT US.
I WON'T LET THEM THREATEN MY SON--
--OR ANY OF THE KIDS AT THIS SCHOOL...
...OR, FOR THAT MATTER, ANY OF MY FRIENDS.
THEY WANT A FIGHT, THEN THE FIRST THING I PLAN TO DO IS DRAG 'EM OUT INTO THE OPEN, SO WE CAN SEE WHAT WE'RE UP AGAINST.
NOT MUCH OF A PLAN.
PLANS ARE EASY, LIFE IS HARD.
JEAN, I...
YES?
I'M TRULY SORRY.
NO LESS THAN I.
NONE OF THIS IS FAIR.
NOT TO EITHER OF US.
YOU'RE WAY TOO RATIONAL, RED. CAN'T YOU BE MORE LIKE LOGAN AND THROW ME A PUNCH?
I WISH IT WERE THAT EASY.
WE WILL
JUST NO
TODAY. INST
WE'LL SAVE
WORLD, LI
ALWAYS.

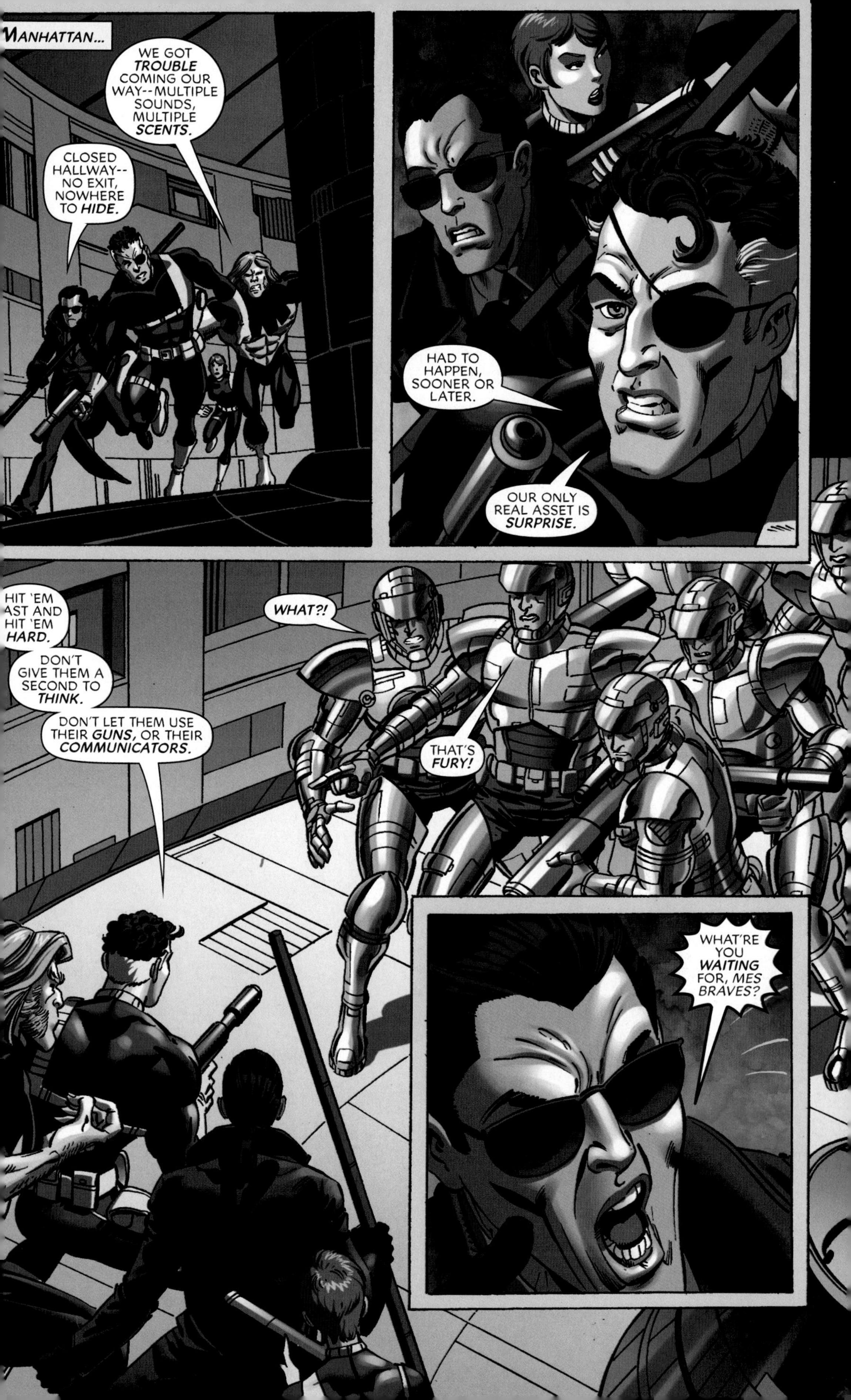
MANHATTAN...
WE GOT TROUBLE COMING OUR WAY--MULTIPLE SOUNDS, MULTIPLE SCENTS.
CLOSED HALLWAY--NO EXIT, NOWHERE TO HIDE.
HAD TO HAPPEN, SOONER OR LATER.
OUR ONLY REAL ASSET IS SURPRISE.
HIT 'EM AST AND HIT 'EM HARD.
DON'T GIVE THEM A SECOND TO THINK.
DON'T LET THEM USE THEIR GUNS, OR THEIR COMMUNICATORS.
WHAT?!
THAT'S FURY!
WHAT'RE YOU WAITING FOR, MES BRAVES?

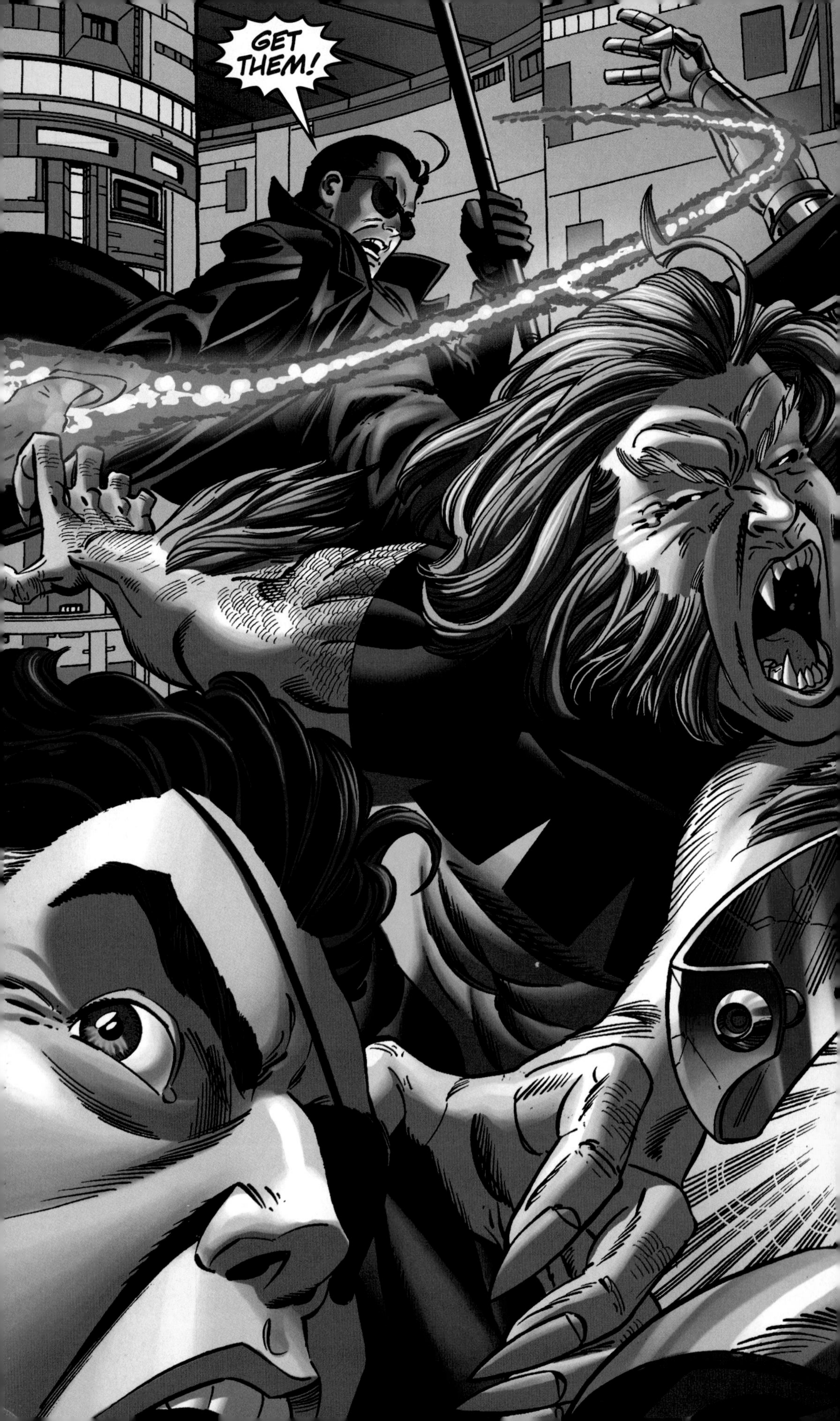
GET THEM!

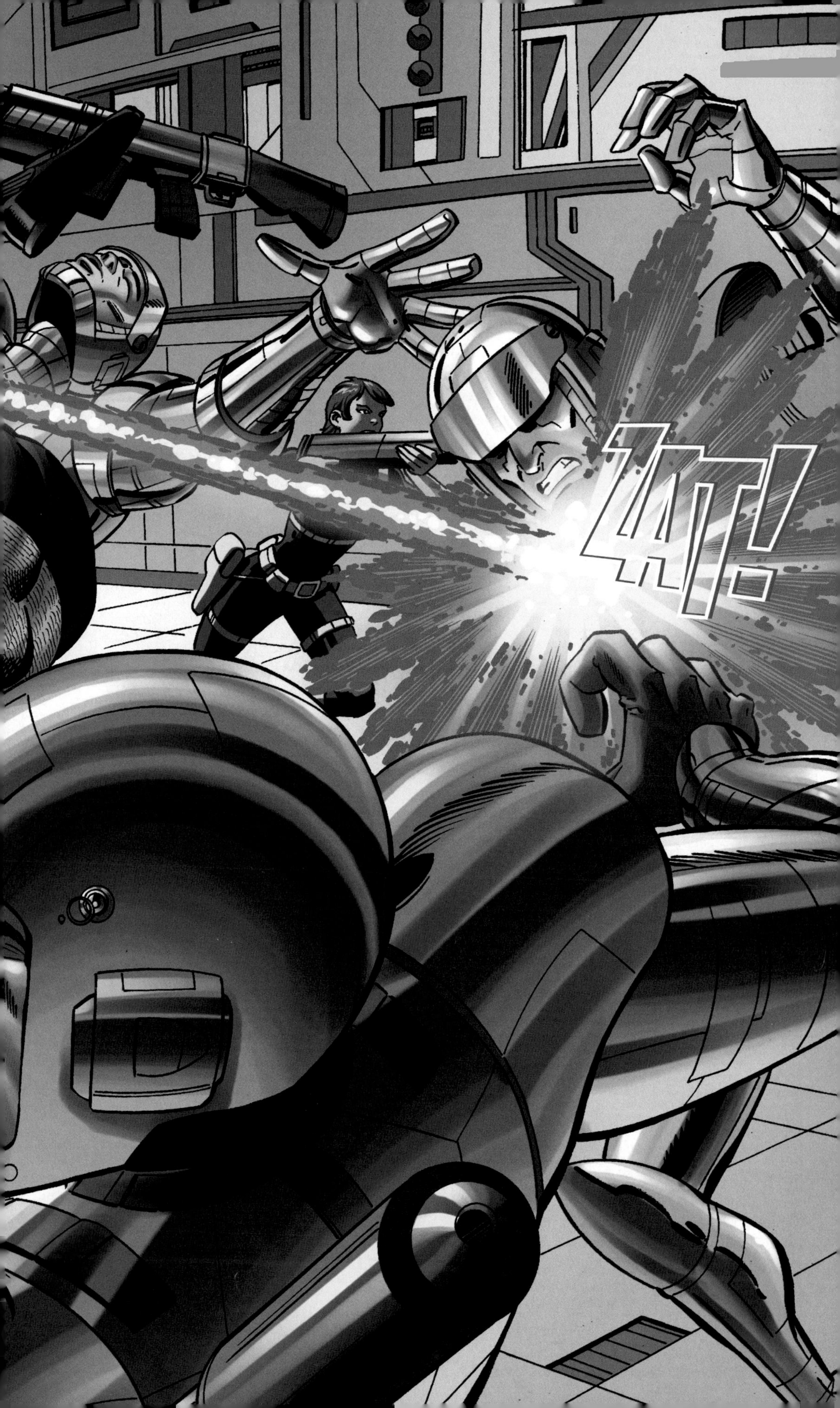
ZAT!

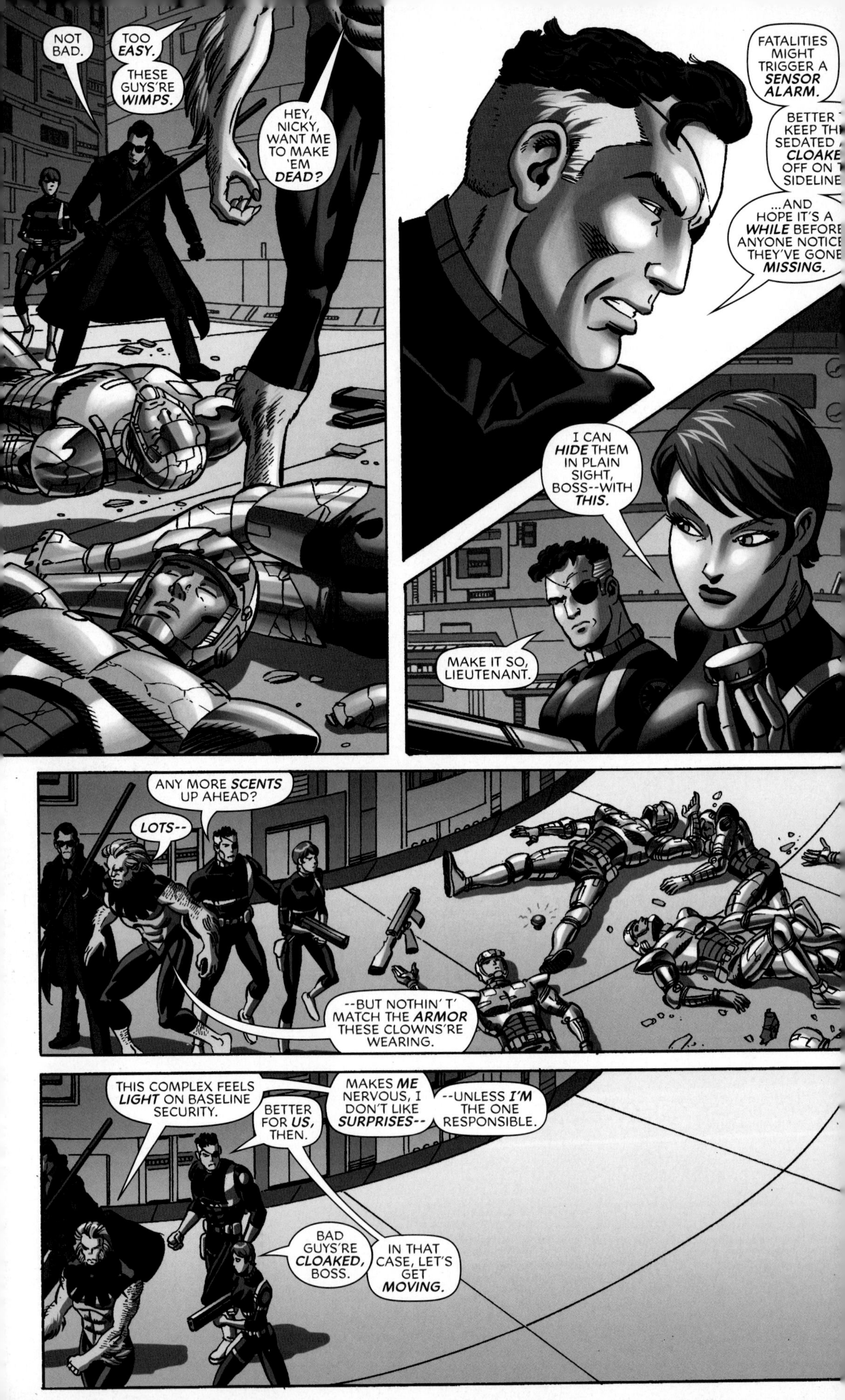

NOT BAD.
TOO EASY.
THESE GUYS'RE WIMPS.
HEY, NICKY, WANT ME TO MAKE 'EM DEAD?
FATALITIES MIGHT TRIGGER A SENSOR ALARM.
BETTER KEEP TH SEDATED CLOAKE OFF ON SIDELINE
...AND HOPE IT'S A WHILE BEFORE ANYONE NOTICE THEY'VE GONE MISSING.
I CAN HIDE THEM IN PLAIN SIGHT, BOSS--WITH THIS.
MAKE IT SO, LIEUTENANT.
ANY MORE SCENTS UP AHEAD?
LOTS--
--BUT NOTHIN' T' MATCH THE ARMOR THESE CLOWNS'RE WEARING.
THIS COMPLEX FEELS LIGHT ON BASELINE SECURITY.
BETTER FOR US, THEN.
MAKES ME NERVOUS, I DON'T LIKE SURPRISES--
--UNLESS I'M THE ONE RESPONSIBLE.
BAD GUYS'RE CLOAKED, BOSS.
IN THAT CASE, LET'S GET MOVING.

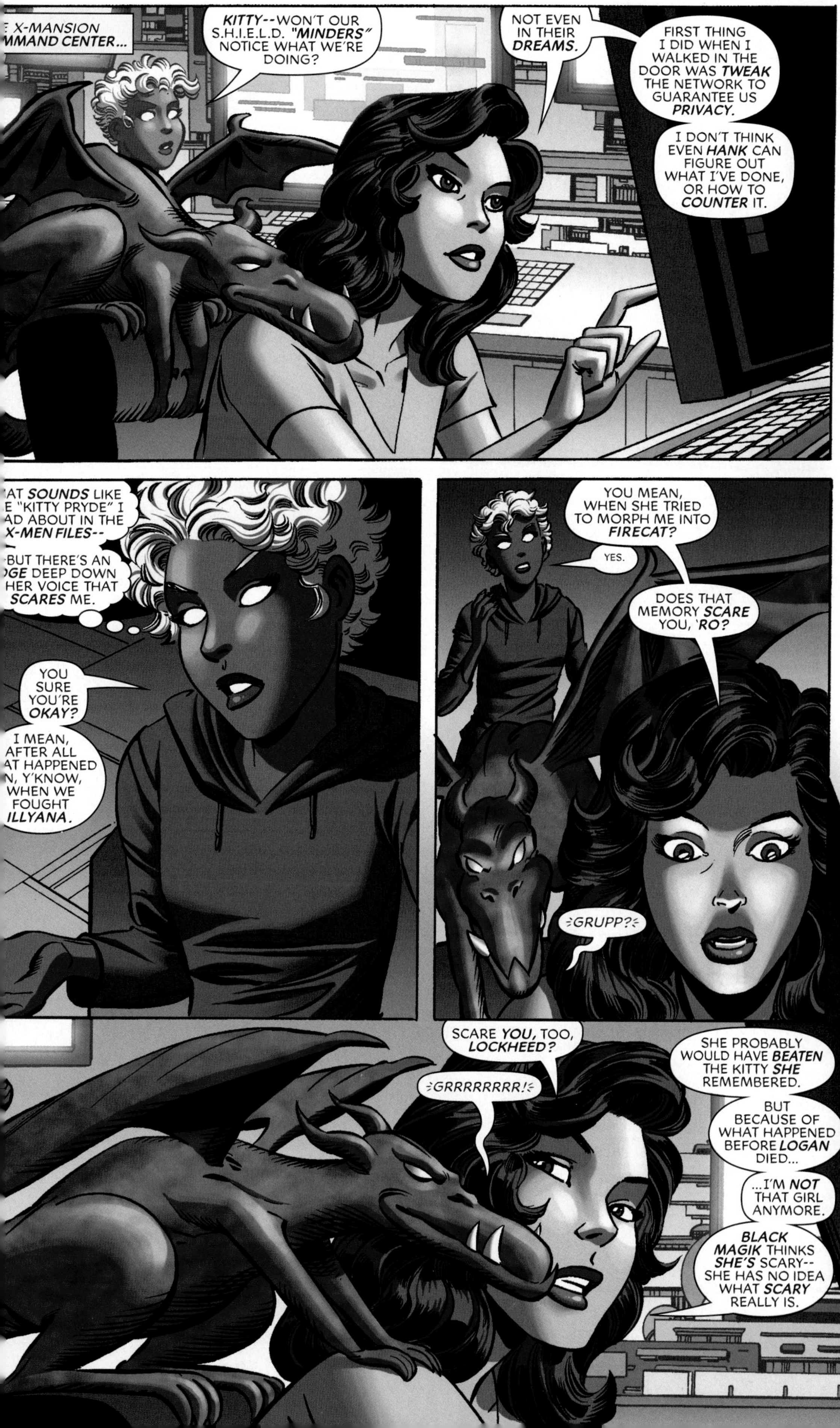

E X-MANSION
MMAND CENTER...
KITTY--WON'T OUR S.H.I.E.L.D. "MINDERS" NOTICE WHAT WE'RE DOING?
NOT EVEN IN THEIR DREAMS.
FIRST THING I DID WHEN I WALKED IN THE DOOR WAS TWEAK THE NETWORK TO GUARANTEE US PRIVACY.
I DON'T THINK EVEN HANK CAN FIGURE OUT WHAT I'VE DONE, OR HOW TO COUNTER IT.
AT SOUNDS LIKE E "KITTY PRYDE" I AD ABOUT IN THE X-MEN FILES--
BUT THERE'S AN GE DEEP DOWN HER VOICE THAT SCARES ME.
YOU SURE YOU'RE OKAY?
I MEAN, AFTER ALL AT HAPPENED N, Y'KNOW, WHEN WE FOUGHT ILLYANA.
YOU MEAN, WHEN SHE TRIED TO MORPH ME INTO FIRECAT?
YES.
DOES THAT MEMORY SCARE YOU, 'RO?
GRUPP?
SCARE YOU, TOO, LOCKHEED?
GRRRRRRRR!
SHE PROBABLY WOULD HAVE BEATEN THE KITTY SHE REMEMBERED.
BUT BECAUSE OF WHAT HAPPENED BEFORE LOGAN DIED...
...I'M NOT THAT GIRL ANYMORE.
BLACK MAGIK THINKS SHE'S SCARY-- SHE HAS NO IDEA WHAT SCARY REALLY IS.

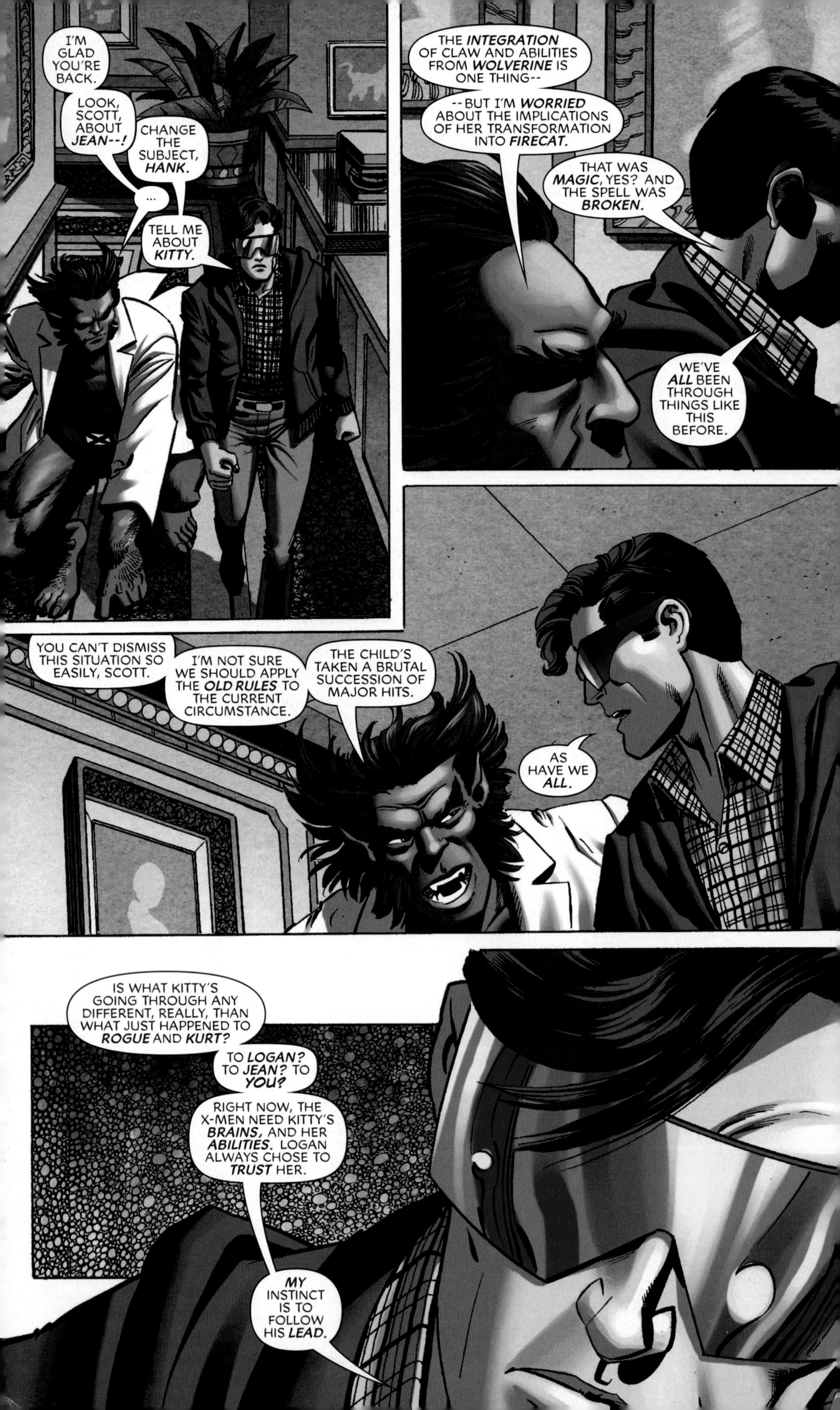
I'M GLAD YOU'RE BACK.
LOOK, SCOTT, ABOUT JEAN--!
CHANGE THE SUBJECT, HANK.
...
TELL ME ABOUT KITTY.
THE INTEGRATION OF CLAW AND ABILITIES FROM WOLVERINE IS ONE THING--
--BUT I'M WORRIED ABOUT THE IMPLICATIONS OF HER TRANSFORMATION INTO FIRECAT.
THAT WAS MAGIC, YES? AND THE SPELL WAS BROKEN.
WE'VE ALL BEEN THROUGH THINGS LIKE THIS BEFORE.
YOU CAN'T DISMISS THIS SITUATION SO EASILY, SCOTT.
I'M NOT SURE WE SHOULD APPLY THE OLD RULES TO THE CURRENT CIRCUMSTANCE.
THE CHILD'S TAKEN A BRUTAL SUCCESSION OF MAJOR HITS.
AS HAVE WE ALL.
IS WHAT KITTY'S GOING THROUGH ANY DIFFERENT, REALLY, THAN WHAT JUST HAPPENED TO ROGUE AND KURT?
TO LOGAN? TO JEAN? TO YOU?
RIGHT NOW, THE X-MEN NEED KITTY'S BRAINS, AND HER ABILITIES. LOGAN ALWAYS CHOSE TO TRUST HER.
MY INSTINCT IS TO FOLLOW HIS LEAD.

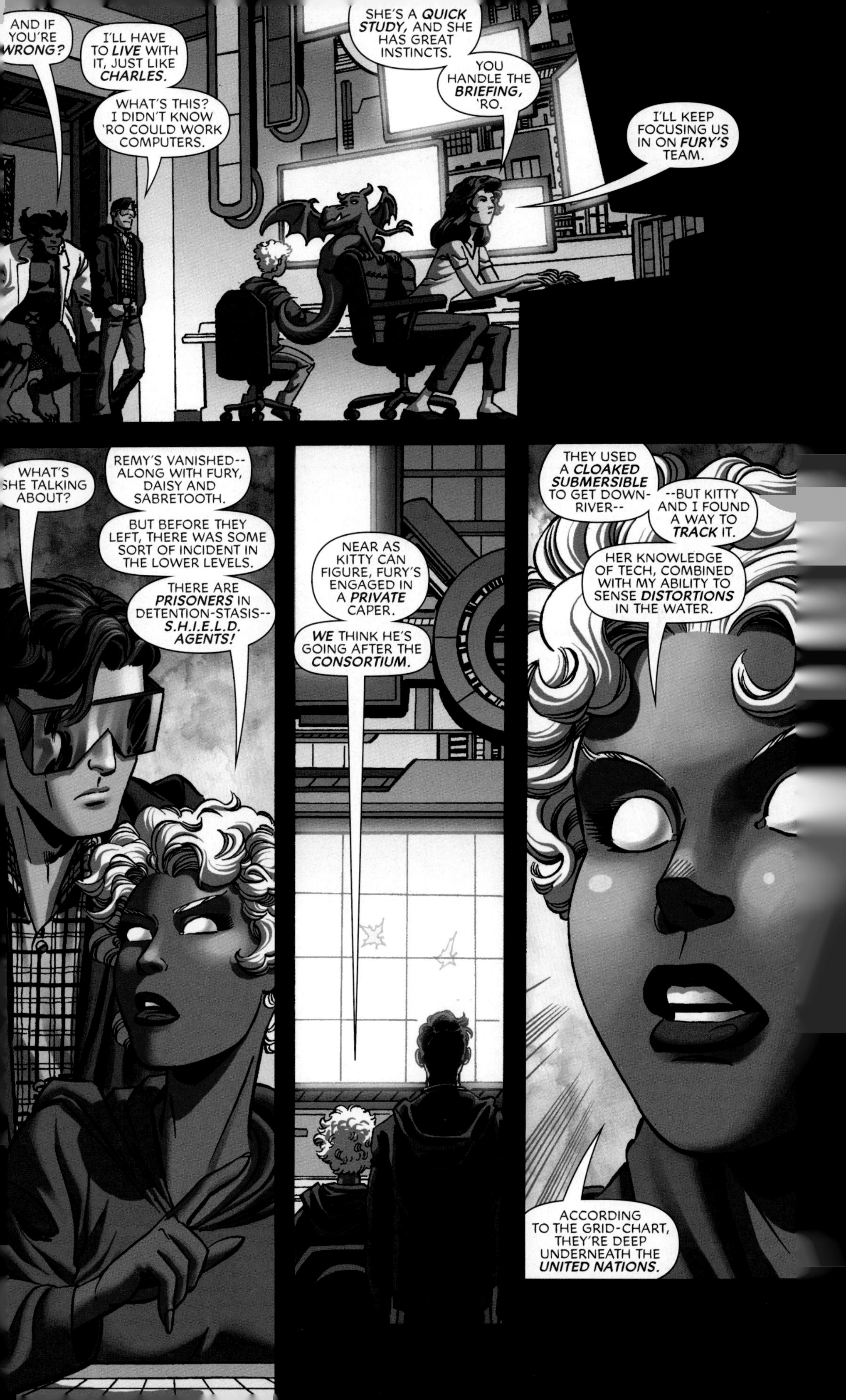
AND IF YOU'RE WRONG?
I'LL HAVE TO LIVE WITH IT, JUST LIKE CHARLES.
WHAT'S THIS? I DIDN'T KNOW 'RO COULD WORK COMPUTERS.
SHE'S A QUICK STUDY, AND SHE HAS GREAT INSTINCTS.
YOU HANDLE THE BRIEFING, 'RO.
I'LL KEEP FOCUSING US IN ON FURY'S TEAM.
WHAT'S SHE TALKING ABOUT?
REMY'S VANISHED-- ALONG WITH FURY, DAISY AND SABRETOOTH.
BUT BEFORE THEY LEFT, THERE WAS SOME SORT OF INCIDENT IN THE LOWER LEVELS.
THERE ARE PRISONERS IN DETENTION-STASIS-- S.H.I.E.L.D. AGENTS!
NEAR AS KITTY CAN FIGURE, FURY'S ENGAGED IN A PRIVATE CAPER.
WE THINK HE'S GOING AFTER THE CONSORTIUM.
THEY USED A CLOAKED SUBMERSIBLE TO GET DOWN-RIVER--
--BUT KITTY AND I FOUND A WAY TO TRACK IT.
HER KNOWLEDGE OF TECH, COMBINED WITH MY ABILITY TO SENSE DISTORTIONS IN THE WATER.
ACCORDING TO THE GRID-CHART, THEY'RE DEEP UNDERNEATH THE UNITED NATIONS.

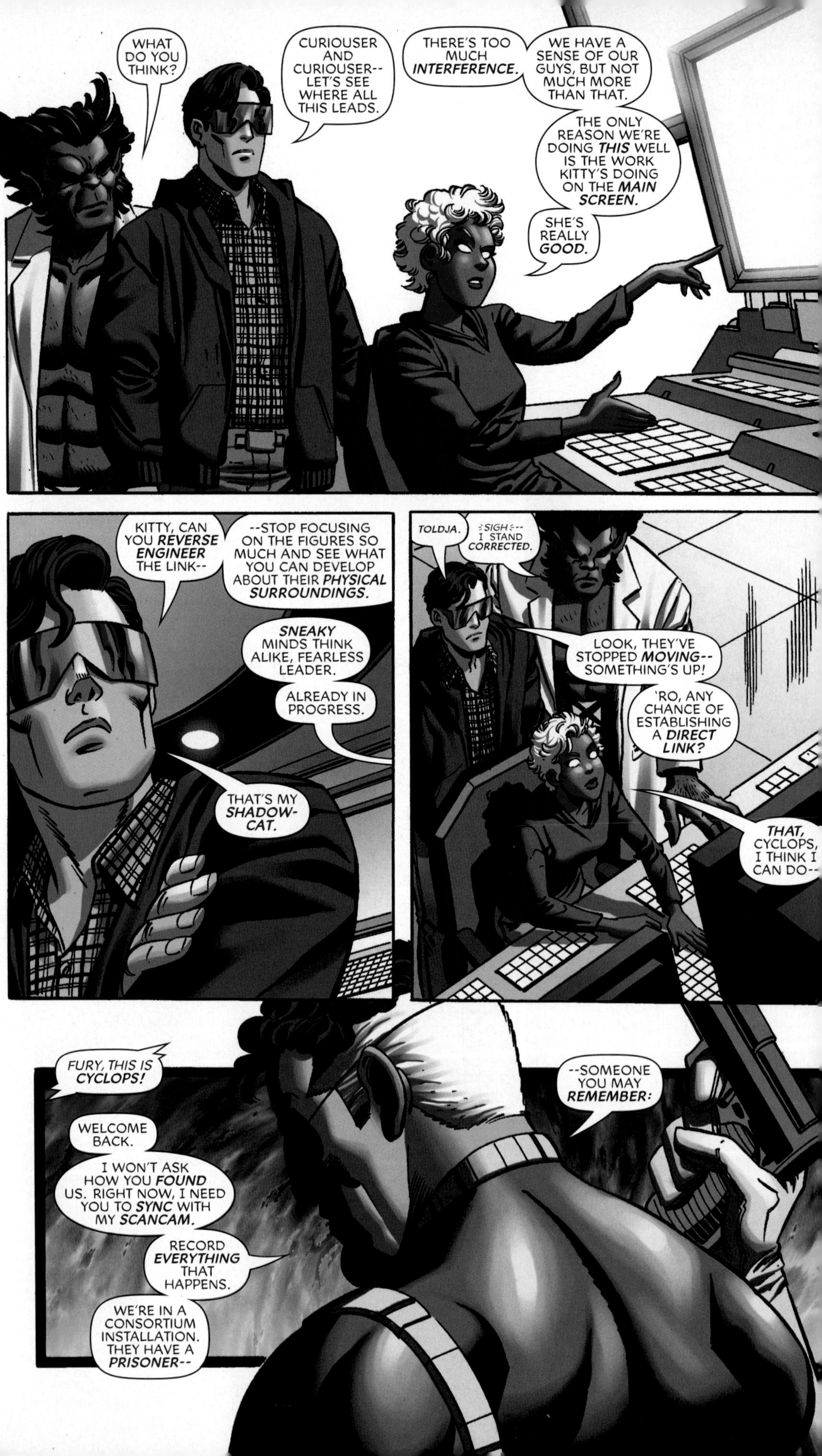
WHAT DO YOU THINK?
CURIOUSER AND CURIOUSER-- LET'S SEE WHERE ALL THIS LEADS.
THERE'S TOO MUCH INTERFERENCE.
WE HAVE A SENSE OF OUR GUYS, BUT NOT MUCH MORE THAN THAT.
THE ONLY REASON WE'RE DOING THIS WELL IS THE WORK KITTY'S DOING ON THE MAIN SCREEN.
SHE'S REALLY GOOD.
KITTY, CAN YOU REVERSE ENGINEER THE LINK--
--STOP FOCUSING ON THE FIGURES SO MUCH AND SEE WHAT YOU CAN DEVELOP ABOUT THEIR PHYSICAL SURROUNDINGS.
SNEAKY MINDS THINK ALIKE, FEARLESS LEADER.
ALREADY IN PROGRESS.
THAT'S MY SHADOW-CAT.
TOLDJA.
SIGH -- I STAND CORRECTED.
LOOK, THEY'VE STOPPED MOVING-- SOMETHING'S UP!
'RO, ANY CHANCE OF ESTABLISHING A DIRECT LINK?
THAT, CYCLOPS, I THINK I CAN DO--
FURY, THIS IS CYCLOPS!
--SOMEONE YOU MAY REMEMBER:
WELCOME BACK.
I WON'T ASK HOW YOU FOUND US. RIGHT NOW, I NEED YOU TO SYNC WITH MY SCANCAM.
RECORD EVERYTHING THAT HAPPENS.
WE'RE IN A CONSORTIUM INSTALLATION. THEY HAVE A PRISONER--

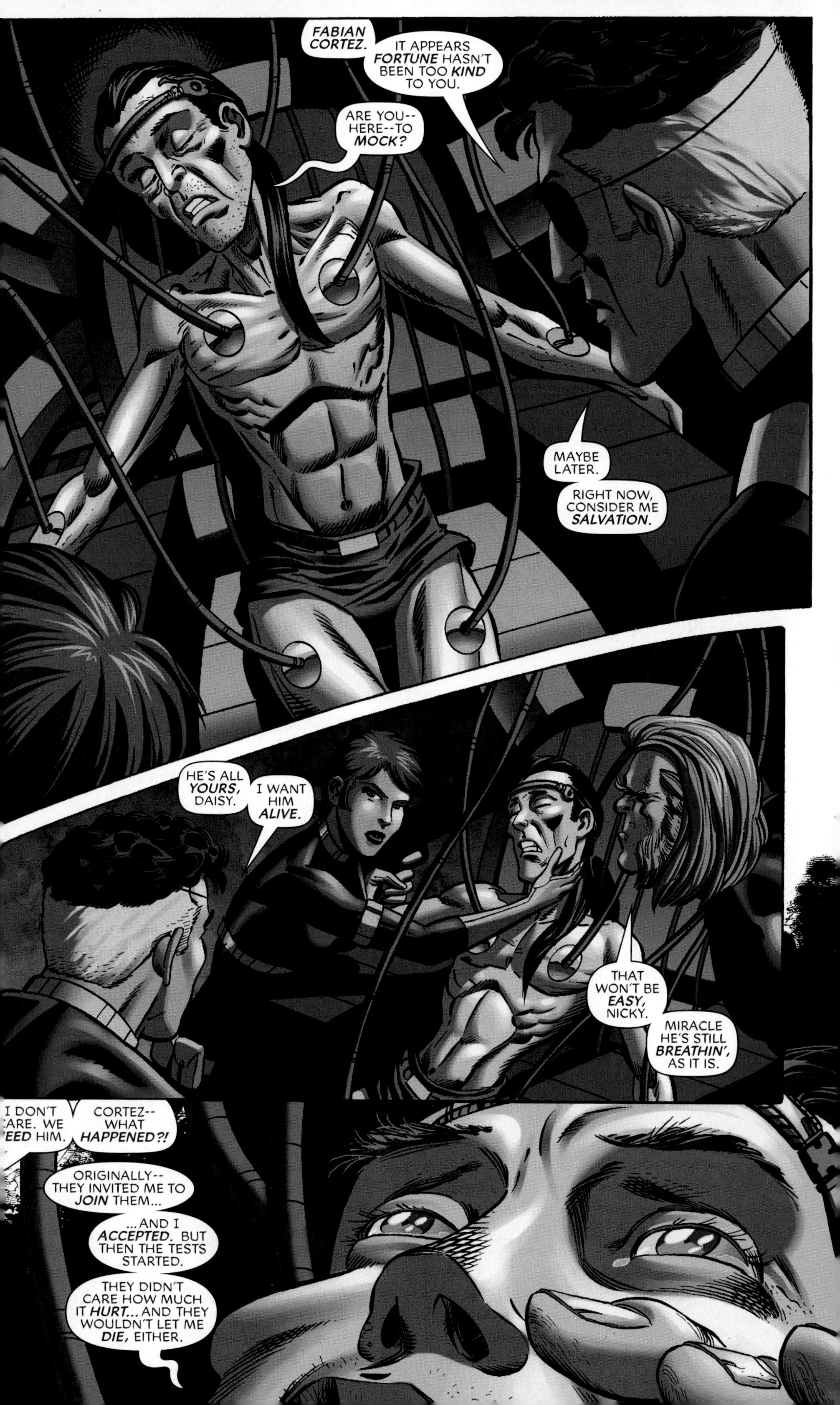
FABIAN CORTEZ.
IT APPEARS FORTUNE HASN'T BEEN TOO KIND TO YOU.
ARE YOU--HERE--TO MOCK?
MAYBE LATER.
RIGHT NOW, CONSIDER ME SALVATION.
HE'S ALL YOURS, DAISY.
I WANT HIM ALIVE.
THAT WON'T BE EASY, NICKY.
MIRACLE HE'S STILL BREATHIN', AS IT IS.
I DON'T CARE. WE NEED HIM.
CORTEZ--WHAT HAPPENED?!
ORIGINALLY--THEY INVITED ME TO JOIN THEM...
...AND I ACCEPTED. BUT THEN THE TESTS STARTED.
THEY DIDN'T CARE HOW MUCH IT HURT... AND THEY WOULDN'T LET ME DIE, EITHER.

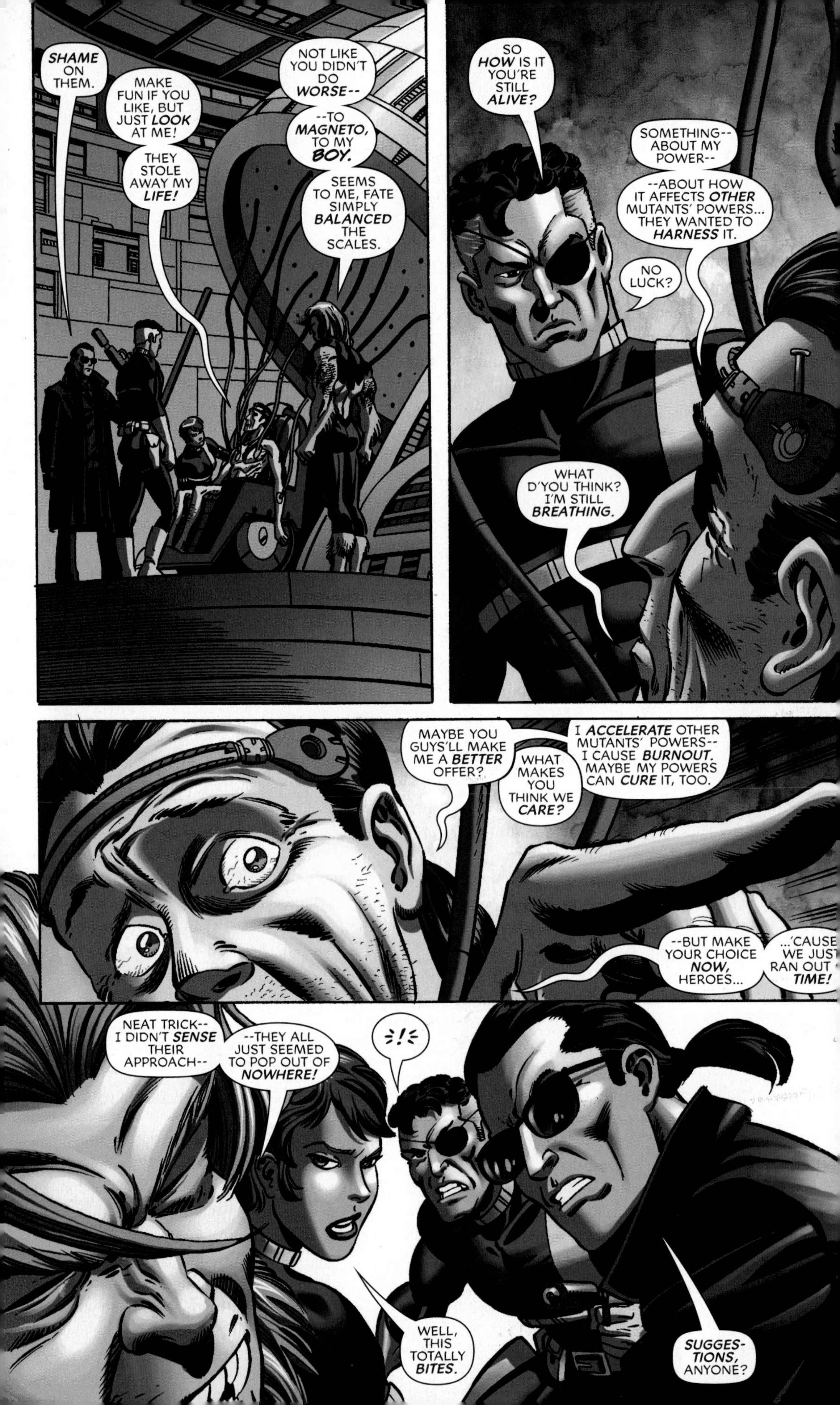
SHAME ON THEM.
MAKE FUN IF YOU LIKE, BUT JUST LOOK AT ME!
THEY STOLE AWAY MY LIFE!
NOT LIKE YOU DIDN'T DO WORSE--
--TO MAGNETO, TO MY BOY.
SEEMS TO ME, FATE SIMPLY BALANCED THE SCALES.
SO HOW IS IT YOU'RE STILL ALIVE?
SOMETHING-- ABOUT MY POWER--
--ABOUT HOW IT AFFECTS OTHER MUTANTS' POWERS... THEY WANTED TO HARNESS IT.
NO LUCK?
WHAT D'YOU THINK? I'M STILL BREATHING.
MAYBE YOU GUYS'LL MAKE ME A BETTER OFFER?
WHAT MAKES YOU THINK WE CARE?
I ACCELERATE OTHER MUTANTS' POWERS-- I CAUSE BURNOUT. MAYBE MY POWERS CAN CURE IT, TOO.
--BUT MAKE YOUR CHOICE NOW, HEROES...
...'CAUSE WE JUST RAN OUT TIME!
NEAT TRICK-- I DIDN'T SENSE THEIR APPROACH--
--THEY ALL JUST SEEMED TO POP OUT OF NOWHERE!
!
WELL, THIS TOTALLY BITES.
SUGGES-TIONS, ANYONE?

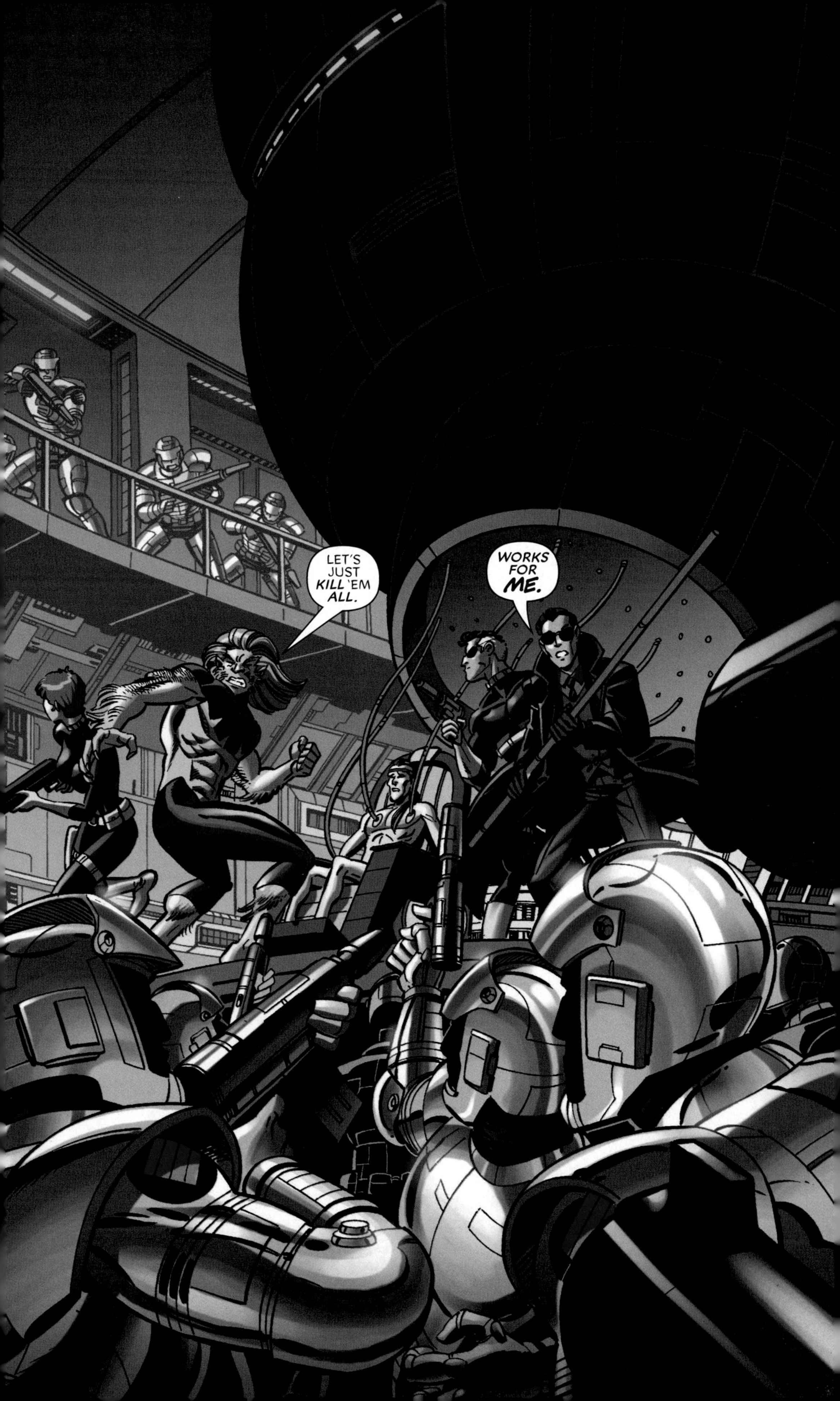
LET'S JUST KILL 'EM ALL.
WORKS FOR ME.

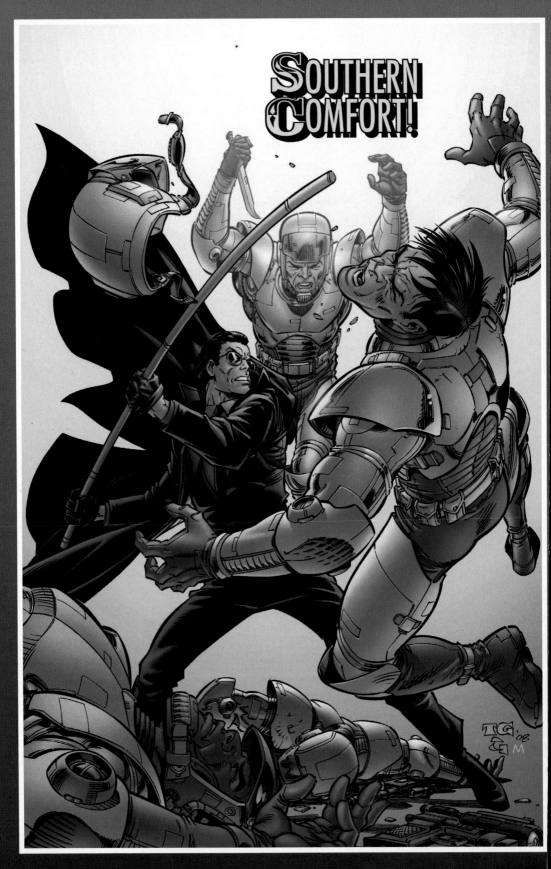

SOUTHERN COMFORT!

TWENTY

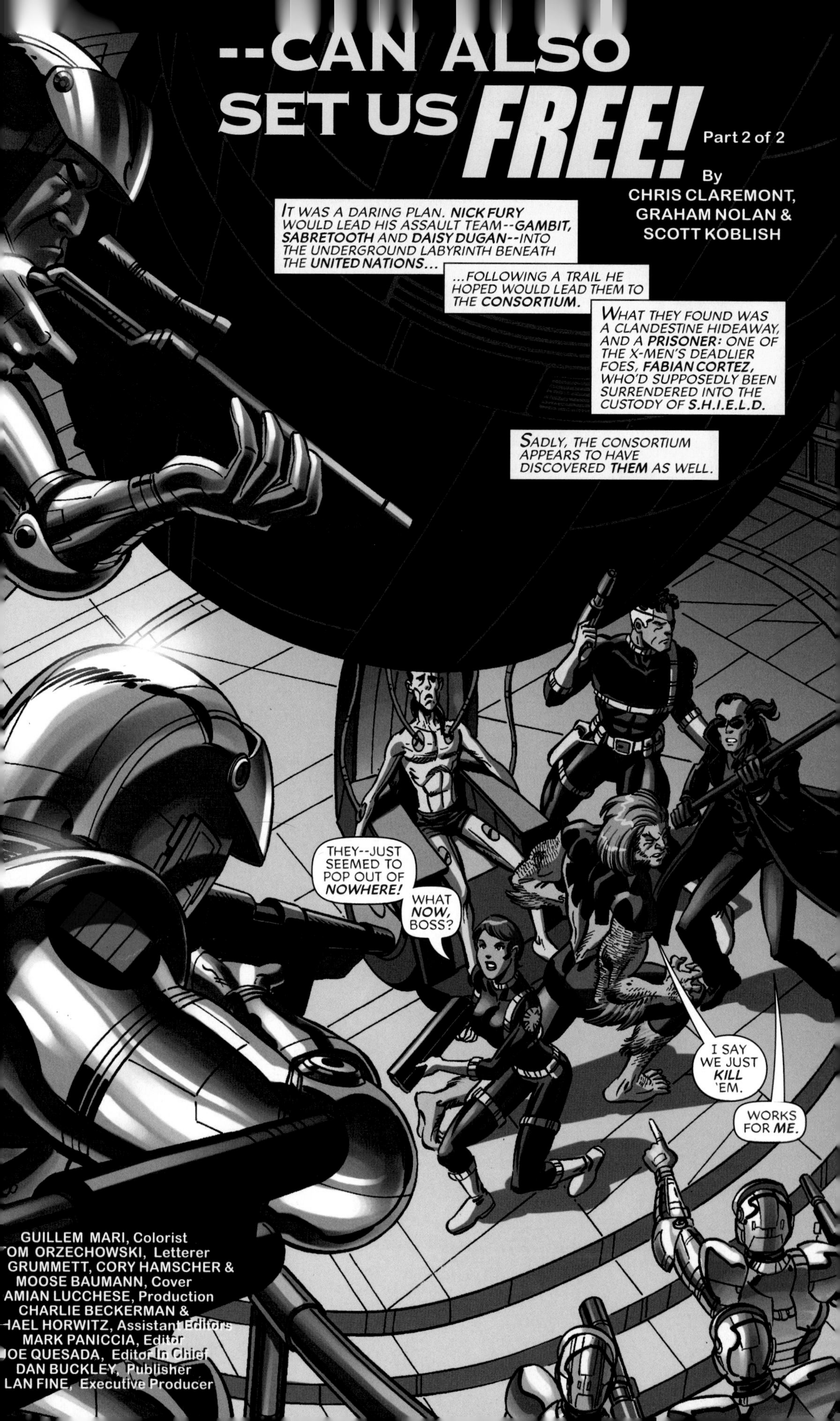
--CAN ALSO SET US FREE!
Part 2 of 2
By CHRIS CLAREMONT, GRAHAM NOLAN & SCOTT KOBLISH
IT WAS A DARING PLAN. NICK FURY WOULD LEAD HIS ASSAULT TEAM--GAMBIT, SABRETOOTH AND DAISY DUGAN--INTO THE UNDERGROUND LABYRINTH BENEATH THE UNITED NATIONS...
...FOLLOWING A TRAIL HE HOPED WOULD LEAD THEM TO THE CONSORTIUM.
WHAT THEY FOUND WAS A CLANDESTINE HIDEAWAY, AND A PRISONER: ONE OF THE X-MEN'S DEADLIER FOES, FABIAN CORTEZ, WHO'D SUPPOSEDLY BEEN SURRENDERED INTO THE CUSTODY OF S.H.I.E.L.D.
SADLY, THE CONSORTIUM APPEARS TO HAVE DISCOVERED THEM AS WELL.
THEY--JUST SEEMED TO POP OUT OF NOWHERE!
WHAT NOW, BOSS?
I SAY WE JUST KILL 'EM.
WORKS FOR ME.
GUILLEM MARI, Colorist
OM ORZECHOWSKI, Letterer
GRUMMETT, CORY HAMSCHER & MOOSE BAUMANN, Cover
AMIAN LUCCHESE, Production
CHARLIE BECKERMAN &
HAEL HORWITZ, Assistant Editors
MARK PANICCIA, Editor
OE QUESADA, Editor In Chief
DAN BUCKLEY, Publisher
LAN FINE, Executive Producer

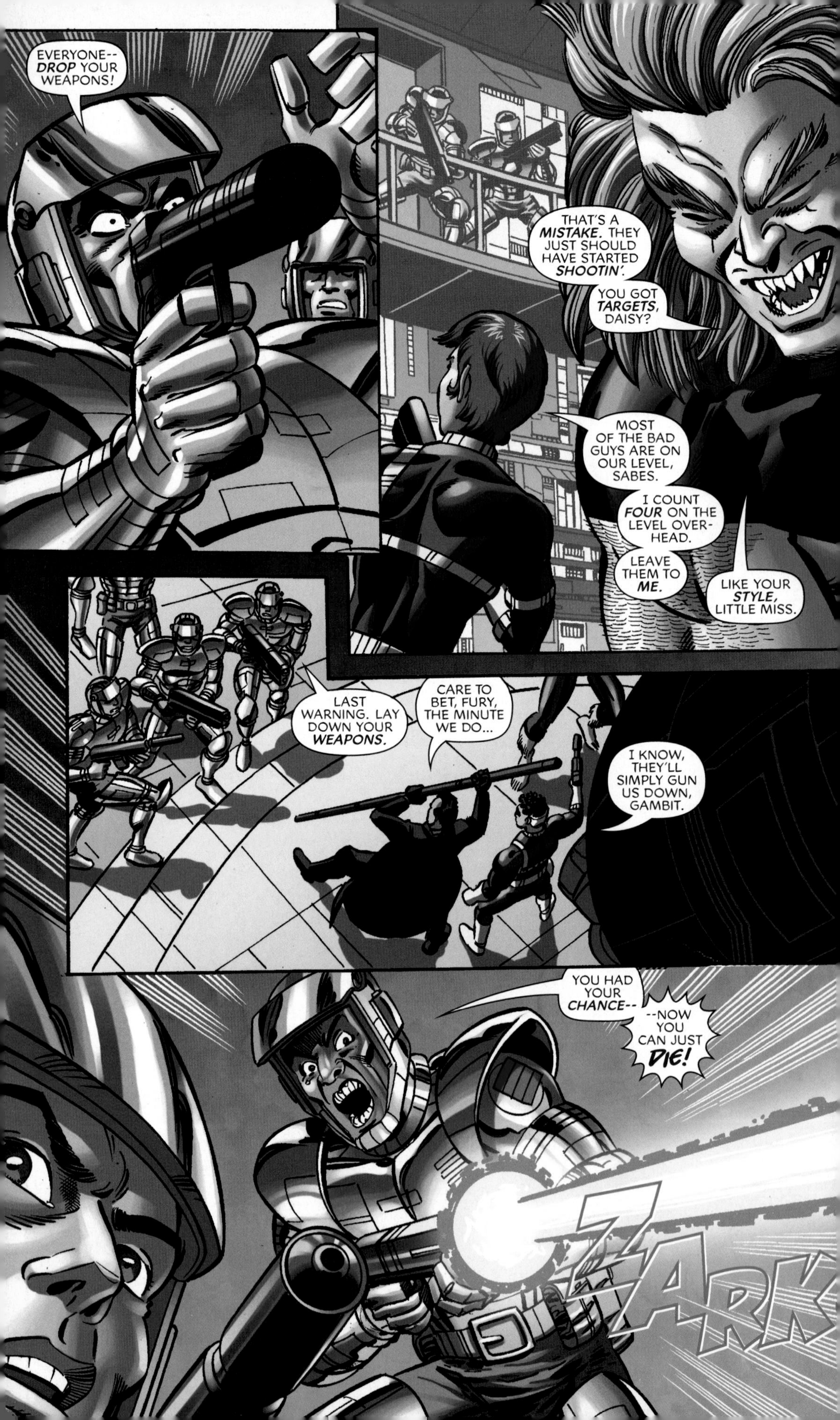
EVERYONE-- DROP YOUR WEAPONS!
THAT'S A MISTAKE. THEY JUST SHOULD HAVE STARTED SHOOTIN'.
YOU GOT TARGETS, DAISY?
MOST OF THE BAD GUYS ARE ON OUR LEVEL, SABES.
I COUNT FOUR ON THE LEVEL OVER-HEAD.
LEAVE THEM TO ME.
LIKE YOUR STYLE, LITTLE MISS.
LAST WARNING. LAY DOWN YOUR WEAPONS.
CARE TO BET, FURY, THE MINUTE WE DO...
I KNOW, THEY'LL SIMPLY GUN US DOWN, GAMBIT.
YOU HAD YOUR CHANCE--
--NOW YOU CAN JUST DIE!
ZARK

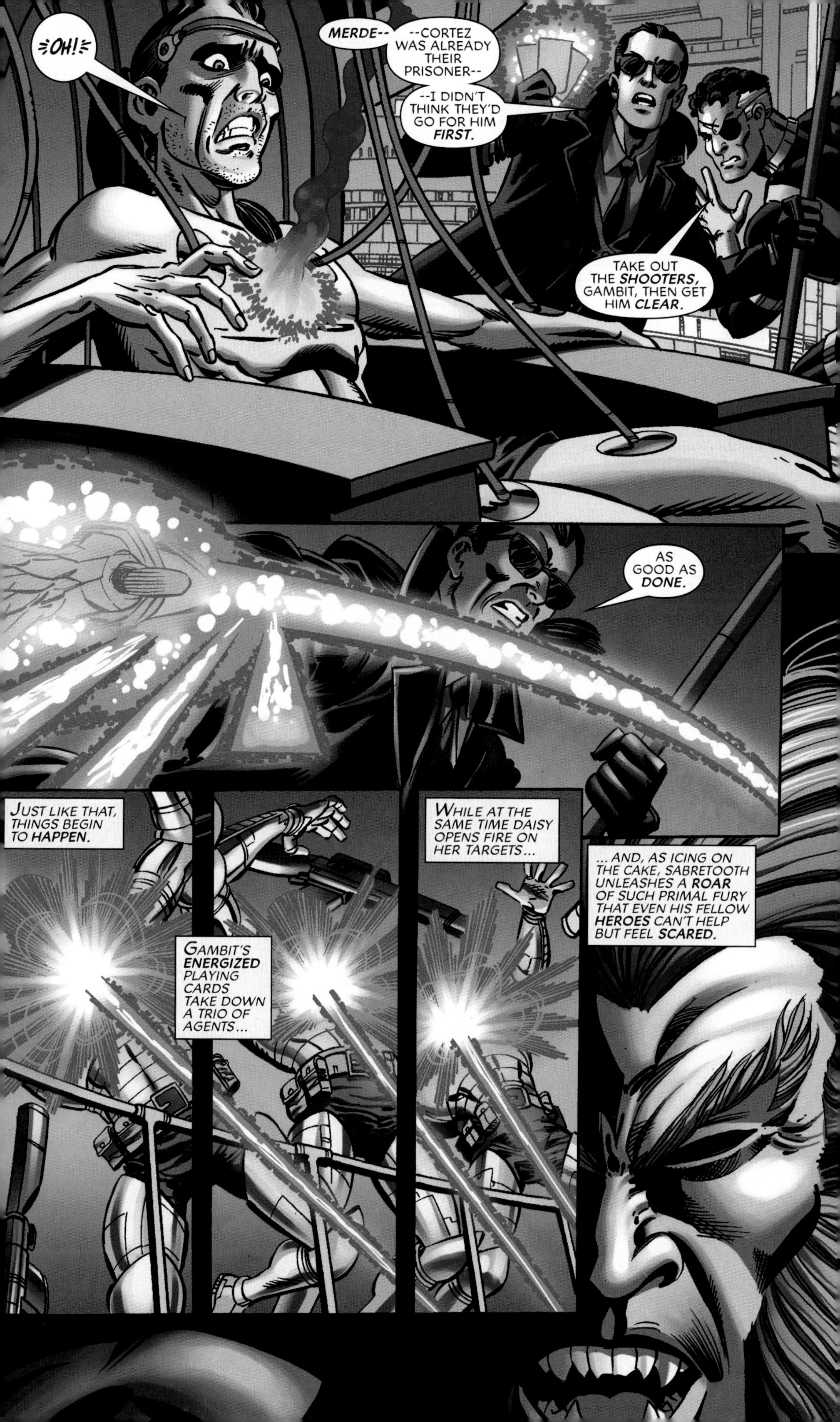

OH!
MERDE--
--CORTEZ WAS ALREADY THEIR PRISONER--
--I DIDN'T THINK THEY'D GO FOR HIM FIRST.
TAKE OUT THE SHOOTERS, GAMBIT, THEN GET HIM CLEAR.
AS GOOD AS DONE.
JUST LIKE THAT, THINGS BEGIN TO HAPPEN.
GAMBIT'S ENERGIZED PLAYING CARDS TAKE DOWN A TRIO OF AGENTS...
WHILE AT THE SAME TIME DAISY OPENS FIRE ON HER TARGETS...
...AND, AS ICING ON THE CAKE, SABRETOOTH UNLEASHES A ROAR OF SUCH PRIMAL FURY THAT EVEN HIS FELLOW HEROES CAN'T HELP BUT FEEL SCARED.

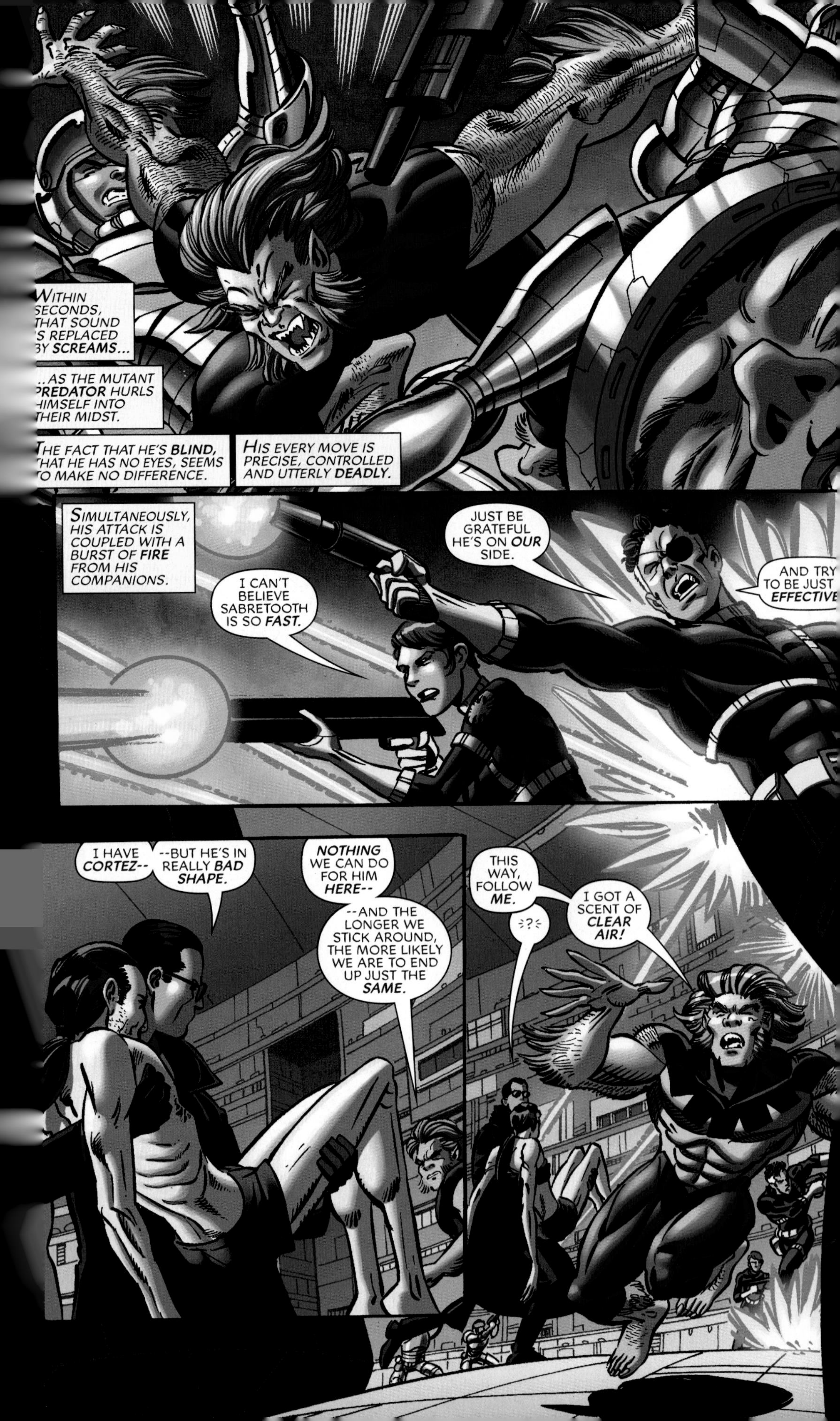
WITHIN SECONDS, THAT SOUND IS REPLACED BY SCREAMS...
...AS THE MUTANT PREDATOR HURLS HIMSELF INTO THEIR MIDST.
THE FACT THAT HE'S BLIND, THAT HE HAS NO EYES, SEEMS TO MAKE NO DIFFERENCE.
HIS EVERY MOVE IS PRECISE, CONTROLLED AND UTTERLY DEADLY.
SIMULTANEOUSLY, HIS ATTACK IS COUPLED WITH A BURST OF FIRE FROM HIS COMPANIONS.
I CAN'T BELIEVE SABRETOOTH IS SO FAST.
JUST BE GRATEFUL HE'S ON OUR SIDE.
AND TRY TO BE JUST EFFECTIVE
I HAVE CORTEZ--
--BUT HE'S IN REALLY BAD SHAPE.
NOTHING WE CAN DO FOR HIM HERE--
--AND THE LONGER WE STICK AROUND, THE MORE LIKELY WE ARE TO END UP JUST THE SAME.
THIS WAY, FOLLOW ME.
?
I GOT A SCENT OF CLEAR AIR!

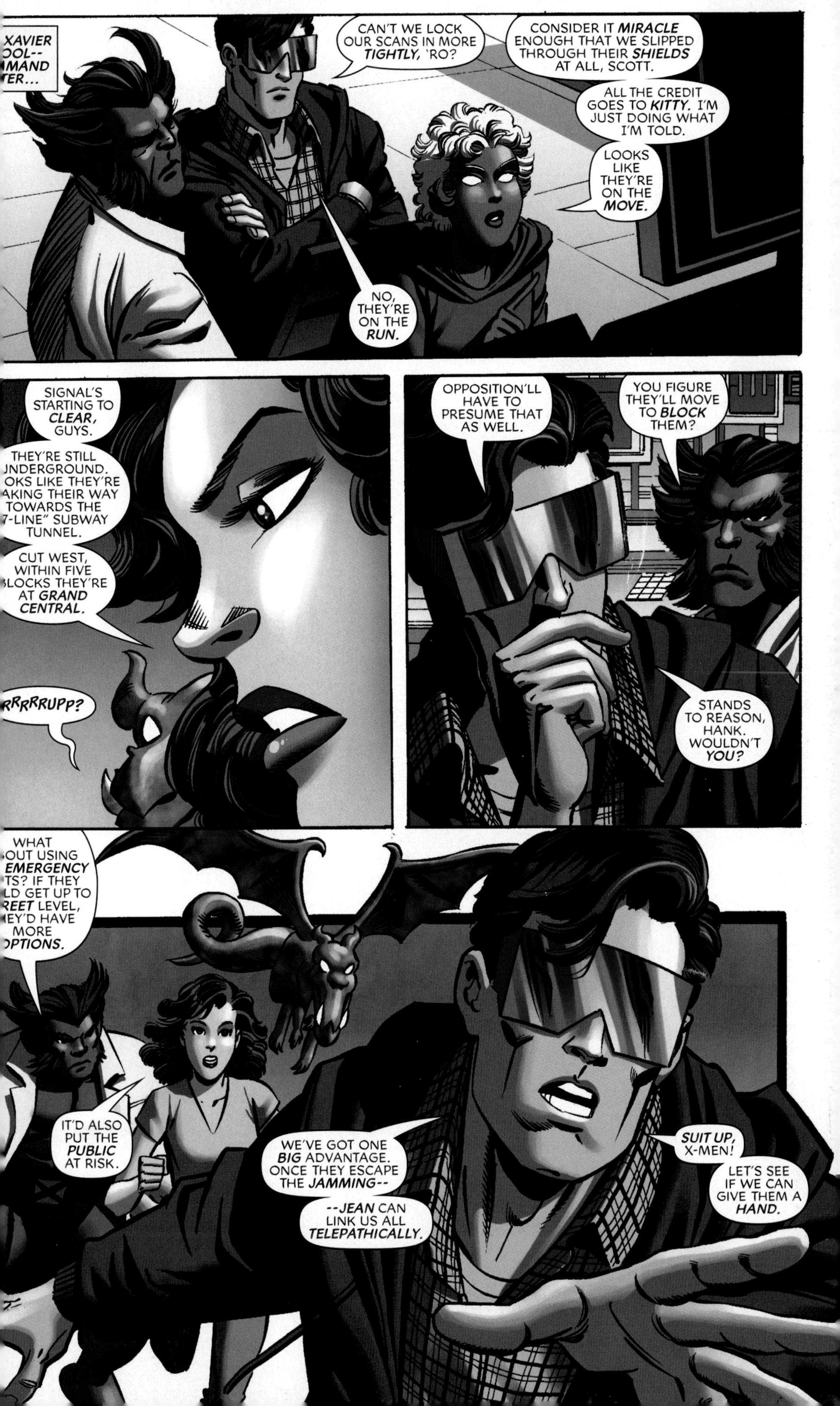
XAVIER
OOL--
MMAND
TER...
CAN'T WE LOCK OUR SCANS IN MORE TIGHTLY, 'RO?
CONSIDER IT MIRACLE ENOUGH THAT WE SLIPPED THROUGH THEIR SHIELDS AT ALL, SCOTT.
ALL THE CREDIT GOES TO KITTY. I'M JUST DOING WHAT I'M TOLD.
LOOKS LIKE THEY'RE ON THE MOVE.
NO, THEY'RE ON THE RUN.
SIGNAL'S STARTING TO CLEAR, GUYS.
THEY'RE STILL UNDERGROUND. OKS LIKE THEY'RE AKING THEIR WAY TOWARDS THE 7-LINE" SUBWAY TUNNEL.
CUT WEST, WITHIN FIVE BLOCKS THEY'RE AT GRAND CENTRAL.
RRRRRUPP?
OPPOSITION'LL HAVE TO PRESUME THAT AS WELL.
YOU FIGURE THEY'LL MOVE TO BLOCK THEM?
STANDS TO REASON, HANK. WOULDN'T YOU?
WHAT OUT USING EMERGENCY TS? IF THEY LD GET UP TO REET LEVEL, EY'D HAVE MORE OPTIONS.
IT'D ALSO PUT THE PUBLIC AT RISK.
WE'VE GOT ONE BIG ADVANTAGE. ONCE THEY ESCAPE THE JAMMING--
--JEAN CAN LINK US ALL TELEPATHICALLY.
SUIT UP, X-MEN!
LET'S SEE IF WE CAN GIVE THEM A HAND.

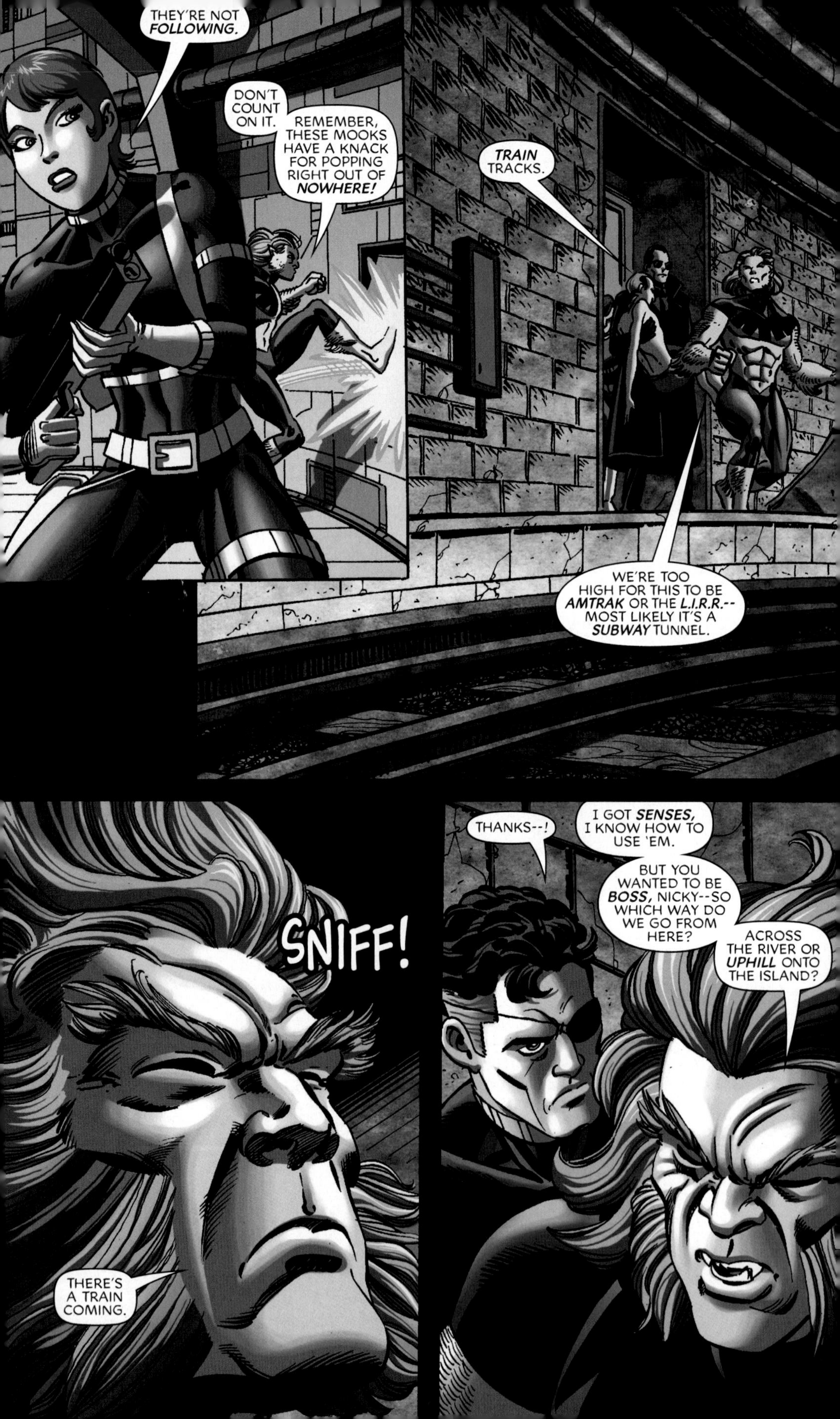

THEY'RE NOT *FOLLOWING.*
DON'T COUNT ON IT.
REMEMBER, THESE MOOKS HAVE A KNACK FOR POPPING RIGHT OUT OF *NOWHERE!*
TRAIN TRACKS.
WE'RE TOO HIGH FOR THIS TO BE *AMTRAK* OR THE *L.I.R.R.*-- MOST LIKELY IT'S A *SUBWAY* TUNNEL.
SNIFF!
THERE'S A TRAIN COMING.
THANKS--!
I GOT *SENSES,* I KNOW HOW TO USE 'EM.
BUT YOU WANTED TO BE *BOSS,* NICKY--SO WHICH WAY DO WE GO FROM HERE?
ACROSS THE RIVER OR *UPHILL* ONTO THE ISLAND?

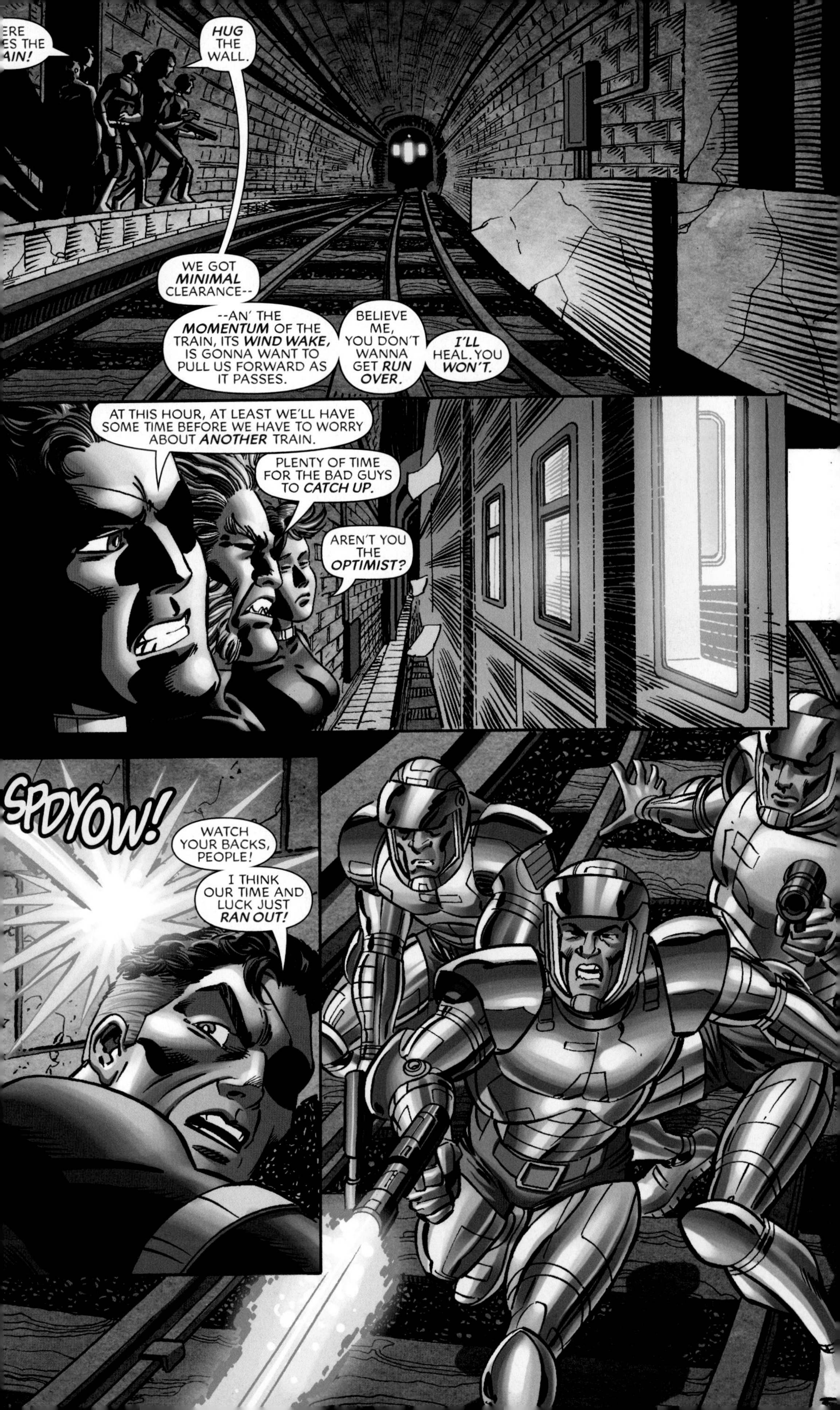

HUG THE WALL.
WE GOT MINIMAL CLEARANCE--
--AN' THE MOMENTUM OF THE TRAIN, ITS WIND WAKE, IS GONNA WANT TO PULL US FORWARD AS IT PASSES.
BELIEVE ME, YOU DON'T WANNA GET RUN OVER.
I'LL HEAL. YOU WON'T.
AT THIS HOUR, AT LEAST WE'LL HAVE SOME TIME BEFORE WE HAVE TO WORRY ABOUT ANOTHER TRAIN.
PLENTY OF TIME FOR THE BAD GUYS TO CATCH UP.
AREN'T YOU THE OPTIMIST?
SPDYOW!
WATCH YOUR BACKS, PEOPLE!
I THINK OUR TIME AND LUCK JUST RAN OUT!

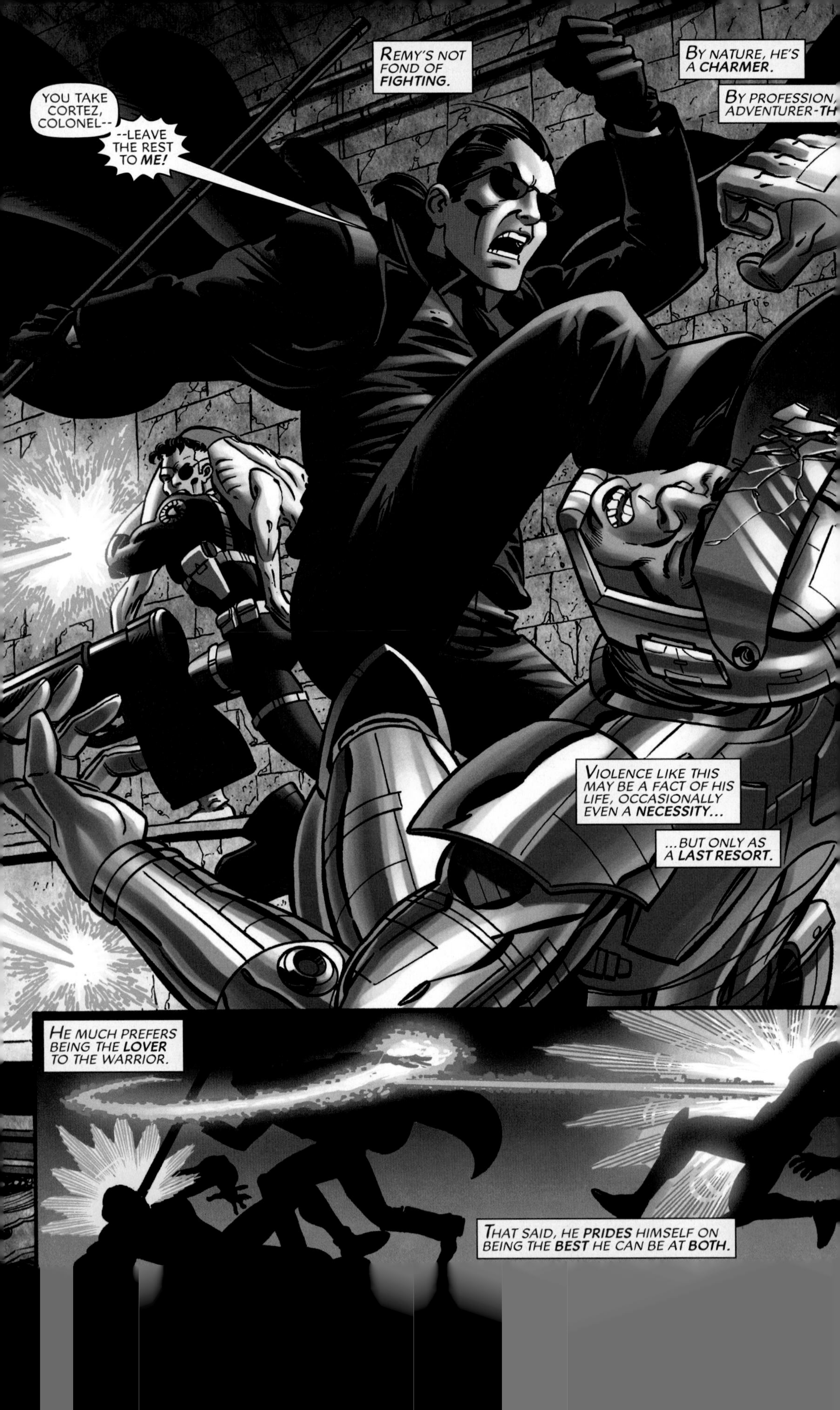

REMY'S NOT FOND OF FIGHTING.
BY NATURE, HE'S A CHARMER.
BY PROFESSION, ADVENTURER-TH
YOU TAKE CORTEZ, COLONEL--
--LEAVE THE REST TO ME!
VIOLENCE LIKE THIS MAY BE A FACT OF HIS LIFE, OCCASIONALLY EVEN A NECESSITY...
...BUT ONLY AS A LAST RESORT.
HE MUCH PREFERS BEING THE LOVER TO THE WARRIOR.
THAT SAID, HE PRIDES HIMSELF ON BEING THE BEST HE CAN BE AT BOTH.

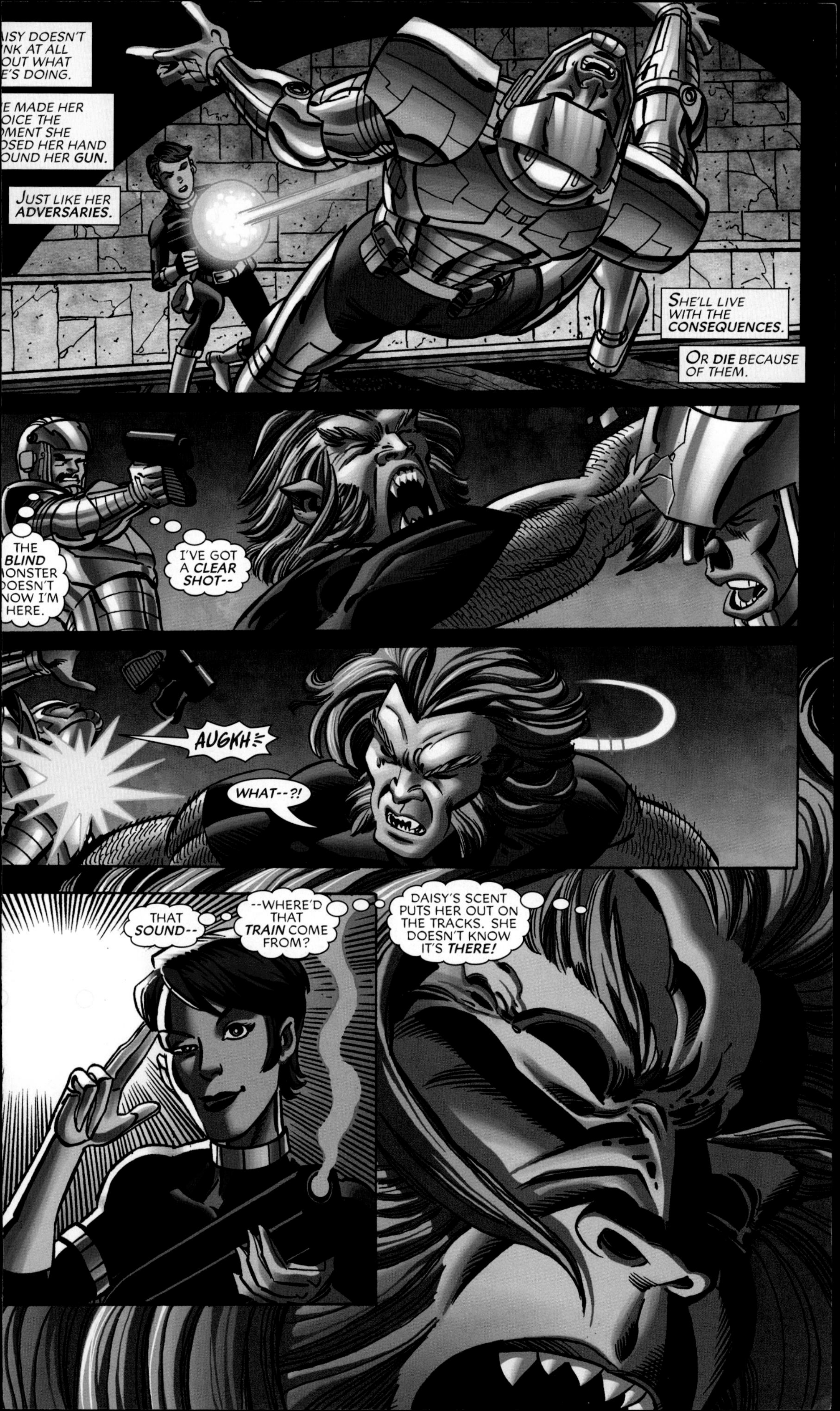
AISY DOESN'T
NK AT ALL
OUT WHAT
E'S DOING.
E MADE HER
OICE THE
OMENT SHE
OSED HER HAND
OUND HER GUN.
JUST LIKE HER ADVERSARIES.
SHE'LL LIVE WITH THE CONSEQUENCES.
OR DIE BECAUSE OF THEM.
THE BLIND
ONSTER
OESN'T
NOW I'M
HERE.
I'VE GOT A CLEAR SHOT--
AUGKH
WHAT--?!
THAT SOUND--
--WHERE'D THAT TRAIN COME FROM?
DAISY'S SCENT PUTS HER OUT ON THE TRACKS. SHE DOESN'T KNOW IT'S THERE!

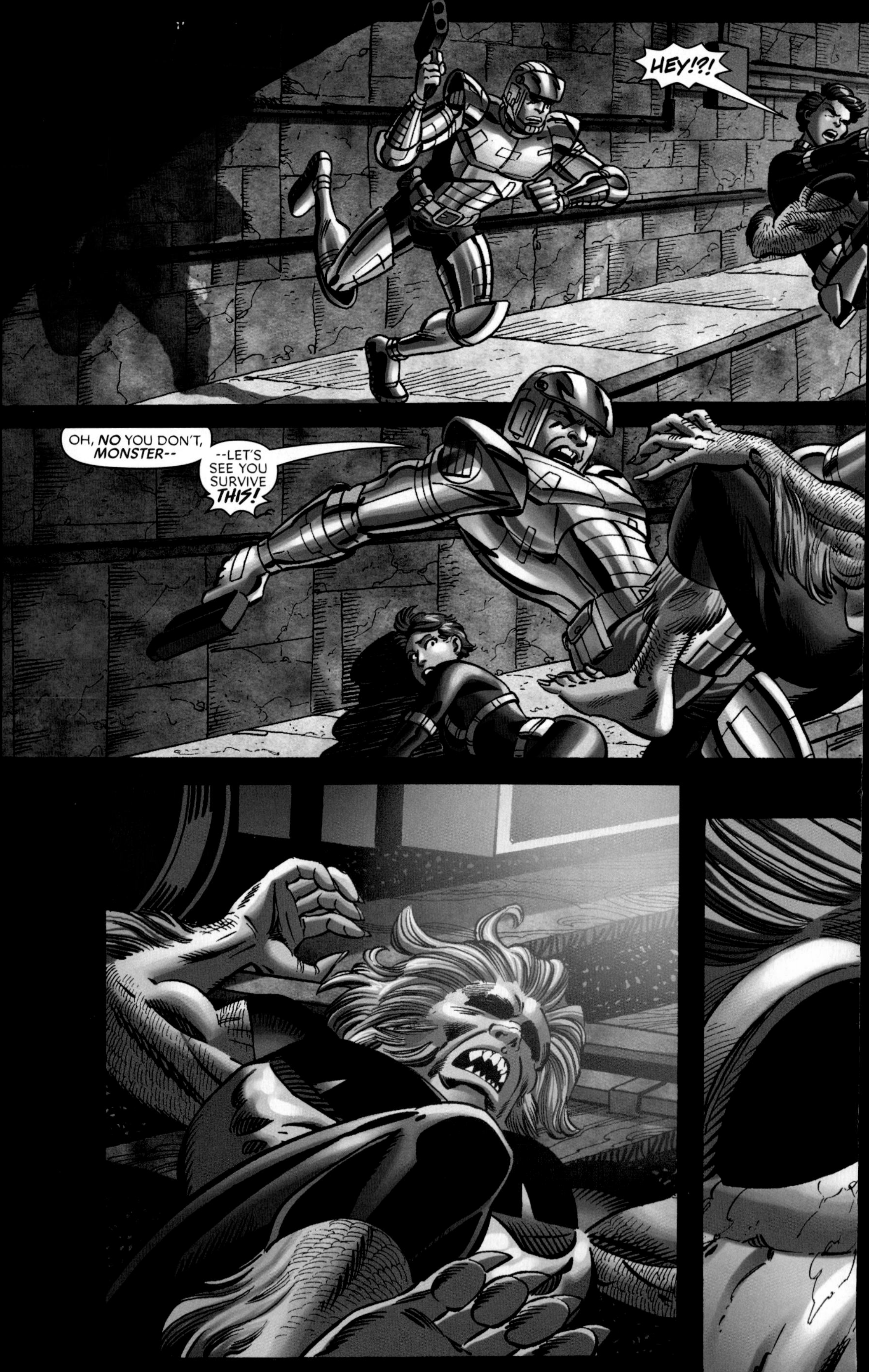
HEY!?!
OH, NO YOU DON'T, MONSTER--
--LET'S SEE YOU SURVIVE THIS!

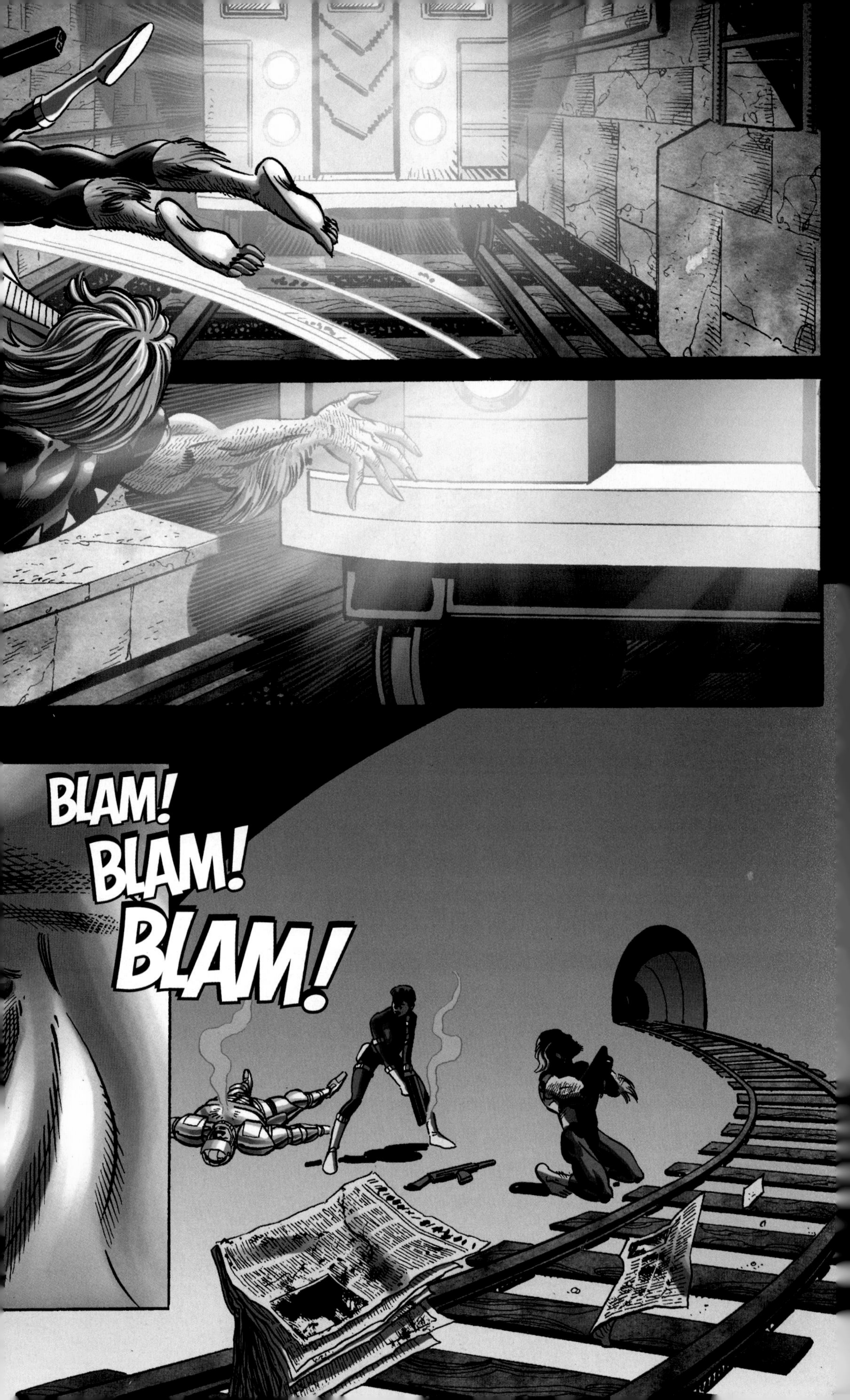
BLAM!
BLAM!
BLAM!

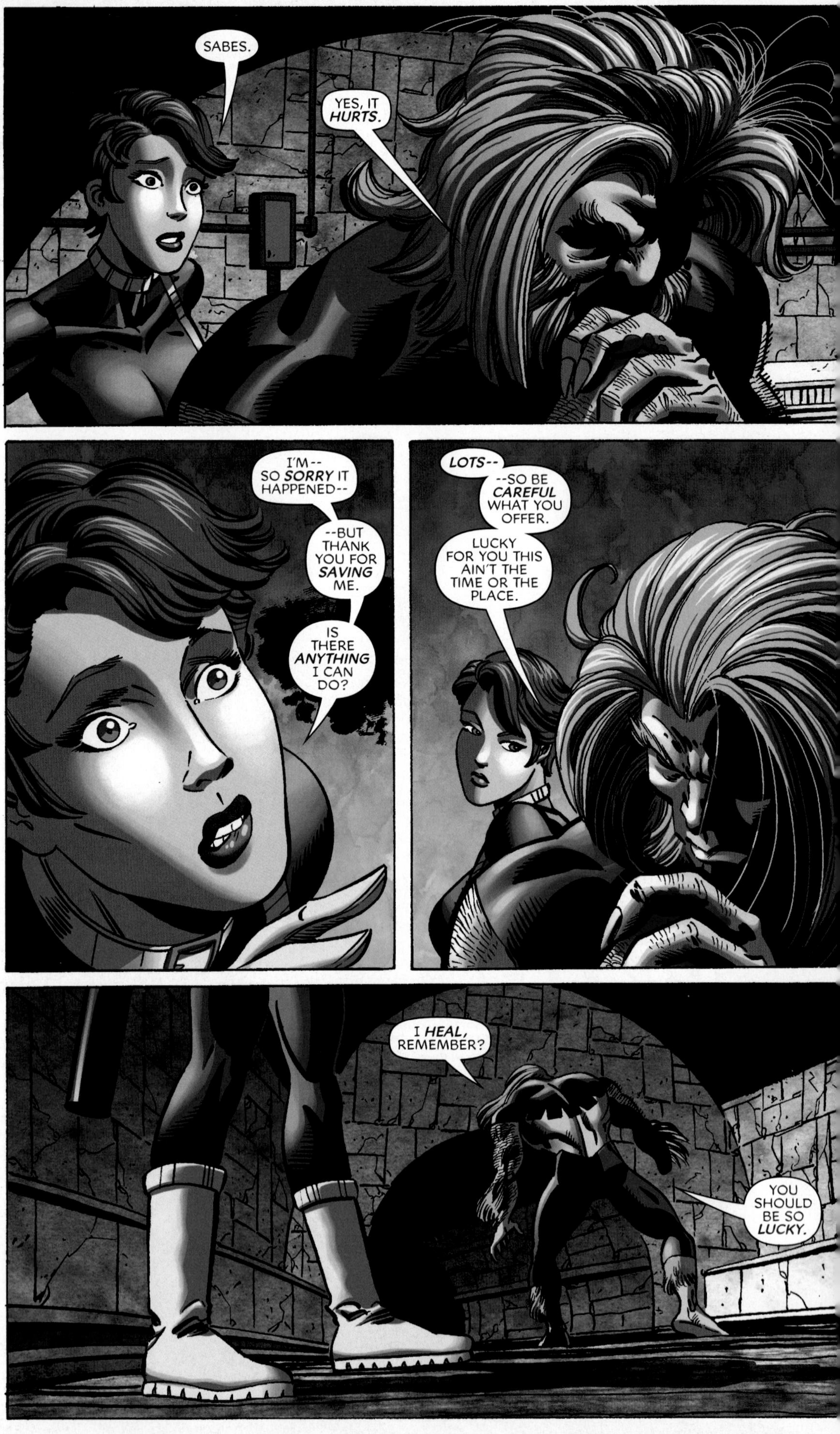
SABES.
YES, IT *HURTS.*
I'M-- SO *SORRY* IT HAPPENED--
--BUT THANK YOU FOR *SAVING* ME.
IS THERE *ANYTHING* I CAN DO?
LOTS--
--SO BE *CAREFUL* WHAT YOU OFFER.
LUCKY FOR YOU THIS AIN'T THE TIME OR THE PLACE.
I *HEAL,* REMEMBER?
YOU SHOULD BE SO *LUCKY.*

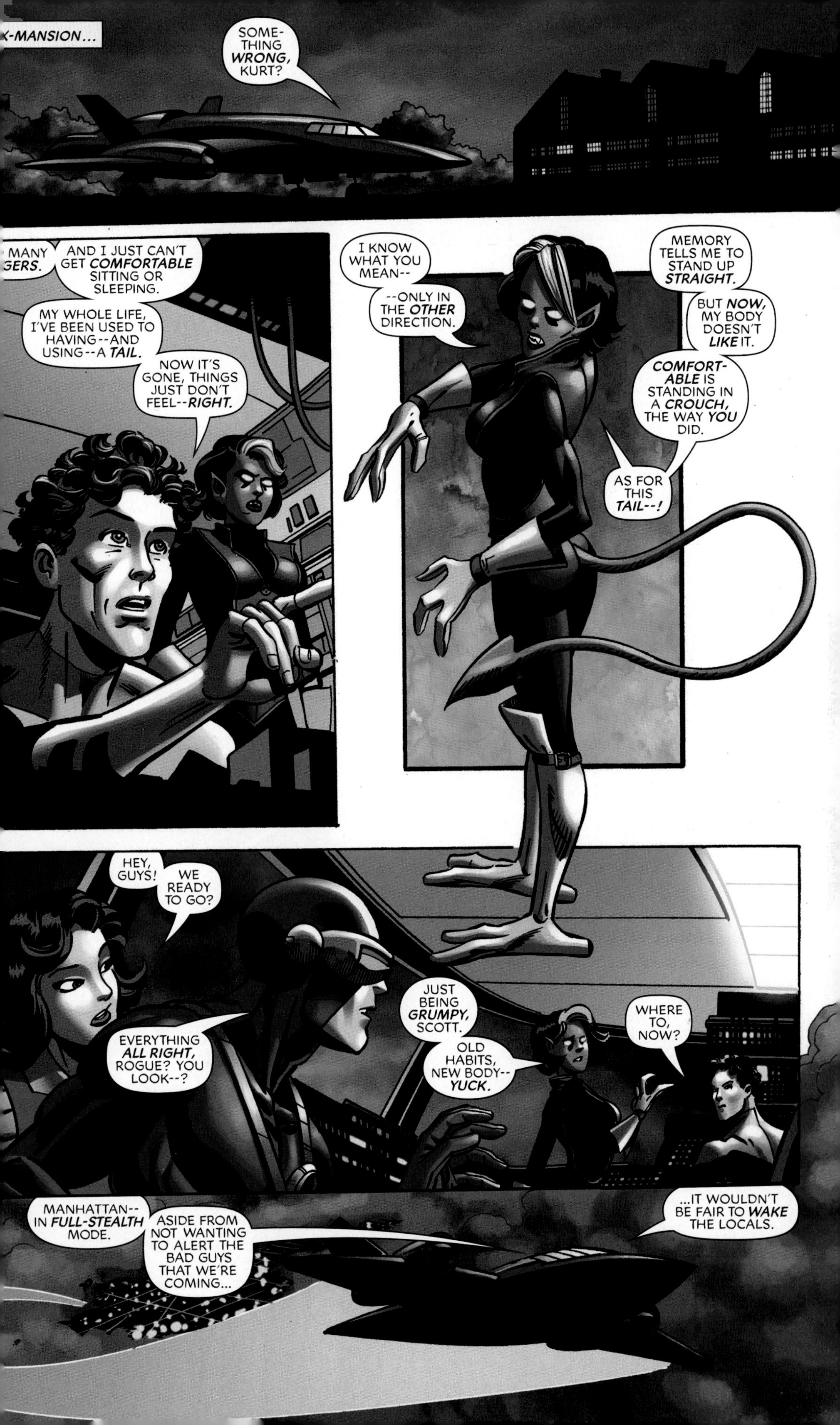

-MANSION...
SOME-THING WRONG, KURT?
MANY GERS.
AND I JUST CAN'T GET COMFORTABLE SITTING OR SLEEPING.
MY WHOLE LIFE, I'VE BEEN USED TO HAVING--AND USING--A TAIL.
NOW IT'S GONE, THINGS JUST DON'T FEEL--RIGHT.
I KNOW WHAT YOU MEAN--
--ONLY IN THE OTHER DIRECTION.
MEMORY TELLS ME TO STAND UP STRAIGHT.
BUT NOW, MY BODY DOESN'T LIKE IT.
COMFORT-ABLE IS STANDING IN A CROUCH, THE WAY YOU DID.
AS FOR THIS TAIL--!
HEY, GUYS!
WE READY TO GO?
EVERYTHING ALL RIGHT, ROGUE? YOU LOOK--?
JUST BEING GRUMPY, SCOTT.
OLD HABITS, NEW BODY--YUCK.
WHERE TO, NOW?
MANHATTAN--IN FULL-STEALTH MODE.
ASIDE FROM NOT WANTING TO ALERT THE BAD GUYS THAT WE'RE COMING...
...IT WOULDN'T BE FAIR TO WAKE THE LOCALS.

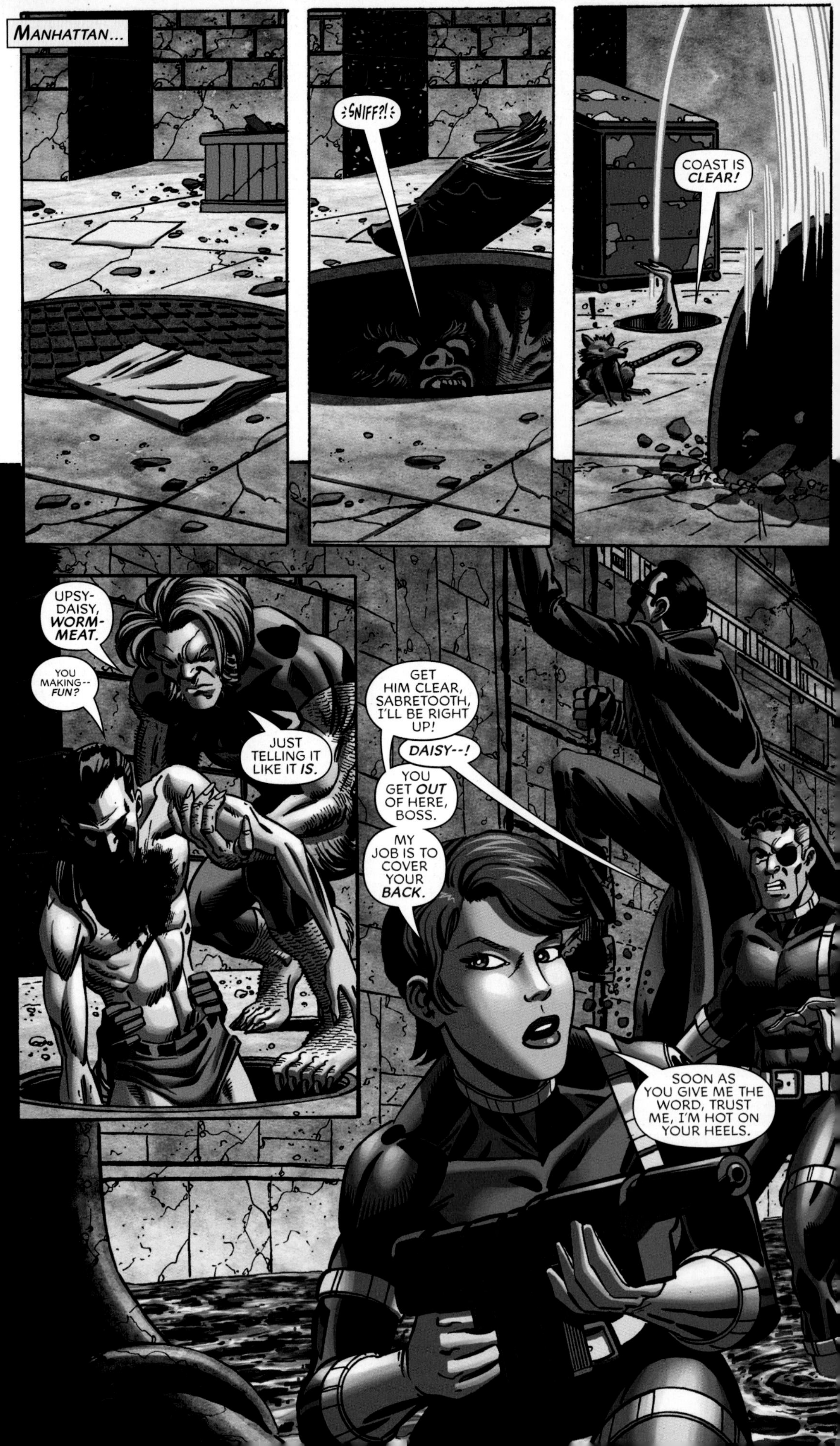
MANHATTAN...
SNIFF?!
COAST IS CLEAR!
UPSY-DAISY, WORM-MEAT.
YOU MAKING--FUN?
JUST TELLING IT LIKE IT IS.
GET HIM CLEAR, SABRETOOTH, I'LL BE RIGHT UP!
DAISY--!
YOU GET OUT OF HERE, BOSS.
MY JOB IS TO COVER YOUR BACK.
SOON AS YOU GIVE ME THE WORD, TRUST ME, I'M HOT ON YOUR HEELS.

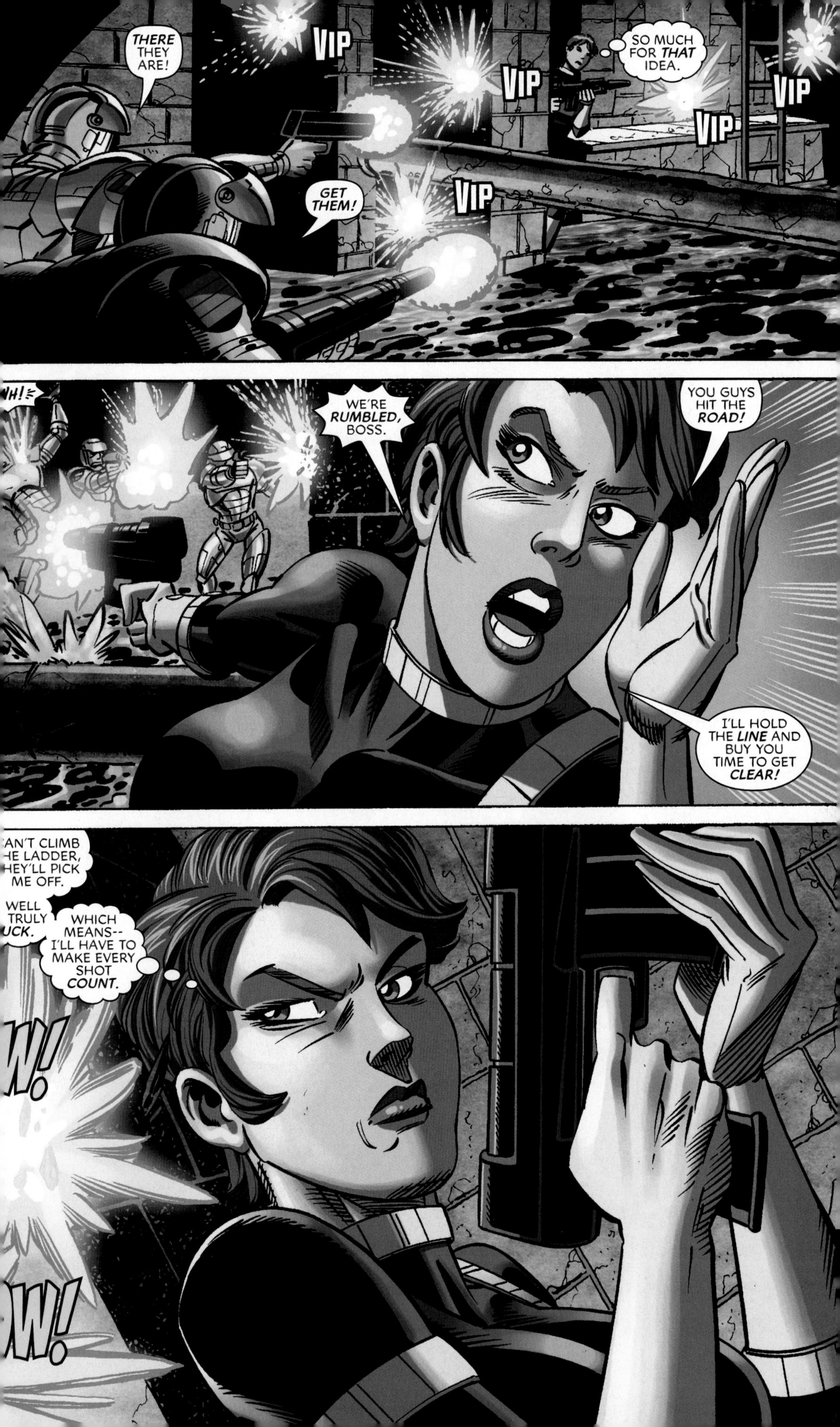
THERE THEY ARE!
VIP
GET THEM!
VIP
VIP
VIP
SO MUCH FOR THAT IDEA.
VIP
VIP
WE'RE RUMBLED, BOSS.
YOU GUYS HIT THE ROAD!
I'LL HOLD THE LINE AND BUY YOU TIME TO GET CLEAR!
AN'T CLIMB HE LADDER, HEY'LL PICK ME OFF.
WELL TRULY UCK.
WHICH MEANS-- I'LL HAVE TO MAKE EVERY SHOT COUNT.

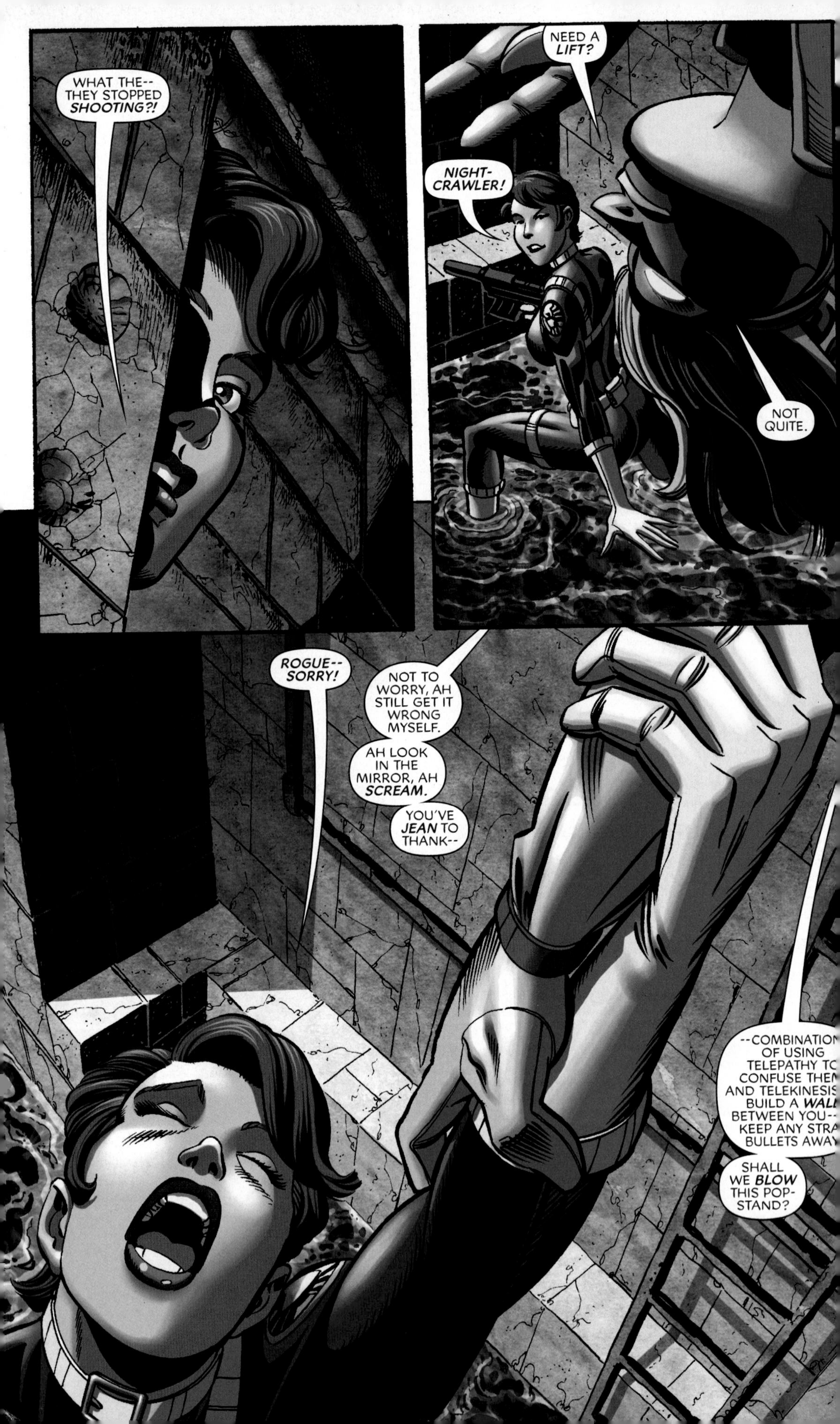
WHAT THE-- THEY STOPPED SHOOTING?!
NEED A LIFT?
NIGHT-CRAWLER!
NOT QUITE.
ROGUE-- SORRY!
NOT TO WORRY, AH STILL GET IT WRONG MYSELF.
AH LOOK IN THE MIRROR, AH SCREAM.
YOU'VE JEAN TO THANK--
--COMBINATION OF USING TELEPATHY TO CONFUSE THEM AND TELEKINESIS BUILD A WALL BETWEEN YOU-- KEEP ANY STRAY BULLETS AWAY.
SHALL WE BLOW THIS POP-STAND?

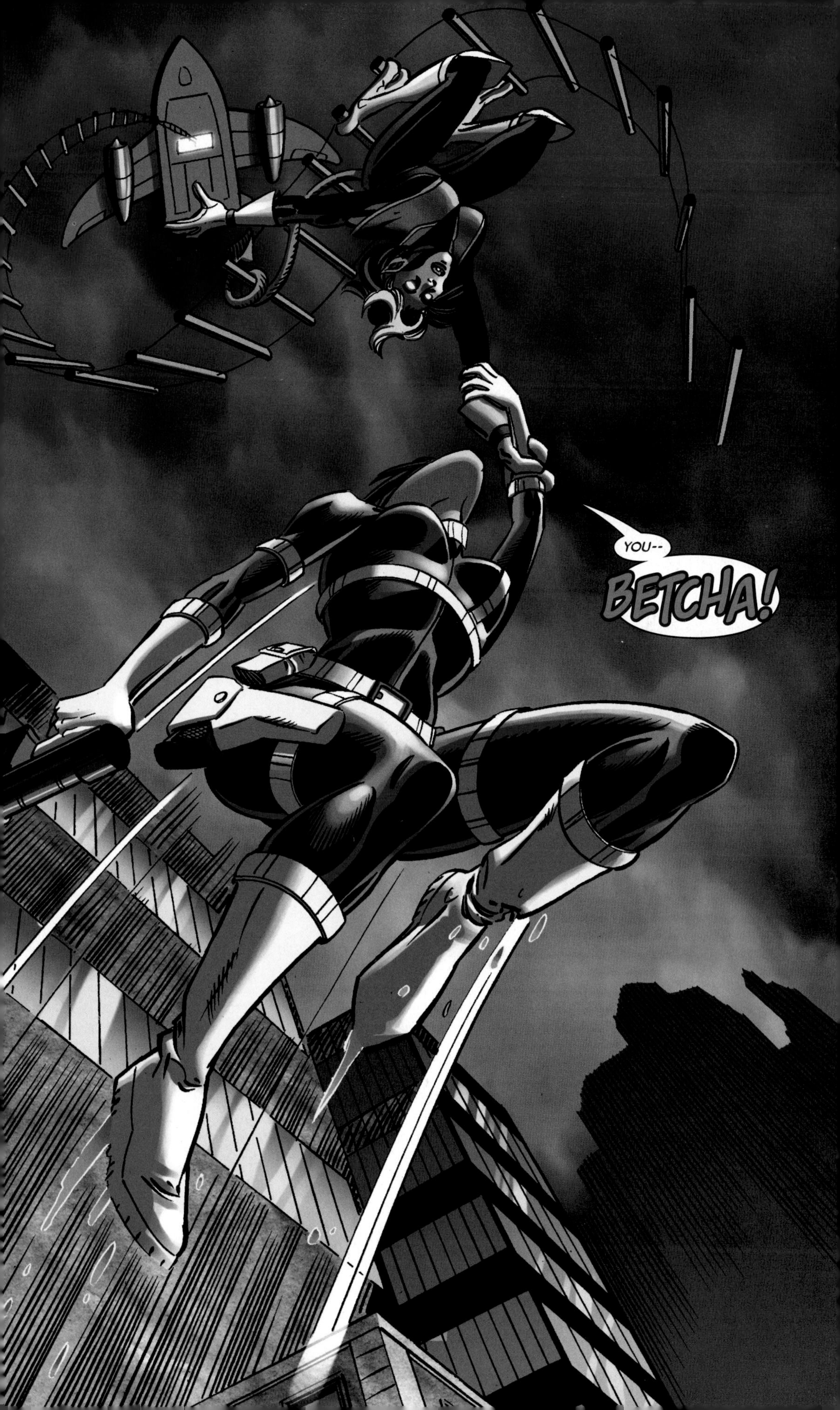
YOU--
BETCHA!

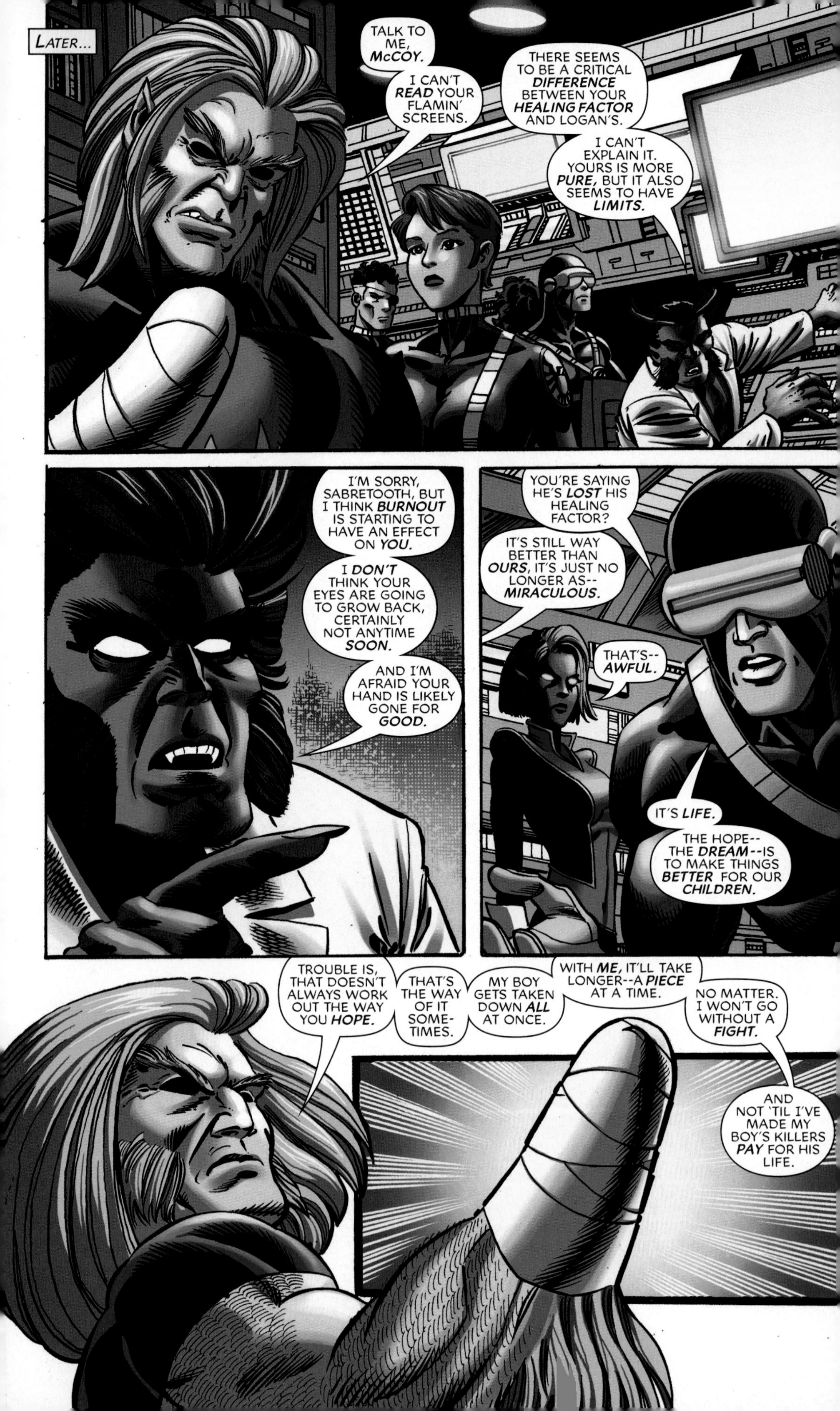
LATER...
TALK TO ME, McCOY.
I CAN'T READ YOUR FLAMIN' SCREENS.
THERE SEEMS TO BE A CRITICAL DIFFERENCE BETWEEN YOUR HEALING FACTOR AND LOGAN'S.
I CAN'T EXPLAIN IT. YOURS IS MORE PURE, BUT IT ALSO SEEMS TO HAVE LIMITS.
I'M SORRY, SABRETOOTH, BUT I THINK BURNOUT IS STARTING TO HAVE AN EFFECT ON YOU.
I DON'T THINK YOUR EYES ARE GOING TO GROW BACK, CERTAINLY NOT ANYTIME SOON.
AND I'M AFRAID YOUR HAND IS LIKELY GONE FOR GOOD.
YOU'RE SAYING HE'S LOST HIS HEALING FACTOR?
IT'S STILL WAY BETTER THAN OURS, IT'S JUST NO LONGER AS--MIRACULOUS.
THAT'S--AWFUL.
IT'S LIFE.
THE HOPE--THE DREAM--IS TO MAKE THINGS BETTER FOR OUR CHILDREN.
TROUBLE IS, THAT DOESN'T ALWAYS WORK OUT THE WAY YOU HOPE.
THAT'S THE WAY OF IT SOME-TIMES.
MY BOY GETS TAKEN DOWN ALL AT ONCE.
WITH ME, IT'LL TAKE LONGER--A PIECE AT A TIME.
NO MATTER. I WON'T GO WITHOUT A FIGHT.
AND NOT 'TIL I'VE MADE MY BOY'S KILLERS PAY FOR HIS LIFE.

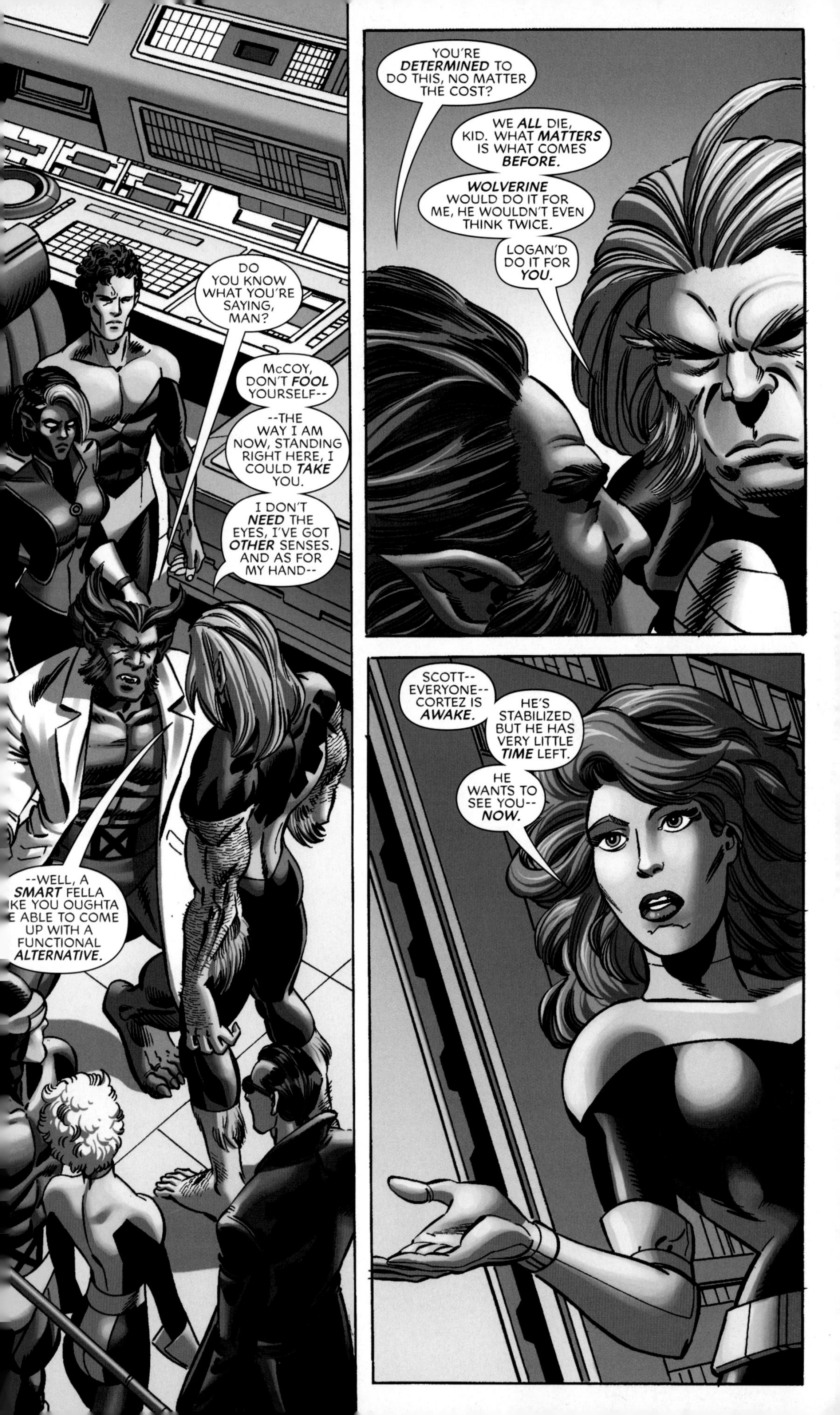
DO YOU KNOW WHAT YOU'RE SAYING, MAN?
McCOY, DON'T *FOOL* YOURSELF--
--THE WAY I AM NOW, STANDING RIGHT HERE, I COULD *TAKE* YOU.
I DON'T *NEED* THE EYES, I'VE GOT *OTHER* SENSES. AND AS FOR MY HAND--
--WELL, A *SMART* FELLA IKE YOU OUGHTA E ABLE TO COME UP WITH A FUNCTIONAL *ALTERNATIVE.*
YOU'RE *DETERMINED* TO DO THIS, NO MATTER THE COST?
WE *ALL* DIE, KID. WHAT *MATTERS* IS WHAT COMES *BEFORE.*
WOLVERINE WOULD DO IT FOR ME, HE WOULDN'T EVEN THINK TWICE.
LOGAN'D DO IT FOR *YOU.*
SCOTT-- EVERYONE-- CORTEZ IS *AWAKE.*
HE'S STABILIZED BUT HE HAS VERY LITTLE *TIME* LEFT.
HE WANTS TO SEE YOU-- *NOW.*

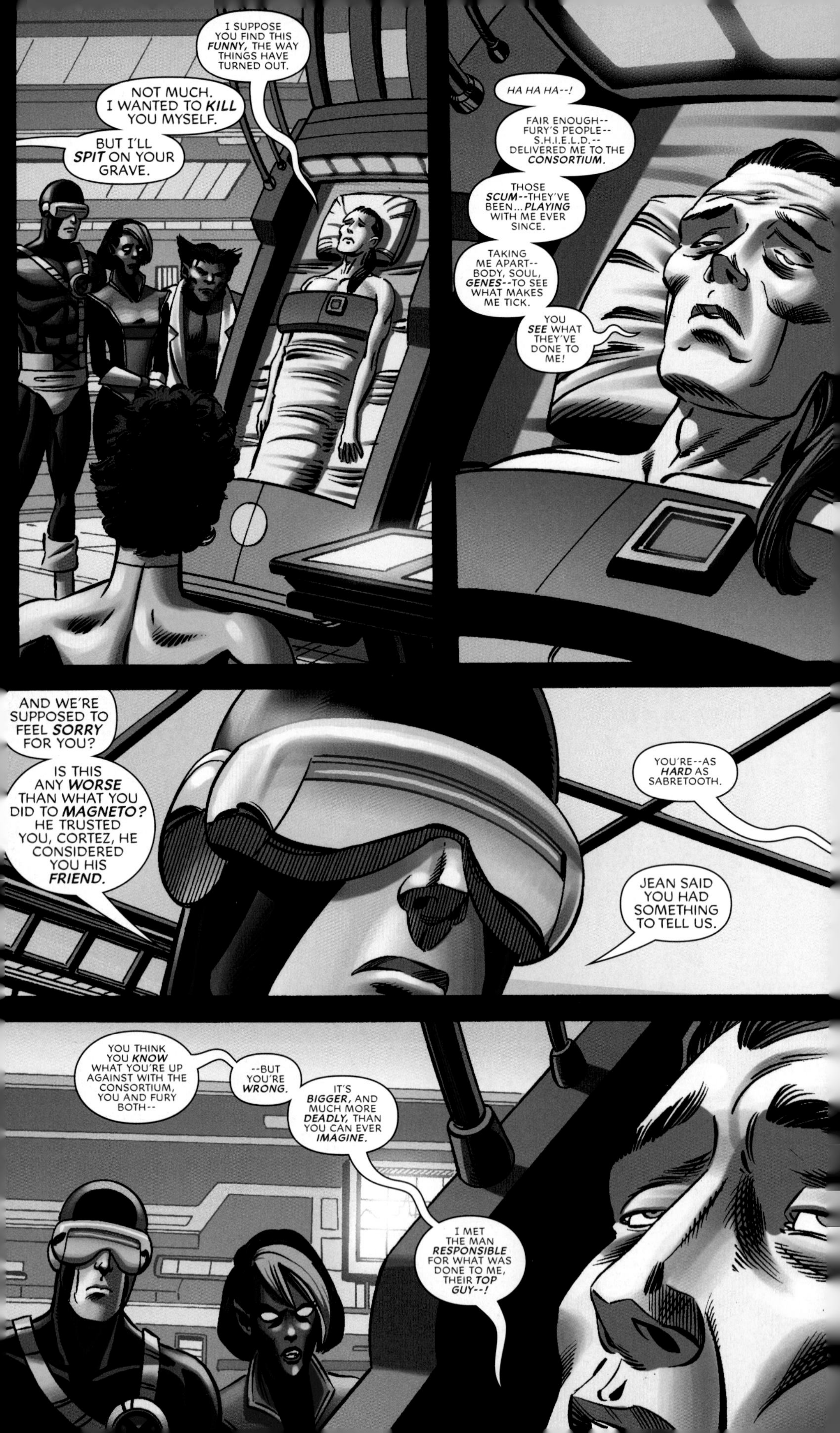

I SUPPOSE YOU FIND THIS FUNNY, THE WAY THINGS HAVE TURNED OUT.
NOT MUCH. I WANTED TO KILL YOU MYSELF.
BUT I'LL SPIT ON YOUR GRAVE.
HA HA HA--!
FAIR ENOUGH-- FURY'S PEOPLE-- S.H.I.E.L.D.-- DELIVERED ME TO THE CONSORTIUM.
THOSE SCUM--THEY'VE BEEN...PLAYING WITH ME EVER SINCE.
TAKING ME APART-- BODY, SOUL, GENES--TO SEE WHAT MAKES ME TICK.
YOU SEE WHAT THEY'VE DONE TO ME!
AND WE'RE SUPPOSED TO FEEL SORRY FOR YOU?
IS THIS ANY WORSE THAN WHAT YOU DID TO MAGNETO? HE TRUSTED YOU, CORTEZ, HE CONSIDERED YOU HIS FRIEND.
YOU'RE--AS HARD AS SABRETOOTH.
JEAN SAID YOU HAD SOMETHING TO TELL US.
YOU THINK YOU KNOW WHAT YOU'RE UP AGAINST WITH THE CONSORTIUM, YOU AND FURY BOTH--
--BUT YOU'RE WRONG.
IT'S BIGGER, AND MUCH MORE DEADLY, THAN YOU CAN EVER IMAGINE.
I MET THE MAN RESPONSIBLE FOR WHAT WAS DONE TO ME, THEIR TOP GUY--!

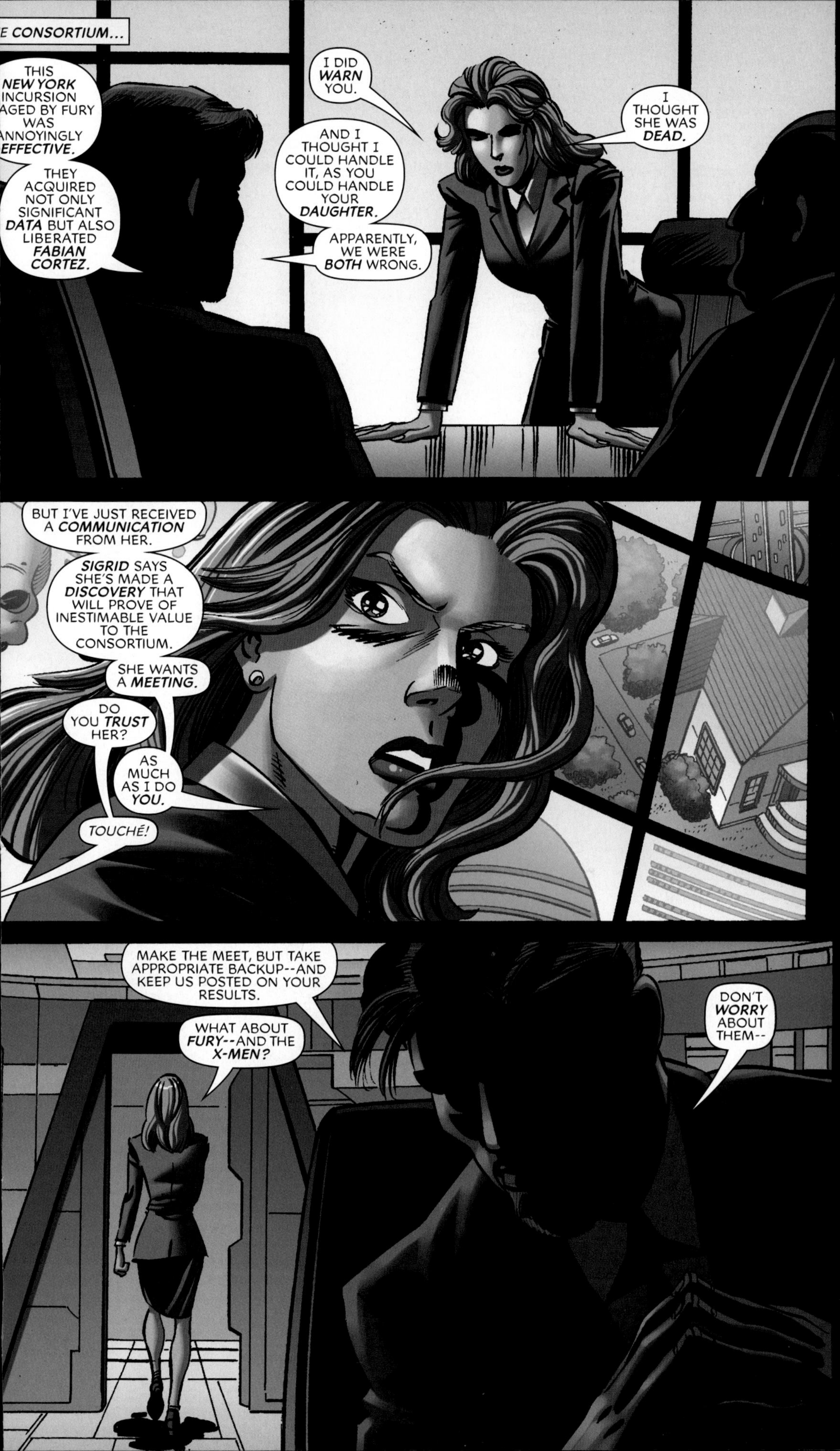

E CONSORTIUM...
THIS NEW YORK INCURSION AGED BY FURY WAS ANNOYINGLY EFFECTIVE.
THEY ACQUIRED NOT ONLY SIGNIFICANT DATA BUT ALSO LIBERATED FABIAN CORTEZ.
I DID WARN YOU.
AND I THOUGHT I COULD HANDLE IT, AS YOU COULD HANDLE YOUR DAUGHTER.
APPARENTLY, WE WERE BOTH WRONG.
I THOUGHT SHE WAS DEAD.
BUT I'VE JUST RECEIVED A COMMUNICATION FROM HER.
SIGRID SAYS SHE'S MADE A DISCOVERY THAT WILL PROVE OF INESTIMABLE VALUE TO THE CONSORTIUM.
SHE WANTS A MEETING.
DO YOU TRUST HER?
AS MUCH AS I DO YOU.
TOUCHÉ!
MAKE THE MEET, BUT TAKE APPROPRIATE BACKUP--AND KEEP US POSTED ON YOUR RESULTS.
WHAT ABOUT FURY--AND THE X-MEN?
DON'T WORRY ABOUT THEM--

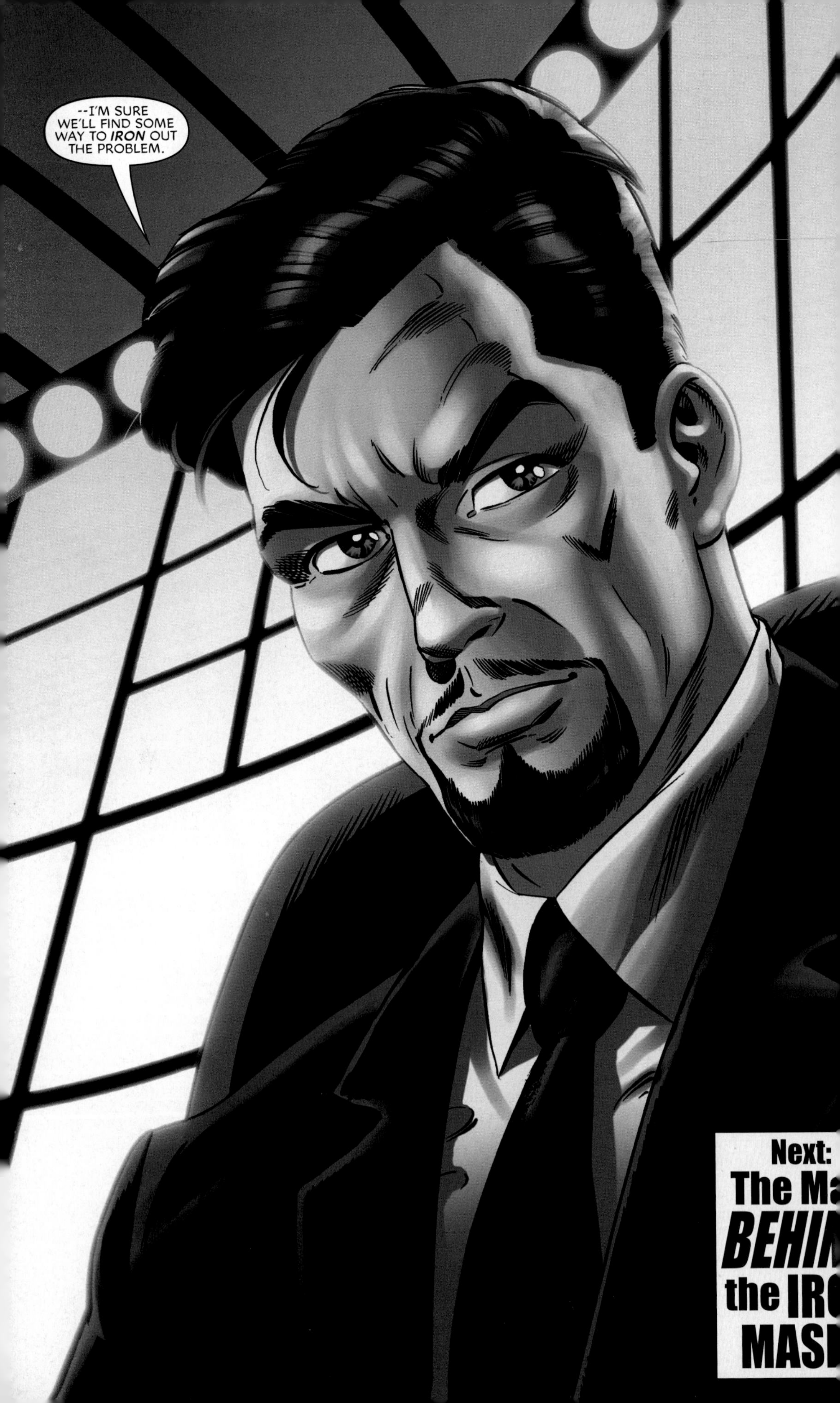
--I'M SURE WE'LL FIND SOME WAY TO IRON OUT THE PROBLEM.
Next:
The Ma
BEHIN
the IR
MAS

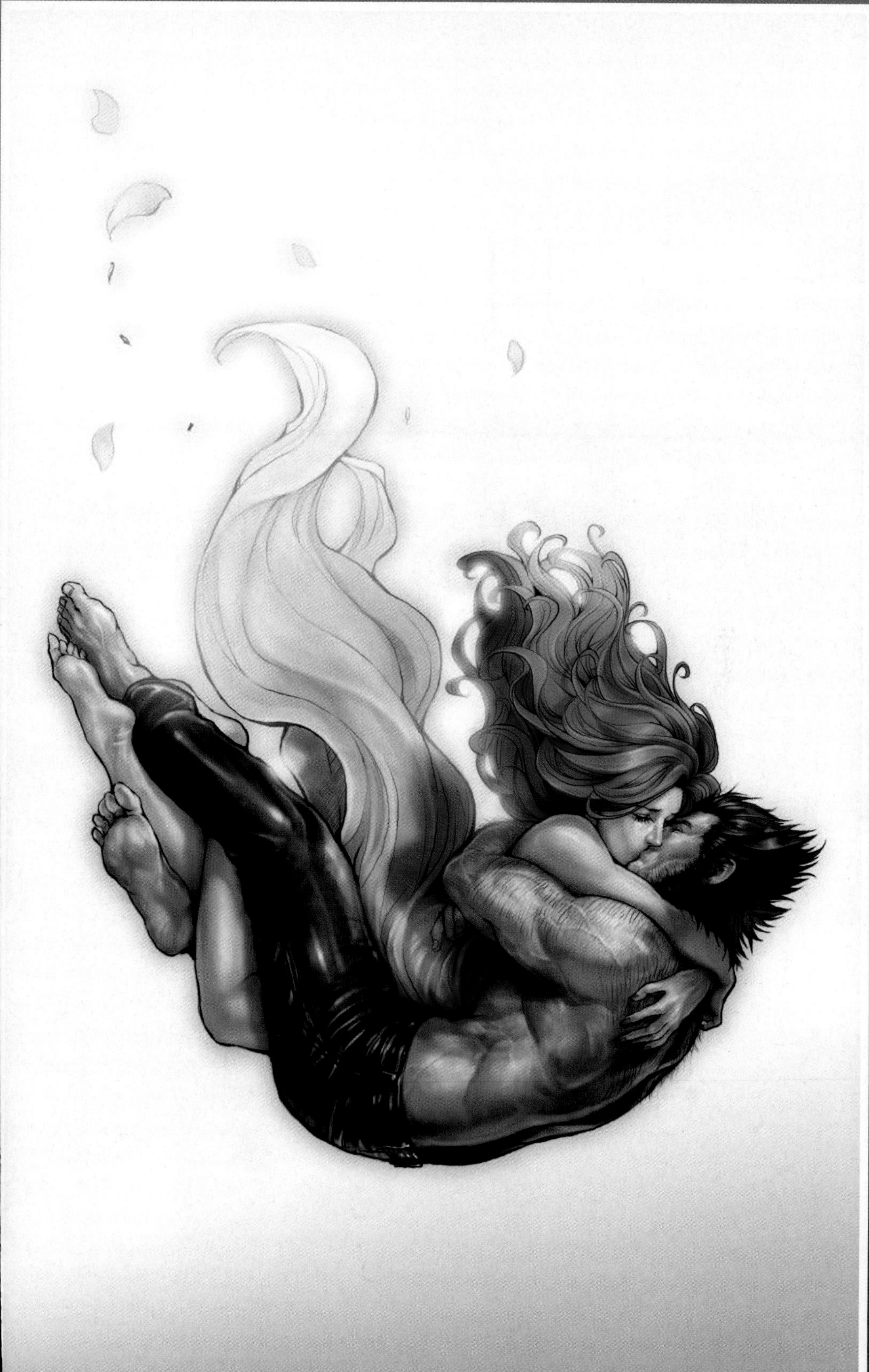

ANNUAL ONE

Comics legend Chris Claremont had an epic 16-year run on ***X-MEN***, which concluc
with ***X-MEN: MUTANT GENESIS #1-3*** in 1991. Now, in an unprecedented comics eve
Claremont returns to his iconic run on the ***X-MEN***.

X-MEN FOREVER

*Jean Grey has had many secrets, but none were so damning as the revelation that
and Wolverine shared an unconsummated romance behind the backs of the X-Men…
completely unbeknownst to her beloved, Scott Summers.*

This is the story of the beginning of that love…

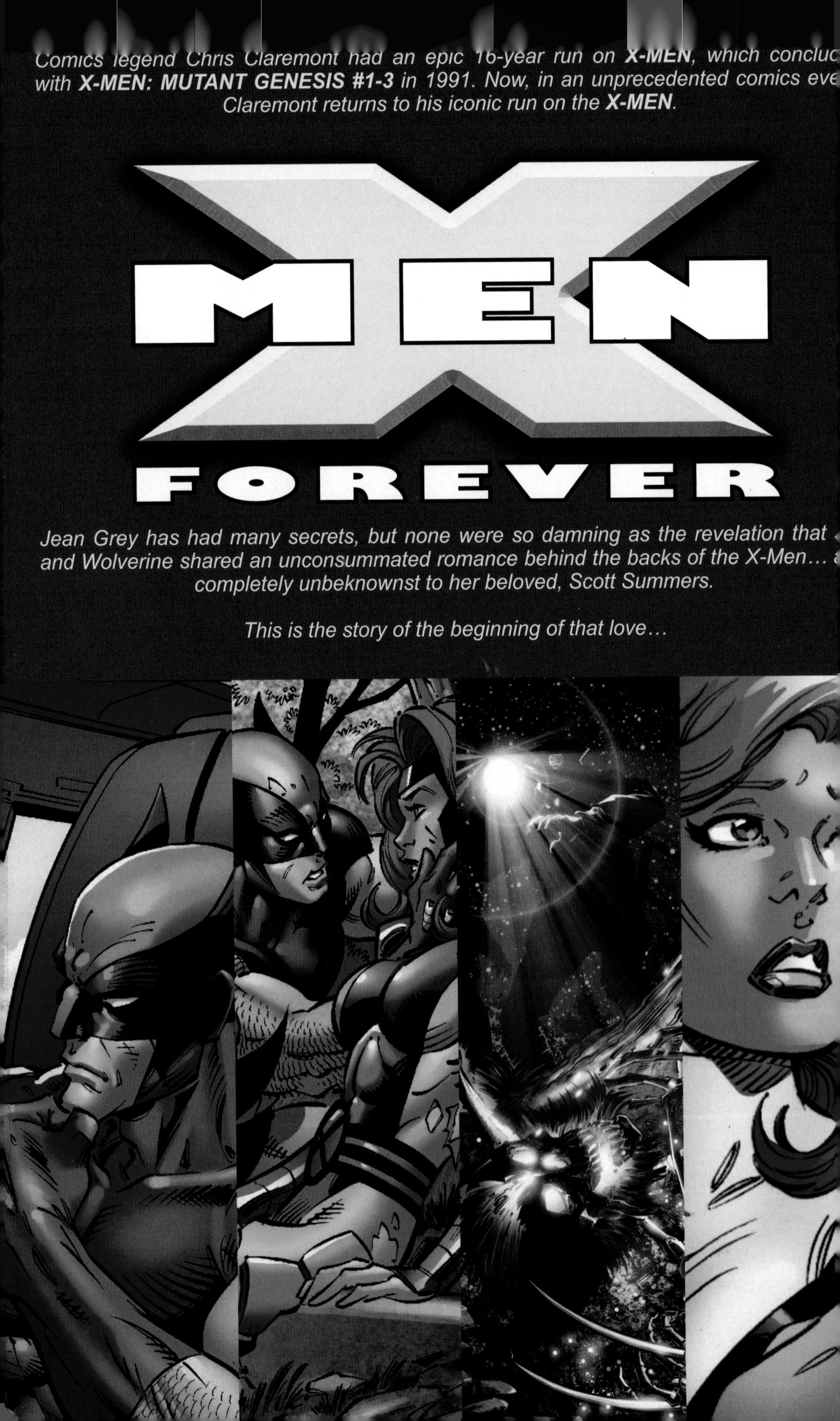

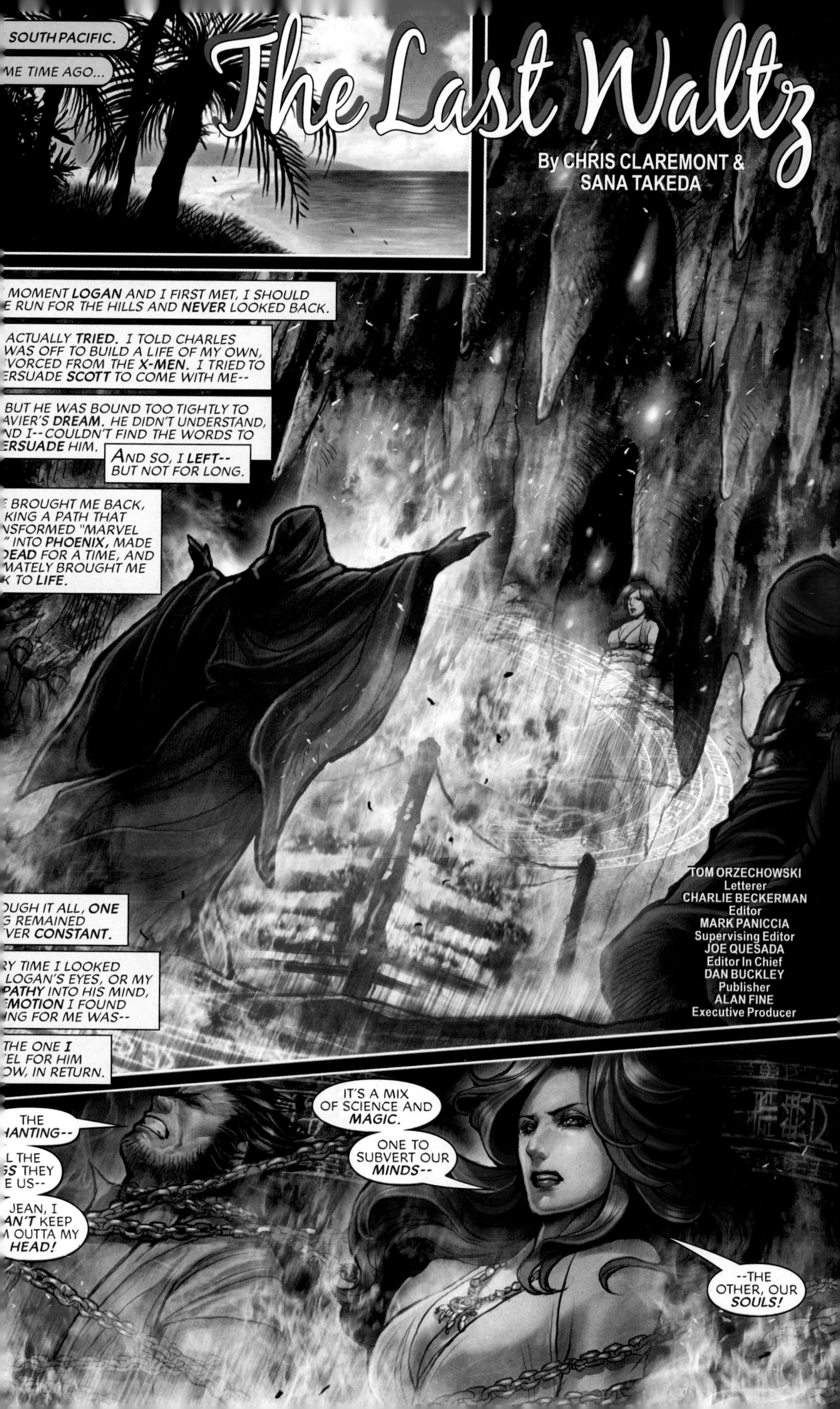

SOUTH PACIFIC.
ME TIME AGO...
The Last Waltz
By CHRIS CLAREMONT & SANA TAKEDA
MOMENT LOGAN AND I FIRST MET, I SHOULD
E RUN FOR THE HILLS AND NEVER LOOKED BACK.
ACTUALLY TRIED. I TOLD CHARLES WAS OFF TO BUILD A LIFE OF MY OWN, VORCED FROM THE X-MEN. I TRIED TO ERSUADE SCOTT TO COME WITH ME--
BUT HE WAS BOUND TOO TIGHTLY TO AVIER'S DREAM. HE DIDN'T UNDERSTAND, ND I--COULDN'T FIND THE WORDS TO ERSUADE HIM.
AND SO, I LEFT-- BUT NOT FOR LONG.
BROUGHT ME BACK, KING A PATH THAT NSFORMED "MARVEL " INTO PHOENIX, MADE DEAD FOR A TIME, AND MATELY BROUGHT ME K TO LIFE.
OUGH IT ALL, ONE G REMAINED VER CONSTANT.
RY TIME I LOOKED LOGAN'S EYES, OR MY PATHY INTO HIS MIND, EMOTION I FOUND ING FOR ME WAS--
THE ONE I EL FOR HIM OW, IN RETURN.
TOM ORZECHOWSKI Letterer
CHARLIE BECKERMAN Editor
MARK PANICCIA Supervising Editor
JOE QUESADA Editor In Chief
DAN BUCKLEY Publisher
ALAN FINE Executive Producer
THE HANTING--
L THE SS THEY E US--
JEAN, I AN'T KEEP M OUTTA MY HEAD!
IT'S A MIX OF SCIENCE AND MAGIC.
ONE TO SUBVERT OUR MINDS--
--THE OTHER, OUR SOULS!

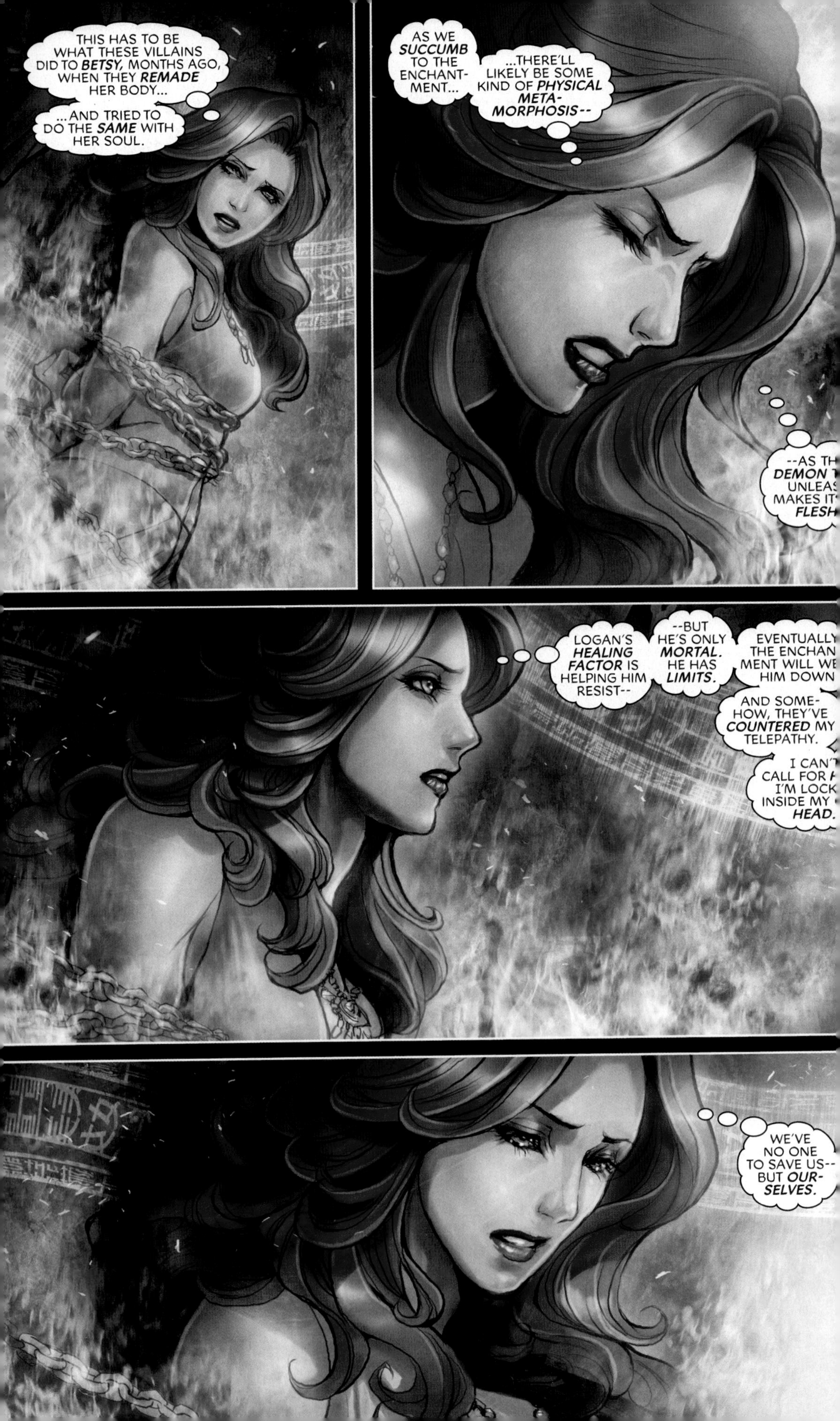
THIS HAS TO BE WHAT THESE VILLAINS DID TO BETSY, MONTHS AGO, WHEN THEY REMADE HER BODY...
...AND TRIED TO DO THE SAME WITH HER SOUL.
AS WE SUCCUMB TO THE ENCHANT-MENT...
...THERE'LL LIKELY BE SOME KIND OF PHYSICAL META-MORPHOSIS--
--AS TH DEMON UNLEAS MAKES IT FLESH
LOGAN'S HEALING FACTOR IS HELPING HIM RESIST--
--BUT HE'S ONLY MORTAL. HE HAS LIMITS.
EVENTUALLY THE ENCHAN MENT WILL WE HIM DOWN
AND SOME-HOW, THEY'VE COUNTERED MY TELEPATHY.
I CAN' CALL FOR I'M LOCK INSIDE MY HEAD.
WE'VE NO ONE TO SAVE US--BUT OUR-SELVES.

"BACK AT THE BEGINNING, IT SEEMED SO *EASY*--JUST ANOTHER MISSION, COURTESY OF *NICK FURY*."

I KNOW YOU PEOPLE HAVE HAD A *ROUGH* TIME RECENTLY, THAT YOU'RE *SHORT-HANDED* WHILE FOLKS RECOVER FROM THEIR WOUNDS...

...BUT THIS IS A *CRITICAL* SITUATION.

IT ALWAYS IS, WHEN *S.H.I.E.L.D.'S* INVOLVED...

"...BUT THE WORD 'ROUGH' BARELY BEGINS TO DESCRIBE OUR SITUATION. FIRST AND FOREMOST IS *CHARLES XAVIER* HIMSELF.

"ONLY WEEKS AGO, HE COULD *WALK*, HIS BODY IN PERFECT PHYSICAL HEALTH. NOW, INEXPLICABLY, HE'S ONCE MORE A *PARAPLEGIC*, AND *NONE* OF US HAVE ANY IDEA *WHY*."

...ND, FRANKLY, ...ROVING HOW ...LUABLE YOU ... BE MIGHT GO ... FAIR WAY...

...TOWARDS ...EVIATING SOME ...BAD FEELINGS AND ...IONS CREATED BY ...EVENTS. I HAVE TO ...U, I'VE *NEVER* SEEN ...UCH ANXIETY IN ...ICIAL CIRCLES--

--ABOUT MUTANTS IN GENERAL, AND THE X-MEN IN PARTICULAR.

WE'VE SEEN IT *BEFORE*, FURY.

TRUST ME, CYCLOPS--*NOT* LIKE *THIS*.

I'M SORRY, COLONEL--THE X-MEN ARE *OFF* THE BOARD.

THE MANSION IS IN *RUINS**. WE'VE *ALL* BEEN THROUGH HELL. THIS TIME, I'M AFRAID YOU'LL HAVE TO FIND *SOMEONE ELSE* TO DO YOUR DIRTY WORK.

SCOTT, WAIT--!

STAY *OUT* OF MY HEAD, JEAN.

MY DECISION'S MADE.

IF YOU'LL *EXCUSE* ME, FURY--HANK McCOY AND I HAVE TO FINISH FIGURING OUT HOW TO GET THIS PLACE REBUILT.

*DESTROYED BEFORE THE MUIR ISLAND SAGA! --CHARLIE B.

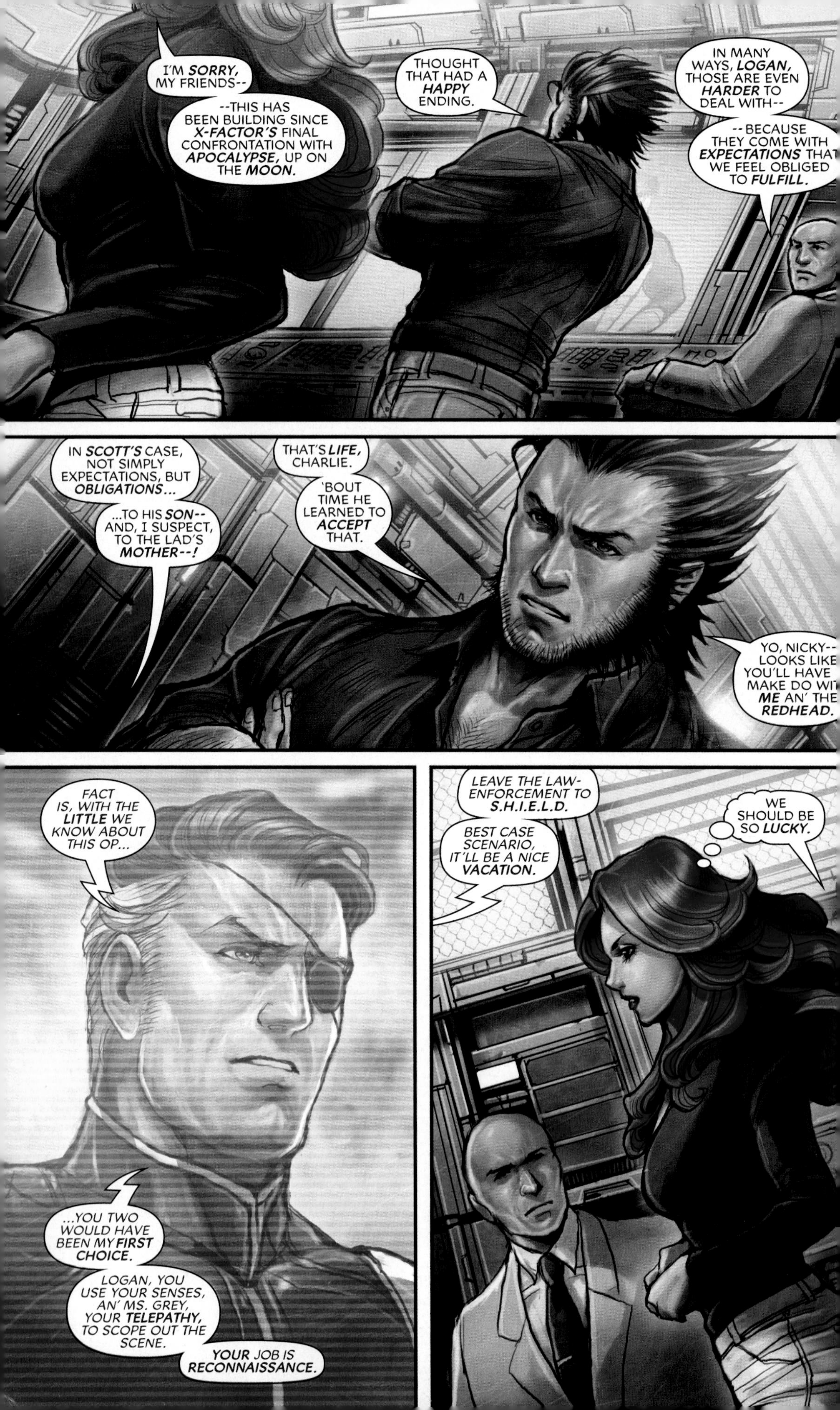
I'M SORRY, MY FRIENDS--
--THIS HAS BEEN BUILDING SINCE X-FACTOR'S FINAL CONFRONTATION WITH APOCALYPSE, UP ON THE MOON.
THOUGHT THAT HAD A HAPPY ENDING.
IN MANY WAYS, LOGAN, THOSE ARE EVEN HARDER TO DEAL WITH--
--BECAUSE THEY COME WITH EXPECTATIONS THAT WE FEEL OBLIGED TO FULFILL.
IN SCOTT'S CASE, NOT SIMPLY EXPECTATIONS, BUT OBLIGATIONS...
...TO HIS SON--AND, I SUSPECT, TO THE LAD'S MOTHER--!
THAT'S LIFE, CHARLIE.
'BOUT TIME HE LEARNED TO ACCEPT THAT.
YO, NICKY--LOOKS LIKE YOU'LL HAVE MAKE DO WIT ME AN' THE REDHEAD.
FACT IS, WITH THE LITTLE WE KNOW ABOUT THIS OP...
...YOU TWO WOULD HAVE BEEN MY FIRST CHOICE.
LOGAN, YOU USE YOUR SENSES, AN' MS. GREY, YOUR TELEPATHY, TO SCOPE OUT THE SCENE.
YOUR JOB IS RECONNAISSANCE.
LEAVE THE LAW-ENFORCEMENT TO S.H.I.E.L.D.
BEST CASE SCENARIO, IT'LL BE A NICE VACATION.
WE SHOULD BE SO LUCKY.

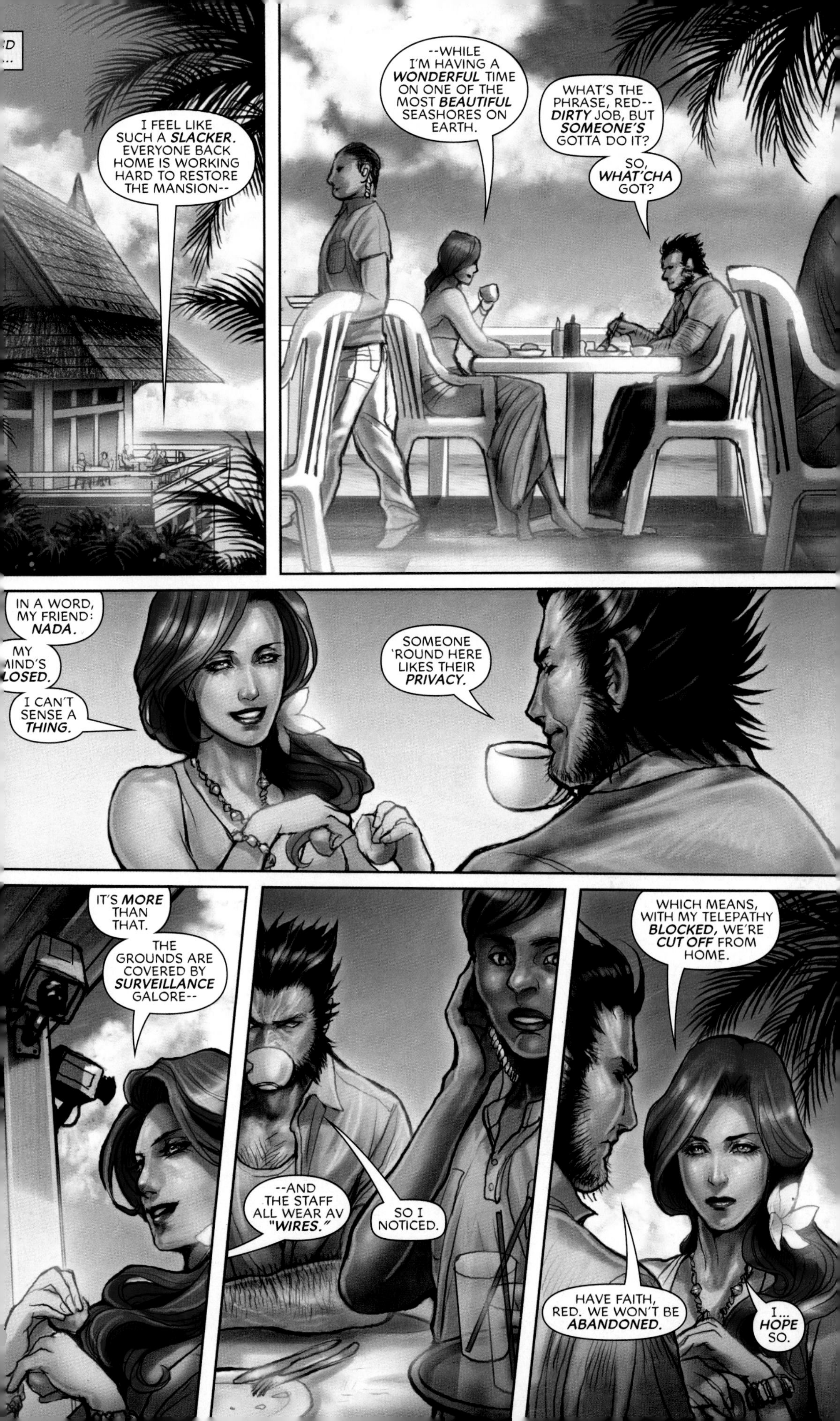
D
...
I FEEL LIKE SUCH A *SLACKER.* EVERYONE BACK HOME IS WORKING HARD TO RESTORE THE MANSION--
--WHILE I'M HAVING A *WONDERFUL* TIME ON ONE OF THE MOST *BEAUTIFUL* SEASHORES ON EARTH.
WHAT'S THE PHRASE, RED-- *DIRTY* JOB, BUT *SOMEONE'S* GOTTA DO IT?
SO, *WHAT'CHA* GOT?
IN A WORD, MY FRIEND: *NADA.*
MY MIND'S *LOSED.*
I CAN'T SENSE A *THING.*
SOMEONE 'ROUND HERE LIKES THEIR *PRIVACY.*
IT'S *MORE* THAN THAT.
THE GROUNDS ARE COVERED BY *SURVEILLANCE* GALORE--
--AND THE STAFF ALL WEAR AV *"WIRES."*
SO I NOTICED.
WHICH MEANS, WITH MY TELEPATHY *BLOCKED,* WE'RE *CUT OFF* FROM HOME.
HAVE FAITH, RED. WE WON'T BE *ABANDONED.*
I... *HOPE* SO.

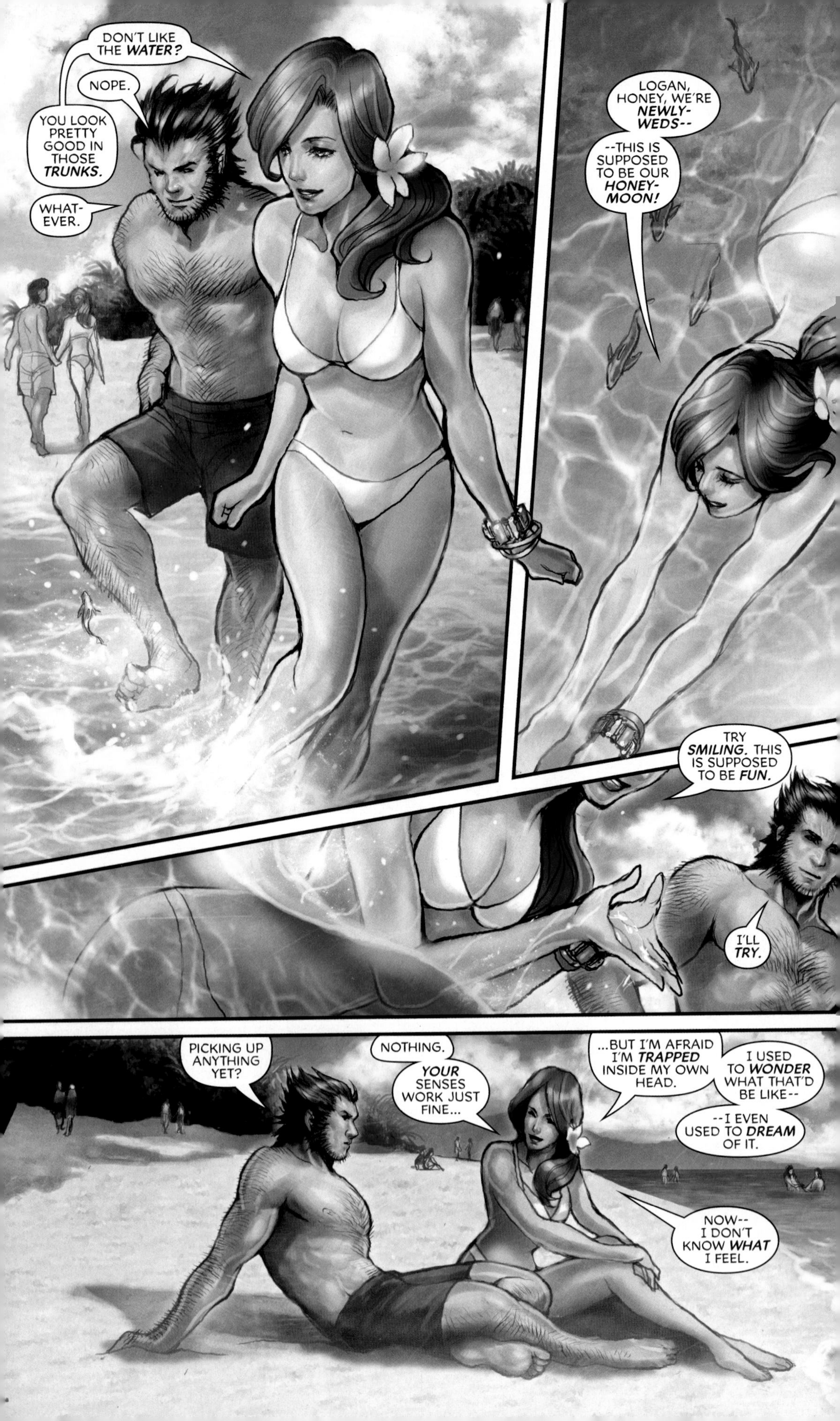

DON'T LIKE THE *WATER?*
NOPE.
YOU LOOK PRETTY GOOD IN THOSE *TRUNKS.*
WHAT-EVER.
LOGAN, HONEY, WE'RE *NEWLY-WEDS--*
--THIS IS SUPPOSED TO BE OUR *HONEY-MOON!*
TRY *SMILING.* THIS IS SUPPOSED TO BE *FUN.*
I'LL *TRY.*
PICKING UP ANYTHING YET?
NOTHING.
YOUR SENSES WORK JUST FINE...
...BUT I'M AFRAID I'M *TRAPPED* INSIDE MY OWN HEAD.
I USED TO *WONDER* WHAT THAT'D BE LIKE--
--I EVEN USED TO *DREAM* OF IT.
NOW-- I DON'T KNOW *WHAT* I FEEL.

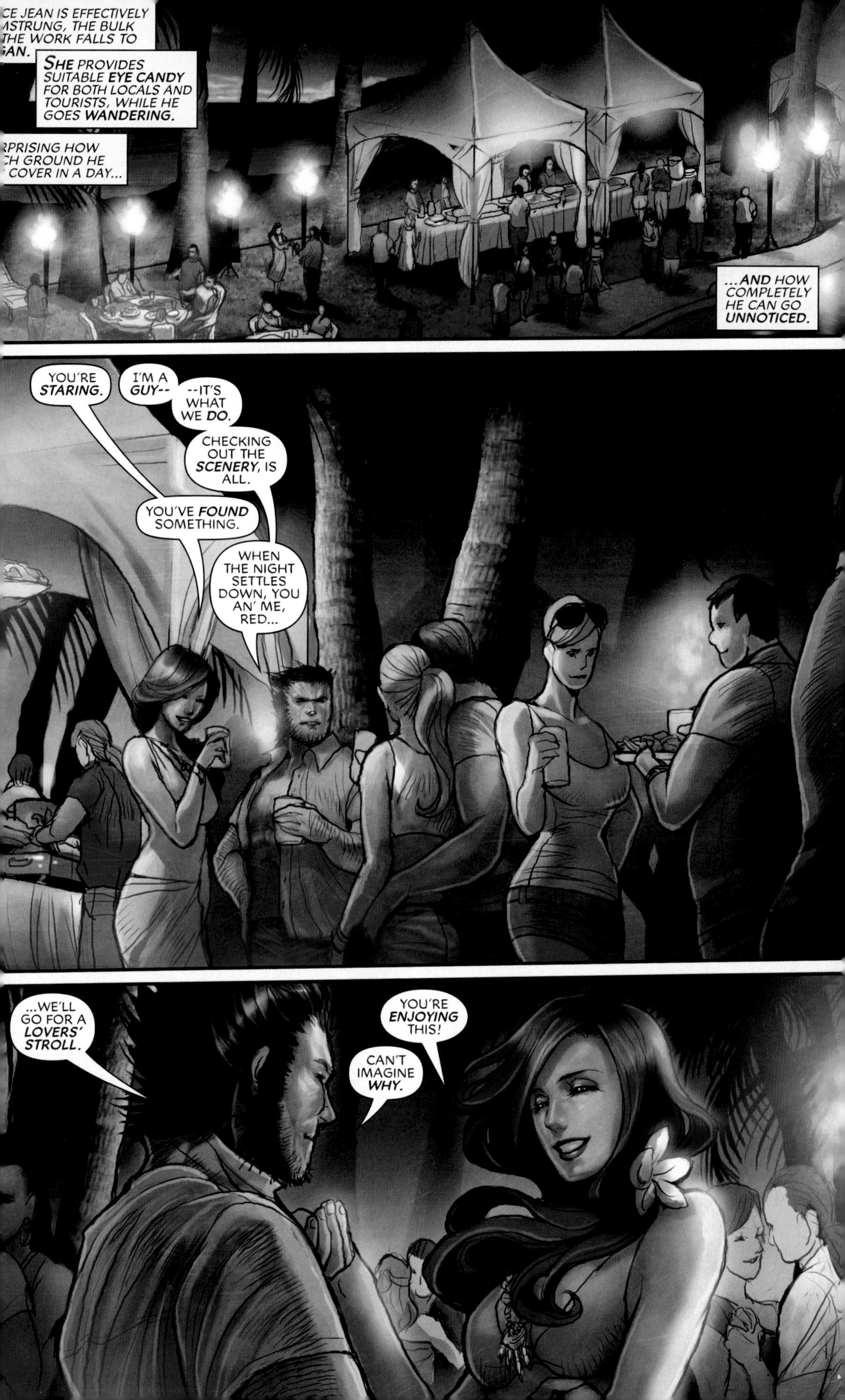

CE JEAN IS EFFECTIVELY
ASTRUNG, THE BULK
THE WORK FALLS TO
GAN.
SHE PROVIDES SUITABLE EYE CANDY FOR BOTH LOCALS AND TOURISTS, WHILE HE GOES WANDERING.
RPRISING HOW
CH GROUND HE
COVER IN A DAY...
...AND HOW COMPLETELY HE CAN GO UNNOTICED.
YOU'RE STARING.
I'M A GUY--
--IT'S WHAT WE DO.
CHECKING OUT THE SCENERY, IS ALL.
YOU'VE FOUND SOMETHING.
WHEN THE NIGHT SETTLES DOWN, YOU AN' ME, RED...
...WE'LL GO FOR A LOVERS' STROLL.
YOU'RE ENJOYING THIS!
CAN'T IMAGINE WHY.

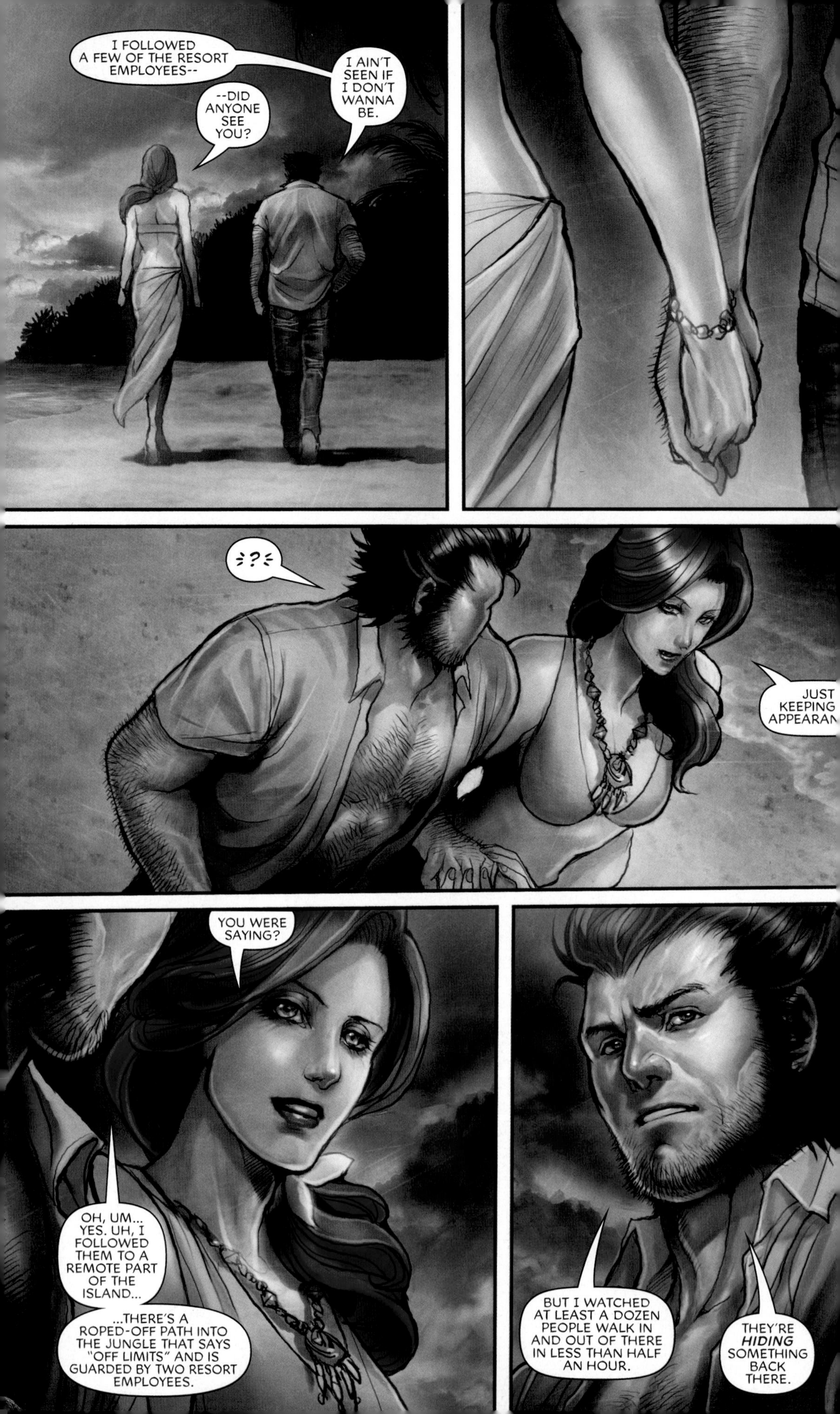
I FOLLOWED A FEW OF THE RESORT EMPLOYEES--
--DID ANYONE SEE YOU?
I AIN'T SEEN IF I DON'T WANNA BE.
?
JUST KEEPING APPEARAN
YOU WERE SAYING?
OH, UM... YES. UH, I FOLLOWED THEM TO A REMOTE PART OF THE ISLAND...
...THERE'S A ROPED-OFF PATH INTO THE JUNGLE THAT SAYS "OFF LIMITS" AND IS GUARDED BY TWO RESORT EMPLOYEES.
BUT I WATCHED AT LEAST A DOZEN PEOPLE WALK IN AND OUT OF THERE IN LESS THAN HALF AN HOUR.
THEY'RE *HIDING* SOMETHING BACK THERE.

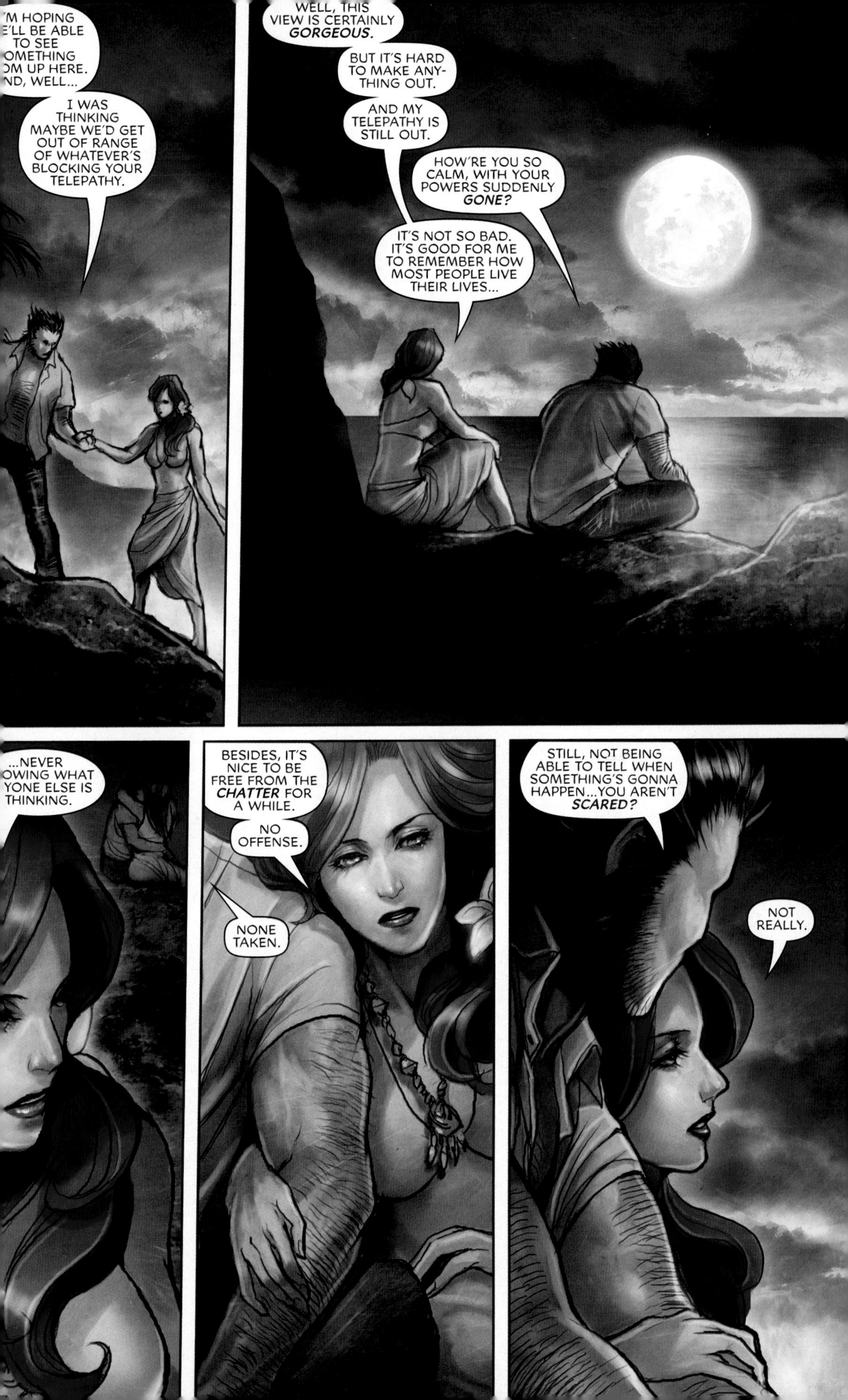
'M HOPING E'LL BE ABLE TO SEE OMETHING OM UP HERE. ND, WELL...
I WAS THINKING MAYBE WE'D GET OUT OF RANGE OF WHATEVER'S BLOCKING YOUR TELEPATHY.
WELL, THIS VIEW IS CERTAINLY GORGEOUS.
BUT IT'S HARD TO MAKE ANYTHING OUT.
AND MY TELEPATHY IS STILL OUT.
HOW'RE YOU SO CALM, WITH YOUR POWERS SUDDENLY GONE?
IT'S NOT SO BAD. IT'S GOOD FOR ME TO REMEMBER HOW MOST PEOPLE LIVE THEIR LIVES...
...NEVER OWING WHAT YONE ELSE IS THINKING.
BESIDES, IT'S NICE TO BE FREE FROM THE CHATTER FOR A WHILE.
NO OFFENSE.
NONE TAKEN.
STILL, NOT BEING ABLE TO TELL WHEN SOMETHING'S GONNA HAPPEN...YOU AREN'T SCARED?
NOT REALLY.

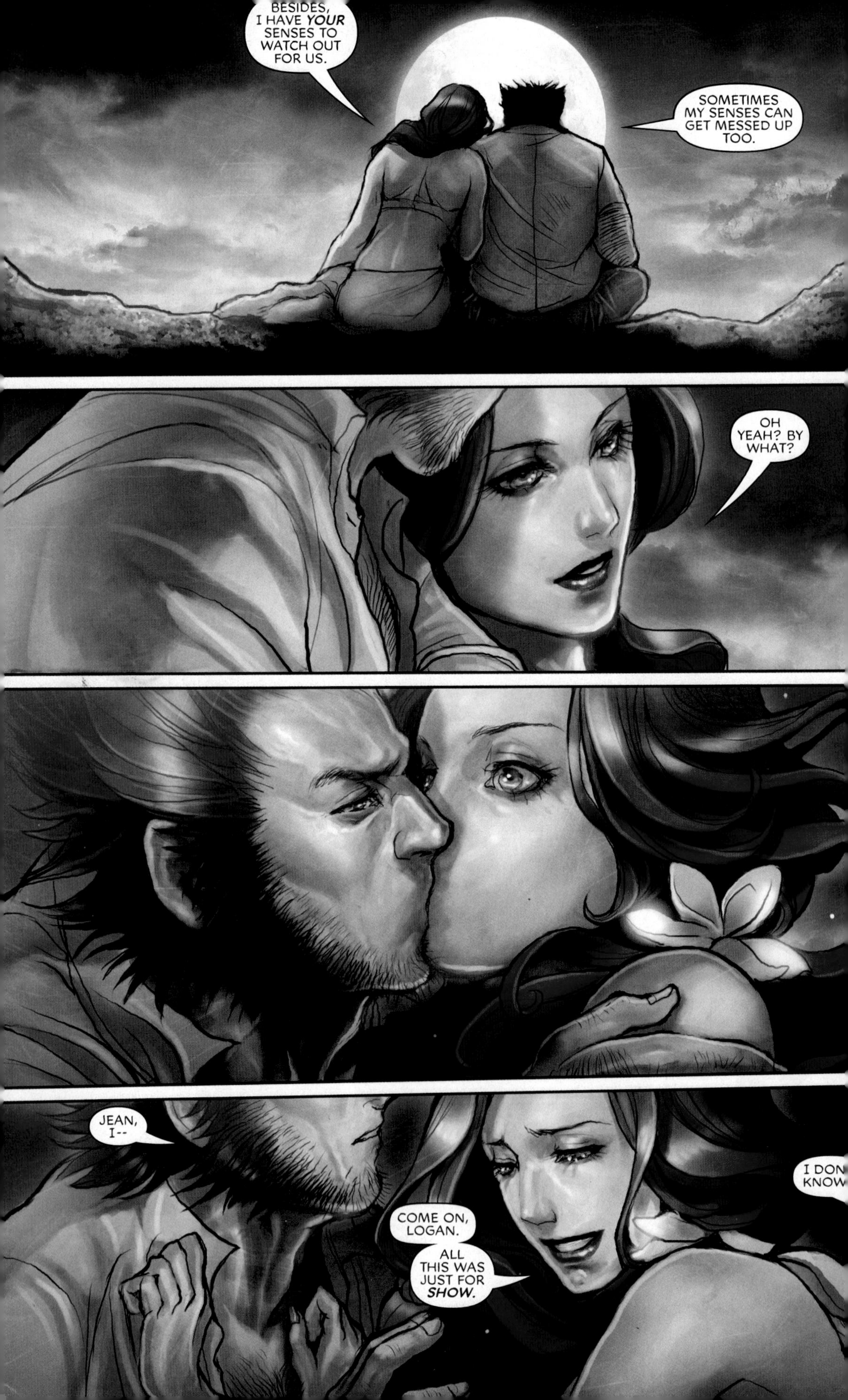
BESIDES, I HAVE YOUR SENSES TO WATCH OUT FOR US.
SOMETIMES MY SENSES CAN GET MESSED UP TOO.
OH YEAH? BY WHAT?
JEAN, I--
COME ON, LOGAN.
ALL THIS WAS JUST FOR SHOW.

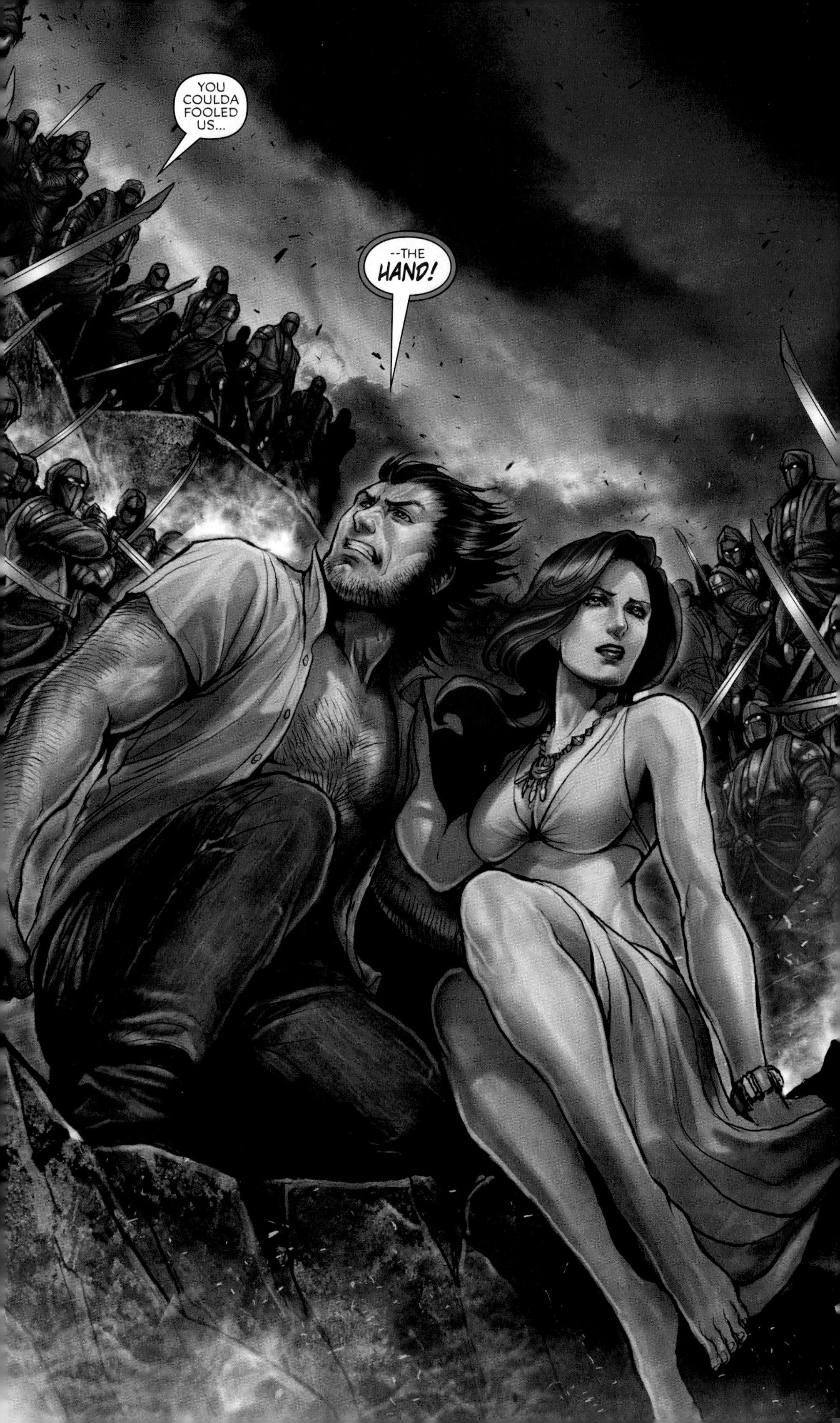
YOU COULDA FOOLED US...
--THE HAND!

NOT SO LONG AGO, THE HAND TRIED TO TURN *PSYLOCKE* INTO THEIR ULTIMATE *KILLER*.

IF NOT FOR *LOGAN*, THEY MIGHT WELL HAVE *SUCCEEDED*.

THIS TIME, THEIR INTENT IS TO *TRANSFORM* NOT ONLY HIM...

...BUT ALSO THE WOMAN HE *LOVES*.

LOGAN'S BEEN THROUGH SO *MUCH* THESE PAST MONTHS.

HE'S FAR *WEAKER* N[OW] THAN WHEN [I] LAST FOUG[HT] THE HAN[D].

AND WHAT'S FAR *WORSE* IS THAT THE *BOND* BETWEEN US MAKES *BOTH* OF US VULNERABLE.

THEY HAVE A WAY TO HIM THROUGH *ME*--

--AND THE SAME, FROM HIM TO ME, IN *REVERSE.*

I'VE HELD MY OWN SO FAR--

--BUT I TRULY DON'T KNOW HOW MUCH *LONGER*--

--WHAT'S *THAT*?!

DON'T YOU DARE *FRET*, JEANNIE.

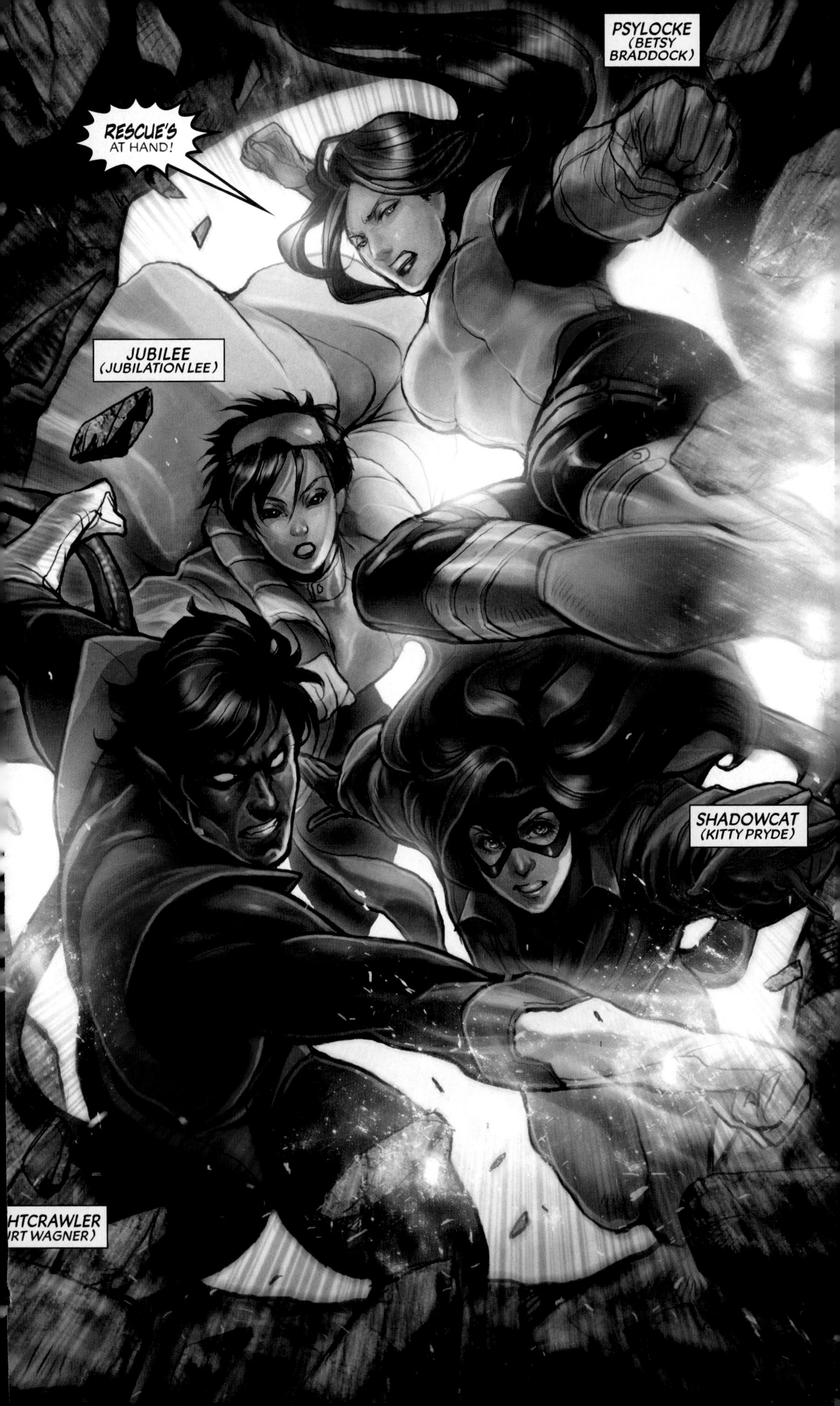
PSYLOCKE
(BETSY BRADDOCK)
RESCUE'S AT HAND!
JUBILEE
(JUBILATION LEE)
SHADOWCAT
(KITTY PRYDE)
HTCRAWLER
URT WAGNER)

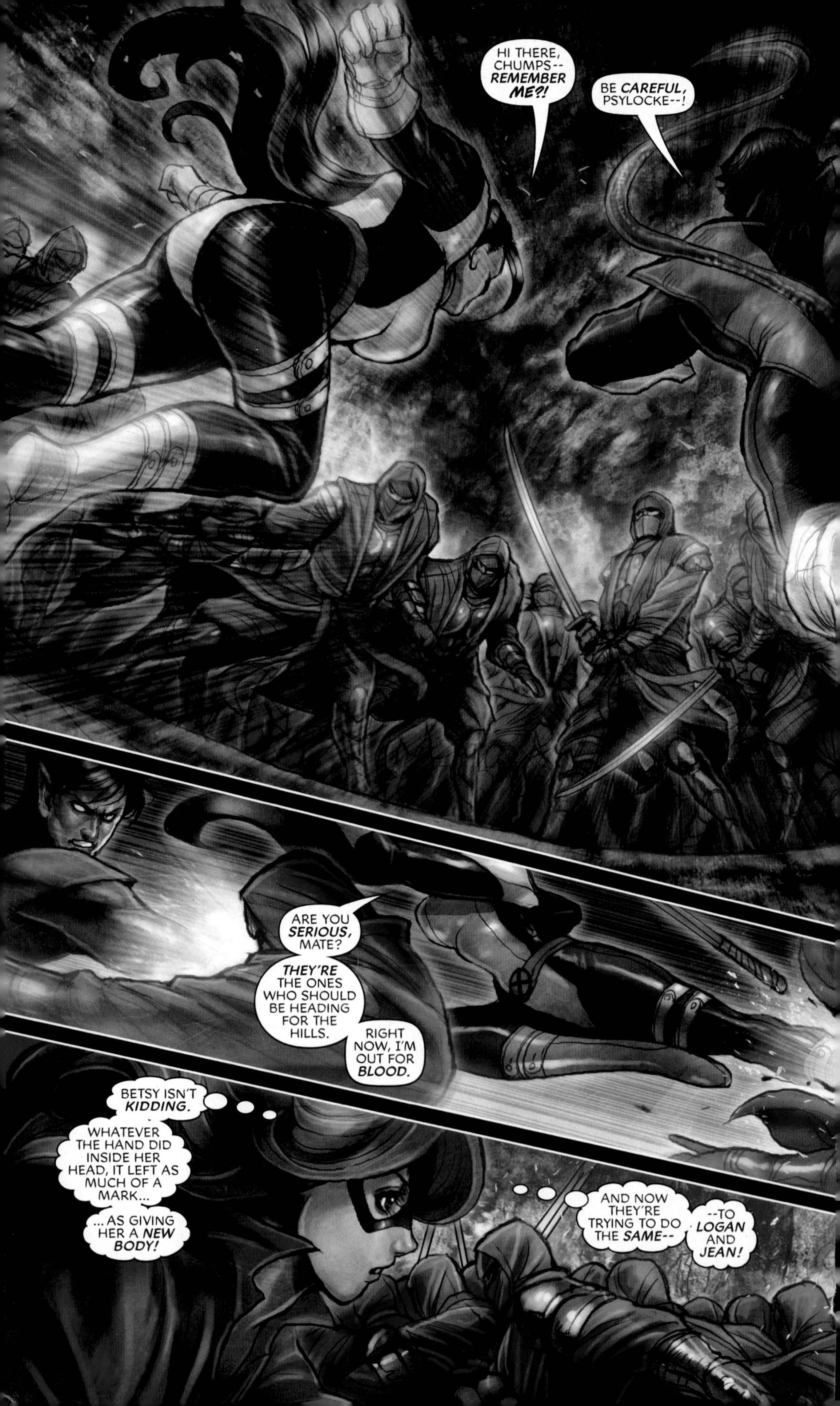
HI THERE, CHUMPS-- REMEMBER ME?!
BE CAREFUL, PSYLOCKE--!
ARE YOU SERIOUS, MATE?
THEY'RE THE ONES WHO SHOULD BE HEADING FOR THE HILLS.
RIGHT NOW, I'M OUT FOR BLOOD.
BETSY ISN'T KIDDING.
WHATEVER THE HAND DID INSIDE HER HEAD, IT LEFT AS MUCH OF A MARK...
...AS GIVING HER A NEW BODY!
AND NOW THEY'RE TRYING TO DO THE SAME--
--TO LOGAN AND JEAN!

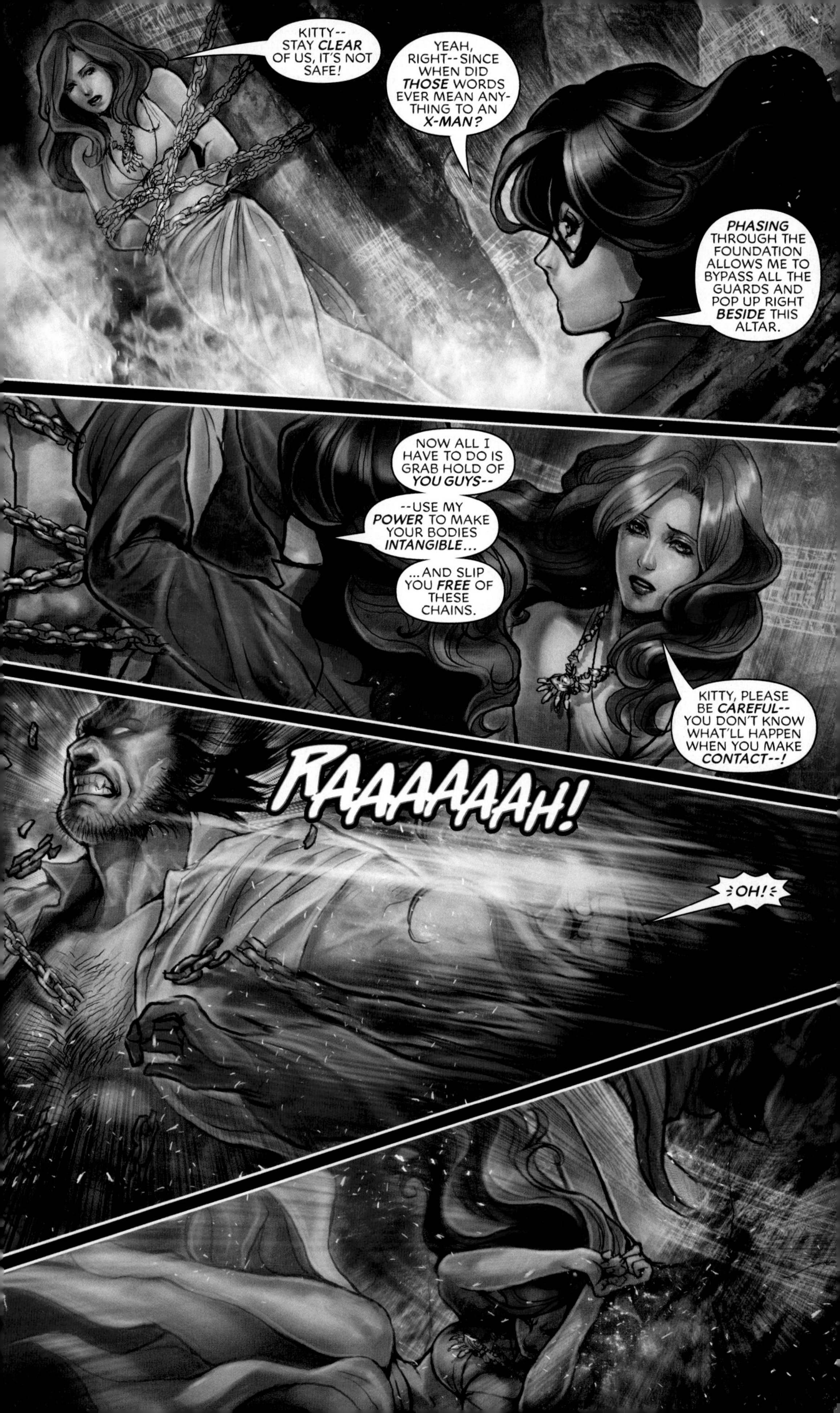
KITTY-- STAY CLEAR OF US, IT'S NOT SAFE!
YEAH, RIGHT--SINCE WHEN DID THOSE WORDS EVER MEAN ANY-THING TO AN X-MAN?
PHASING THROUGH THE FOUNDATION ALLOWS ME TO BYPASS ALL THE GUARDS AND POP UP RIGHT BESIDE THIS ALTAR.
NOW ALL I HAVE TO DO IS GRAB HOLD OF YOU GUYS--
--USE MY POWER TO MAKE YOUR BODIES INTANGIBLE...
...AND SLIP YOU FREE OF THESE CHAINS.
KITTY, PLEASE BE CAREFUL-- YOU DON'T KNOW WHAT'LL HAPPEN WHEN YOU MAKE CONTACT--!
RAAAAAAH!
OH!

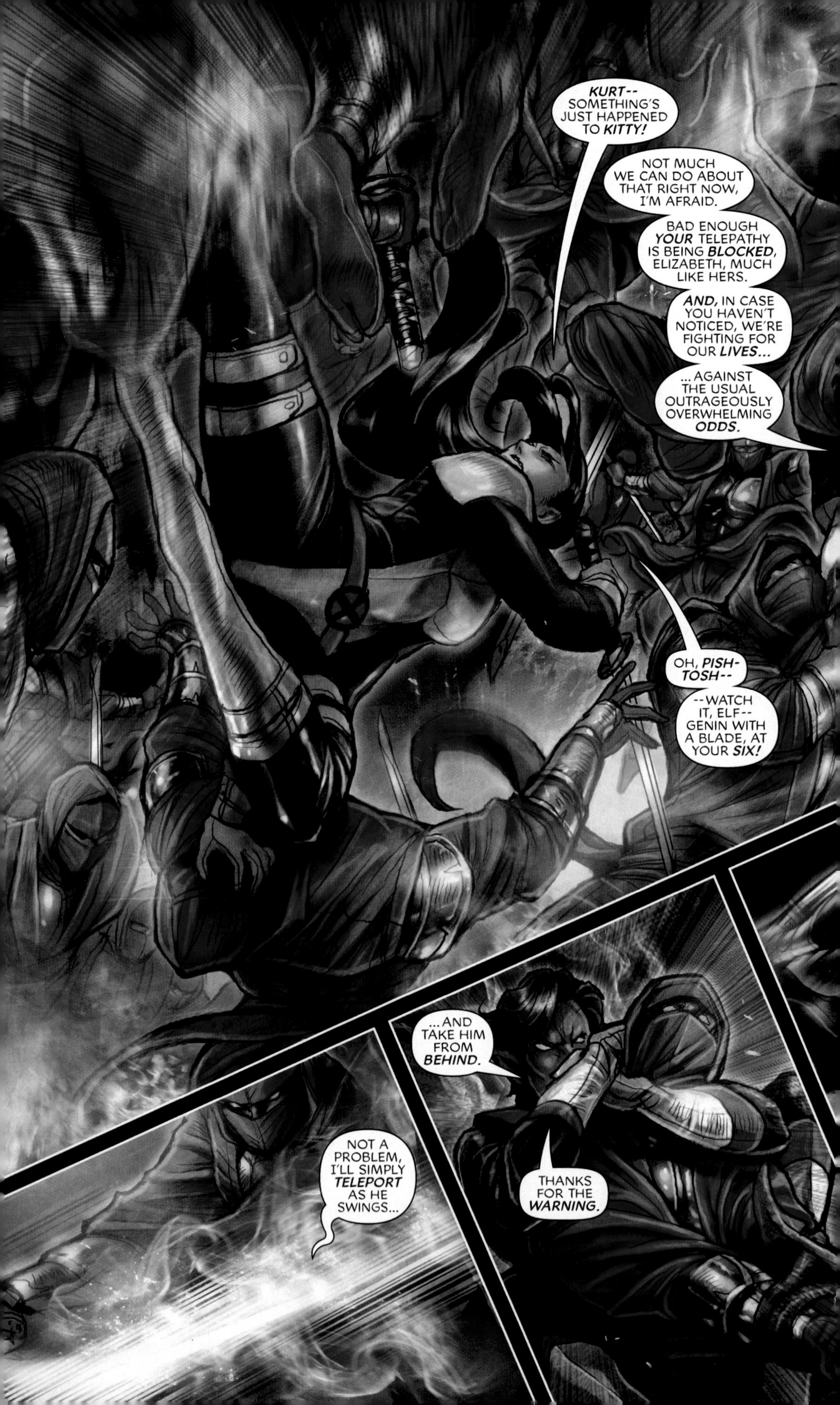

KURT-- SOMETHING'S JUST HAPPENED TO KITTY!
NOT MUCH WE CAN DO ABOUT THAT RIGHT NOW, I'M AFRAID.
BAD ENOUGH YOUR TELEPATHY IS BEING BLOCKED, ELIZABETH, MUCH LIKE HERS.
AND, IN CASE YOU HAVEN'T NOTICED, WE'RE FIGHTING FOR OUR LIVES...
...AGAINST THE USUAL OUTRAGEOUSLY OVERWHELMING ODDS.
OH, PISH-TOSH--
--WATCH IT, ELF-- GENIN WITH A BLADE, AT YOUR SIX!
NOT A PROBLEM, I'LL SIMPLY TELEPORT AS HE SWINGS...
...AND TAKE HIM FROM BEHIND.
THANKS FOR THE WARNING.

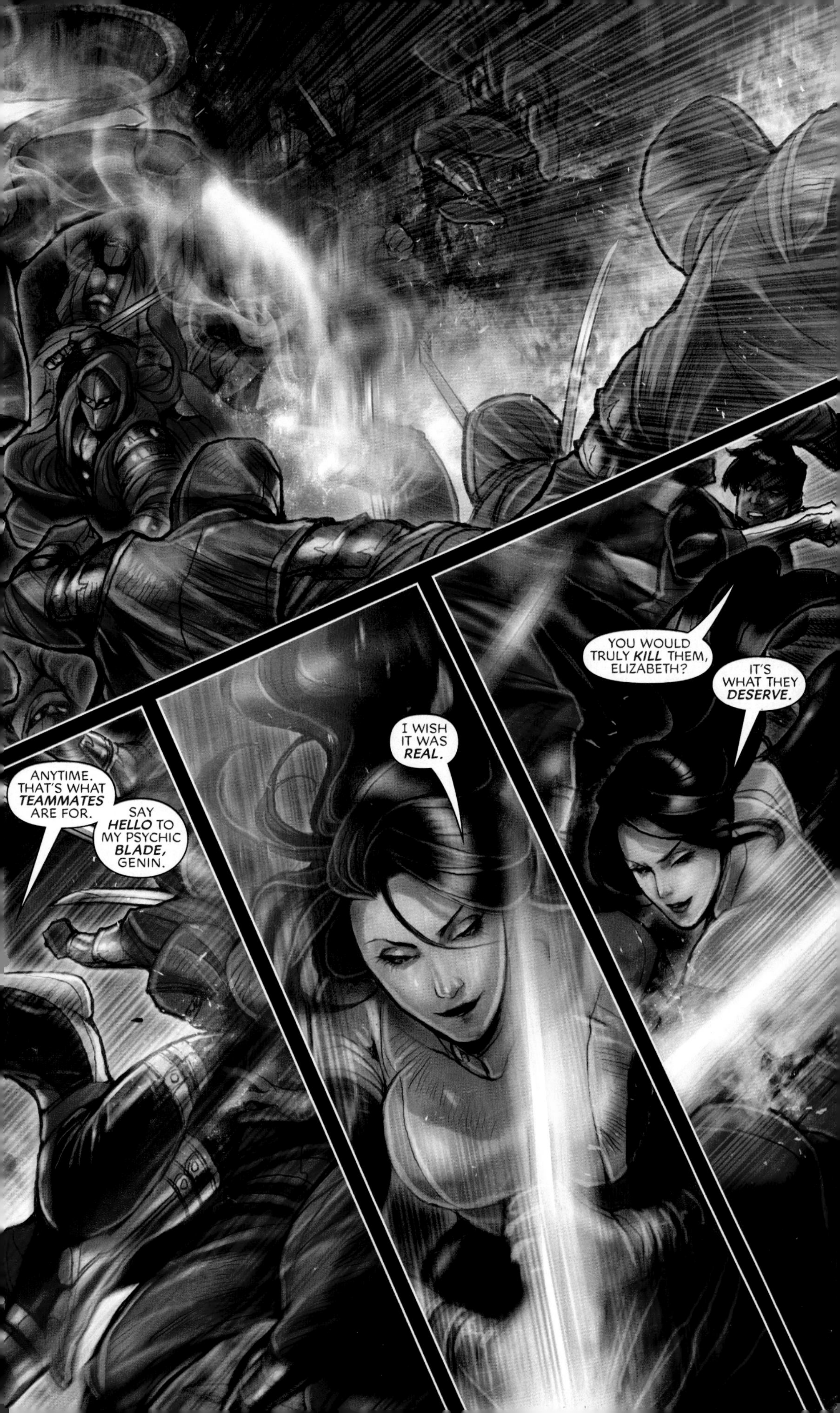
ANYTIME. THAT'S WHAT *TEAMMATES* ARE FOR.
SAY *HELLO* TO MY PSYCHIC *BLADE,* GENIN.
I WISH IT WAS *REAL.*
YOU WOULD TRULY *KILL* THEM, ELIZABETH?
IT'S WHAT THEY *DESERVE.*

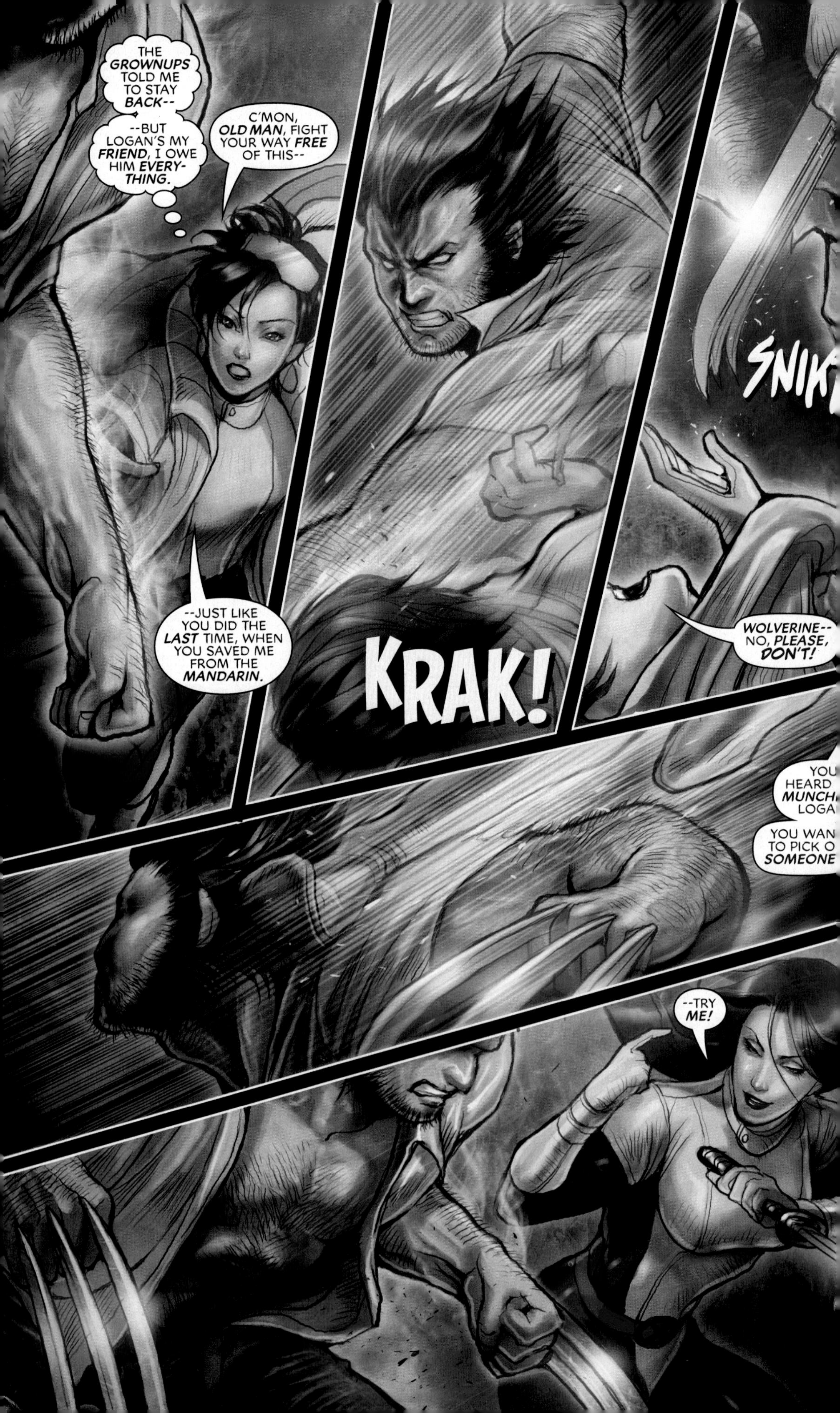
THE GROWNUPS TOLD ME TO STAY BACK--
--BUT LOGAN'S MY FRIEND, I OWE HIM EVERY-THING.
C'MON, OLD MAN, FIGHT YOUR WAY FREE OF THIS--
--JUST LIKE YOU DID THE LAST TIME, WHEN YOU SAVED ME FROM THE MANDARIN.
KRAK!
SNIK
WOLVERINE--NO, PLEASE, DON'T!
YOU HEARD MUNCH LOGA
YOU WAN TO PICK O SOMEONE
--TRY ME!

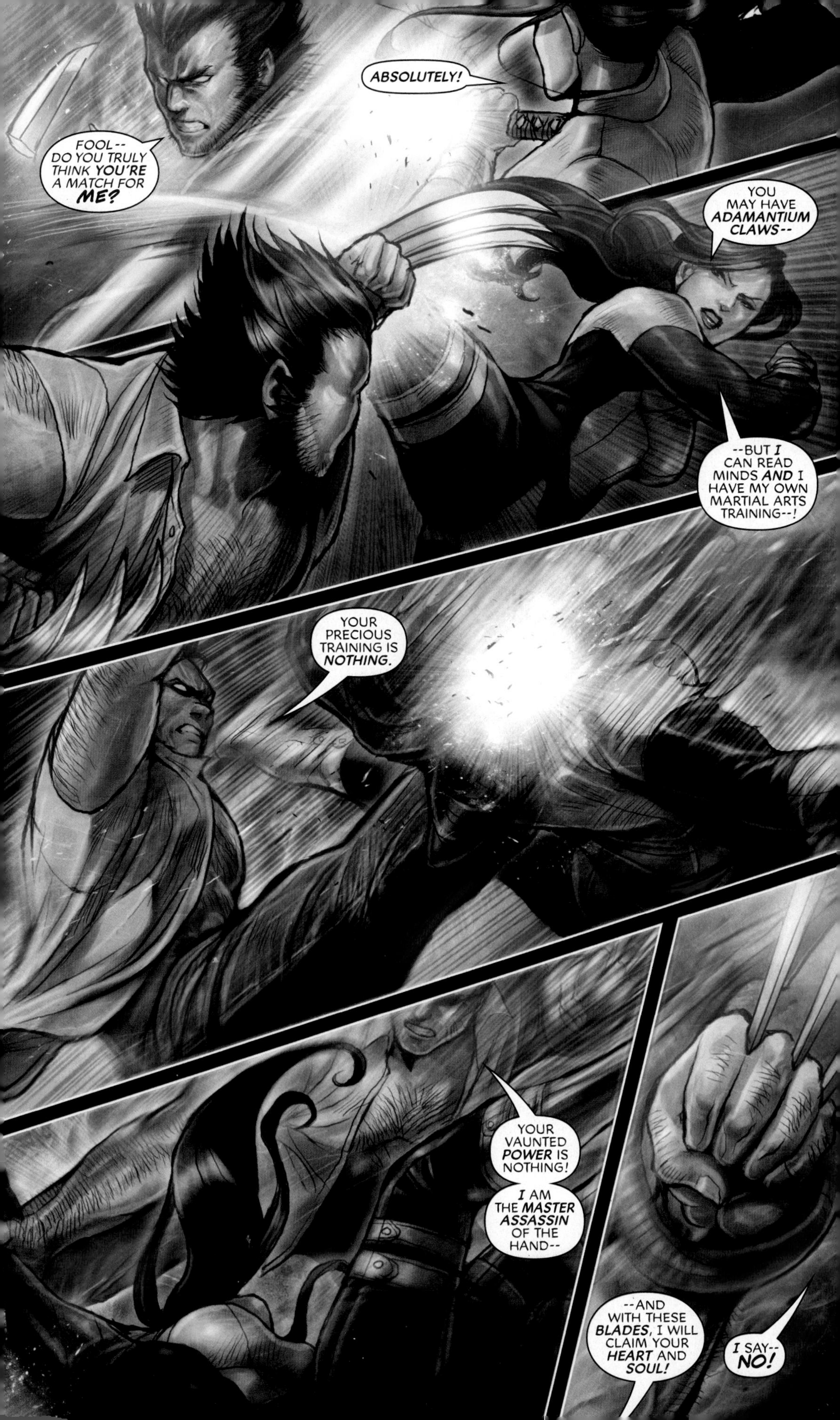

ABSOLUTELY!
FOOL-- DO YOU TRULY THINK YOU'RE A MATCH FOR ME?
YOU MAY HAVE ADAMANTIUM CLAWS--
--BUT I CAN READ MINDS AND I HAVE MY OWN MARTIAL ARTS TRAINING--!
YOUR PRECIOUS TRAINING IS NOTHING.
YOUR VAUNTED POWER IS NOTHING!
I AM THE MASTER ASSASSIN OF THE HAND--
--AND WITH THESE BLADES, I WILL CLAIM YOUR HEART AND SOUL!
I SAY-- NO!

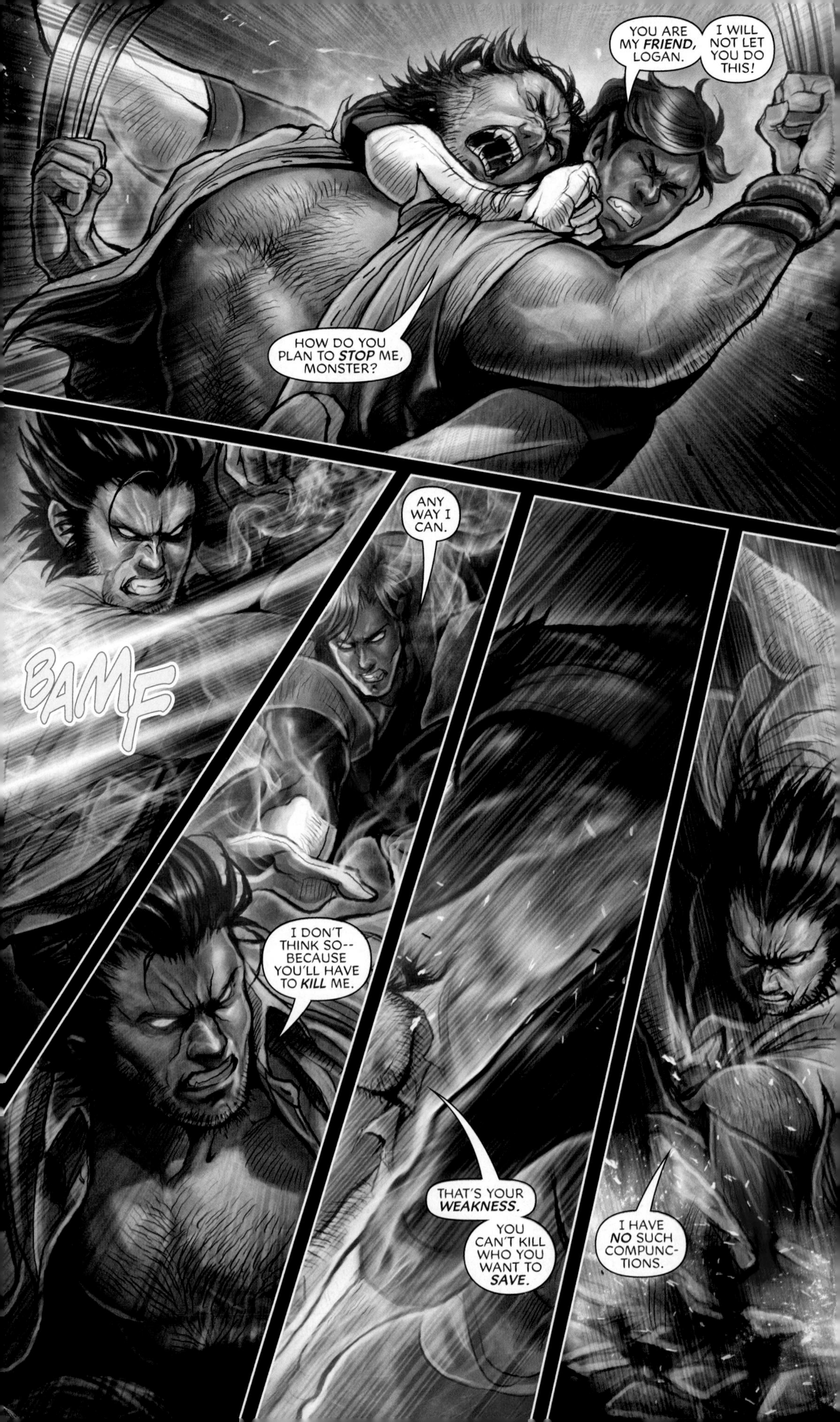
YOU ARE MY FRIEND, LOGAN.
I WILL NOT LET YOU DO THIS!
HOW DO YOU PLAN TO STOP ME, MONSTER?
BAMF
ANY WAY I CAN.
I DON'T THINK SO-- BECAUSE YOU'LL HAVE TO KILL ME.
THAT'S YOUR WEAKNESS.
YOU CAN'T KILL WHO YOU WANT TO SAVE.
I HAVE NO SUCH COMPUNC-TIONS.

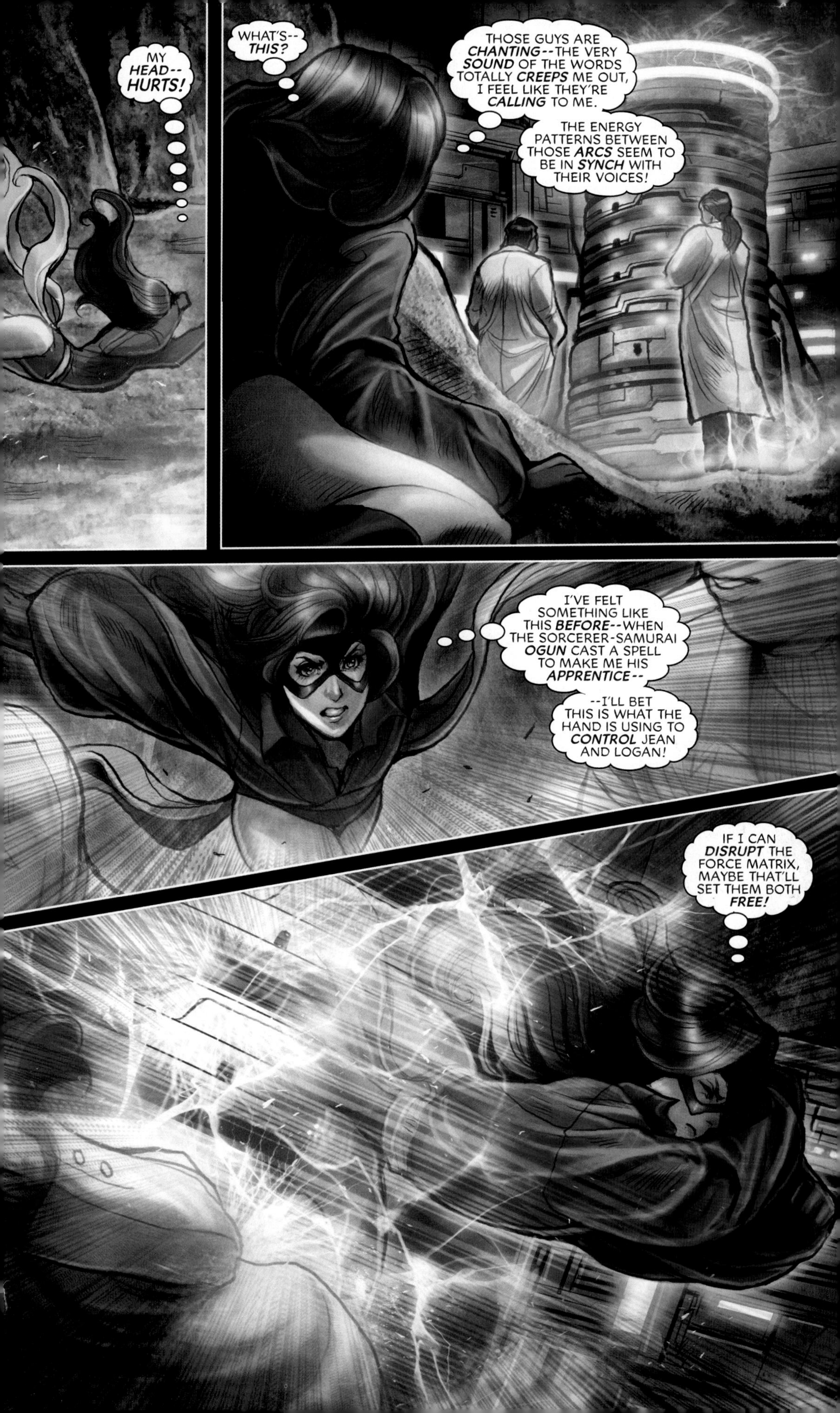
MY HEAD--HURTS!
WHAT'S--THIS?
THOSE GUYS ARE CHANTING--THE VERY SOUND OF THE WORDS TOTALLY CREEPS ME OUT, I FEEL LIKE THEY'RE CALLING TO ME.
THE ENERGY PATTERNS BETWEEN THOSE ARCS SEEM TO BE IN SYNCH WITH THEIR VOICES!
I'VE FELT SOMETHING LIKE THIS BEFORE--WHEN THE SORCERER-SAMURAI OGUN CAST A SPELL TO MAKE ME HIS APPRENTICE--
--I'LL BET THIS IS WHAT THE HAND IS USING TO CONTROL JEAN AND LOGAN!
IF I CAN DISRUPT THE FORCE MATRIX, MAYBE THAT'LL SET THEM BOTH FREE!

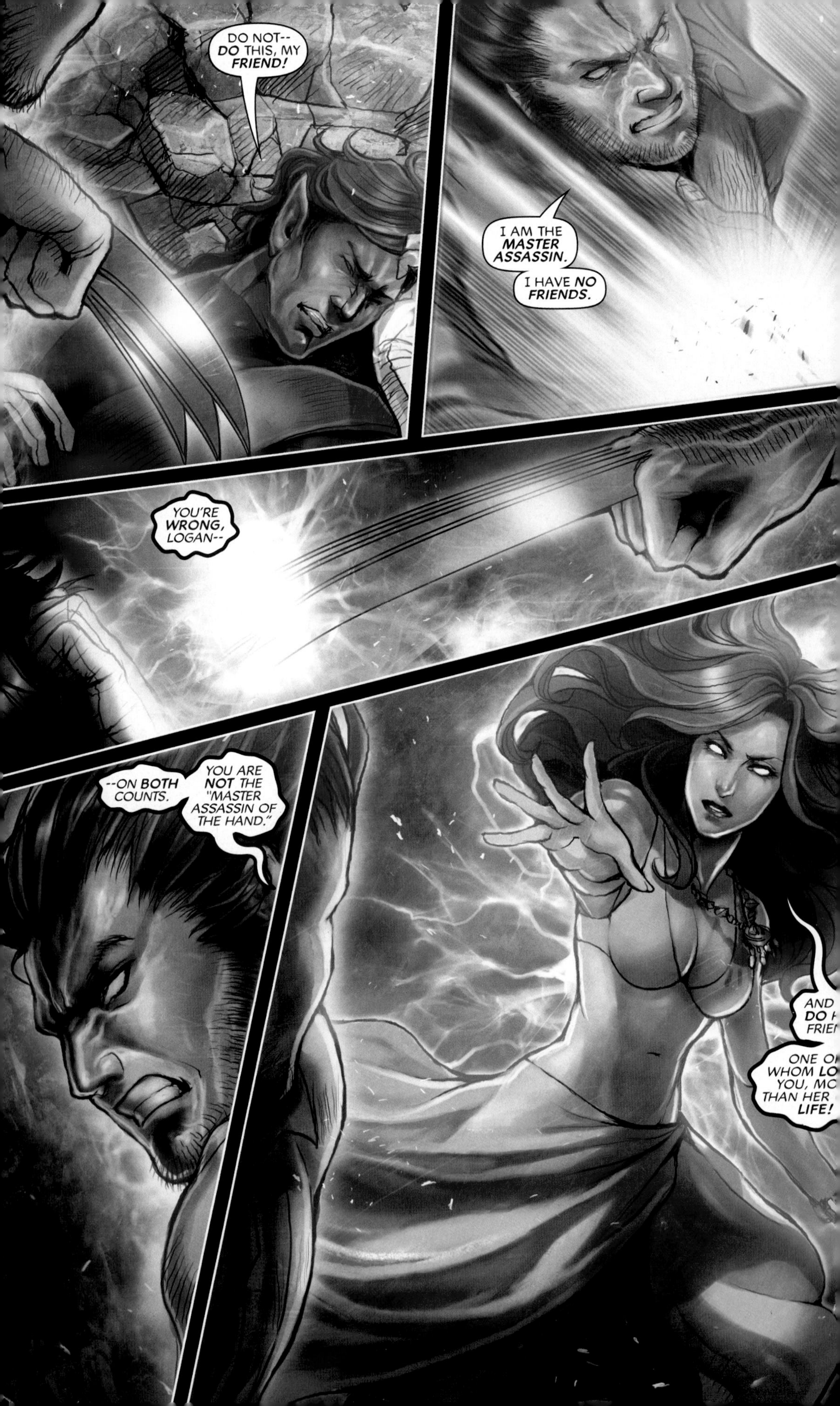
DO NOT--
DO THIS, MY FRIEND!
I AM THE MASTER ASSASSIN.
I HAVE NO FRIENDS.
YOU'RE WRONG, LOGAN--
--ON BOTH COUNTS.
YOU ARE NOT THE "MASTER ASSASSIN OF THE HAND."

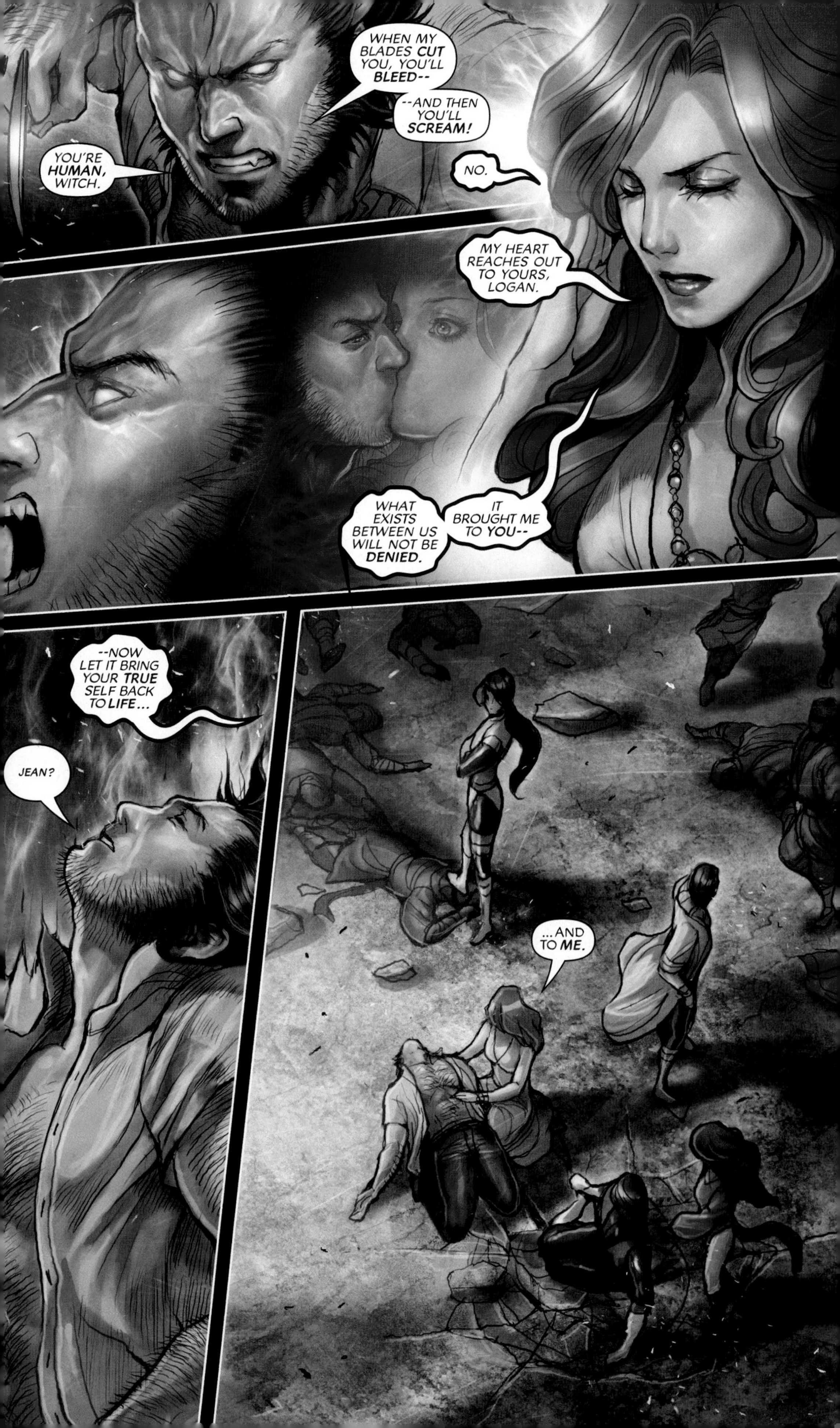
WHEN MY BLADES CUT YOU, YOU'LL BLEED--
--AND THEN YOU'LL SCREAM!
YOU'RE HUMAN, WITCH.
NO.
MY HEART REACHES OUT TO YOURS, LOGAN.
IT BROUGHT ME TO YOU--
WHAT EXISTS BETWEEN US WILL NOT BE DENIED.
--NOW LET IT BRING YOUR TRUE SELF BACK TO LIFE...
JEAN?
...AND TO ME.

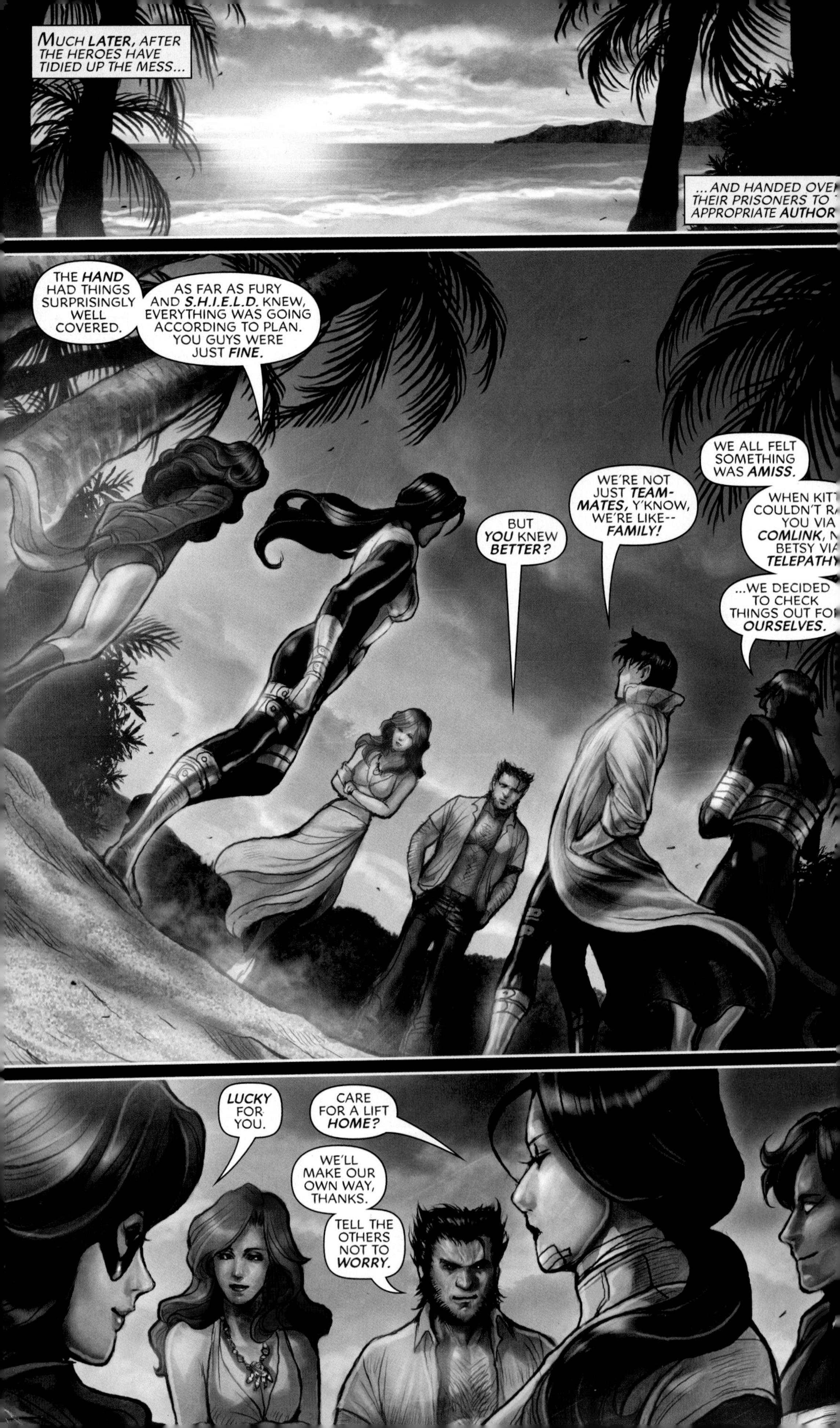
MUCH LATER, AFTER THE HEROES HAVE TIDIED UP THE MESS...
...AND HANDED OVE THEIR PRISONERS TO APPROPRIATE AUTHOR
THE HAND HAD THINGS SURPRISINGLY WELL COVERED.
AS FAR AS FURY AND S.H.I.E.L.D. KNEW, EVERYTHING WAS GOING ACCORDING TO PLAN. YOU GUYS WERE JUST FINE.
BUT YOU KNEW BETTER?
WE'RE NOT JUST TEAM-MATES, Y'KNOW, WE'RE LIKE-- FAMILY!
WE ALL FELT SOMETHING WAS AMISS.
WHEN KIT COULDN'T R YOU VIA COMLINK, N BETSY VIA TELEPATHY
...WE DECIDED TO CHECK THINGS OUT FO OURSELVES.
LUCKY FOR YOU.
CARE FOR A LIFT HOME?
WE'LL MAKE OUR OWN WAY, THANKS.
TELL THE OTHERS NOT TO WORRY.

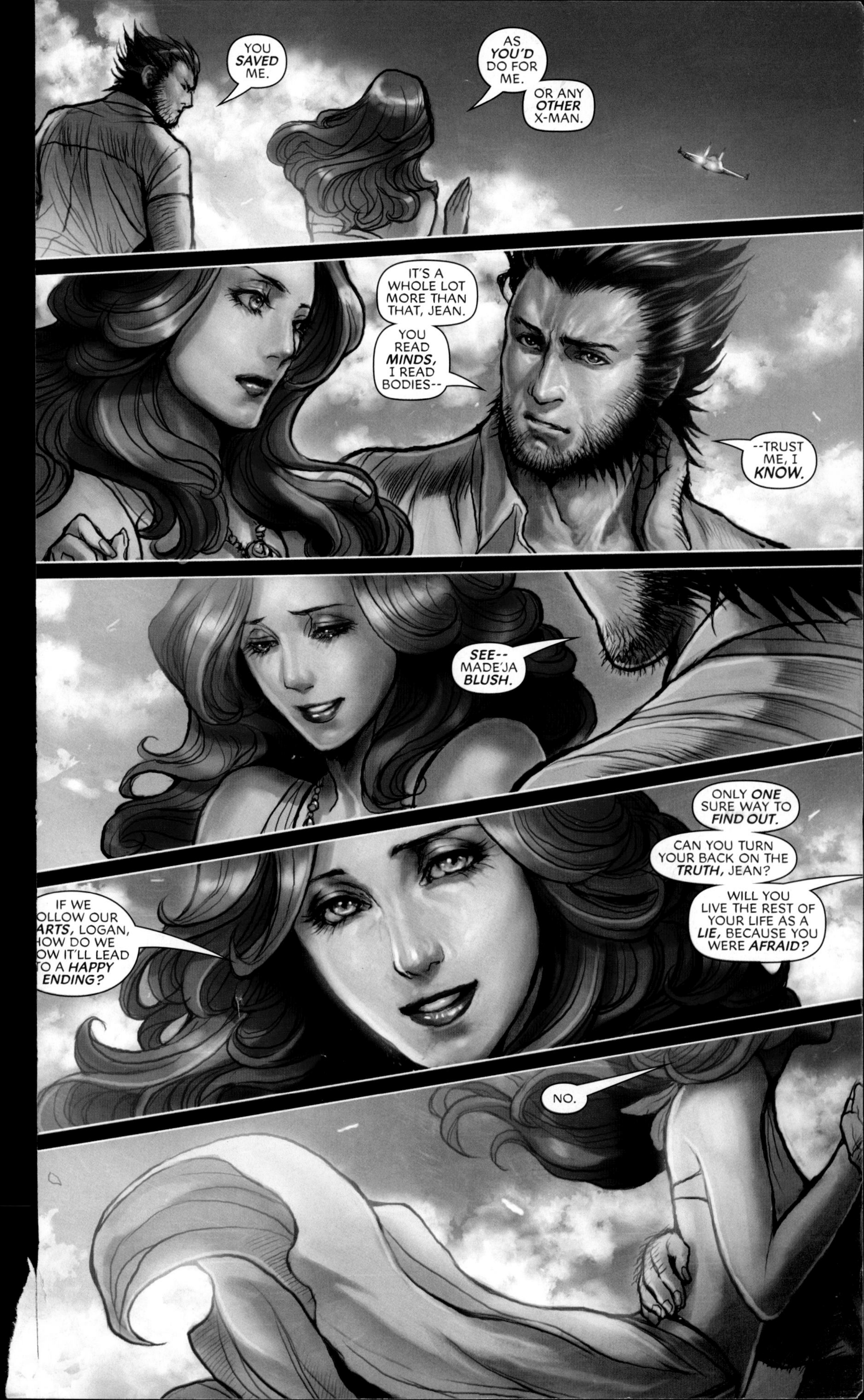
YOU SAVED ME.
AS YOU'D DO FOR ME.
OR ANY OTHER X-MAN.
IT'S A WHOLE LOT MORE THAN THAT, JEAN.
YOU READ MINDS, I READ BODIES--
--TRUST ME, I KNOW.
SEE-- MADE'JA BLUSH.
IF WE OLLOW OUR ARTS, LOGAN, HOW DO WE OW IT'LL LEAD TO A HAPPY ENDING?
ONLY ONE SURE WAY TO FIND OUT.
CAN YOU TURN YOUR BACK ON THE TRUTH, JEAN?
WILL YOU LIVE THE REST OF YOUR LIFE AS A LIE, BECAUSE YOU WERE AFRAID?
NO.

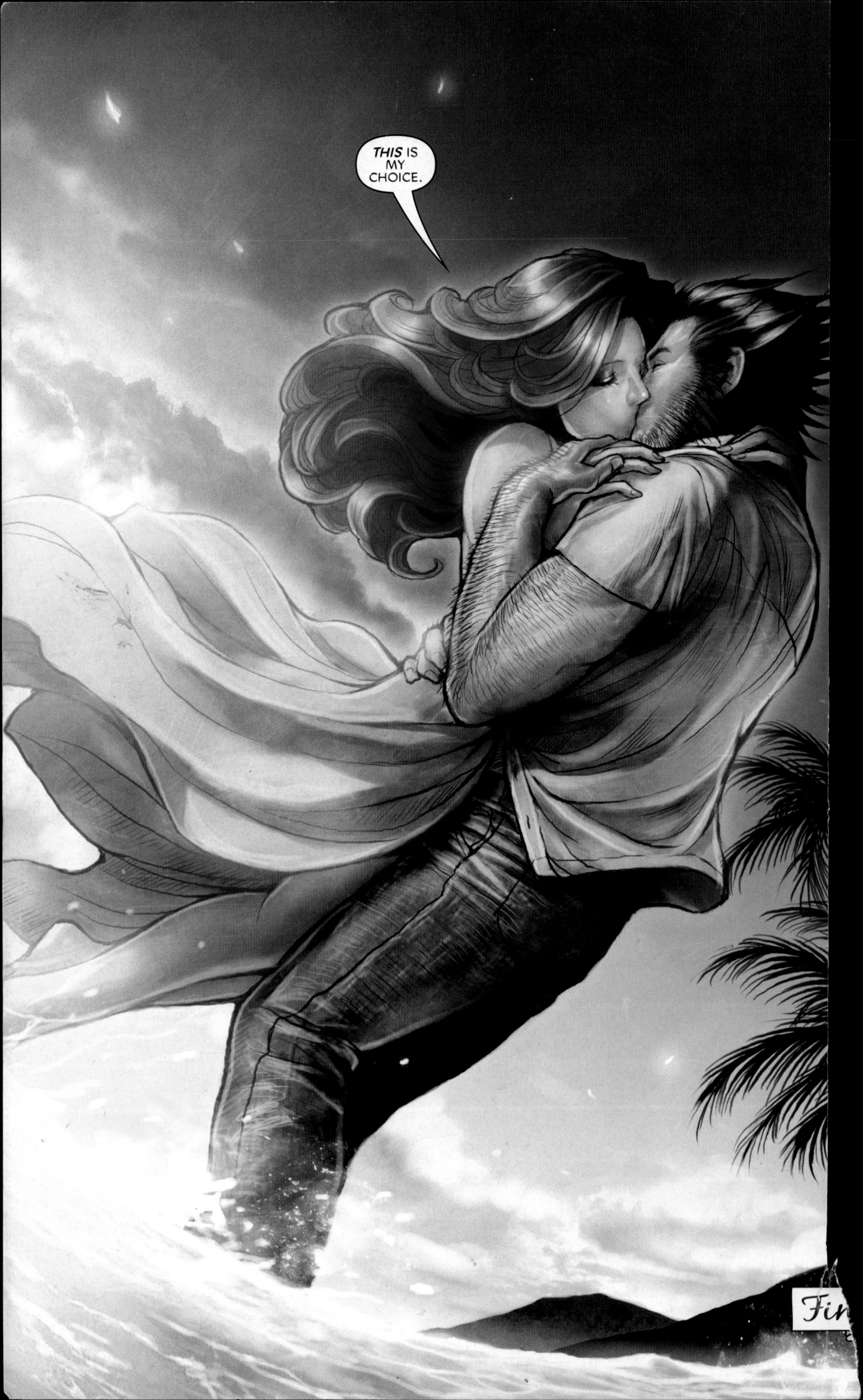
THIS IS MY CHOICE.

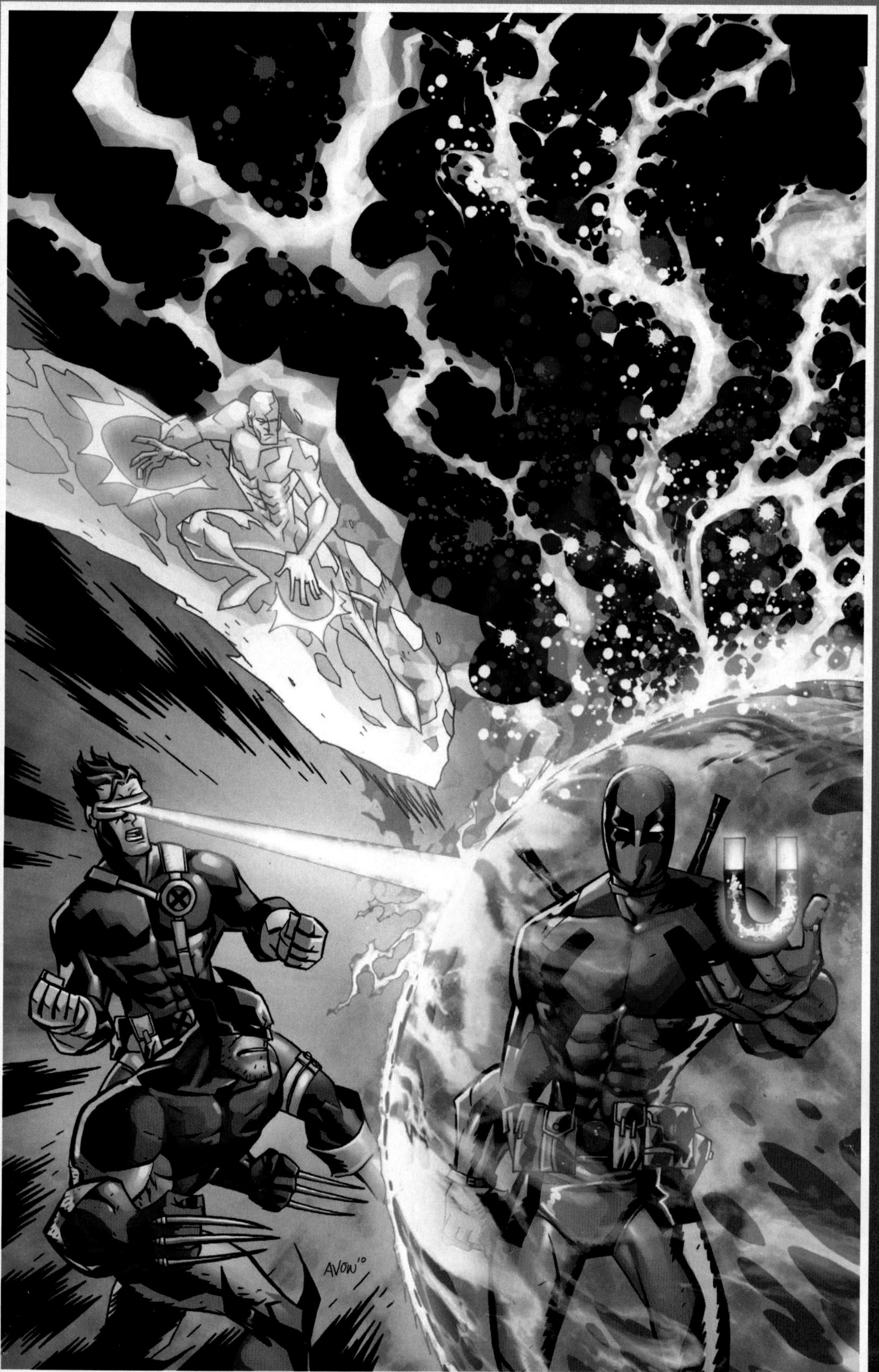
AVON '10

SEVENTEEN DEADPOOL VARIANT
BY MICHAEL AVON OEMING

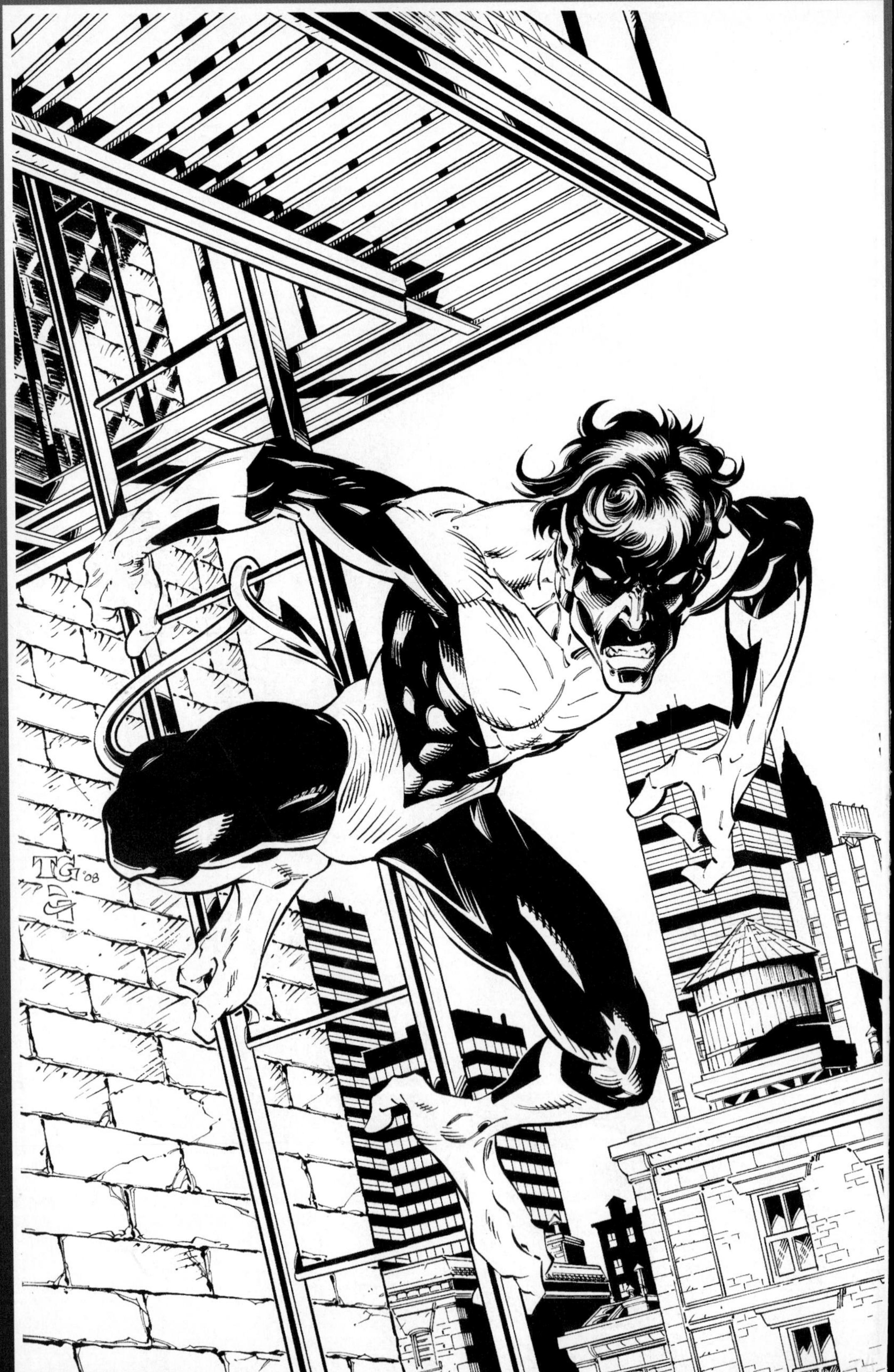

SIXTEEN COVER INKS
BY TOM GRUMMETT

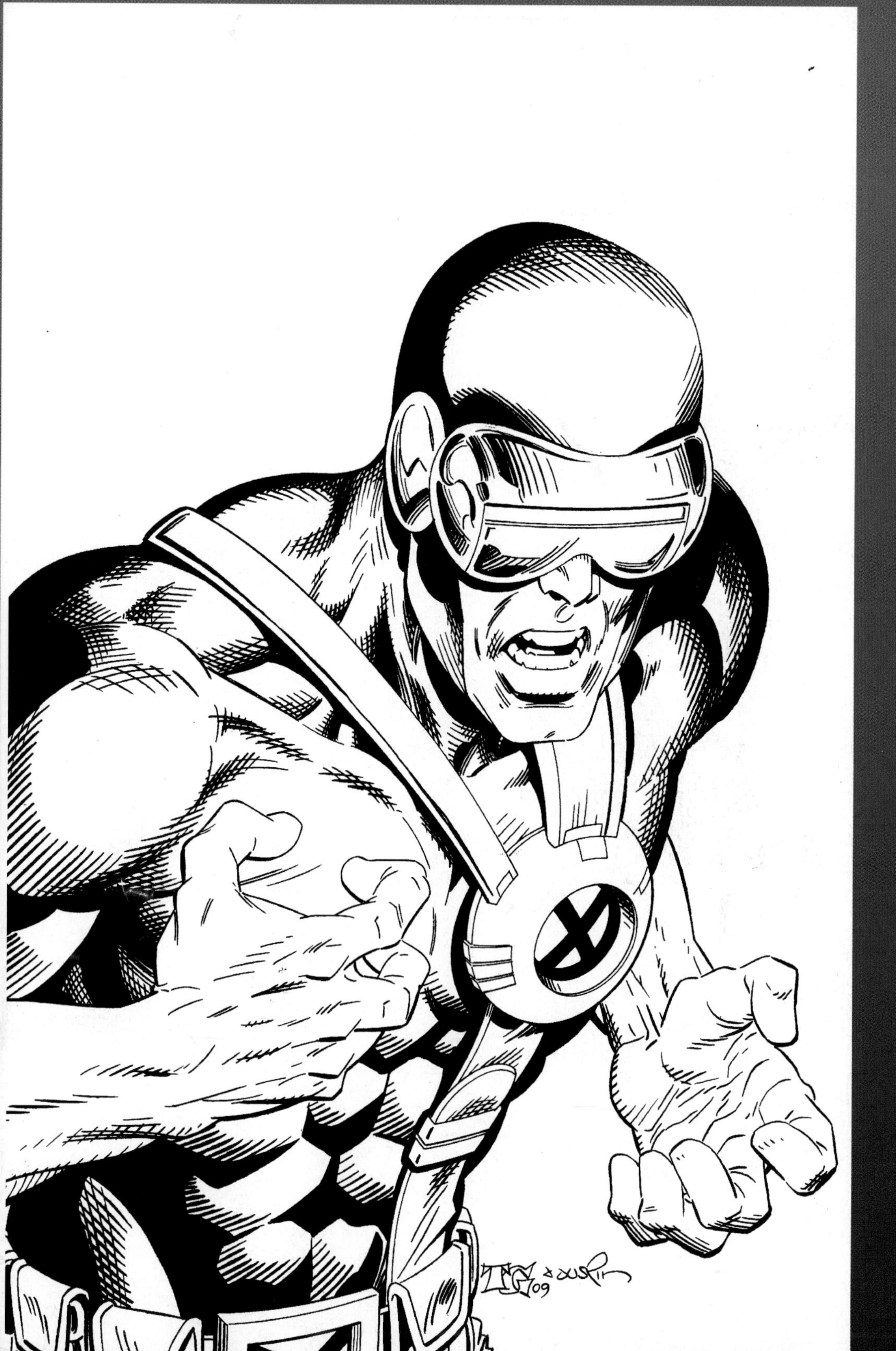

EIGHTEEN COVER INKS
BY TOM GRUMMETT

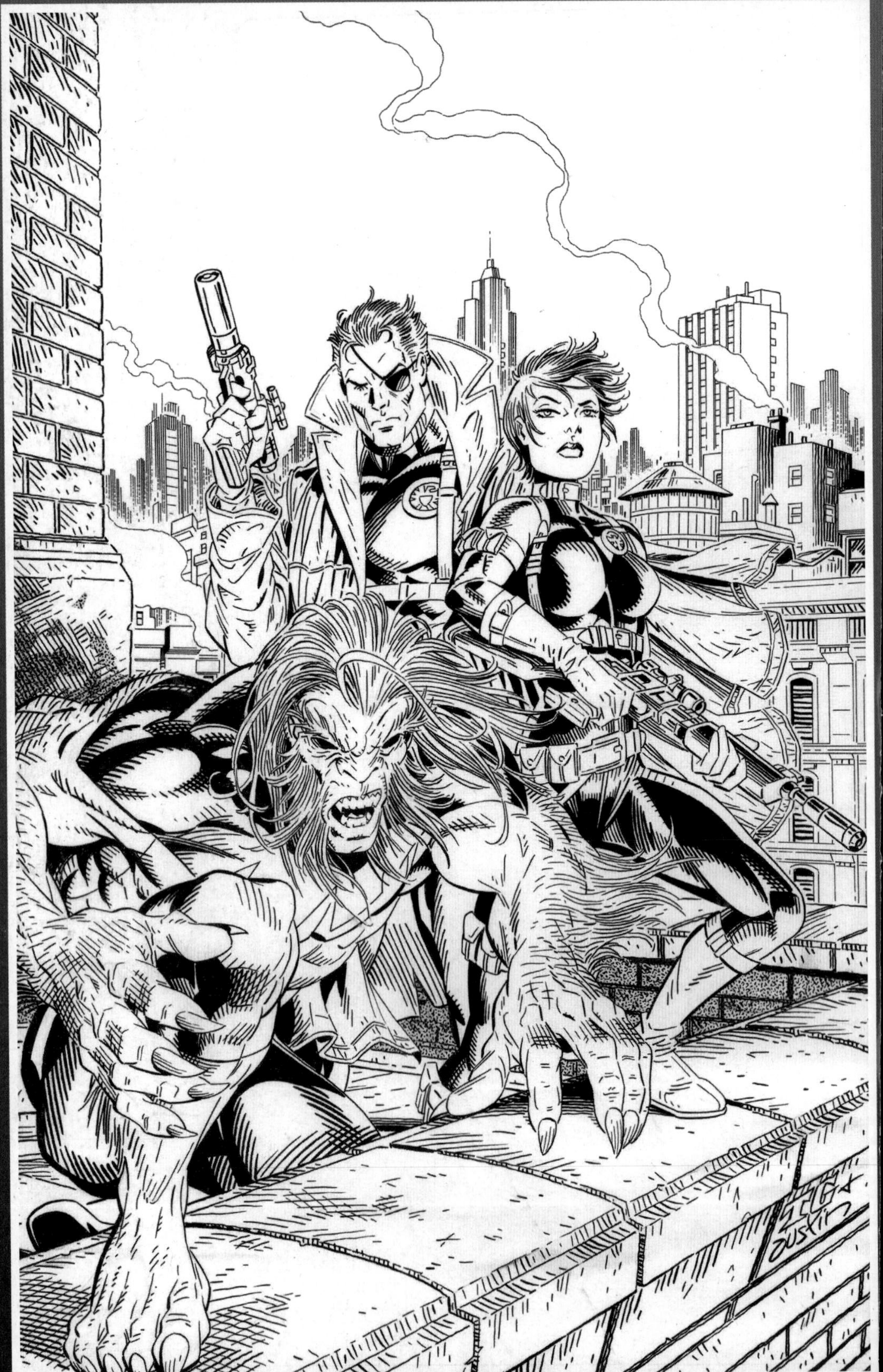

NINETEEN COVER INKS
BY TOM GRUMMETT